Uncommon Ground

for Michael Finnissy

by Harry Gilonis

air's susurrus
through the rushes:

the gaps matter
as much as the stems,

the stalks, all
quavers in the wind

Uncommon Ground

The Music of Michael Finnissy

Edited by
HENRIETTA BROUGHAM,
CHRISTOPHER FOX
and IAN PACE

Ashgate

Aldershot • Brookfield USA
Singapore • Sydney

Published by

Ashgate Publishing Limited
Gower House, Croft Road
Aldershot
Hants GU11 3HR
England

Ashgate Publishing Company
Old Post Road
Brookfield
Vermont 05036–9704
USA

British Library Cataloguing in Publication Data

Uncommon Ground: the Music of Michael Finnissy.
1. Finnissy, Michael, 1946– —Criticism and interpretation.
2. Instrumental music—20th century—History and criticism.
I. Brougham, Henrietta. II. Fox, Christopher. III. Pace, Ian.
780.9'2

ISBN 1–85928–356–X

Library of Congress Cataloging-in-Publication Data

Uncommon ground: the music of Michael Finnissy/edited by
Henrietta Brougham, Christopher Fox and Ian Pace.
p. cm.
Includes bibliographical references and index.
ISBN 1–85928–356–X (hardcover)
1. Finnissy, Michael—Criticism and interpretation.
I. Brougham, Henrietta. II. Fox, Christopher, 1955–
III. Pace, Ian.
ML410.F456U53 1997
780'.92—dc21 97–40494
CIP
MN

ISBN 1 85928 356 X

for Michael Finnissy by Harry Gilonis was previously published in the anthology *Vertical Images 9* (London) and in the Canadian magazine *west coast line*; *Song 9 (for Ian Pace)* first appeared in *Shrike* and was reprinted in the programme for Ian Pace's 1996 complete Finnissy piano music concert series.

This book is printed on acid free paper

Printed in Great Britain by Galliard (Printers) Ltd, Great Yarmouth

Contents

Introduction

The genesis of this book can be traced quite precisely. On a dark February evening in 1995 Paul Archbold and I drove across the Pennines to Manchester to a symposium on 'Internationalism and Nationalism in new music' at the Royal Northern College of Music. The symposium was promoted by the International Society for Contemporary Music (ISCM) and opened with a piano recital by Michael Finnissy, the President of the ISCM. Then came a panel discussion, with Gerard MacBurney talking about Russian music, Rodney Sharman decrying the collapse of arts funding in Canada, and other contributions from Steven Pruslin and the Mexican composer Ana Lara; then lively exchanges between panel and audience.

After the symposium some of us found our way to an Indian restaurant further down Oxford Road and the talk continued over beer and food. I lamented the fact that my 40th birthday was only a month away; Michael Finnissy replied that in March 1996 *he* was going to be 50. The conversation moved on, but once Michael's attention was elsewhere Rodney Sharman and I returned to the subject of birthdays. 50 is an age at which useful provisional assessments of a career can be made; we knew (since we were among them) that Michael's music and his advocacy of other people's music had many admirers: something ought to be done to mark the event.

In the following weeks I talked to Cathy Graham, administrator of the British Section of the ISCM, and to Helen Thomas, from Oxford University Press, Finnissy's current publishers. We all agreed that some sort of celebration of Michael's work - perhaps including tributes both musical *and* musicological - should be attempted. That this idea had a more general currency was borne out when I was phoned by Ian Pace: did the magazine, *Contact*, of which I had once been an editor, still exist and if so would we publish an article he was planning to write about Michael Finnissy, which would be linked to a series of concerts of the complete Finnissy piano music which he was going to give in London during 1996? I told him that *Contact* was no more but that I too had plans for the Finnissy 50th and as we talked the project gained momentum. Shortly afterwards there was a further acceleration when Cathy Graham drew my attention to a correspondence between the ISCM and Scolar Press, who were interested in developing their coverage of new music.

I made contact; they were interested; I wrote a proposal; they agreed to publish. While that process moved along, Ian Pace and I developed ideas about the other contents of what was now going to be a book. The choice of contributors was easily made: Ian Pace's enthusiasm for the music is, like his piano-playing, prodigious and has spilt out into two long articles for *Tempo* even during his work on the book; Roger Redgate's practical experience of the chamber music, gained over many years of work with Finnissy in

Ensemble Exposé, adds an invaluable dimension to his analysis of this music; Julian Anderson is a writer, both of brilliant music and of insightful words about music, who I knew to be a Finnissy enthusiast; I had a longstanding interest in Finnissy's music, going back to 1985 when it suddenly burst into my consciousness, and a particular interest in exploring his recent choral music; Henrietta Brougham came to the project fresh from cataloguing Xenakis and with the inside knowledge of one who works for United Music Publishers, Finnissy's publishers until 1987.

Writing on Finnissy's work had, as he points out in the interview with which this book opens, been a scarce commodity. Until very recently Richard Toop's long article, 'Four Facets of the New Complexity' in *Contact 32* was the only significant piece of musicological work on the music. During the work on the present book a long awaited issue of *Contemporary Music Review*, *Aspects of Complexity in Recent British Music* has added a superb article by Richard Barrett to the literature, as well as stimulating discussions of the theatre music and a valuable first attempt by Tom Morgan at a complete catalogue of Finnissy's music. The inclusion of a second attempt at such a catalogue in the present volume has allowed an up-dating to October 1997, as well as providing an opportunity to add more contextual detail.

The decision to divide our discussion of Finnissy's work by medium was made for a number of reasons. In the face of so much music and such a variety of music, even a short account of every single work would fill more space than was at our disposal and such an approach can often seem closer to trainspotting than musicology. One of the most interesting questions about a composer like Finnissy, whose music has undergone a number of apparently quite major stylistic upheavals, is the very nature of these changes: what do they constitute? are they simply changes in manner or do they reflect changes in subject too? Each contributor in this volume offers their own view, the medium in question imposing subtly different refractions on each occasion. In selecting just some of the possible works for discussion (the hardest choice of all!) each of us is also constructing his own 'Finnissy'.

The decision to open the book with a long interview was also spurred by a number of considerations. I have wanted to correct Finnissy's omission from Paul Griffiths' *New Sounds, New Personalities* ever since that fascinating 'state-of-the-nation' collection of interviews with British composers was published. I had also enjoyed the long interview with Luigi Nono that begins Enzo Restagno's collection of Nono writings; the opportunity of reading how another composer, *in media res*, sees his life and his work seemed too good to miss when one's subject can talk as fluently as Michael Finnissy. The interview was recorded over two successive days in May 1996. The first tapes were made on a cold, dark Friday afternoon in the Barbican Centre, London, as the rain streamed down outside; Michael's answers to Ian Pace and my questions ride a background clatter of cups and saucers, spoons and cake-knives. The next day we recorded in Michael's home in Steyning, near Brighton; there was coffee, tea, cakes from the village bakery; the sun shone and we ate lunch in the garden; in between we (and Henrietta Brougham too) continued the interview, covering new ground as well as revisiting, clarifying and extending topics from the previous day. Although both Ian and I are fans of the *interview verité* style of Walter Zimmermann's book of conversations with American composers, *Desert Plants,* we decided to edit the resulting transcripts, eliding the two days' work into a single text and (Griffiths-style) offering our subject a chance to make his own final corrections and improvements.

Initially we hoped that we could publish during Michael's fiftieth birthday year and Richard Steinitz, who was featuring Finnissy in the 1996 Huddersfield Contemporary Music Festival, generously offered us a space within the festival schedule to launch the book. We also wanted to include within the book a series of short piano pieces, written as tributes by an extraordinary cross-section of Finnissy's fellow composers and premièred in a birthday concert given by Ian Pace at the British Music Information Centre on 11 July 1996. In the end, unfortunately, our aspirations to topicality were overwhelmed by the demands of scholarship and by the difficulties which attend all collaborative ventures. A briefer record of the BMIC celebrations can be found here, however, in Appendix A which lists the birthday pieces and their composers and in the poetry of Harry Gilonis and Ken Edwards which was read at that occasion.

As in any collaborative venture there are many people to thank. Paul Archbold and Rodney Sharman were in at the conception; Cathy Graham provided the vital links and much encouragement; Helen Thomas at Oxford University Press, Christopher Saward at United Music Publishers, Miranda Jackson at Universal Edition and Frederike Zimmermann at Edition Modern have been unfailingly helpful in providing material; James Erber provided invaluable music-processing services for a number of music examples; my wife, Amanda, and my children, Ben and Anna, put up with me; my fellow contributors met their deadlines with remarkable punctuality. In particular I would like to thank my fellow editors, Ian Pace and Henrietta Brougham, for their hospitality and the energy with which they have driven this project (and their co-editor) along. Ian's virtually comprehensive Finnissy library has been an essential resource and without Henrietta's zeal in transcribing, cataloguing, collating and preparing this text for publication there would be no book. Finally I must thank Michael Finnissy whose music has been a constant source of wonder to me ever since, in 1985, I finally arrived on its wavelength. I love the passion of his music just as I love the passion of Michael's engagement with the world, its music and the people who make that music.

Christopher Fox

CHAPTER ONE

Conversations with Michael Finnissy

Christopher Fox: When did you decide to be a musician rather than anything else? Can you date that?

Michael Finnissy: Not easily because as far as I remember, from the age of four anyway, I'd played the piano and I think I only gradually drifted towards thinking that I might want to do it for the rest of my life. But I'm sure there were moments when I was steered towards other things. I wasn't consciously pursuing a career as a composer but I suppose throughout secondary school it was something I did better than anything else. I appeared in school concerts, I joined the local theatre centre, not to act but to provide music. When I left school I applied to Teacher Training Colleges as an English teacher. They all thought I was unsuitable in one way or other. But I found one, in Bath, where they said, 'we do an English-and-Music course, would you like to try for that?' I said yes, and they gave me a bit of sight-reading to do: the first of Debussy's *Trois Chansons de Charles d'Orléans*. Perhaps I should have found this an odd choice, but I read the first couple of pages - singing the bass part - and the examiner said, 'You should be at music college.' I went back home and told my father. We'd only the money to apply to one,[1] so I chose the Royal College of Music in London - partly because it was near one of my favourite museums, the Victoria and Albert. I sat the exam, did an interview with Herbert Howells in which he made me play an orchestral piece I'd written [*Symphony*] from memory, and they put me on a B. Mus. course and awarded me a Foundation Scholarship. I think that was when I really knew that it might be feasible to become what is laughably called in England a 'professional composer'. Which really means having a full-time *hobby* as a composer.

Ian Pace: Going back a bit, when did you first become interested in music of this century?

Probably about eleven or twelve, although I've got an old school diary from when I was about eight which records a 'Music and Movement' [2] class in which we were played Ravel's *Bolero*. Up until that time I had never been so excited - *physically* - by a piece of music. My main guidance came through listening to Antony Hopkins,[3] usually surreptitiously, because if there was anything at all modern my Dad would turn it off. I think he did a programme talking about Ives and Varèse and played a bit of the *Concord Sonata*, and again there was this physical (now I'd call it 'sexual') excitement. I asked for the music and got it for my twelfth birthday present from Largs in Holborn and I'm sure I was aware by then that this was music of our century.

LINES AND TRANSCRIPTION

IP: I've noticed in your scores a distinctive calligraphic quality, especially in the early works. I wondered if at any time you considered a career in the visual arts?

Well that's what I was streamed into. Having failed the eleven-plus,[4] I was put in the technical school, which was completely ghastly because I was such an 'artistic and sensitive' child! They got it really badly wrong. Instead of technical drawing the art master, who was the father of Peter Frampton the pop singer, said 'why don't you do graphics? It would be useful to you and help you write music out.' He made sure that I learnt penmanship which was indeed extremely useful. I think, although I am sensitive to colour, I still prefer pen and ink drawings and lithographs to painting. Now, by analogy, I pursue the sense of line, rather than colour and texture, in my own work. It's something I do consciously, though I'm not sure if it started like that. It's interesting that Cézanne, or maybe Degas, on going to visit the great nineteenth-century painter Ingres, was told, 'line, line, line, line, line is what you need to master'. For me the same applies to music, though it may be different for other people. Line is what I learnt from drawing and line is what I pursue in music.

IP: How do you see the distinction between line and melody?

Melody is the sort of line more people remember.

CF: Is there a link then between a fascination with drawing and the idea of transcription?

Perhaps. Most people know Klee's words about 'taking a line for a walk', or 'rendering things visible' rather than simply 'reproducing the already visible'. Composition is like that: you *reveal* sounds, write them in order to hear them, and the writing springs from deep inside: from emotions recollected in tranquillity... passionate tranquillity! You can make a lot of analogies between music and the other arts at this sort of 'conceptual' level, so - perhaps - transcription is like still-life or representational art in some way. Of course transcription is not simply 'writing down', but creating webs of allusions, playing with sub-texts, cultural codes; it's a discourse on the 'already extant' if you care to try to differentiate it from 'free' composition.

CF: Transcription is a concept which a lot of people would regard as being principally to do with the great pianistic hey-day of the end of the nineteenth century.

There's the essay[5] in which Busoni refers to *all* musical composition as a kind of transcription. I don't know when I read it - certainly before I went to the RCM - although Bernard Stevens re-emphasised the importance of Busoni's aesthetics to me very early on when I was working with him - between 1965 and 1968. Having learnt aesthetics from the work and writings of visual artists such as Hokusai and Leonardo da Vinci, it didn't come as any big surprise to me that Busoni was being 'inclusive' rather than 'exclusive'. He says that you 'transcribe a thought', which I think is a very meaningful expression to anybody who's been through the experience. You 'transcribe it', because in a sense you realise that you can never literally write it in the way it initially comes to you; *writing* it is also changing it, thinking through, imagining. One should enjoy this, and not feel frustrated that something has gone or somehow disappeared. You create tensions between invention and convention; a meaningful dialectic. As with language: a large vocabulary, or in any case a 'good ear', would be useless without the capacity to find imaginative and novel connections between words or sounds.

IP: But when you say in terms of the process of composition that any art work is the transcription of an abstract idea, I don't imagine you would see your work as merely a form of representation.

No I don't, but I'm never sure when the composition starts and when the transcription as such stops. Because I don't have a particular fetish any more for generating original material, I often, even in pieces I don't acknowledge as transcriptions, take the material from somewhere else because how can you have an original idea in something as socially determined as music? All the notes have been used before, all the combinations have been used before, so at best you can deceive yourself that you are starting from scratch, but you never are. I wouldn't say that if I started a transcription, *deriving* the material from Machaut, Beethoven, Wagner, that I view the composition *with* that material any differently. Composition remains the same business of actually discovering what that object is and revealing what your perceptions are, what your insights are about that object.

IP: And by analogy also the ways in which you work on material, the ways in which you transform it?

I discovered that more easily by doing transcriptions because I could always go back to the original material, not confusing it with subsequent explorations, variations, and treatments. I could be clearer about the *Durchführung* because I could readily and objectively identify the *Grundgestalt*. I was less concerned about damage, not wanting to ruin my 'precious' material! I need distance. I need to be able to step back, otherwise it gets too claustrophobic.

CF: Have you been involved with transcription ever since you started composing?

That's how I started I think, because I wasn't taught what composition was. Composition could be anything and the first piece that I ever wrote - at least to my knowledge and unfortunately it's disappeared in several moves of house - was called *The Chinese Bridge*. My great aunt had a set of willow pattern plates. She used to tell the story of the willow pattern which at age four made an enormous impact. I was also taken to the theatre a lot, so narrative and theatrical performance were always very alive in my house. This piece *The Chinese Bridge*, which was one line long, was an attempt to tell the story of the willow pattern plate. Is that a transcription because it's based on a narrative? Or an original composition? I had other material too: folk music, where I stole the tunes and messed them around a bit. I learnt very gradually that opus numbers had to go in sequence, but before that I thought they were simply something that you added to a title. If you liked opus number 323 that's what you added to the title! If we had pieces of music they were usually single sheet copies and on the front, in those days, they used to put adverts, short excerpts from other pieces. I thought that was the whole composition, never imagining that it ought to be longer than four bars. Some pieces were very long because they were longer than one page. As a child I wasn't aware that it was in any way deficient to write a piece of music that was only one line long, because there were plenty of them on the front of the pieces of music that we had in the piano seat.

IP: When you were coming of age, in the sixties, composers like Berio, B. A. Zimmermann and Kagel were writing with many references to other musics. Was this in any sense an influence?

I've never been particularly close to compositional orthodoxies. I never went through a serialist phase, or felt it necessary to carry a banner for any *one* type of contemporary music. When I was a student I was made fun of by the other composers who were my contemporaries, because I liked Tchaikovsky and I was ready to defend composers like Tchaikovsky, Bellini and Verdi who were - and probably still are - out of favour with the modernists. Later, in 1969, I met Elliott Schwartz, and I told him that, playing for ballet classes, I really enjoyed improvising that style of music yet I also liked to go to concerts of Webern. I said, 'do you find that odd?', because Americans are a bit more open and I could talk to them more easily than I'd been able to with English composers. Schwartz said, 'no, why don't you try and synthesise the two things?'

IP: Has this idea of synthesising seemingly irreconcilable opposites been a major preoccupation through your compositional career?

I don't try to *reconcile* them because I like oppositions and setting up one thing against another. We talk about music as if it was a series of objects but it isn't, it's a series of processes from a composer's point of view. If you treat materials as objects it becomes like making a collection of skulls or a collection of penises in formaldehyde or whatever it is that you happen to be into - they're just a collection of objects which you then arrange and fetishise. Everybody has a different life so everybody theoretically can have a different way of coping with that life as a model for musical composition. I think I find 'search and discovery' a more important issue than 'are you doing the correct thing with these notes?'

CF: But in the 60s and 70s that was quite a radical decision, because there were a lot of composers around then, in the wake of post-war serialism, and of Stravinsky as well, who were fetishising musical objects. There was a tendency for that sort of attitude to be regarded as the norm

and while some composers decided they were interested in material, you were more concerned with processes.

I preferred Cage, Busoni, Satie, Weill and Ives. I liked what Cardew was doing politically, not least because it was in line with socialist principles I acquired from my father, and Marxism which was approved of by Bernard Stevens. I wanted to study with Nono. A few months before I was due to go, Nono was imprisoned and the RCM insisted I went elsewhere. When I was working for London Contemporary Dance Theatre I was sucked into the orbit of American, rather than European, ideas - so I played Terry Riley and was fed La Monte Young and Meredith Monk. I'm more intuitive than analytical: I hadn't started to isolate 'processes' from material in a conscious, decisive way. In fact, none of this was radical decision-making on my part. Just me being stubborn. I prefer to go my own way, blundering into things by accident and trying to puzzle them out. It's more interesting, less calculated, less like painting by numbers.

IP: In your first mature, acknowledged works, I've heard you say that many ideas came from the cinema.

I wanted the first work that I acknowledged to be a kind of marker-post for things in the future, and the choice of a poem by Rimbaud was deliberate. I identified with Rimbaud: a homosexual, an outsider, his senses deranged and intoxicated. I was nineteen and he was my role model. I treated the poem - it's in fact a rather classical sonnet - as a film-script. I let the lens of my imagination capture the words as a sort of 'montage', roving across the poem as a series of images, actions and gestures. At the end the words get lost in the 'river' flowing out of the instruments. You hear the two bullets being fired - as a flashback - certainly it tries to go beyond the conventions of 'good word-setting' where it's possible simply to create a redundant mimesis of the text. In my head the key-word was 'montage' - from Sergei Eisenstein or Pudovkin. I can't have been thinking of practicality because it's scored for string quartet and three keyboard instruments - celesta, piano and harpsichord - with a mezzo soprano voice that goes from low C four leger lines below the treble stave to the high A one leger line above it! Nonetheless, Josephine Nendick, who remained a champion of mine right up to her retirement, sang that piece beautifully.

IP: How much have these ideas continued throughout your work?

For a serious composer I trained myself with the wrong kinds of aesthetics, which all came from the visual arts and I still wasn't training myself in an orthodox way as a composer when I went to sixth form. When I was in a very formative period, when I was correcting or re-balancing or re-aligning my compositional sympathies during my time studying at the College, I was also going to the National Film Theatre and the Arts Labs a lot to see experimental film. I was particularly taken with film makers like Stan Brakhage, Gregory Markopolous, Jack Smith, the film makers of the American underground during the 1960s/70s. If I tell you there is a particular

Markopolous film in which very very brief snatches of beautifully lit castles in Italy alternate with very long passages of completely black screen, you can see how it would be very stimulating to somebody thinking about how to place sounds. Perhaps it's a poetic/painterly approach, but I immediately see analogies to composition because film happens in time, unlike painting, and the controlled revelation of a vision is possible in that way. Markopoulos would speed things up, slow things down, shoot from odd angles, light things in unusual ways. Films like Jack Smith's *Flaming Creatures*, an ecstatic, totally overblown, kitschy drag ball, have any number of illicit pleasures going for them, but the editing style has a slightly frenetic quality that I find everywhere in things like *English Country-Tunes*. It's an accurate measure of a particular psychological state of mind, a kind of hyper-sensitivity, hyper-neurosis which I want in the music, like exposed nerve-endings. That was the crucial door which opened through film: editing, forming.

IP: Does the manner in which, say, you sometimes have abrupt changes in textures, whereas at other times they dissolve into each other, come from film editing?

Yes, and I still read film scripts (you can see a pile of Dennis Potter scripts on the floor) more than musical scores I suppose, for clues on modes of perception. Pasolini is a director who has shaped narrative in a particularly interesting kind of way, and whose responses I often quote to students. Somebody asked if, in *The Gospel According to St Matthew*, he was trying to tell a biblical story in an up-to-date kind of way? He said no, this was a story *plus* 2000 years of Christianity. Film makers are so much more intelligent about what they say than most composers are.

CF: Yes, but how do you find a musical equivalent of the hand-held tracking shot in *Mean Streets* when they come down the bar?

I teach a film techniques and musical composition course at Sussex University, where I might start with Kenneth Anger and Hitchcock or David Lynch. We talk a lot about correspondences between the controlled observation of camera work and how you control the ear when you decide on a certain course of events in music. You can speed things up and slow them down and you can do perspective because, as in cinema, there are long, medium and close-up shots in music. For example, *Thérèse Raquin* is nearly all in close up, like Dreyer's film *Le Passion de Jeanne d'Arc*. You have to understand its musical perspective, because the piece is claustrophobic by design, there is no medium and long shot at all and it's intensified by nearly always being in the treble clef. Consequently when Laurent's voice first appears in the first scene, it's an aural shock, it's the first note any distance under middle C. I spend a long time thinking about these sorts of things, where to place this or that, or how what I do is like a camera movement. Eighteenth-century rationalism and dogma is less charged with possibilities: it's geometric and controlling the universe, dominating nature. It may be an attractive and comforting prospect to try to maintain, but it's blinkered and a lie about the universe.

EDUCATION

When I went to College, I was 18 years old, I didn't know anything about how a fugue was put together. I knew what fugues were but I didn't know how you went about writing one. It was a great surprise to me, the business of tonic and dominant. Once I'd absorbed that, I became very keen on mediant modulation (not going up a fifth but up or down a third) which I found hugely exciting and looked through all the books to find other composers who liked it as well. I didn't know anything about Palestrina so I was given R. O. Morris,[6] and it was like learning ABC again. But Stevens was a good teacher - what he taught were not methods but principles. Tools not recipes. Counterpoint was top of his list. It contains everything else, depends on imaginative handling of rhythm and harmony. One was never just told to avoid parallel fifths, there was always an explanation, a rationale. Parallel fifths can be a very attractive option, but changing the interval between the notes gives more energy and variety. I'm upset that we never really discussed his own work. He put himself slightly outside his teaching. The only time I can remember him referring to his work - I think he was just tired or disillusioned like anybody who works for institutions gets - was when he said, 'you know, I feel like the member of a lost generation', meaning the ideals that he'd grown up with had been discarded by the musical establishment - perhaps he meant Glock at the BBC. He was interested in the way I felt able to make transitions between modal or diatonic material and atonality or even microtonality. He happened to have heard one of the first performances of Alois Hába's *The Mother* on the occasion that I went in ready to challenge him on quartertones - because he was always one step ahead - and he thought it was odd that I didn't discriminate between that kind of musical language and serialism.

IP: What did your study with other teachers, Humphrey Searle and Roman Vlad, involve?

I only remember one conversation with Searle about the piano music of Liszt and Alkan. I told him I knew their work, he was absolutely delighted, then fell asleep! I bought his book on Liszt which is a delight.

I remember going up in the rickety elevator on the outside of Vlad's house - that's the way they are in Rome - and being terrified because I'm scared of heights. I got out of the lift at his floor, opened the door and there were two or three Mirò originals facing me. There were also Calder drawings, he just loved the arts. His wife was an archaeologist and he was - at that time - the intendant of the Rome Opera House, so I got lots of cut price tickets to see opera - that's how much of my time was spent. I bought myself an opera-cape and went to the opera looking like Bela Lugosi! I saw the most wonderful selection of stuff: at one moment it was Berio doing a triple bill with Cathy Berberian, then the next it was the Hamburg Staatsoper with *Die Frau ohne Schatten.* In *Fedora*, an opera completely unknown to me but not to the audience, they all stood up and joined in an aria with the heroine at one point. I can still remember the appearance of the lights going down - it was all pink in those days - and it was like the last moments of a sunset before it becomes dark. It was an absolutely magical, beautiful place. But I didn't study anything very serious with Vlad.

We talked about Nono (I think he was very hurt because he knew from Searle, who put me in touch with him, that I had originally applied to go to Nono). When I first went to meet him I had analyses of a number of Nono pieces and wanted to talk about them, as if Nono was all that was happening in Italian music. I was embarrassingly arrogant and stupid but he was very understanding!

IP: Perhaps in the early scores you were influenced by the calligraphy of Italian figures such as Bussotti?

My best friend from the ages of 11 to 13 was Roderick Scott. His parents were keener on the arts in a more informed kind of way than mine (not that mine were obstructive) and were determined for Roddy to have an artistic background and education. As most of the kids at the technical high school were what I would describe now as 'fast-lane drivers on the motorway' they weren't interested in sissy stuff like the arts, so Roddy and I teamed up and went round the music publishers. We found Bussotti's *5 Pieces for David Tudor* and I immediately started writing pieces like that. Perhaps the initial attraction came from the visual elegance of the scores, though as they were never played I had no idea what they sounded like. When years later I actually heard a score of Bussotti, it sounded like a kind of marzipan! Sweet and sticky. It drifts about, sometimes rather morosely, sometimes like someone waving sequinned chiffon, and then: nothing - just air. The bad air of the sewer, I would be tempted to say, but I think that's too consciously what Bussotti's about. It's more the kind of fake bad air that's been captured in bottles and is thrown in your direction through very sophisticated devices. 'Smell the sewers...', that's what the *Passion selon Sade* is about - it's an elegant trip into sexual deviance. You come away completely unscathed, rather than lacerated.

CF: I believe you also studied with Nadia Boulanger.

Nadia Boulanger used to come to do Easter courses at the RCM when I was there, and all the composers were asked to go, although some didn't actually show up. She was a terrifying old lady. I remember the first session: she came into the room, announced, 'we're going to begin with a little bit of ear training', thumped out a cluster with surprising ferocity, and imperiously demanded, pointing arbitrarily around the room, 'what pitches did I just play?' You'd never know what she was going to do, she'd ask us to come up one by one and play something that we'd written and then sink her fangs into it. The sort of questions she would ask were 'why is this an F sharp, not an F? Do you think this is shape? Couldn't this phrase be improved somehow?' Basically you didn't learn very much because she made herself so intimidating that we just sat there and shat ourselves. I found her much more interesting when she was talking about other people's music, like Beethoven. She did an afternoon session, which I was obliged to attend as a second study pianist, and she talked about his piano sonatas. She was ten times more interesting about composition when she was talking about pieces that weren't new. I don't think she had much command over the idioms and modes of expression that young people in the '60s, who were after all a good 50 years younger than her, were using. She was formidable and had the reputation for being so, advertising herself as such. Some people liked that, there are a lot of masochists around in the music game, and they wanted to put on their CV that they studied with Nadia Boulanger.

CF: Who else, apart from your formal teachers, do you regard as a major influence?

I think Ives was the composer who really shifted the way I think. Just the general principles of Ives's music, its inclusiveness and the way it reflects man's thoughts and ideas, remain a kind of totem for me.

CF: Does your pantheon change from time to time?

I get crushes on composers and buy everything I can, listen to it, play it. Bartók was an early crush, Feldman, Bernd Alois Zimmermann, Brahms at one stage, Xenakis, Castiglioni, Berwald, Messager... but I distinguish these 'crushes' from more lasting, or much deeper, influences as they tend to be a bit temporary in their impact: you might be able to detect it in one or two pieces rather than permanently. I'm also fortunate in having many composer friends whose work I prize very highly, and whose work undoubtedly influences mine. It's a long list: Chris Newman, Andrew Toovey, Luke Stoneham - all very close friends. Laurence Crane, Chris Dench, Richard Barrett, Rodney Lister, Elliott Schwartz, James Clapperton, Judith Weir, Brian Ferneyhough, you [Fox], Howard Skempton, Loong-Hsing Wen, Karin Rehnqvist! If you want to indulge in a bit of time travel - Hildegard, Abbess of Bingen, Chaminade (Maxwell-Davis told someone he thought my work was a bit like Chaminade 'on speed'!), that's apart from those composers to whom I've rendered homage and thanks in the form of short pieces: Grainger, Nancarrow, Lutyens, Handel, Smyth, Tutev, Stevens, Cardew, Cage, Tippett (in *Folklore*) - I could go on - Szymanowski, Enescu...

CF: I remember you saying in the Toop interviews[7] that you grew up knowing Gershwin songs. Within your works they don't appear formally until the *Gershwin Arrangements* of the 80s.

I knew Gershwin amongst the many Broadway songs that my parents played. But I wasn't immediately conscious of the possibility of using them as 'raw materials' for composing - or for a 'critique'. The first versions of the *Gershwin Arrangements*, which I've since torn up, were absolutely terrible, as were the first versions of the *Verdi Transcriptions*. They were terrible and primitive. Too close to the originals. No profile. No insight.

I was brought up with people who were much older than me. My Auntie Rosie, for example, who taught me the piano, was 40 years older than me. When I befriended Lutyens she would say, very meaningfully, 'I can't remember yesterday but I can remember 40 years ago.' When I found I could remember Gershwin at that sort of distance, curiously, I found a way of using that memory.

CF: So does it always take a long time for your musical digestion to work things through?

I'm often just too close and it takes a lot of time.

CF: But there have been some things which come quite quickly, like the Australian pieces.

I set myself a specific task, it was a research programme. 'The first time I go to Australia I'm going to be an Aboriginal', I said to myself as I got onto the plane at Heathrow airport, terrified at such a long flight. I had planned out my life and I was going to lose everything - getting on the plane was shedding a skin, 32 hours later there I was in Melbourne 'naked'. The next time I went back as a colonial settler and wrote the *Australian Sea Shanties*, *Botany Bay*, *The Eureka Flag*. There's actually less from that period - colonial settling is not as interesting as being an Aboriginal!

PIANO

CF: Who taught you the piano?

I began playing the piano when I was about four, maybe even before. Anyway, there was a piano in the front room, which I took to and played duets with my great aunt Rose Louise Hopwood. She taught me how to play and then couldn't keep up. So when my parents moved from my grandparents' house in about 1951, when I was five, I was sent to the local piano teacher up the road, Mrs Conrath, a very timid woman. I was an awful pupil - I never practised at all, never did scales, and she was despairing. But she used to have these little soirées, where the children who were very good at scales played abominably, because they got very nervous, while I, who had been a show-off since the age of whatever, could sit down and play Chopin Mazurkas that I'd only practised once. This used to drive her to distraction, and after a while she told my parents that she was very sorry, but she couldn't teach me any more - I was unteachable. My parents were a bit upset about this and after a couple of years without a teacher they sent me to a man, because they thought he'd be able to keep me more in line. I went to Mr Ellis, a friend of Peter Racine Fricker, from the time I was about twelve to sixteen. When the time came to go to the College I think my father went to see him and asked who I should study with. He of course recommended Fricker, so they filled his name in on the application form, but Fricker was by that time resident in the States. The registrar asked who else I wanted to study with and I asked for the only other person I recognised on the College's rota, Humphrey Searle. As he was away for a year, they said I could go to Bernard Stevens who didn't at that time have any composition students. Stevens was the teacher I needed. I think it was one of the best things that ever happened to me.

IP: The sort of characteristics of some of your piano writing, especially in the earlier works, such as wide leaps and the use of all seven octaves of the piano seemingly simultaneously, especially the extreme registers, do they relate to the way you learned the instrument?

It's the way I sit [indicates hands as if in extreme registers] I don't sit like that [indicates hands close together in central position] because it hurts my tummy. I didn't learn properly - they probably tried to teach me but I just made up what I did! I suppose if you've got a bit of a musical imagination and you go to somebody and say, 'these are fairies and these are elephants' hitting the top and bottom of the keyboard, they say, 'oh yes, what a clever child', which encourages you a bit and you continue along those lines. The piano was just an adventure playground for me! It didn't surprise me at all when they said, 'aren't you inventive with the keyboard, you don't just use the middle register', because it's all there so why not use it? It never occurred to me that it was forbidden to use the outer octaves of the keyboard. People said 'you can't hear what the notes are'. If you teach yourself, you can.

I am not a piano virtuoso - I did piano studies at College as a second study. I studied with Edwin Benbow: we never really worked on anything because I could sight-read really well. The first thing I played in Benbow's lessons was Bax's *Moy Mell* - about a thousand notes in each bar. We just went for joy-rides through all this two piano literature each week. When I left College it was natural to go into repetiteuring because what I couldn't sight-read I thought I could make up. If you've had to invent most of the polyphonic ensemble at the end of Verdi's *Falstaff* - singing one bit and bashing the rest out on the keyboard - you'll know how I play! My real interest in 'virtuosity' apropos of the piano, is in turning that one instrument into a whole orchestra - a multiplicity of timbres.

IP: But in the early days, you were writing works such as *Autumnall* which contained what would then have seemed transcendental difficulties.

Yes, but not to be a virtuoso. They were written for Alexander Abercrombie who could do those sort of things. He used to live in Lewes - a short train ride from Brighton - and we used to attack Holleyman and Treacher [music shop in Brighton] for their stock of Godowsky transcriptions, Tausig and the like. I liked them because they were interesting textures - and because tonality was less perceptibly stable in virtuoso piano music than in some other more highly-esteemed areas, and I rather like that slippery approach to harmony.

CF: This may not be true, but I remember hearing James Dillon introducing a tape of you playing his solo piano piece *Spleen* and his

explanation for the level of virtuosity in that piece was that you had specifically requested something transcendentally difficult.

Not true! But it gets competitive if you're around and known as a bit of a whiz on the keyboard. Dillon had sent his first piano piece, *Dilug-Kefitsah* to Chris Dench. Chris showed me this private letter which said something along the lines of 'you can show this to old Finnissy but he's not likely to be interested'. Of course he knew perfectly well that I would be! I wonder what he'd have done if I hadn't contacted him but told Chris that I thought it was rubbish! I also knew *Once Upon a Time* because Kris Donovan and I had done a duo recital at York, at the SPNM Composers' Weekend[8] where that piece was done, by an ensemble conducted by Peter Wiegold. I thought that piece was very exciting, but realised that if Dillon was going to write a piano piece it wasn't likely to be a five-finger exercise! I played *Spleen* though he was never very complimentary about the way I played it. In fact the most he said was, 'you played it in a very pragmatic sort of way'. I had to look pragmatic up in the dictionary.

CF: Nevertheless there is a certain commitment to the idea of things not being easy and simple.

The commitment I have is for doing what composers want. Ronald Lumsden phoned in about 1976 to tell me that the SPNM had suddenly noted the dearth of piano music from British composers. John Woolf[9] wanted him to do a programme which consisted of the Liszt-Beethoven Fifth Symphony, Ives' *Concord Sonata* and he also wanted to include my piece *Ives*, and this would apparently encourage lots of composers to write lots of pieces. I thought of a simpler solution and got on the phone to all the composers I knew and told them I would book a hall if they would like to write me a piano piece. I got *Sonya's Lullaby* from Oliver Knussen, pieces from Nigel Osborne, Jennifer Fowler, Robert Saxton and Howard Skempton. I did my debut concert at the Schwarzes-Klöster Gallery in Freiburg and repeated it at the Stedelijk Museum in Amsterdam. Of course I couldn't get a concert here in this country - no one was interested in what I was doing - but Ronald went on an SPNM tour with the Ives *Concord Sonata* and Beethoven-Liszt Fifth Symphony. After that I just kept on asking people, falling in after a while with younger composers like Dench and Dillon who knew me as a pianist. A little band was already gathering round who thought that if I could play this then I could do *Spleen* [Dillon], *Pas de Cinq* [Chris Dench] and all the other things that got written for me over the next few years. I enjoyed working at them, they're super pieces which I really love. I'm proud that some of these composers' best music was first performed by me. It's absolutely the best thing you can ever do as a performer. I wouldn't have dreamt of telling those composers to hold back, I just told them, 'go as far as you like', which they did! They were competitive too and wanted to 'out-do' me.

IP: Was that the situation with the piano part in Richard Barrett's *Coïgitum*?

He somewhat over-estimated how good I was, particularly in the last pages of which I had to make a transcription - the more literal kind of transcription! It was the same with Dench in *Enoncé*. There are now quite a few people around playing that kind of music, though when you write it as a young man, publishers say, 'we couldn't possibly take this - nobody can play it'. That was the reputation that Ferneyhough and I had from 1969 to 1979, that we were unperformable.

IP: Is the fact that there are now a number of pianists who play this kind of repertoire, a reason why you no longer play the works of Dillon, Dench and so on?

There are a lot of people who can play it a lot, lot better than I ever could. If you act as midwife to those pieces it doesn't mean you have proprietary rights over the children. I'm very happy to let them go, and I'm also very happy to let my own pieces go to other pianists who can play them better. The insights are different if you play as a composer, which is something Nadia Boulanger pointed out to me. Composers and non-composers play differently, because they're looking for different things. It's like actors reading Hamlet - people accept that actor A and actor B are not going to read and intone the part in the same way - yet they expect pianists to sound like the one greatest recording as revealed by so-and-so the leading critic - that's complete nonsense. In the better days of the Third Programme [the precursor to BBC Radio 3], there were late night concerts where composers were encouraged to play. I remember Maxwell Davies doing the Chopin G minor Ballade, it was a marvellous performance, and certainly like no other I've ever heard. What you lose in sheer keyboard pyrotechnics you gain immeasurably through other kinds of insight.

IP: One of the biggest difficulties in playing your music is simply reading the voluminous amount of information in the printed score. You must find, when playing your own music, that the familiarity of the notes makes things much easier than when playing other music of a similar level of density.

Possibly, but I've never found it very difficult to read. I can read orchestral scores at the piano too, which is how I got to know a lot of music. In the days before CDs and 24 hour Radio 3, I had to go and hunt music out, and if I couldn't find recordings of pieces I would play them through at the piano. That's how I got to know the huge range of music that I do. It's terrible that so few composers today are sufficiently good musicians to be able to do that. Long before Verdi's minor operas were being produced I bought all the vocal scores and played through them.

IP: One thing that surprises me is how rarely you use extended instrumental techniques.

The sounds which result tend to draw attention to themselves, and away from the overall discourse. They lack that malleable anonymity which is my preferred 'tabula rasa': I feel better about any old A sharp than I do about wind multiphonics that listeners identify as 'abnormal' or may contextualise as neo-Holliger. There is the performer problem too, discomfort, self-consciousness. When I played pieces which involved those sorts of things, I felt embarrassed, wiggling my bottom around in the air and grinding around inside the piano. In the days of London Contemporary Dance Theatre I used to be more often inside the piano than out. Eventually I decided that compositionally it was very hard to integrate unusual timbres in a piece; you either have to make the whole piece about that or you do something very clever. I was never happy with my pieces which involved extended techniques, so I stopped using them.

IP: But in *Lost Lands*, they are almost the subject of the piece.

They are allowed and encouraged to intrude on and fracture the surface of the piece, which is about those types of operations on surfaces. They are necessary, but very intrusive. I prefer the *Art of Fugue* approach to instrumentation. I had a conversation with the Welsh composer Denis Ap Ivor around the time *Le Dormeur du Val* was written. He thought the instrumentation was 'interesting'. I said, 'but it could be anything else', to which he responded, 'this is absolutely incomprehensible, how could you have such an attitude?'

IP: How have things changed since the arrival of a generation of younger performers, starting with James Clapperton, who have been playing a substantial amount of your music?

I have lived out of suitcases my whole life, on tour with London Contemporary Dance Theatre during the 1970s and more recently doing solo concerts. I hate it, I want to be at my desk, writing. So I don't mind yielding that position. It also gives me a different perspective on what I write for the keyboard.

IP: It makes a difference for people like me knowing your own recordings of your piano music, which present something authoritative. But how do you feel when we want to do things differently to yourself?

I think my recordings are useless. I can't listen to them, I get so frustrated with all the mistakes I make. If you get anything out of them, that's fantastic; but I feel I've done what I set out to do by writing music which can be played by somebody else. I don't think you will ever appreciate how much it means to me that people have taken those pieces up. I've been slapped down so often for how unplayable they were and continually asked, 'why don't you take a more realistic attitude towards performers, why don't you do this, why don't you do that!' You can't imagine how often that has been said. Now things have suddenly changed and gone in the completely opposite direction. I don't know whether it will make any difference to the way I write, I'm too cussed and stubborn for that. I'll probably go on the same way. But the awful worry I have is what will happen if you all change your mind? I'll have to practise those Czerny scales again and get back to that keyboard!

CF: You said earlier that when people weren't asking you to write things you wrote for the piano; but just now you were saying that that's changed because of a new generation of pianists like James and Ian. Does that alter the way you think about the piano?

I know Ian can do lots of things on the piano that I can't! Of course I know what my limitations are in terms of contrapuntal delineation of voices, wrist attack or finger agility. Even if I'd prefer that it wasn't the case, that knowledge filters out certain possibilities if I'm writing for myself. I don't just simply go in there blind. Now that Ian in particular, who has a far greater technique than I do, is playing my music, it gives me a lot more possibilities. And Nicolas Hodges, for example, has recently asked me to do what, in effect, is a series of technical studies looking at the right hand only, the left hand only and then the possibilities of contrapuntally combining them. I would never think of doing this for myself; knowing the restrictions of my own left hand technique would mean I would have to do it within a certain framework. I've never written a piece for the left hand alone, although there are many such pieces in the piano literature. To have pianists provoke particular responses to the instrument is extremely interesting and challenging.

THEATRE

IP: I gather there are quite a number of scores either for film or for theatre which no longer feature in the catalogue.

The film scores are rubbish, which I'm unhappy about because it's a medium which interests me very much. I got the thin edge of the wedge with film because I was working with people who wanted something like the Hovis advert, or a bit of Satie. So if I sketched anything else and played it to them to see if they liked it, they would say, 'eh, no, can't you do us a *Gymnopedie*'. Rather than argue, I did something like a *Gymnopedie* and threw it away afterwards. It was the same in the London Contemporary Dance Theatre: I remember Robert North doing a piece called, rather unfortunately, *Brian.* He wanted 'a score rather like the Bach *Brandenburg Concertos* mixed in with the Beach Boys'. You do get people who ask you to do that sort of thing and if you can do it... but it makes for bad feeling eventually. At the Theatre Centre in Beckenham I was allowed a freer hand. I wrote the music to *The Happy Haven* by John Arden, who himself came to the performance of the piece, because at that stage he wasn't a frequently performed playwright. He hated it because he had instructed the music to be performed unaccompanied by the actors and there I was behind the piano. That was a slap in the face. Finally there was a director who asked me to write music for *Camino Real* by Tennessee Williams. At the first rehearsal, when I played the music, he had a dreadful temper tantrum. He said, 'you are trying to upstage the play', to which I replied, 'with this play that isn't hard to do.' He thought that was such a monstrous thing to say about Tennessee

Williams and I was ordered off. I kept the music to *The Happy Haven* because I think it's very good; *Camino Real* I actually lost somewhere. Then I did music to school plays - I improvised an organ score to *Richard II.* So some of it was never written down.

IP: Then you did quite a lot of work with individual dancers.

Always for companies though, and as far as the music goes, never yet with much degree of fulfilment or satisfaction on my part. I don't work well in collaborative contexts.

CF: The collaboration with Kris Donovan, although I only saw it once, seemed to work.[10]

I think of that as an entirely different genre, happily free of entrepreneurs, theatre managements, easily irritated dancers complaining that they couldn't 'feel' the beat or count the choreography. It was just the two of us. Very tight focus. We agreed territory first. We liked each other, we were friends, it worked very well. Kris was very insightful and happened to say meaningful things about my work. I trusted her and wrote many pieces for her. She's a fabulous choreographer.

CF: Watching that, it felt like a duo.

We modelled it on lieder-recitals: opera on a small scale - this was a dance-theatre for small spaces. I was able to apply what I learnt to other theatrical pieces I was writing.

IP: Did these theatrical works relate to a particular view of theatre, one which rejects conventional narrative?

The kind of spoken theatre I was interested in was that of Brecht and Artaud which is not notably narrative, at least not in the conventional Terence Rattigan sense of the word. There usually isn't a plot, and if there is it's there for other reasons, to be commented on and drawn attention to. I thought, why can't opera be like this? It didn't seem to me to be such a radical notion but everybody threw up their hands in horror, saying 'Opera is this way'. Even recently, one of the critics who was sent a pre-performance copy of *Thérèse Raquin* sent the libretto back saying, 'this is not a proper opera libretto, it's not in rhyming couplets', and I don't think he was trying to be funny! People think that opera libretti have to be in verse to be singable. 'Why aren't you interested in number-opera?' somebody asked me. Number-opera refers to balanced, symmetrical successions of closed forms. A Metastasio-world where order is paramount. Not the world of the twentieth century, perhaps not of previous centuries either since composers like Handel (in *Orlando*) and Rossini (in *Ermione*) subvert this structural metaphor for 'order and stability' into a madder, more romantic, view. I prefer a more through-composed, symphonic, open-ended basis to start from. It's metaphors and symbols embedded in structural hypotheses. Number-opera is just one of many possibilities. Not the sole or ideal one.

IP: Pieces like *Vaudeville* and *Soda Fountain* are close to something like a number-opera.

There are numbers, yes! Part of the initial process of coming to terms with the operatic genre is looking at it critically and saying, 'well do you like what you see?' I worked at the Royal Opera House and I didn't like what I saw. I'm not interested in perpetuating that kind of out-of-date, trundling old circus with lots of people getting rich off the pickings of nineteenth-century opera. They never think about it as a provocative or challenging medium. I was involved in performances of *Taverner* by Maxwell Davies the second time it came round and the management really couldn't have cared less about the piece. Indeed, I had an organ transplant on the stage of the Royal Opera House! At the dress rehearsal, having never rehearsed it before, they moved the portative organ which I was playing on stage. This was during a scene change which also involved complex manoeuvres of the big iron set which had been designed by Koltai. It happened in a blackout, the dancers got the position of the organ wrong and an enormous iron ring came down right on top of the organ and demolished it! I had the presence of mind to jump backwards and was saved from the jaws of death. Ted Downes in the orchestra pit uttered the immortal line, 'carry on as if nothing has happened'. He didn't want to delay the rehearsal, but the only accompaniment during that scene was provided by me and Steve Pruslin on the other side of the stage. I spent the rest of the run living in fear and trembling that it would happen again. The only other time anything ever went wrong was during the broadcast, when the plug came out of Steve's regal organ just as it went on stage. By the first performance the opera house had spent £10,000 on another organ and they would have spent another £10,000 if the ring had come crashing down on it again but never thought to check the positioning or re-do the staging. At-five-to-two the orchestral representative says 'five more minutes chaps' and they get to within two bars of the end of the score and stop. They wouldn't go one second over because they're into overtime - this is an opera house for you! And the future of the arts lies in the hands of these people.

IP: Would you ever be tempted, like some German and French composers, to set an experimental text, by someone like Heiner Müller for example?

Well Heiner Müller writes very seductive texts so the answer has to be yes. But people tend not to ask and you've got such a fight on your hands to get anything going here. I've had two full-length stage works produced - one, *The Undivine Comedy*, by the Almeida in 1988. I went round cap in hand to various opera companies and an eminent producer at ENO saw me for about three minutes. All he could say was, 'oh, I enjoyed *The Undivine Comedy* very much', by which I knew - from his intonation - that he'd hated every minute of it, 'but your music is much too marginal for an ENO audience'. The second stage work I did, *Thérèse Raquin*, came about mainly through my friendship with Wilf Judd and Lynne Williams - it was co-produced by the

Garden Venture and Eastern Arts Touring Agency. We opened in Bury St Edmunds. The press were a bit sniffy at making such a long journey, and a few were very peeved at not being accommodated at the best hotel. One of them asked at the reception if the wine was château bottled. They have very high standards and lost no time in revealing that we were beneath them. Fortunately the audiences enjoyed it.

IP: And we've had very little experimental theatre here.

It's usually brought in from Europe. I can see the paucity of writing, having done courses in which writers and composers are brought together. It's always, unfortunately, the writing component which lets the courses down, as people are obsessed with narrative, telling stories... straight from A to B.

IP: As they are in literature as well.

It's like the English novel, has it advanced since Dickens? Discuss!

IP: As B. S. Johnson said, most English writers act as if *Ulysses*, let alone *The Unnameable*, had never happened.

Joyce and Beckett are Irish and regarded as freaks. An Australian student of mine recently went to a composer's workshop at Sussex University and told the little gaggle of students he was with that he was studying with me, with some degree of pride (stupid idiot!), to which they replied 'oh, Finnissy's freakish!' I wonder how much this was a received impression from the rest of the university staff. If you're marginalised, you're just a freak, an eccentric, a maverick or any of the more polite words people will choose to basically say 'you don't belong'.

IP: It's a very English thing, labelling people as 'eccentrics' to trivialise and thus marginalise their work. This happens to Chris Newman as well, which is why he moved to Cologne, where they are more open to innovation.

Well it's a survival tactic as well. You can either be an English eccentric or quite isolated. When given that kind of ultimatum I'd rather be an English eccentric.

CF: It's interesting that the European theatrical mainstream is at such a distance from what goes on in the theatre here.

We are at rather a distance from Europe in aesthetics. If those works are performed here it's OK because they're European, but if an English person wrote them they'd be rapped over the knuckles, as there's an English art which by definition has to be at least 200 years behind the times.

CF: But it's interesting that both the *Undivine Comedy* and *Thérèse Raquin* are, in theatrical terms, small to medium scale productions, and that's also the scale at which the English theatre allows anything remotely experimental to go on. It's the sort of scale of theatre companies like IOU, and before them Impact or Theatre de Complicité.

It's alright as long as you don't go beyond that. The worst that can happen is when they peel off the directors and put them in the National Theatre, where they can do Shakespeare.

Those works of mine I mentioned earlier are both fairly conventional narratives - *The Undivine Comedy* perhaps less so.

IP: If the *Undivine Comedy* and *Thérèse Raquin* do follow an overall narrative structure, nonetheless there are features which seem to me to involve an element of critique. In the *Undivine Comedy* you incorporate texts from Hölderlin and de Sade, and in *Thérèse* you actually have the pianist on the stage as if he were one of the characters. Both these elements seem a departure from naturalistic conventions.

The on-stage piano in *Thérèse* was just practical because the venues were too small to put the piano anywhere else. It was also on-stage to show that I wasn't trying to hide it, and as a distancing device like having on-stage posters announcing the time and the place in Brecht.

IP: The idea that a drama might be multi-dimensional, in the sense that one might introduce elements that are not essential to the linear flow of a narrative, seems to be anathema to modern English theatrical practitioners, and to establishment British composers' ideas of temporal flow and 'tightness' in a work of music too.

You can hang any number of elements on a line, test how far you can go before the line breaks, but up to that point you surely do as much as you can. Then there's a 'golden rule': less is more. It's not just about text of course. But the right words are crucial, even if it's as much a question of what to leave out as it is what to put in. I'm a believer in textual anthologies and certainly not being over-respectful of the writer - if I don't like two lines of a poem I cut them out. Why set the whole thing? You'd only set them badly and it's not a 'comprehension' test. In *Whitman* (although I haven't finished this piece yet) what I did was to cut chunks out of the poems. If people want to read the original poem they can buy a book!

FORM

IP: It seems in your work that many lines move in a multiplicity of directions and are eventually pushed towards a goal, which makes an interesting comparison with Richard Barrett's work, where you have these hemmed-in lines struggling to break out. I'm thinking in particular of his string quartet *I Open and Close* which seems like a musical analogy of free-will thwarted by coercive forces.

Isn't that a kind of objectification of the material, making you aware of the form in a way?

CF: The feeling in the middle of any of your pieces is that anything is still possible whereas in something like *I Open and Close* you know damn well what's going to happen.

I try to make form active, conspiratorial, mobile, disturbing - but above all, audible. You're not supposed to have worked it out before the end. In early pieces - the first set of *Songs* and things like *Afar* - there is a fast section and a slow section. I don't think you'd ever be sure what the proportions of those sections were, or when they were going to end. I do plant little clues: the unison chord at the end of *Afar* is the only time that the trumpets ever play together in that section, so you know it must be the end. Otherwise I prefer to just close the door, as if the music is still going on behind that door.

CF: In that sense, the open-ended Finnissy cadence seems always to imply the teeming life of the music can carry on, but we just can't hear it any longer.

It's a fear of death. It's a fear that the world will come to an end. I'm presenting an optimistic view. Life must go on and beyond a piece there is life. It's false to tell the audience 'This is the end'. It isn't, they go home on the bus after the concert.

CF: A lot of baroque forms are beautifully symmetrical but that doesn't imply closure either, because it's part of the 'divine plan'.

Musical metaphors also propagate the world-views of their particular era. From the beginning of a Handel piece, you can see how the people walked, you can see the clothes and you know what their attitude to the world was, at least the attitude that they wanted to have. But my world is not the same as Handel's. I don't even wish that it was. Other metaphors have to be found.

IP: In works of yours such as *As when upon a trancèd summer night* or *all.fall.down*, you seem to offer an alternative to symmetrical baroque forms, by starting at one point and ending at quite another. Obviously the work goes in many other often tangential directions on the journey but eventually gets there. Does this reflect an idea of music as a non-closed entity?

Yes. People are off-centre; we dream of finding the perfect man or the perfect woman but they don't exist, nor do perfect ideas, they've always got one leg shorter than the other. Deliberately flaw your work. Only God is perfect. And perhaps...

IP: Are those artists who hearken for the past in reality yearning for an idealised world which never actually existed?

In Alan Bennett's *The Madness of King George III* he shows how success at court actually depends on ignoring what's going on around you. The level of pretence is quite horrific to maintain that status quo, but therein lies success. Not in achieving but almost in refusing to achieve. You get further by not rocking the boat than you ever do otherwise.

CF: In 1985 when I came across all this Finnissy, having encountered it ten years earlier and not got the plot at all, it was the amazing optimism in the music that struck me.

Tippett says you have to be optimistic to be an artist, otherwise you wouldn't write anything. You do it with a certain energy and a certain commitment which either succeeds in putting life into a work or is perceptibly taking it away. Compare recent Ligeti with Nancarrow. Whereas Nancarrow is teeming with energy and the very stuff of human existence, Ligeti sounds very nihilistic. It's as if something is being erased in front of you, and the composer isn't rushing to save it, or has not realised the poignancy of the moment or even what indeed is there. It becomes a mechanistic thing. Uninterestingly deviant.

IP: A problem I have with the Ligeti pieces stems less from the works themselves than with the trappings they have attained through the sort of people who have been playing them - those of mechanistic competition playing.

That's almost what they were destined for anyway. I dislike music where there's 'just enough' to be interesting - but not more. Thin, tepid, mean music. Or music which plays to the gallery, wringing its hands and tearing at the collective soul. Usually those composers are control-freaks with bad tempers, selfish beyond the limits of tolerance, like Stockhausen or Kurtág. I feel exploited, not given the freedom or opportunity to decide for myself. For me the greatest measure of a work of art is whether it makes me feel uncomfortable or excites me sexually. Ligeti doesn't do either of those things and neither does Kurtág.

CF: Going back to James Dillon and transcendental difficulty, within your own work there's a preoccupation with the concept of transcendence isn't there? You start off with material in one form and then, through transcription it is transformed.

The first use of the word 'transcendence' I remember was describing Thoreau's philosophy. It's also a religious concept - shamans transcend their own body in meditation or ecstatic trance. It's not to be confused with 'escapism'... the idea being that you can attain a higher level of awareness, of consciousness. It's implicit in Rimbaud, or the other drug-taking imagists of nineteenth-century literature. I think it's important we go beyond the notion that composing is akin to furniture-making. It is about insight and imagination - illumination: the white light that St Augustine writes about. I'm attracted to metaphysics and mysticism, to the inexplicable. I'm not so interested in answers, more in questions. I also, in spite of all the loose talk about 'autobiography', try and lose myself, transcend myself, in my writing. The autobiographical element should be understood as me-*as*-my-music or me-as-composer.

CHURCH

CF: More recently your music has become quite specific in religious terms.

Music to me has always been more than simply the technical mechanisms; there also needs to be a spiritual and aesthetic apparatus in place. I think this not only enriches the music but also adds symbolism and metaphor where musical devices alone may or may not perform that function. It also makes my life more interesting, as I feel my responses to things are widened and deepened. Religion contextualises music.

IP: It seems, in view of some of the sources and texts you have set, that your recent work reflects a new type of religious experience.

For me circumstances always affect things: I live with, and love, the choir master and musical director of an Anglo-Catholic church and I want to be with him in his work so that means that I had either to consider his work seriously or ignore it. Spiritual activity for me also covers what other people would call tribal or ritual activity. Those are all under the same umbrella for me - ritualised and collective music making: hymn singing and the Mass in parts of Western Europe.

IP: Do you feel closer to aspects of Christianity now than, for example, when you wrote the *Mysteries* in the 1970s?

No, not really - I'm more active within a specific church community at St Paul's, West Street in Brighton - but I serve that community primarily as a musician. I have faith, but I have doubts too.

CF: Some people who have known your work for a long time have found the more recent work difficult, especially the way in which you started to locate the choral pieces in a very specific tradition. I don't think it's so surprising when you think of what you did in the past, particularly with plainsong and that tradition.

I grew up listening to Maxwell Davies when he was most prominently making use of medieval compositional devices and deriving a lot of works from plainsong. The central use of cantus firmus devices and drone devices, which is quite familiar from Max's work and medieval music, is very important in my work too, and when I got an opportunity to address it directly rather than obliquely I grasped the nettle. I think many people in a predominantly secularised society find 'religion' unacceptable. They find the word 'tradition' symbolic of capitulation. Surely these words are not that inflexible. We have lived to see people pour scorn on the 'tradition' of modernism too. I'm not trying to maintain a 'status-quo' choral tradition: otherwise I wouldn't have chosen plainsong (symbolic of Catholicism, idolatry, Popishness). In Lindsay Anderson's film *If...* hymn singing has definite connotations, which he exploits quite wonderfully - it's criticism and not nostalgia. Plainsong has connotations which one can exploit, it's rather more fertile territory than the note-row of Messiaen's *Mode des valeurs....*

CF: I think lots of composers, confronted with the problem of cohesion, would come up with some sort of grand, abstract scheme to make the whole piece work.

Test that in reality: you know what those grand, pre-compositional schemes can amount to. I've seen enough compositions in my time where the plethora of pre-compositional schemes have produced something absolutely sterile or void. You can spend 25 years labouring on a piece but it doesn't necessarily make it better than anything written in 25 days, or even 25 minutes. Perhaps it's just a pompous illusion which people who suffer very badly from a form of constipation promote!

CF: Isn't it quite an English thing to do as well? There's quite a strong tradition within twentieth-century English music of pieces that belong explicitly to special circumstances, whereas German, French and Italian composers cover their tracks more carefully...

Why should one have to 'cover up' tracks? To make the arrival seem more miraculous? Surely most composers are located, or locatable in a particular culture. Maybe many don't make it explicit but have grander scenarios to enact. I'm becoming defensive. Stockhausen's *Mikrophonie* or *Gruppen* locate themselves in a period, people tend not to use those titles any more, or *Formel* or *Carré*.

CF: But *Carré* isn't called *Australian Sea Shanties*, or *Maldon*.

I wouldn't call something 'Square': a colloquialism for ponderous and old fashioned! Supposing, since I believe it is part of the material, *Momente* were called 'My Life with Mary Bauermeister and other women' - you de-emphasise the structural level... Stockhausen is emphasising the structure in his choice of title.

CF: But 25 years after *Momente* people still talk about Klang- and Melodie- moments and these quasi-serial concepts, but in your case they say, 'He's gone completely soft, he's writing these drone pieces, he's turned Catholic and is writing about Essex villages.'

Is that something real composers don't do? Why not write about Essex villages, or - in the case of *Maldon* - their history? If that was all I was doing, maybe you should dismiss it as limited and provincial. 'The Battle of Maldon' is a well known Anglo-Saxon poem. You don't become a better writer by confining yourself solely to the grandest topics, or loftiest moments of world history. Look at Emily Dickinson: is she less of a poet than Tennyson?

IP: People wouldn't suggest that *Ulysses* was only of interest to Dubliners.

But I have heard it said that it's impossible to understand *Ulysses* unless you've been to Dublin. People will say anything they like if they want to cut a work down to size, that's democracy for you!

IP: In what sense do you see a political or socio-critical dimension to your work? Are you thinking while you're writing, as some composers do, that your music is in some sense a force for change or reflects a certain state of society?

I usually feel pitifully impotent in the face of those big scale changes in society. What can you possibly achieve in that sense by writing a piece of music which 14 people are going to listen to in a closed venue in London? That's the real power politic isn't it? To an extent my work with amateur groups - non-professional players and singers, people who make music because they enjoy it rather than to make money - my work with them is part of a political and social drive. But we live in a society which minimises your capacity to act politically because it cuts everything down to size. Look how we all treat Birtwistle now he's suddenly become big; we pick holes in his work until we hope he's going to collapse under the weight of all the adverse criticism that's suddenly appeared. I'm just waiting for it to happen to me: it's already happening with the religious music. It's just an irresistible temptation to make light of it. Stop it getting too big for its boots!

IP: How valid are the questions of the relationship between new music and society, and the way they were treated by Wolff or Nono or Cardew?

Cardew, Wolff and Nono are just the tip of an iceberg and three very different responses to the question! I was taught by a composer who was very left-wing, who - for a while - was a card-carrying member of the Communist Party, and a Marxist thinker. He and many of his generation, who had fought the Second World War, were very disillusioned with the kind of policies that were afterwards current in Britain. They were influenced by Hindemith, Eisler and Dessau - music for the proletariat, 'Lehrstücke'. They had ideals, their work was admired in some places, discriminated against in others. They felt betrayed, but nobody wanted to listen to them - they were then old fashioned Marxists, arm-chair Commies, and they were swept away by Maoists who were swept away by Trotsky-ites, and so on. I have a cause to fight, although I don't always fight it very effectively. *Folklore* is as much a political piece as something called *Remember what happened in Auschwitz*. *Folklore* is perhaps more all embracing than something to do with Auschwitz, but it isn't asking you for a shocked emotional response; rather to consider issues critically. Some people might think it's 'more cultural imperialism' - Finnissy tours the world, picks up these folk music tunes and bungs them all together into some spineless piano piece which goes on for 85 minutes.' It's titles again. Should I have called it 'Remember what happened in Cambodia, in Rumania, in Korea, in Belfast, in...?'

CF: But you've made a conscious aesthetic decision, which is also familiar especially in the visual arts, to be present in the work at a much higher, more obvious level than lots of other composers are.

I get that from painting. My background in aesthetics came from painters who will do things like make self-portraits. People like David Hockney were very visible at a time when politicising my sexuality was also very important, so I began to think along the same lines as those people - I could probably quote you more Hockney than I could Stockhausen. I don't think one should have to stand aside from one's work; in my case I'm quite prepared to take responsibility for it. I am present in it in many different ways: *Folklore* is an investigation of different modes of presence. I have had a lot of discussions with friends who also use folk material in their work. Many of my Bulgarian friends are horrified because they were forced to write folk music under Soviet domination in a way which turned them into caricatures of Bulgarians. They wouldn't use folk music now but a blander, more universal kind of system like minimalism, which they think is world music. *Chacun à son goût.*

LIVING IN BRITAIN

IP: Have you never been tempted to leave the country?

Yes, because living here is such a disaster for a composer and I have had offers. During the early 1980s, when I was at such a low ebb, there was just no work at all, I contacted friends all over the world. I tried Carol Plantamura and American friends of mine on the West Coast and also an old college contact, Richard David Hames in Australia, who came up with a job: a three month residency. I fell in love with Australia partly because they made me welcome and treated me so seriously. By the time I had to come back I was weeping on the plane because I didn't want to leave at all. I went again the next year as there was still no work here. Fortunately by the time I returned there was. More recently I was offered a job in Amsterdam to head the composition department at the Conservatorium. But they wanted me to be a full time resident in Amsterdam which would not have worked for personal reasons. Recently again I had the offer of a job in New York but I didn't want to take that both for the same reasons and because I still have important issues to address here: bigotry, racism, fear and ignorance.

IP: Without wanting to press these comparisons too far, I think of the fact that, for example, Ferneyhough hasn't lived in this country for about the last 25 years, Richard Barrett lives in Amsterdam, Chris Dench lives in Australia, and so on. I've heard people compare you to them; they would say your music is more 'English'.

Isn't it strange that 'English' is a tactful euphemism for 'second-rate' or worse a limited and limiting culture? I don't have many illusions left about English culture or society, except perhaps that I could meaningfully contribute to it. I feel a responsibility towards it. It's probably a waste of time in terms of fulfilling personal ambitions, but that's not the only, or even the dominant, issue in culture. These are the fading echoes of concepts like the Welfare State to most people, after we've had nearly twenty years of smash and grab Thatcherist greed. I know where the brick wall is... feel the bumps, see the scars, it's a great show!

CF: What are the questions posed by this culture?

There are many. Populism is an ongoing question for the English; the question of music and whether it has any role to play in society at all. Why should 'composer of contemporary art-music' be perceived as somewhat less important than an average cricketer or someone who has the ability to kick a football from one side of a piece of grass to another? I enjoy serving amateur musicians and children, which is part of our culture to an extent which it is not elsewhere. I enjoy the contact and the freshness and the challenge of it. Coping with a particular kind of imported Americanism which other cultures in Europe, perhaps with the exception of Holland, have managed to resist. The ongoing questions of contextualising music in life in fact. For me the landscape is still a potent contextualisation for music.

IP: The 1960s, when you were composing the first works that you still acknowledge, was a flourishing time for the arts, with figures like Cardew, B. S. Johnson, Peter Brook and others whose work has had a lasting reputation and impact both here and abroad. That period of British cultural history seems particular in that sense.

It was a wonderful time, but you mustn't be nostalgic, you have to move on. The trouble is we've retrenched rather than progressed - people have forgotten what it was to be awake.

IP: Yes, but it's noticeable from the multiplicity of sources of musics or texts or anything else I might mention, the sheer range of arts that you were able to encounter then. For today's generation this is no longer the case.

It gets out of hand for governments you see. Too many people with too many ideas - it's too hard to control so it has to be clamped down on. Stay on the kerb, don't try and cross the road.

IP: When you made your move to Australia was the recent election of a radical right wing government here a factor?

It certainly had some significance. I knew there was nothing for me here and I felt frightened. I needed space and there was nothing to keep me here. Unlike now.

IP: Do you think that all the talk of Victorian Values and so on had an effect on the musical scene?

Quite a few people were still entrenched in original Victorianism, ignoring the twentieth century altogether. Obviously very few people had read

Mayhew or seen Doré's engravings of Victorian London. It only sounds good: Queen Victoria was a powerful woman, and people admire (without necessarily questioning) power. One major Victorian value consisted of the rich exploiting the poor. Others include hypocrisy, imperial despotism, superciliousness. Naturally the musical climate has been changing and mostly worsening since Thatcher tempted and caught us with our own greed. Being 'accountable'. Insufficient 'profit'. 'Market' forces. Lots of jargon has entered the musician's vocabulary: mostly connected to finance, less to do with quality. We're dominated by class issues. Too ready to bow and scrape to the toffs. 'God save me from the Porkers' and so on.

IP: In recent pieces you've been more explicit with subtexts to do with the questions of sexuality. Do you think, perhaps, sexuality actually affects the type of music one writes?

If people don't know, what assumptions do they make? Once they do know they may say 'I suspected that'! Hans Keller was a great champion of Jewishness in music, suggesting that you can hear that Schoenberg and Mendelssohn are Jewish! I think the moral or political crusades on which one might go are a rather small part of what one's doing anyway, but as the situation becomes worse one either becomes more open about it or not. I'm being more open now because I think the situation has become worse and I have a responsibility to younger artists who don't want to be terrified of their sexuality and not be dominated by, entirely bogus as it happens, heterosexual politics. I'm not against heterosexuality, that would be equally stupid - it's just about equal rights. The fact that Cage or Barraqué or Tippett are also homosexual doesn't make their music sound stereotypically homosexual. As far as the English go that would mean limp-wristed, handbaggy, shrieking hysterically - in other words: a caricature. I was taught that all composers were straight, white-skinned, and male. Ha Ha Ha. Recent revelations about Handel and Schubert are apparently provoking controversy: so you see, it does make a difference. It is definitely not good to be gay, or to be black, or a woman. You can climb up the ladder far more easily with a mask on, so people don the mask rather than tell the truth.

IP: Perhaps amongst the advocates of doctrinaire, hard-line modernism there is a certain amount of machismo involved.

It would be wrong to assume that gay men are incapable of being macho: but maybe some people, and certainly the tabloid press, prefer to envisage us all as 'sissies'.

IP: I think of the way in which your works aren't completely taut and absolutely focused in one direction, the way in which they are prepared to move out in lots of directions and include elements which aren't necessarily of paramount importance to the overall flow of the piece, even decorative elements. I wonder if you might see that on one hand reflecting those forces which have recently resulted in an interest in

Anglo-Catholicism, and also perhaps a difference from a very puritanical, 'straight' mode of composition.

'Straight' in the sexual sense?! I think my pieces are digressive certainly and maybe technically incompetent. I think it would be wrong to ascribe any kind of motives to that from Anglo-Catholicism; after all the people who started it, like Cardinal Newman and Pusey, were Oxford Dons and extremely straightlaced, at least that's what the history of the Oxford Movement suggests. I don't think digressiveness and lack of focus can be attributed to Anglo-Catholicism or indeed to feminine or masculine modes of thinking or effeminate modes of thinking. D'Indy's explanations of sonata principle, in which the masculine first subject eventually overcomes the feminine second subject, so that she (the feminine) can assume her rightful place in society where men are always in control - Yuck! But that was taken on board by generation upon generation of Paris conservatoire students right up until 1920 or so. Nobody questioned it!

IP: I was citing this non-tunnel-visioned way of writing as a strength.

Thank you, but I am tunnel-visioned, obsessive.

IP: But it is evidently the work of a human being in the world, not just some private mythology which in the long run would never really be of true interest to anyone other than the person who actually perceived and created it.

No man is an island.

FOLK MUSIC

CF: How do you select the folk musics which crop up in your work? I'm not aware of a proliferation of *Lederhosen* tunes for instance! How is the decision to make a piece around Polish or Sardinian folk musics made?

It depends on the contact I have with it. My parents had contact with Polish people during the war so there were books of Polish folk music on the piano from when I was a child, which I made use of in early pieces and which then led into Chopin. The first things I liked of Chopin were the Mazurkas which are folksy and there are some with very strange modalities. Their strangeness mirrored my strangeness. When I was playing piano for ballet classes I was working for a Macedonian dance teacher who had a lot of Macedonian folk music which I used to transcribe for displays - it was on tape. Often the contact comes from going to those countries where I find I am attracted to the folk music. In general it's part of a quest for irregular things (perhaps it has something to do with sex as well) like irregular modalities, irregular scale patterns, irregular metric organisation. The folk musics which have these properties are those to which I am attracted. If you want to explain the absence of *Lederhosen* tunes it's because they're rather four-square: though *Lederhosen* are gorgeous - on the right man!

CF: But on the other hand you've used English folk tunes.

When I discovered Grainger's notations of English folk music, I was struck by the irregular barring, quite unlike Cecil Sharp's whiter-than-white fascist versions of it. They're astonishingly expressive, very highly decorative and very close to Bartók's notations of Turkish and Rumanian folk song. I was looking for confirmation that my own intuitions and beliefs about 'art' music were actually born out at folk music level, so that I could feel what I was doing was more authentic. It helps to combat other forces in the music world which are asking you to conform to this or that, as was the case with serialism, for example, when I was a student.

IP: In the series of works which are based on Kurdish folk music, were you also attempting to say something about the contemporary situation about those people?

No, that would be patronising. I'm not sufficiently aware of Kurdish politics to attempt to articulate them in music - though 'oppression' and 'tyranny' are common enough here to register correspondences - the use of any folk material is to redress imbalance and neglect, the idea that folk music is 'trivial' or 'irrelevant.'

CF: When you're working on a piece which uses a folk music model, is the feeling one of writing your music on a Sardinian hillside?

The main topics in folk music - birth, love, work, death - are pretty much those I would address even in pieces without a 'folksy' component. So I empathise with the folk musician, rather than his or her location, and don't see myself as different from them: the same useful tension between intuitive individual response and received convention exists in both types of music. You offset one with the other: your ideas *vis-à-vis* inherited and established ideas.

CF: It seems to me that in a lot of those pieces there's a very subjective engagement with the material which is quite different from the way in which a lot of other composers use folk material where there's a sort of critical distance - 'I'm using folk material but I'm showing you that I'm using folk material'.

I am subjective, empathic and socially gregarious, qualities I take from my mother. I find it very easy to make contact with people. It's not that my work is entirely devoid of critical distance because there is also the issue of bringing those thoughts back into a Western European, fairly moneyed living room, very different indeed from the sources which produced them. There's a certain amount of guilt and shame in doing that. I'm not pretending they're settings of folk song, in the way that Grainger and Grieg pretended that the nature of their folk-song settings produced an authentic atmosphere. I hope they convey something more 'problematic' - an internalisation of my contact with them, transcending mere depiction.

IP: In your experience of investigating folk musics and folk cultures, has it led you to the conclusion that in modern industrialised Western European society we've thrown the baby out with the bath water? Is there in a sense something lacking?

There's certainly something lacking, but I think that whatever it is you can't just recapture it by pretending to be a Sardinian folk musician. It's another kind of poignant tug, towards Arcadia or lost innocence, like the wish to go back to childhood. Some people have children to try and re-experience childhood. Perhaps it's nostalgia, 'I remember the good old days', the good old days of Arcadia. It was never there! Nostalgia is also present in Christian mythology through the garden of Eden, which was Arcadia until the snake came along - 'have a bite of this apple my dear!' Trying to capture a lost innocence, a lost virginity. The flesh sags, the wrinkles grow. The stuff (and nonsense) of folk culture!

IP: Maybe in the process of industrialisation we're losing knowledge of the real nature of rural life.

Read Blake, that's all about that, dark satanic mills! Industrialisation's been happening for such a long time, but we still pin all our hopes on this three-quarter inch square of all that is left of rural England - get out there and sniff the buttercups, it will make you feel better. We're not addressing the real problem are we?

IP: There are some who would say that, despite the industrial revolution, in the twentieth century England has been a nation that yearns for a pre-industrial, pre-urban age - you can see it in the architecture for example. Some people would say that your exploration of folk music reflects that.

Exactly so.

CF: So on the other hand, where does the spectacular savagery come from? That's the counter-argument to the idea that by writing a piece called *English Country-Tunes* you're indulging in some sort of smock-wearing nostalgia: in reality that piece is full of outbursts of psychotic violence.

Savagery and violence are everywhere, not least in my temperament: Eros and Thanatos. The single fine white line down the middle of a bright red canvas by Barnett Newman. Suicide. The *Liebestod*. Where do they come from? From inside. From outside. From every damn place on earth: the real chaos of the universe breaking through our pathetic rationalisations of it. Across the still and snow-swept landscape a deep chasm opens. BAM! The sun disappears behind a cloud. A hurricane suddenly tears across southern England at two in the morning. Relish the unpredictability of such events - even while lamenting the terrible destruction. They should render us somewhat more humble. It's not new in music, shock and surprise figure largely in Haydn, Schubert, Berlioz...

IP: I remember playing one of the *Verdi Transcriptions* to someone and they said, 'this man must really dislike Verdi'.

That's like what some wit said about Stravinsky's *Symphonies of Wind Instruments* which ends with the chorale he wrote *in memoriam* for Debussy: 'I never knew Stravinsky disliked Debussy that much!' People confuse dissonance and even more overt kinds of aggressive tactics in music, with dislike, anger, hatred and so on. That's why I use the word passion because we all probably know from experience that passion can entail a certain amount of violence.

CF: In things like the outbursts in the *Verdi Transcriptions*, *English Country-Tunes*, the *Third Piano Concerto* and lots of other pieces, it is a sort of sexual excitement with the material.

Absolutely.

CF: Some people find it difficult to follow everything that you do all the way.

RETROSPECTIVE

CF: Looking across your career, are you aware of, comparatively speaking, a golden age?

No. Frank Lloyd Wright, when asked which of his houses was his favourite, answered 'the next one', and that applies to my works as well. I have favourites amongst pieces, but I don't see them as representing golden ages. They might be associated with events I've remembered with particular pleasure. But the important one is the one I'm working on - or the next one.

CF: I also meant the circumstances in which your work was made.

The writing of any piece is enjoyable, even if frustrating on occasion, or maddeningly slow to complete itself. Critical response has often driven me to extreme despondency, wanting to give up - though anger soon wells up and drives despair away. I've mostly been lucky with performers. There was one hideous experience with the London Sinfonietta with *Alongside*, I waited ten years to hear it properly done (Olly Knussen revived it at the 1988 Almeida Festival, a wonderful performance of a piece I'd grown to hate). Orchestras do their best to intimidate you: they deserve to be extinct.

Henrietta Brougham: Isn't what you're writing now very much dependent on what you're asked to write? Many commissions seem to come from choirs and local groups and, although there are any number of ensembles who would like to commission you, very often they're not able to raise the commission fees. Does this shape what you're able to do, and might this explain the number of religious pieces?

I don't mind what I do so long as I'm working. If I'm not writing anything for anybody specifically then I'm probably writing piano pieces for myself to play. Don't assume that getting religion necessarily changes the way you write, it doesn't for me. I had this fantasy about the sea for a number of years and two of my orchestral pieces, *Offshore* and *Sea and Sky* are actually about it. As soon as I moved to Brighton, people would say, 'now you're living by the sea you'll be doing even more seascapes', but I didn't write a single piece about the sea! It's like, 'now you're living in Steyning you can do another *English Country-Tunes*,' when nothing could be further from my mind.

HB: So it wouldn't have mattered if you'd been commissioned by Steyning Choir or by Elision, the preoccupations would have been the same?

Absolutely. They're couched in different terms technically but it doesn't mean the vision is in any way different. Does it to you [Fox]?

CF: No, you do whatever you're doing at that time.

IP: Surely the capabilities of the performers you're writing for has some bearing on the piece you write? There are different possibilities in writing for an amateur choir than for a very experienced ensemble.

Of course there are, but I don't find one more limiting or frustrating to my creativity than the other. *Wee saw footprints* was just as interesting to write as *Pathways of Sun and Stars*: it's your problem if you think one is 'better' or 'more characteristic' than the other.

IP: So why then do you write *Wee Saw Footprints* on one hand and then the recent seventh *Tango* which, on one page, has a kaleidoscope of notes? If the conceptions are not so different, why are the pieces so dissimilar? Or do you think they're not?

I'm interested in apples and oranges and I try not to confuse them. If I'm drawing an apple with music then I don't draw an orange. Some people only produce one or the other. Can't we have both black and white - gay and straight? Probably not, eh? Someone has to be best of all!

IP: People used to open your scores, see 77-in-the-time-of-62 and lots of notes which don't seem to follow any regular pattern, and be unable to see the piece beyond that level.

Poor them.

CF: That was the curse of the 1980s: the great Darmstadt experience was to see susceptible young people opening scores aghast, 'look, I've seen the biggest irrational; no, there's one over here even bigger, look at this'.

Size queens! Whether the notation contains any irrationals or none at all is rather secondary, even tertiary, to other concerns. Sound remains of paramount importance. Exploring the 'psychology' of notation is more revealing - how you precipitate certain kinds of response by either writing half-notes or sixty-fourth notes. How much detail? How clearly can you hear or envisage a sound? Notation is about choice and degrees of exactitude, reality-unreality. I can best illustrate this if I refer to Monet trying to paint light, which he found very difficult because light always changes and the brush can't capture it fast enough. What one ends up doing is not capturing it, but putting up with the frustration and finding other means which possibly even suggest that frustration. The notation of music is like that if you start from the premise of sound - when you impose the conventions of music on it, you're imposing a filter, which we do all the time. The filter of our understanding, or our tolerance or our prejudice or whatever it happens to be. Filters upon filters upon filters. What is eventually left is a choice of what to do, but music notation is quite limited.

CF: You talked just now about notation as unreal and earlier you talked about the composition process as being some sort of mediation between things that are real and unreal. I wasn't sure earlier whether the unreality was the world of the piece, the music, and the reality is us here now, or whether it was the other way round.

It's so tempting to leave it ambiguous, but the real is the here and now of us sitting around a table and the unreal is the world of the imagination, the transcendent world, the parallel universe, the attainable through music, if that clarifies it. They're not very good words, one involves the other as well, either as a potential interference, not necessarily total but as a flicker of presence.

CF: They are sort of gateless gates into one another.

Screens, windows, the mirrors in Cocteau's *Orphée*.

CF: There are Finnissy fans who like this period but not that, and there are a lot of people who can't make it into the pieces at all: this huge range from a single stream of very slow notes to a plethora of notes is simply too challenging.

What was it Joyce said about *Finnegans Wake*? 'If it took me thirty years to write it why would it take less time to read it.' I've been thinking about these things for many, many years, whereas most listeners haven't been with the pieces for so long. Also, there hasn't been any body of received critical opinion, until recently, to help them on that road. I'm glad I had to wait because it's now come with a bit of background and sense, whereas a lot of writing about composers' work is instant and wrong. Most music doesn't yield up its secrets in one listening, and listening is what is really important. When you see the scores they have another thing to contribute - the notation, and the appearance of the notation can be attractive - but they're not about the notation, the notation is a way of enabling the performer in some way to produce an audible result. The sound of the music has had to be around a number of years before people have started to take it seriously and not think it was a deviant form of somebody else's writing. I'm aware that my work is an uncomfortable, often by design, synthesis of many things, stemming from often very diverse forces, but they're unified by this sexual thrust.

IP: There is also the spectrum from works like *Alongside* or *Sea and Sky* or *Fast Dances, Slow Dances*, which certainly have a large number of notes on the page but are actually quite direct, to highly enigmatic works like *Nine Romantics* or *Folklore* or some of the early stuff. People who claim to be interested in 'complex' music often come unstuck when the complexity is not about having lots of notes on the page but about extreme discontinuities, non-closure and other complex ideas.

'Complexity', if it is meaningful and not merely sensational, is surely operating deep in the structure - within the processes of composition itself, and not on the surface of the score in thick tangles of notes. Of course I can choose an image from nature which suggests complexity: but do I choose a simple-looking complex phenomenon (the night-sky for example) - or a tangled-hedgerow where the eco-system and the appearance are both complex? It's a mistake to assume Mozart is simple, or that Skempton is simple, in comparison with Reger or the stormier pages of Roslavets. Complexity is too often simply a question of detail, why assume that superfluity of detail equals complexity?

IP: When I did the first concert in my series of the complete Finnissy piano music,[11] almost everybody I spoke to found the *Verdi Transcriptions* very immediate and were really taken aback by them, but a lot of people didn't know what to make of *Nine Romantics* as a piece.

Well, I think the *Verdi Transcriptions* are actually very easy to understand because they're very direct and you have the original material up front in quite a lot of instances. Anyway, you have some idea as to who Verdi was, you know he was a nineteenth-century opera composer. Some people might even know his political affiliations and all the rest of that stuff so you have plenty of material there to deal with. In *Nine Romantics*, listeners can be resistant to the word 'romantic' (which is a good reason for using it in the title), and one might not know, not having been told, that it is - covertly - about Simeon Solomon, so there's less material to go on. There's only a rather puzzling musical surface which is nowhere near as obvious, gesturally, as the *Verdi Transcriptions*, and is actually far more despairing and pessimistic. I think there are private and public rhetorics. People go more for the public rhetoric, the circus, and less for the private, difficult, internal things.

IP: As Nono found in his last years.

I think people find Nono's late works a lot harder to deal with than *Il canto sospeso*, which is hard enough! But those late works really demand that you listen and think, and it's the thinking that drives people crazy. But anything benefits from a bit of thought, doesn't it? If you think about what Tchaikovsky was doing in the *Pathétique Symphony*, you get more out of it than if you just let it all wash over you like a great big warm bath. 'Oh my God, I didn't come to this concert to think, I left my brain at the office at five o'clock, why do I have to think about music?' But it might change the way you think about the world: 'Oh no, I don't want it to make any difference to my preconceptions'.

IP: A lot of people find it surprising that you're a regular advocate and performer of composers like Howard Skempton, Chris Newman and that you probably perform their music more often than composers whose work has similar degrees of surface detail to yours.

Well, I like and know Howard and Chris and I believe in their work passionately, whereas the work of some composers of similar persuasion to myself I can't relate to in the same degree.

IP: Do you think there are any similarities between Newman and Skempton's work and your own?

Yes, I don't see it as any different. We are all dealing with large topics like fragmentation of life at the end of the twentieth century, the despair and nihilism of people's responses, the dark cloud of annihilation hanging over us all. I don't think Skempton or Newman do this particularly differently from me. The surfaces of the music might seem different, but not the inner necessity.

IP: If on the page much of Howard's work looks sparse, within the notes, chords or indeed any sort of sound there is an infinity of detail and activity. Maybe the only real difference between his work and yours in this respect is that you make this detail more explicit.

The number of notes becomes irrelevant, doesn't it? That's just not the point. In a piece like Howard's *Even Tenor*, the circle is not being closed. It's a harmonic sequence which stops one bar short of closing a circle, which I find exactly the same as the kinds of processes I'm interested in. He does it one way and I do it another, but one should rejoice in the capacity of two human beings to be so dissimilar and nonetheless enjoy each other's work. There are more important things than notes or even diatonicism versus atonality or pan-tonality or whatever, those are all surface factors. It's the philosophical concerns of these people which interests me. Nothing makes me back off a composer's work more quickly than to find out that they're some kind of fascist - all they're trying to achieve in asking me to play their work is to control me in some kind of way. So there are composers whose work I've played and no longer do. Sometimes I like them as people but not their work very much, either because of what it may or may not come to stand for, or because I'm intolerant in more than one way.

IP: Which composers were your contemporaries from college days?

David Fanshawe, Douglas Young, Richard David Hames. Brian [Ferneyhough], who is three years older, had just finished at the Academy or was doing a fourth year - we did have an overlap period. We also had a mutual friend in the pianist Philip Pilkington with whom I used to play two-piano music. He knew Brian and John Tavener. When I finished College, Brian, I think for the second year running, went to Gaudeamus where I met him, and that set the seal on a very long friendship. I also met people like Brian Chapple and Jenny Fowler.

CF: What about younger composers, and people you've taught? I read in an interview with you that you said teaching was just composition time wasted. But you have taught quite a lot of people, or at least shaped quite a lot of people's impressionable years.

I do feel bad about the amount of time that goes into teaching when I think of how much time is lost from composing, but that's only in one of my more selfish frames of mind. Of course it's very exciting to encourage young compositional talent and see it flower, particularly if other people haven't seen the possibility in it and I can somehow bring it to life. That was the case with Luke Stoneham who to all intents and purposes had been something of a drop-out at Sussex University. He came to me as an MA student and I manage to unlock whatever it was that was there. He'd been with people like Alison Cox who had encouraged him, but since university days it had all gone into retreat. He's a very instinctive person. There were many, almost non-verbal moments of 'realisation' - ideas dawning, epiphanies. It was the same with Andrew Toovey. I can't claim to teach composers of that calibre, only give them permission. It's not a very easy thing to define what composition teaching is, and also you should remember that you can't make a silk purse out of a sow's ear. If a student has no talent you can't turn them into a good composer. I have had only two students whom I told to go because I didn't think I could cope with them at all. I didn't like them at all either; I didn't like their psychology or their approach to composition although funnily enough both wanted me to change the way that they wrote. I would never set out to do that - I think all composition is self taught. You go to somebody for confirmation that your beliefs are the right ones and they either encourage you or they slap you down and try and change things. I have slapped a few students whom I thought were really stupid, but not so many - I've had some good people.

IP: So you don't teach people the ways of handling material?

I open up as many possibilities as I can for them. A lot of the time teaching is un-teaching, making students un-learn things that they've been told by idiots who really don't know what composition can - potentially - be. They've taught a limited rule-book and while you need to understand some of the rules, you have to know the principles behind composing. That's what I said earlier about Stevens' teaching, he was always concerned to reveal the principle behind something rather than tell you what the rule-book says. So you learn codes of conduct and responsibility towards material, audience and music.

IP: If an eighteen year old composer comes to you now and asks your advice on how to make a living writing music, what do you say?

Frankly, I'd be concerned at anyone wanting to make a living from writing music. You'd need a great deal of luck and, usually, patience. England is not ready for the notion of art being a real job: it's something people do in their free moments and, indeed, is on the level of making models with matchsticks or growing prize marrows. In my experience most eighteen year olds are not that far-sighted, they're idealistic and soaking-up ideas. If the question of 'making a living' was over-riding I'd probably advise the student to try elsewhere: my annual income (averaging £16,000) is only about thirty per cent from what I write, most of it comes from teaching, doing concerts, broadcasts and so on: so I'm not a good example of 'making a living' as a composer - although you could say that all the other things I do, Beethoven did too (except broadcast!). The Royal Academy of Music in London offers a commercial music course, perhaps their students learn how to make a living. I usually look at the music and, in spite of the political-socio-economic babbling of the foregoing answers to your questions, I spend most of a tutorial dealing with purely technical issues.

WORKING METHODS

CF: In the Toop interview, there's a disagreement between the two of you about how prolific you are.

I write all the time.

CF: Has there ever been a period when you didn't?

No, not for any extended period, not since I was a child. If I'm not writing on paper I'm writing in my head.

CF: No two year long silences?

No, I'd explode!

IP: So how much is there a continuation from one piece to the next?

When I started writing I tried to join the end of each piece to the beginning of the next. I don't do that any more, although I do think of my works as a path through my life, not one-offs.

CF: Do they overlap? Do you have one piece on your desk and other pieces starting to happen in your head or in a sketch book?

I can only ever work on one piece at a time. Sometimes towards the end of pieces I start thinking about the next one, if I know what that's going to be, but usually I've only got one commission to work on at a time, so I work on that until I finish it. If you think of composers like Bach, Telemann and Mozart, then I'm comparatively slow but then if you look at somebody like Webern... On the other hand, as we know now, Webern wrote twice as much music as was actually acknowledged during his life-time, he just discarded it. If you listen to some of those discarded pieces you wonder why, they're not worse than those he kept. But some composers have weird fetishes, like grouping things in threes, so if they happen to write a fourth and very good song from a set of three, they cut it out anyway, and then it's for the wrong instrumentation to go into the next.

There is the prejudice that if you write a lot, it follows that it can't be any good, you must be doing it sloppily, not thinking deeply enough about the individual works. That's another stigma that you have to bear. I take solace from the fact that Rossini wrote *The Barber of Seville* in two weeks and in a similar period of time Schoenberg wrote *Erwartung*, and if you can say the Rossini sounds like the product of two weeks' work, then *Erwartung* certainly doesn't. It's possible to write maybe in a white heat for two weeks, then have three weeks off. You could do ten pieces a year on that kind of basis.

CF: And there are an awful lot of composers who don't work hard enough and would be a lot better if they worked harder!

Well, you can go into print saying that, Mr Fox, I'm glad I didn't! Of course I agree with you, there are a lot of composers who are very lazy.

CF: Feldman says somewhere in the *Essays* that all these young European composers are always on the phone, or doing this or that, when they should be at their desks.

Well, Feldman was no slouch when it came to writing pieces, neither was Cage. If you spend your life conducting and swanning around going to parties, getting commissions and all that stuff, then you can't expect to spend that much more time writing, can you? We've only got a limited amount of time. I'd rather be writing than talking to the right people to get jobs writing the right sort of pieces. If the right sort of jobs come along, then hooray, but otherwise I'm happy to write the wrong sort of pieces.

IP: But many young composers in their twenties are desperate to find enough money to pay for the heating and end up having to do menial jobs, and often don't have the time to compose. Surely in this day and age, when our social security system does nothing at all to help artists starting out, it's necessary now to spend large amounts of time building up any possible contacts, in the hope of getting commissions, just to make enough money to survive.

Don't rely on the social security, the whole system is collapsing, being phased out. When I was that age I was working full time at a dance school and had one day a week, Sunday, to do my composing. Ives lived quite a lot of his life doing that. You can do as much in one day as some people can in seven, if you just spend less time staring out of the window feeling precious. I suppose that makes me a snob in another way. I think the work ought to come to me more often than it does, and sometimes I do go out and get it, but I don't hunt work down the way I see a lot of young composers doing it. They want to be as famous as Mick Jagger. It would be nice to have lots of money in the bank but that's not the be-all and end-all. I think you have to start by being able to offer something that's decent when you write it. A lot of these guys don't even care about that: 'we'll do a deal, you give me a lot of money and I'll give you a lot of notes'. I prefer quality control!

IP: At the age of 50, what do you really want to do next?

Make 51! If I knew what the future was then I could have some hopes for it, but I'm not a soothsayer. I'm only a composer and when the future's there I'll respond to it as best I can, but I really don't know what will happen.

CF: You don't have a *LICHT* coming over the horizon?

Heaven forfend! I would like to write more vocal music because I think I have an aptitude for doing that and I enjoy working in the theatre. Otherwise, I don't have a grand plan. I never did, that's probably what's wrong with the work, and the problem for people trying to promote it. I don't have any ambition except to do what I'm doing at any particular moment as well as I can. There are works I've had to let go - particularly in the early days: around 1970 I was invited to write for Donaueschingen: Yvonne Minton and the London Sinfonietta were to be involved in this project *Re-organised elements of Opera*, funnily enough - including a very elaborate piano-fantasy on Donizetti's *Lucrezia Borgia* - I kept the sketches for ages then chucked them. Heinrich Strobel instigated that and he was really one hundred per cent behind it, unfortunately he was also extremely ill and he died before all the paperwork was in place. Nobody else gave a shit about the project. So... maybe I could wish in some instances that I'd had a bit more encouragement but it's no good being too bitter about that. I'd like to try and answer a question of yours [Fox's] in a review of Darmstadt some years ago.[12] You said you were never worried about being bored in my music because even if you didn't like the particular thing that was happening you could be pretty sure that a more interesting one would come along. That's an interesting reflection on how I perceive work as I'm writing it, which ties in with the idea of pre-compositional plans. I try to step back, as a painter might do from their canvas, to keep a sense of perspective when writing and not to have a scheme dictating where you are supposed to be at every point. I think, as music can re-define time, distort it, that such a sense of perspective, of spacing and timing, only comes about when you've actually begun to write the score down and discover things through interaction of brain and pen. I change tack when I feel I've had enough of a particular kind of thing. I am quite relentless with some kinds of material, monolithic, obsessive... but I also reject ideas, when writing, that might have seemed OK at the planning stage. It's a sensual response to the work, cutting, rearranging, dropping inserts in.

CF: In a way that's a bit like a film director sitting next to the editor; all the material has been shot but when you actually see that the scene in sequence doesn't work it ends on the floor.

I do, sometimes, generate a lot of material first and then edit it. New possibilities are opened up at that second stage. When Feldman quotes Rothko (or Rauschenberg maybe) 'let the paint do the work' that includes 'watching' or watching out for new possibilities, rather than military campaign tight-arse organisation. Let the notes do the work, let the sounds out, listen to them. It's one reason I'm so devoted to random numbers and statistical spreads of alternatives: I get excited by sudden discoveries.

IP: Where do you get your numbers from?

I've got a print-out in book form, *Tables of Random Numbers* by Lincoln E. Moses and Robert V. Oakford, published in 1963, which I bought for 33/6 [£1.68] from Joseph's in Charing Cross Road. It consists of random permutations of limited numbers of digits: 1-9, 1-16, 1-20, 1-30, 1-50, 1-100, 1-500, 1-1000.

CF: Do you have favourites?

1-20 is good, but I always open the book at random.

IP: Perhaps, like a sculptor who starts with a block of stone, you create a lot of notes and you sculpt them into the form you want.

I find that easier; once I can see something it's easier to correct it. With folk music it's the same thing, it's there already. With self-generated material, sometimes I write pitch and rhythmic configurations separately, then combine the two to see what happens. You can always displace them and do something else if they don't work out and you still have the original material. It's a very exciting way to compose because everything becomes an adventure.

CF: And you do things that you would never otherwise have done, which is always exhilarating.

Yes, composition should be exhilarating shouldn't it? Composers that grizzle on about it being such a terribly painful experience, maybe they have Messiaen leering over one shoulder and Boulez looking over the other one. How on earth can you do anything under those kind of circumstances?

IP: I've read your talk about musical 'archetypes'. Would you mind explaining those again?

Archetypes are 'ur-modellen': the original prototypes. You can find discussions of them in Jung: the deep rooted fundamental experiences of all humankind - birth, sexual attraction, anger, despair, death. The word can also indicate cultural codes, recurrent symbols in mythology or art. Recurrent musical patterns occur in folk music, in art-music too: the 'weeping' descending semitones in Baroque music. Because hypothetical audiences share your knowledge of these symbols you can use them as 'signifiers'.

IP: How did that relate to your ways of treating folk materials?

Maybe because I imagine that the behaviour of folk musicians is less conditioned by the whims of fashion, good taste or Christian morality (bowdlerised English folk culture is not a good indicator); and if these musicians are better able to express, through melodic or rhythmic codes (archetypes), their own, or the community's feelings about birth, marriage, death then it's worth some research, some investigation. I'm totally disgusted with the results of commercialism and monetarism.

Folk music exists through necessity, it has to be there, nobody asks it to be there, pays for it to be there. It has a real function within society which art-music either does not have, because civilised urban society is so fragmented and dissolute, or is not perceived to have. Art-music crawls up its own arse to please the purchaser.

IP: But a lot of art-music has evolved to serve a purpose, through the patronage of the church.

Latterly, the church's patronage of music has been far from enlightened: Vatican II, the repudiation of 900 years of service from Machaut, Obrecht, Ockeghem, Tallis, Byrd, Bruckner - down the toilet and replaced by anodyne trash-pop. The holier-than-thou superiority-complex of English cathedrals. What purpose does music serve there? A balm and a salve, a cup of Horlicks to make the congregation sleep better.

CF: You mean that if you're working in a field, work songs arise because they make the business of doing that work marginally more bearable; they have a degree of necessity, whereas if you're Louis XV you don't *have* to have Lully's music?

Exactly. In a religious experience, music unlocks a lot of things which words perhaps don't, which is possibly why priests are always so suspicious of music - it often has a far more immediate effect on their congregation than a sermon and seems to them to offer glimpses of heaven or indeed hell fire which sermons don't. So the practice of music within a tribal and totemic society can be a very meaningful part of life whereas here in Great Britain it's become a kind of aural chewing gum. People are so frightened of silence they chew on music, but it doesn't serve any useful function. Out of that you get rather strange responses to the arts: people don't expect music to be anything except chewing gum and they think you're at fault if you think otherwise. I don't see any difference between being a folk artist and being an artist working in a society as a so-called professional: you look for what you can do to make life better, to share and understand, because that's what you want yourself. You do what you can. Don't you?

Notes

1. Finnissy is referring to the practice in British conservatoires of charging prospective students an audition fee.
2. 'Music and Movement' was a BBC Schools radio programme.
3. Antony Hopkins presented a BBC series called 'Talking about Music'.
4. Until the mid-1960s the English educational system required children to take exams at 11 years to determine whether they went to grammar school, a secondary modern school or, in some cases, a technical school. Courses in

grammar school were more 'academic', those in the other schools less demanding.

5. Ferruccio Busoni, 'Value of the Transcription', *The Essence of Music and Other Papers* (New York: Dover Publications) pp. 85-9.
6. R. O. Morris, *Foundations of Practical Harmony and Counterpoint* (first edn 1931, reprinted Westport, Conn., Greenwood Press, 1980), one of the standard texts for teaching counterpoint in the 1960s.
7. Richard Toop, *Four Facets of 'The New Complexity'*, Contact 32 (Spring 1988).
8. The SPNM (Society for the Promotion of New Music) is an organisation devoted to the encouragement of new music. In the 1960s and '70s it organised a summer conference, the Composers' Weekend, at which new works specially composed for a guest ensemble were rehearsed and performed.
9. John Woolf was Administrator of the SPNM from 1966-80.
10. A performance at the 1979 SPNM Composers' Weekend at York University, including *all.fall.down*.
11. Conway Hall, London, 26.1.96; subsequent concerts were on 29.2.96, 10.5.96, 28.6.96, 4.10.96 and 5.12.96.
12. Christopher Fox, *Plural Darmstadt: The 1986 International Summer Course*, *New Music 87*, eds. R. Wright, M. Finnissy, pp, 102-5, Oxford, 1987.

CHAPTER TWO

The Piano Music

Ian Pace

Michael Finnissy's piano music represents, at around 70 works, the most substantial section of his output. It has also generated the most attention, in part as a result of Finnissy's own activities as a performer. As a composer who writes continuously, not merely in response to commissions, Finnissy seems to have treated the piano as the most immediate receptacle for his ongoing concerns, at least since the mid-1970s.

Finnissy views the piano, an instrument which he knows as intimately as any, as a 'neutral' vehicle for fundamentally 'musical' concerns, timbral considerations receding from the foreground as a result of familiarity. Such a conception is in marked contrast to that which portrays him as the last in a long line of virtuoso pianist-composers, such as Liszt, Busoni, Rachmaninoff, Godowsky, Grainger and Sorabji. Yet several of these figures admitted to performing primarily by virtue of necessity, in a desire to enable both their own work and that of others they admired to be more frequently heard and understood. They ideally would have liked to concentrate their energies on composing, which is to some extent true of Finnissy as well. Beyond the restless harmonic experimentalism and proto-atonality of Liszt, the tonal objectification of Busoni, as well as his expression of inner tension through the differing pulls of the Germanic and Italianate traditions, or Grainger's ideas of 'free music'; these factors all have parallels in Finnissy's work that are in my opinion of much greater significance than those of mere virtuosity.

That said, it is hard to deny that Finnissy's piano music bears the hallmarks of a very distinctive approach to the instrument. Although Finnissy writes away from the piano, often taking a work to the instrument only in order to check the possibility of what has been written, he nonetheless would seem to have his own particular characteristics as a performer in mind. This may be unconscious on his part, but it is apparent to others who take up his work. However, virtuosity is, except in a few works, essentially a means to an end, which Finnissy uses to communicate his conceptions of the diversity, asymmetry and polyvalency of human beings and the world.

The works, as well as being huge in number, are enormously diverse, and encompass each different area of focus throughout Finnissy's compositional career. I have chosen to divide the works into categories partially determined by chronology, partially by preoccupations. There are clearly many other possible categorisations and I wish every bit as much to discuss the works as individual, autonomous entities, as by the extent to which they exemplify aspects of Finnissy's aesthetic and technical development.

Early Works - From the Juvenilia to *Wild Flowers*

The very first music that Finnissy wrote is a (currently lost) one line piano piece called *The Chinese Bridge* (1950). After this followed numerous, mostly short, piano pieces written during childhood. In recent years Finnissy has been prepared to let some of these be performed and published (some are collected in the Appendix to *Wee Saw Footprints*, others in the *Collected Shorter Piano Pieces Volumes 1 & 2*). If obviously limited in conception and realisation, these pieces do foreshadow ideas which were to be enacted in a more concrete form in Finnissy's mature work. The *Polskie Tance Op. 32* (1955/62)[1] show a certain indebtedness to the music of both Szymanowski and Bartók, but also an interest in close intervals and a blurring of tonality through continually changing chordal structures and bass lines.

Example 2.1 *Polskie Tance Op. 32, 1. Kujawiak-Kozak*
Reproduced by permission of Oxford University Press

The second of the *Two Pasodobles* (1959) consists of overlapping strings of long held pitches with broad, expansive contours that seem like a premonition of the luminosity of *My Bonny Boy*, from *English Country-Tunes*, and passages from *Fast Dances, Slow Dances* and other pieces, as well as anticipating the style of many later vocal works. The *Romance (with Intermezzo)* (1960) hovers around different keys, although nominally it is in E flat/C minor. By contrast, the Intermezzo is more or less twelve-tone, taking Brahms' *Intermezzo Op. 118 No. 2* as a rhythmic model, and a 'note-row' based on an inversion of the opening bars of the Romance. The second part of the Romance then leads to a climax close to A flat, which is thus made all the more striking, though the piece immediately dissolves once more, ending in a tonally ambiguous manner.

The first piano pieces Finnissy acknowledges as part of his mature output are the *Songs 5-9* (1966-68). A more electrifying entry into the arena of piano literature could hardly be imagined. Finnissy burst onto the scene with huge rapid gestures encompassing the whole keyboard, wild streams of grace notes, but also very long sustained chords and silences. Extremes are everywhere, of dynamics, range, angularity, continuity/discontinuity, notation, transcendental virtuosity (Example 2.2). Despite the stylistic pluralism of the 1960s, an original voice like no other had emerged, writing music that did not fit into any of the established categories. Where had it come from?

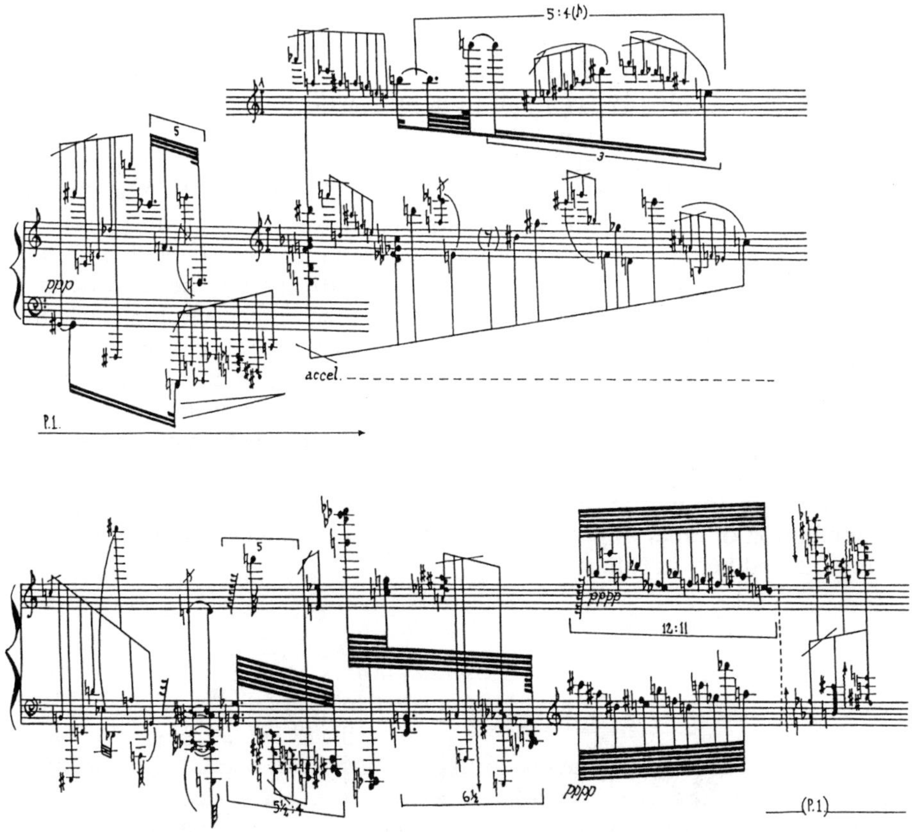

Example 2.2 *Song 5*
Reproduced by permission of Oxford University Press

Finnissy was dissatisfied with what he perceived as the predominance of 'poetic' forms in music, and sought alternative structural models from painting, the cinema and anthropology. The ideas underlying the *Songs* stem primarily from several of Finnissy's interests: a series of short experimental films by the American film-maker Stan Brakhage, from which the pieces take their titles; Warhol's early cinematic work; and Levi-Strauss's belief that man's cognitive abilities are structurally reducible to a series of 'binary oppositions'. Brakhage's films consist of extremes of camera position, focus, lighting, etc. in such a way as to present familiar phenomena in unconventional ways, stressing the essential strangeness of what is often perceived as ordinary. As Robert Kelly said of Brakhage:

> It is a totality of making so intense it becomes a systematic exploration of the forms and terms of the medium itself. To explore the form without exhausting the form.[2]

Warhol's early films were often made merely by switching a camera on at one point, then off at another, so that the film would be precisely whatever occurred in between.

The *Songs* are in no sense naturalistic representations of these films; rather it is the formal cinematic features that are Finnissy's key concern. Each of these pieces is explicitly sectional in nature, with the emphasis on gesture, this mode of composition serving to illuminate one level of the music as clearly as possible. In *Song 5*, the performer can make his or her own choice for the ordering of the sections. The pieces are also noticeably 'non-circular' in that they end at a point which has progressed considerably from the opening. Pitches seem to be determined more in terms of density and range than by harmonic considerations, and durations by the contrasts of meticulously notated rhythms, rapid series of grace notes and long sustained pitches or chords. Dynamics are of an equally archetypal nature; either extreme *fff* or *ppp* or *crescendo/diminuendo* between the two. *Song 8*, unusually, makes use of both cluster *glissandi* and *pizzicato* on the piano strings, in opposition to 'conventional' use of the instrument, as another structural dichotomy.

The ways in which Finnissy constructs a work from a syncretic accumulation of binary oppositions can be seen from an examination of *Song 7*, reproduced here in full:

SONG 7

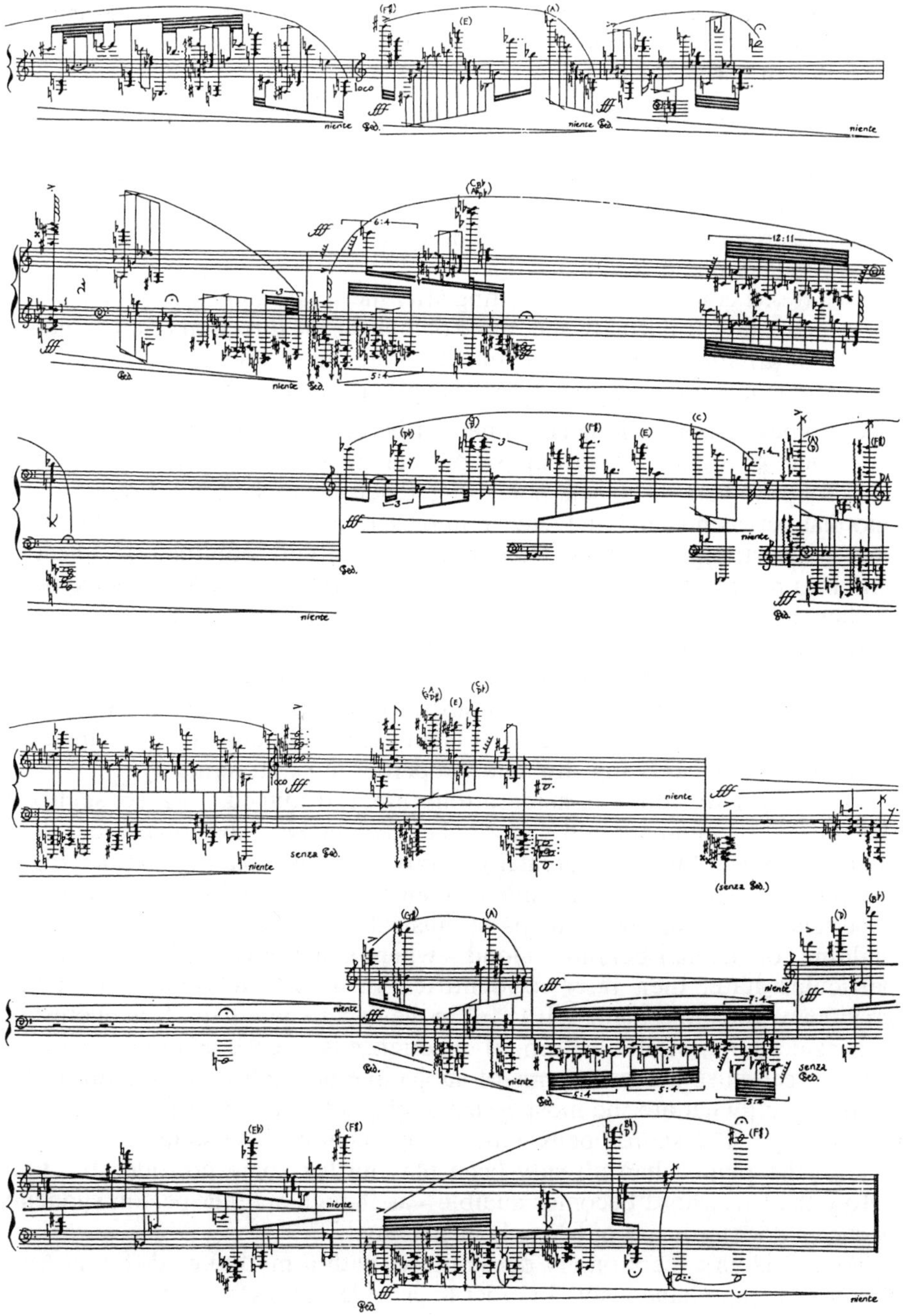

Example 2.3 *Song 7*. (Note that Bar 9 contains a transposed passage from *Song 5*, see Example 2.2, second line.)

There are 16 fragments, separated by bar lines, which are made clear to an uninitiated listener through a diminuendo from *fff* to *niente* in each bar. In the first bars, each of which seem to be in bi-partite form, one might notice the following properties:

Bar 1: (a) bass, single notes/chords, (b) treble, albeit tempered by the last few pitches, single notes/clusters.

Bar 2: (a) irregular rhythms, (b) regular. Each interrupted by grace notes. In a registral sense, (b) is inverse of bar 1.

Bar 3: (a) regular pulses with grace notes, (b) arch of chord/cluster/notes of indeterminate duration.

Bar 4: If one conceives (b) as starting after the single C natural, then (a) and (b) differ in density and, more obliquely, the direction of arpeggiation in (a) alternates, whereas in (b) it is regular (down). In both (a) and (b) the non-grace note figures have a statistical *ritardando.*

These types of oppositions continue, but become less obvious in bar 9, and from there onwards. Other oppositions can also be discerned between bars and groups of bars. The held pitches/rapid activity dichotomy is transformed into that between sound and silence in bars 12 and 13, to an extent that both are 'made strange' and, perhaps as a result of the polarisation, the two extremes might be seen each to contain the other (a consideration explored further in the ensemble work *Afar*). *Song 7* can be listened to on several different levels; indeed the bars might well have been written in a different order. It is for the listener to derive their own conclusions from this work which, at the time of writing, demonstrated the trans-cendentalist's aim to venture beyond the conceivable. It is an essentially abstract, perhaps even 'formalist' work, stressing structural properties most prominently.

With *Song 9*, other considerations are introduced. In 16 sections, demarcated by numbers in the score, the piece makes substantial use of long silences (indeed there is a greater quantity of silence than actual playing in the piece). These were intended as an attempt to realise in music the experience of certain phenomena in musical terms - a car passing behind a building, or the sun behind a cloud - where something is observed in one particular state, then later re-identified in a state advanced from that previously, the mind being left to fill in the experiential gap. It is interesting to consider how, when this form of experience is re-enacted in music, one is able to recognise the two forms of subjective perception as relating to the same object; what are the most essential characteristics that give this object its identity? The score opens with the instruction, 'The song must start as though the pianist had already been playing for some considerable time before the first chord becomes audible - as though another person suddenly opened a door to the room where he is playing.'

Song 9 is an exceptionally dense piece, with a myriad of different lines progressing simultaneously. In order to provide some sort of 'ruler' for these to be measured against, in the first section Finnissy introduces a series of notes and chords to be accentuated and optionally paused upon, 'focal points' which serve the function of a *cantus firmus.*

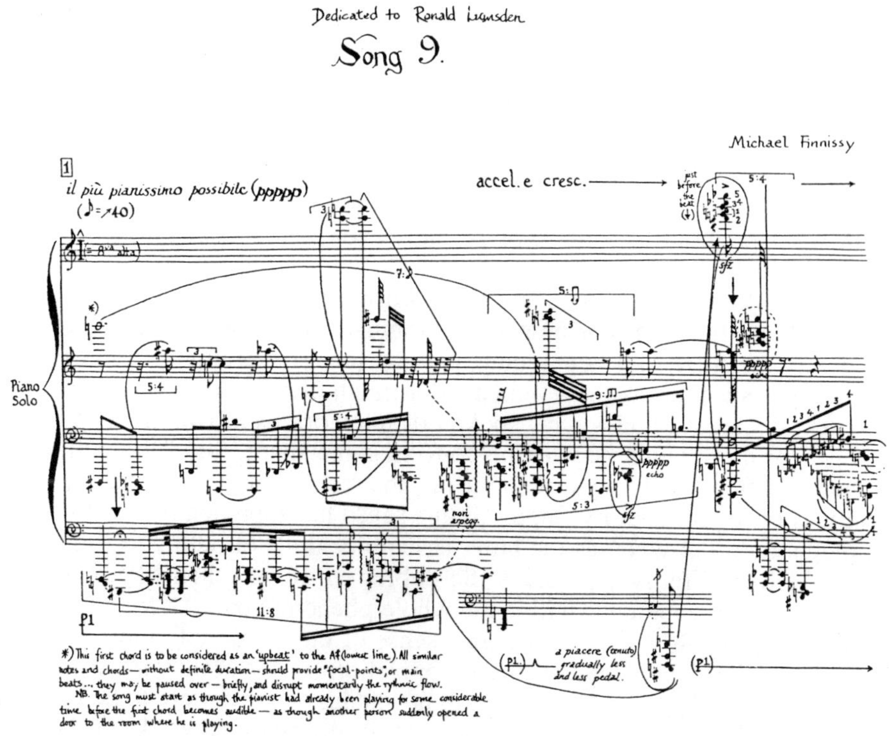

Example 2.4 *Song 9*

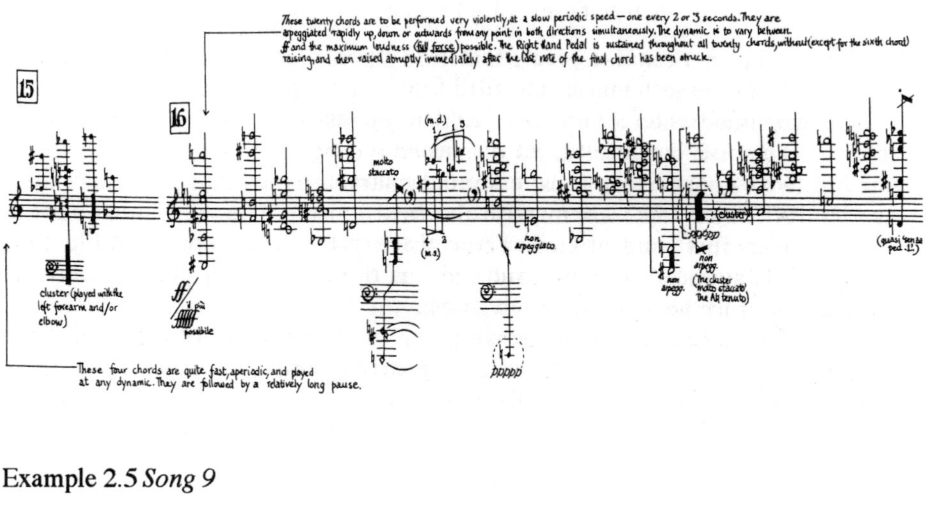

Example 2.5 *Song 9*

In other sections, Finnissy makes use of lightning-like flashes of activity, which disappear as immediately as they are made apparent, sometimes near, sometimes distant, a quasi-pointillist series of multiple lines where each note has a different dynamic (which is equally soon homogenised, perhaps an expression of Finnissy's reaction to a particular 'tradition'), and a series of strident periodic chords at the end, a counterpart to the opening, but foreshadowed in a previous set of chords, which are 'quite fast, aperiodic and played at any dynamic', thus sharing only the most essential characteristics with what is about to follow, or perhaps even demonstrating the arbitrary nature of such categorisation (Example 2.5).[3]

One might say that for music to be born again, it has first to die. The *Songs* clear the air for a new type of music to emerge. They are self-evidently the work of a young man, making the most dramatic of entries and defining in stark terms the boundaries of much of his later work, at least for the next decade. Finnissy has spoken of his work as inhabiting a 'post-Big Bang' world, in which he attempts to form some shape out of the millions of particles which are flying around the air, the residue of the musical explosion that was brought about by Cage. In this sense his approach relates to that of Ferneyhough, but whereas the latter assembles units of debris to form some sort of entity, Finnissy presents the debris en masse, then like a sculptor creates areas of coherence within the whole phenomenon.

The 'archetypal' (in Levi-Strauss's sense of the word, not Finnissy's as he would explore it later) nature of the oppositions in the *Songs*, the theses and antitheses, the blacks and whites, with no shades of grey, were to be revisited in a very different manner in some of the folk-music based works of the early 1980s. However, for a self-critical and continually developing composer, as Finnissy was and is, it was inevitable that some degree of synthesis of the polarisations of the early *Songs*, different structural models and extensions of the methods for articulating longer continuities begun in *Song 9*, would ensue. These came about with the piano pieces *Autumnall* (1968-71) and *Snowdrift* (1972).

Autumnall takes its title from John Donne's poem 'The Autumnall':

> No spring, nor summer beauty hath such grace,
>   As I have seen in one autumnall face.
> Young beauties force your love, and that's a rape,
>   This doth but counsel, yet you cannot scrape
> If 'twere a shame to love, here 'twere no shame,
>   Affection here takes reverence's name
> Were her first years the Golden Age; that's true,
>   But now she's gold oft tried, and ever new.
> That was her torrid and inflaming time,
>   This is her tolerable tropic clime.
> Fair eyes, who asks more heat than comes from hence,
>   He in a fever wishes pestilence...

The piece represents Finnissy's reactions to these words, an attempt to re-think the ideas and emotions expressed in the poem through his own set of preoccupations. Whilst it does not consciously follow the narrative structure of the poem, the piece nonetheless has a greater sense of linear motion than some of the *Songs*. From the beginning, Finnissy makes use of three types of material intercut with each other:

Section (A) (all section delineations are my own interpolation):

1. Rapid, angular gestures, interspersed with grace notes, in the treble register.
2. More spacious lines, with longer durations.
3. Long sustained notes, whose durations are given in seconds.

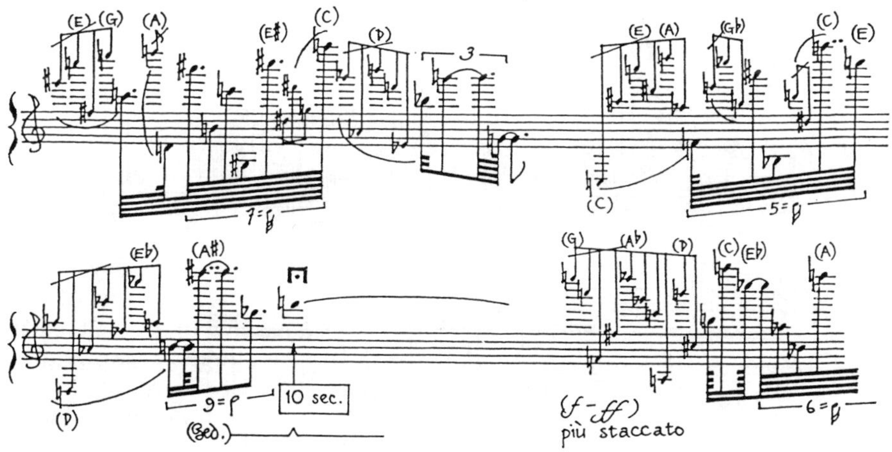

Example 2.6 *Autumnall*
Reproduced by permission of Oxford University Press

The following is an outline of the progress of the work:

Section (B): Crotchet = 120

Extension of (A1) to cover the whole keyboard, with addition of clusters, arpeggios, and differing dynamics for different notes. First use of *ppppp* notes, written in dotted circles, recalling Ives' *Concord Sonata.*

Section (C): *Fulminato*

Combination of materials (A1), (A2) and (B), in continuous form. Extraction of more extended single line of type (A2), in high treble interrupted at end by (A1) and (A3).

Section (D): *Immobile tranquillamente, molto meno mosso*

Fragmentary line - single isolated pitches, a musical equivalent of the experience of objects glimpsed through gaps between clouds. Parallel progress of *ppppp* line. Interrupted towards end by burst of rapid arpeggios.

Section (E): *come prima*

Further progress of (A1) and (A3), the latter usurping the former with longer durations. Quick *crescendo* of (B) material.

Section (F): Crotchet = 104

Spacious line of type (A2) now spread over whole keyboard, *crescendo* from *p* to *fff*, but tangents provided by continual interruptions of *pppp* and *sfz* notes, structurally equivalent to the progress in section (D), but here with three lines instead of two. Sudden cut to a few low, indistinct chords. Silence.

Section (G): *not too violent*

Very rapid multiple lines of types from (A), (B), (C) (Example 2.7). Sudden *appassionato* outburst, equally suddenly wiped out by quick, fading away, *pppp* gesture.

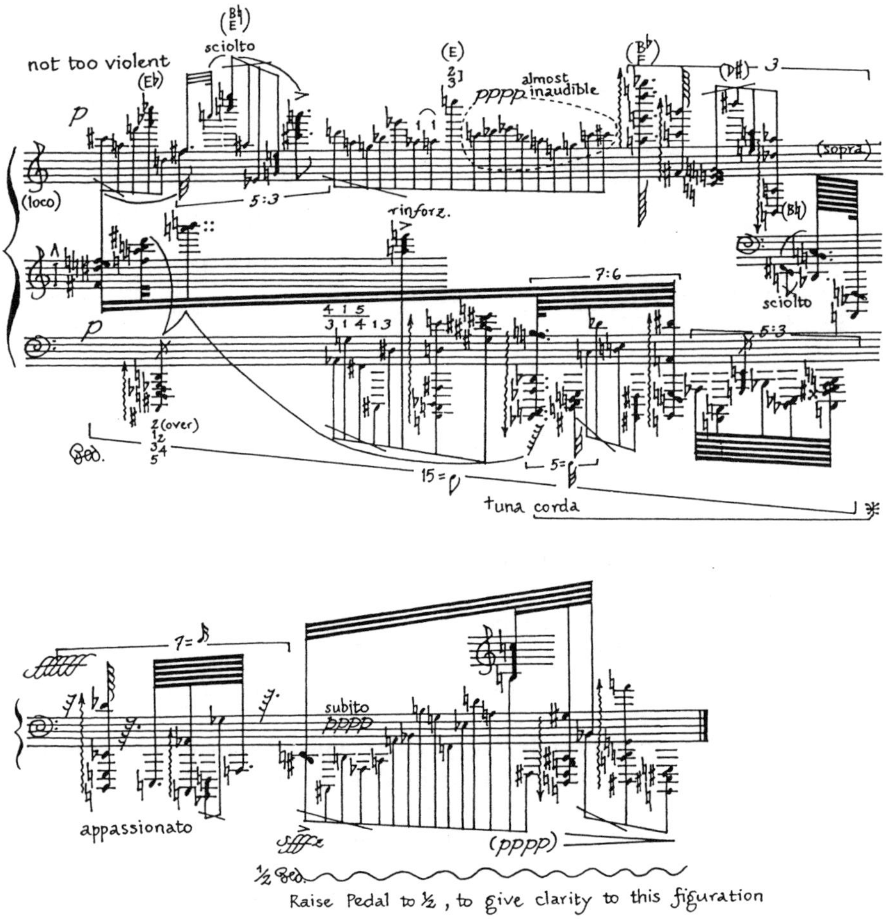

Example 2.7 *Autumnall*
Reproduced by permission of Oxford University Press

It is unlikely that a listener would hear clear boundaries between sections in this way; this description is intended rather to break the score down into manageable units. The most important point to note, I believe, is the extent to which the differing material types are allowed to extend, then suddenly cut away. This can be seen in terms of the relationships between, for example, sections (D) and (F) as well as in the frenzied opening of (G), which is an amalgam of much that has gone before. The inherent *violence* of seasonal change, coupled with a sense of loss (always a consideration for a contemporary composer) seem to be factors which inform this work. Yet, like Donne, Finnissy is also able to find hope in the passing of the familiar, positive inspiration in the concept of transience.

While *Autumnall* is both radiant and violent, the following work, *Snowdrift* (1972) seems a (relatively speaking!) more still and translucent affair. It too takes its title from a poem, here William Sharp's 'The White Peacock', which inspired Charles Griffes's work of the same name and includes the following lines:

> Here as the breath, as the soul of this beauty
> Moveth in silence, and dreamlike, and slowly,
> White as a snowdrift in mountain valleys
> When softly upon it the gold light lingers

Two features, which might be seen as opposite ends of a spectrum, stand out in this work: a series of major thirds or minor sixths (the two intervals most fervently proscribed by the 1950s serialists), or their equivalents with octave transpositions, and long series of grace notes.

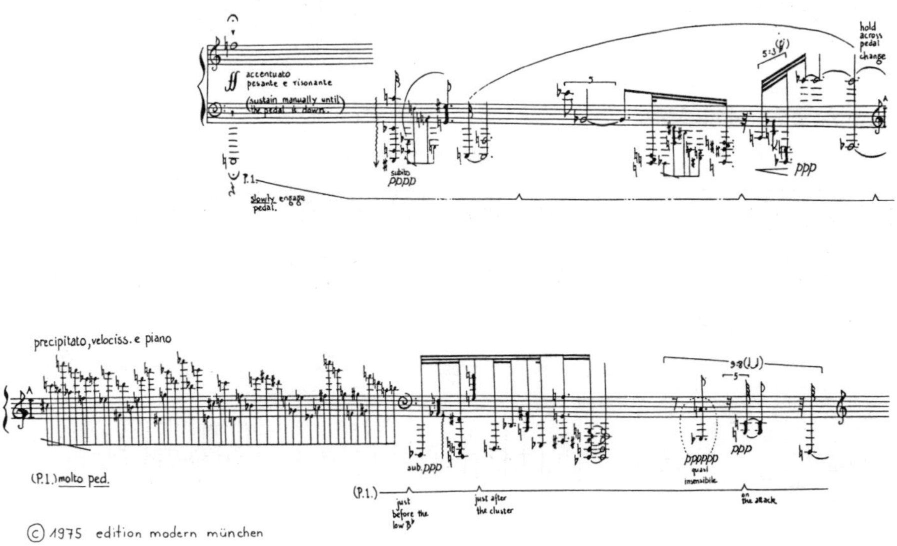

Example 2.8 *Snowdrift*
Reproduced by permission of Edition Modern

Through the piece, the intervals are reiterated at various points in different voicings, in particular within an ongoing progression of chords. They are more discreetly smuggled into other types of gestural material, while the grace notes follow an overall progression towards an extended series near the end (though in the sketches this comes after the first chord). Other elements are juxtaposed and intercut in a manner similar to ***Autumnall***, but with a much more extended melodic line, which while at various points is briefly interrupted and subject to 'commentaries' in the bass register, nonetheless is given a considerable amount of space to progress. This uninhibited use of long line was to become an important feature of both Finnissy's instrumental and vocal writing, reflecting his humanity and consequent love for the human voice, so different to the desiccated, fragmented vocal gestures which had become such a feature of much post-Second Viennese School vocal and instrumental writing.

Finnissy makes use of a wide repertoire of cinematic technique, including the use of 'jump cuts' (Example 2.9a), 'dissolves' (Example 2.9b) or expressions of 'distance' (Example 2.9c).

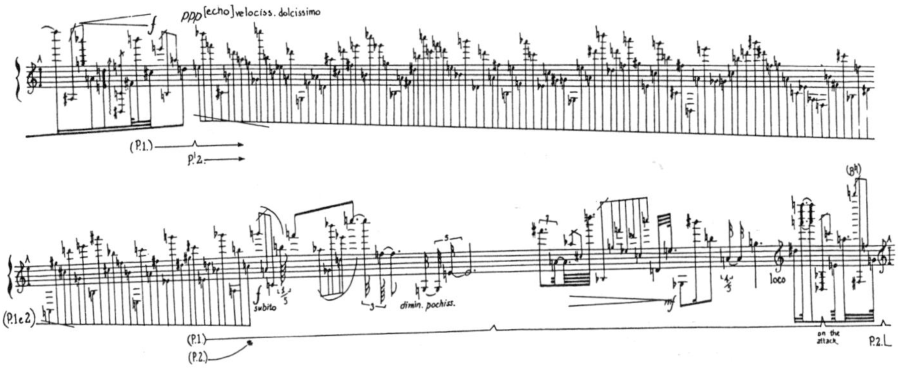

Example 2.9a *Snowdrift*

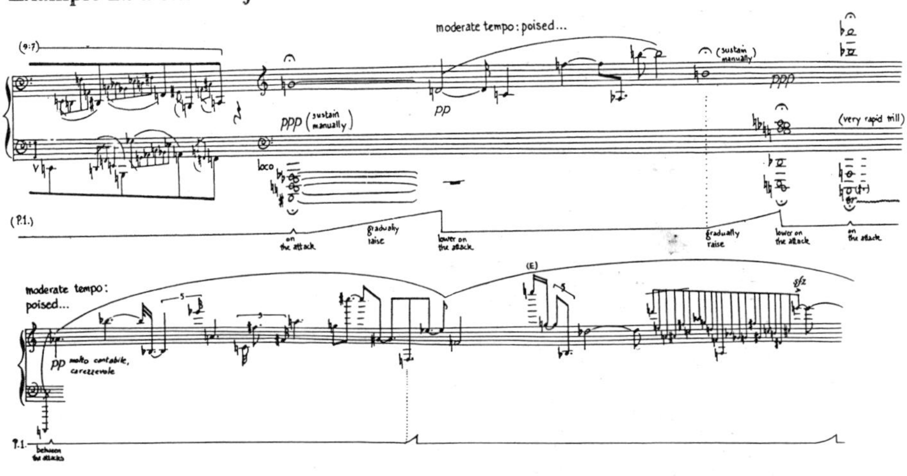

Example 2.9b *Snowdrift*

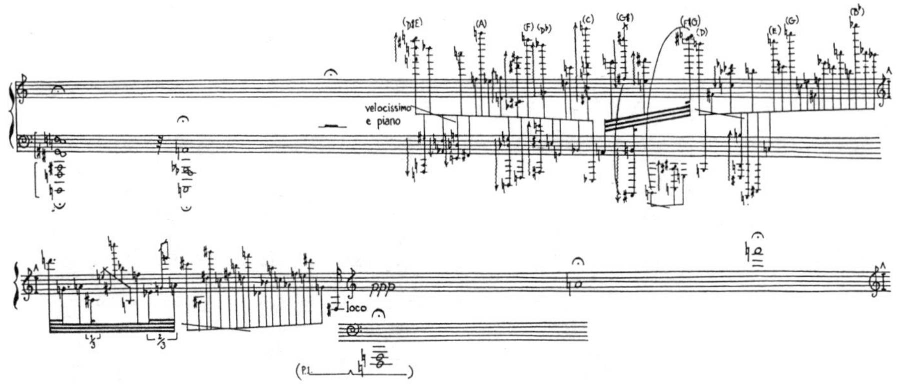

Example 2.9c *Snowdrift* (a) p. 2, (b) pp. 3-4, (c) p. 7
Reproduced by permission of Edition Modern

The sudden interruptions create a sense of dynamism and also serve the montage-like function of 'distancing' the material, showing its particularity by virtue of there being something else with which to compare it to.

There are obvious connotations of a 'snowscape' in the blizzards of grace notes but otherwise *Snowdrift* resists a clear programmatic explanation. Finnissy was more interested in the creation of new modes of expression than in mere narrative, or copying a pre-existing formal model which would have been incompatible with his requirements (though he would soon find ways of rejuvenating older forms). This is also true of the two-piano work, *Wild Flowers* (1974), a further literary-inspired work. The title here is taken from William Blake's *Auguries of Innocence*:

> To see a World in a Grain of Sand
> And a Heaven in a Wild Flower
> Hold Infinity in the palm of your hand
> And Eternity in an hour.

Such a coming together of extreme opposites extends the structuralist concerns of the *Songs* to the post-structuralist notion that binary oppositions inevitably contain the roots of their own inversion (perhaps this conclusion cannot be escaped in the earlier works either). The piece makes much of the distinction between hyper-stasis and hectic activity as if to demonstrate the reality of this conception, especially in its use of sustained chords and clusters near the beginning. Moments like that shown in Example 2.10, the shattering of a state of relative tranquillity by a glancing blow to the keyboard by the first pianist, have the power to disturb intensely even an initiated listener, as has been demonstrated in successive performances.

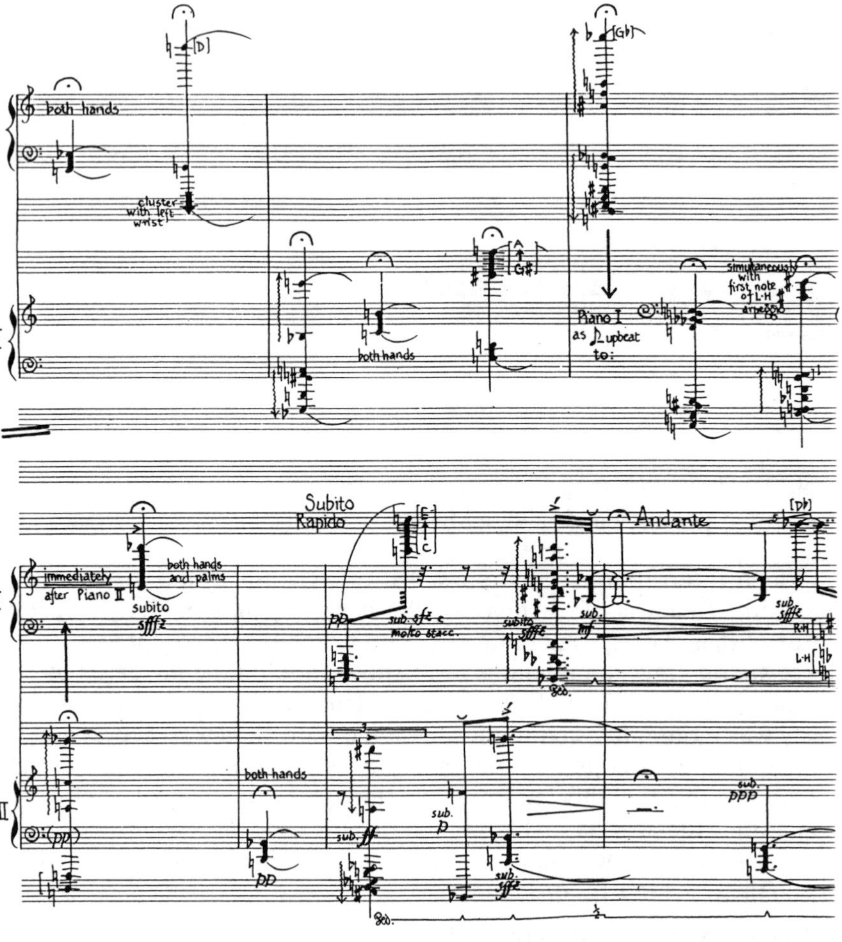

Example 2.10 *Wild Flowers*, p. 2
Reproduced by permission of Edition Modern

The piece is made up of a series of quite long sections, within each of which material or ideas are allowed to run their natural course. An extremely beautiful extended melodic line starting on the second page, echoes the similar passage in *Snowdrift* and also includes many intervals with clear consonant properties. Elsewhere a continuous stream of accelerating notes work their way up the bottom half of one keyboard, are transferred with an overlap onto the other half and progress further towards the top register.

Finnissy makes ample use of the antiphonal possibilities of the two-piano medium, as when the second piano echoes key notes within the melodic line of the first.

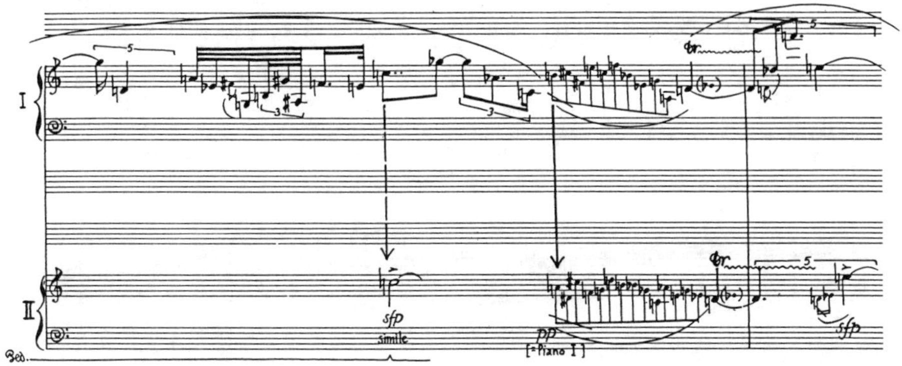

Example 2.11 *Wild Flowers*, p. 3
Reproduced by permission of Edition Modern

Yet the work was initially conceived for solo piano, a 'super-piano' exceeding in scope anything that had previously been thought possible (this would have to wait for the 3rd and 4th *Piano Concertos*). The use of multiple lines in different metres is made the more clear, however, when divided between players, who consequently need 'divide' their minds only half as much!

Wild Flowers contains much less of the intercutting that was such a striking feature of *Autumnall* and *Snowdrift* and consequently the large-scale design of the piece is easier to grasp. The shift from an assemblage of clearly defined components, as in the previous works, to a series of longer sections whose boundaries are clearly audible, thus allowing a greater emphasis upon material itself and its development (again receiving its prototype in *Song 9*), was to become a major feature of the next period of Finnissy's work. It parallels the development in cinematic history from the almost exclusive use of montage to a greater concentration on *mise-en-scène*.

From Improvisation to Abstraction

For much of the 1970s, Finnissy worked as a pianist and repetiteur for opera and dance companies. His work as an improviser for Matt Mattox's dance classes was to be reflected in a number of piano pieces, while others were written for choreography by Siobhan Davies and Kris Donovan, among others.

Freightrain Bruise (1972/80) is the first piano work clearly indebted to Finnissy's improvisational work. The piece opens with rhythms, gestural contours and, more obliquely, harmonies derived from the blues, with a mostly regular beat, but within an essentially atonal context.

Example 2.12 *Freightrain Bruise*
Reproduced by permission of Oxford University Press

The aura of the music, the sensation of distance and alienation from the generic source comes about as a result of other factors as well as the atonality; Finnissy also uses a filtering technique, in the manner of *Song 9* but on a more small-scale level, to produce silences, gaps in the texture, and occasionally compresses or otherwise modifies the beat. He describes the distortions as ''bruises' on its surface, places where the ripe fruit of jazz hit the cold floor of late twentieth-century 'angst'!'. It would be easy for these types of transformation to become predictable, but in the end the piece is irreducible to any processual schema. The subsequent works in this vein were, however, to use much more monolithic structural models.

Kemp's Morris (1978) takes its title from the actor Will Kemp, who Morris-danced for nine days from London to Norwich. Finnissy has the pianist wear Morris bells around the knuckles, which produce sympathetic jangling, to correspond to the bells that a dancer like Kemp would have worn around their calves. The piece is in nine sections (one for each day of Kemp's dance) the first five of which both allude to and are derived from the twenty-sixth melody in Playford's *English Dancing Master* (1651), by a process of sub-division and subsequent re-construction and modification. This type of technique, and the meaning of different levels of allusion and derivation, will be explained in more detail when considering *G.F.H.* and other transcriptions later. The culmination is a wild dance around the keyboard with the right hand, accompanied by a more regular bass line:

Example 2.13 *Kemp's Morris*, p. 5
Reproduced by permission of Oxford University Press

From the sixth to ninth sections, the textures become more fragmentary, and the bells are shaken independently of any notes being played on the keyboard, their long tremoli eventually usurping the piano lines. However, the material within the sections often moves in various directions, or relates to other material, in ways which are tangential to the overall direction of the work, as when an echo of the melody from the beginning is briefly glimpsed in the eighth section.

The pounding bass line with a leaping right hand in the fifth section of *Kemp's Morris* is given a very different colouration in the final version of *Boogie-Woogie* (1980/81/85/96) (the last revision is a minor re-writing after the final page was lost), the first piece of a 'dance' trilogy with *Jazz* (1976) and *Fast Dances, Slow Dances* (1978-79). Here the left hand has a 'boogying' line which pulverises the bottom register for most of the piece, against which the right hand alternates a frenetic mixture of accented staccato notes and chords, and short two and three note/chord phrases, with more continuous monodic, but intervallically angular, lines, which later develop into two such lines simultaneously. A coda at the end consists of a quick *pppp, staccatissimo brilliante* flurry of notes. While most of *Boogie-Woogie*'s structural and textural elements have clear predecessors in earlier works, it is the particular 'flavour' of this piece that gives it its distinct identity, deriving from the jazz-inspired characteristics of the smallest scale elements.

In the initial draft of *Jazz*, Finnissy was more explicit about this, stating that 'Pianist should remove tie and play throughout as closely to the style of

Jelly-Roll Morton as possible: Blues and Stomp in alternation'. To provide a container for his creative imagination in this piece which, like *Freightrain Bruise*, was inspired by his improvisational work for Matt Mattox, Finnissy turned to a pre-existing structural model, the series of tempos in Beethoven's *Sechs Bagatellen Op. 126*:

1. *Andante con moto / L'istesso tempo / (non troppo presto)*
2. *Allegro*
3. *Andante: cantabile e grazioso*
4. *Presto*
5. *Quasi allegretto*
6. *Presto-Andante amabile e con moto-Tempo 1 (Presto)*

He then delineated three categories of material (my descriptions):

(A) Melancholy, bluesy. Generally in top two and bottom two octaves of keyboard, sometimes with accentuated line in middle, providing *cantus firmus*, a little like the opening section of *Song 9*. Progressively getting slower.

(B) Fantastic, macabre plundering of bottom of keyboard, first as a stomp, then as series of trills and tremolos, with clusters.

(C) Stomp around whole keyboard, at first with ratios of 10:9 between the hands. Progressively getting faster.

The first of each of these material types is shown in Example 2.14.

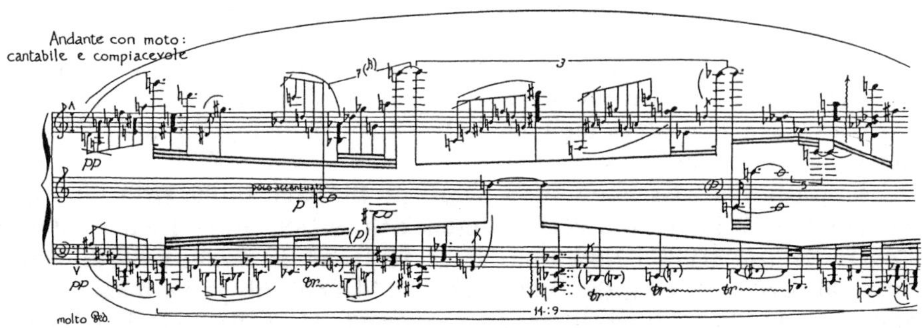

Example 2.14a *Jazz* material type (A1)

Example 2.14b *Jazz* material type (B1)

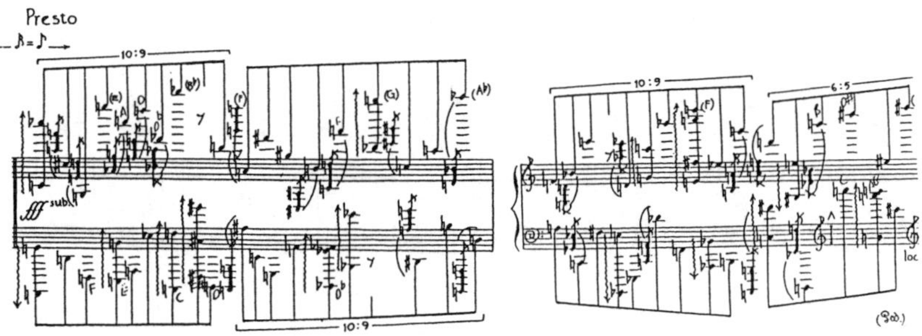

Example 2.14c *Jazz* material type (C1)

The development of materials (A) and (C) is thus in opposite directions. The work is then shaped as follows:

(A1) *Andante con moto: cantabile e compiacevole*
Transformation A1-B1 (a) *l'stesso tempo*
Transformation A1-B1 (b) *(non troppo presto)*
(B1) *Allegro*
(A2) *Andante: cantabile e grazioso*
(C1) *Presto*
(B2) *Quasi allegretto*
(C2) *Presto*
(A3) *Andante amabile e con moto*
(C3) *Presto*

One of the most noticeable characteristics of this work is its use of extreme registers of the piano for extended passages. Finnissy has said that this pianistic idiom derives from his sitting position at the piano (see Interview), but, for me, the sensation it produces is akin to being confronted by stalagmites and stalactites, or mountain peaks and deep pits; the melancholy and free improvisatory qualities of the work are given a larger-than-life portrayal. Finnissy's use of the very bottom of the piano in section (B1) was taken a stage further in *We'll get there someday* (1978) which is entirely in this register, except for the final staccato chord which acts as an ironic form of objectivisation.

The move to a high degree of abstraction was shown in *all.fall.down* (1977). Taking its title from the well-known nursery rhyme 'Ring-a-ring of roses' (which also appears in the stage work *Vaudeville*), the work is in three corresponding sections. The first, *all*, uses all the notes of the piano with both hands in rhythmic unison. Development is effected by the use of white note/black note filters which produce differing chromatic/diatonic/pentatonic harmonic fields, as well as occasional registral filters and tempo changes, interspersion of contrary motion scales, arpeggiation and grace notes. On a more mundane level, this section is also notable for its frightening difficulty of execution:

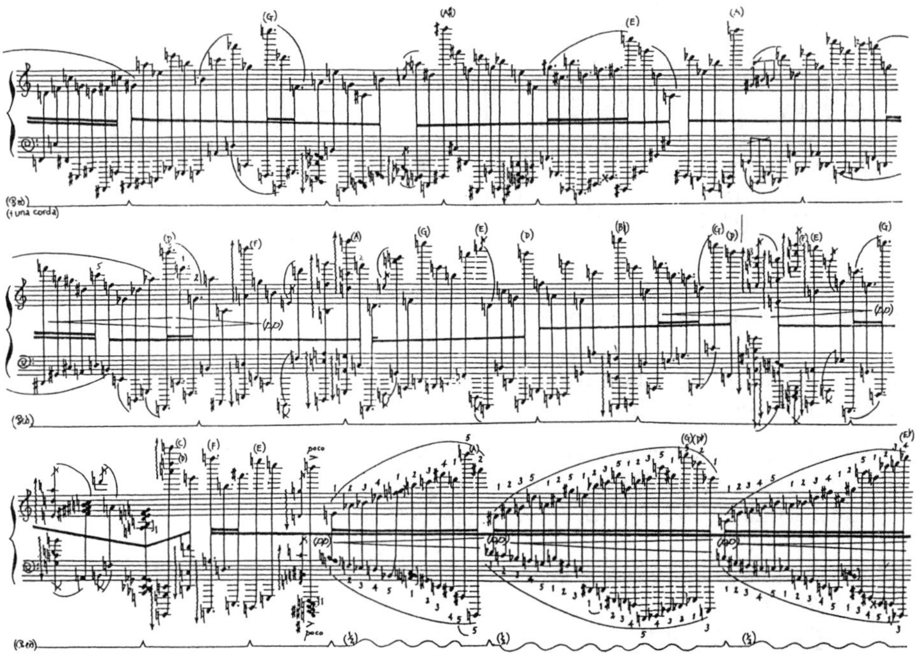

Example 2.15 *all.fall.down*, p. 2

Towards the end of this section, the left hand works its way up the keyboard for *fall.* Here two lines of chords gradually move down the keyboard, though with other forms of modification along the way, towards *down,* which is exclusively in the bottom register. This is notated in terms of metrical ratios for time signatures between the two hands, so that the left hand is proportionally slower than the right by a ratio of, for example, 13 to 19. Simultaneous developments here include overlays of silences, the reduction of continuous lines to single *sfffffz* chords and back to lines again with progressively less dense chords, and 'stepwise' *diminuendo* (jumps from subito *ff* to subito *f*, subito *mf*, etc., without any other quietening in between).

Fast Dances, Slow Dances similarly took Beethoven's *Elf Bagatellen* Op. 119 as its structural model, but the resultant piece is quite different from *Jazz*:

(1) *Allegretto*. Two lines at top of keyboard, the upper line monodic, ornamented with grace notes, the lower beginning in chords, then thinning down to single notes. Interruption of overall *staccato*, *fff* with pedalled *ppp* segments. Interspersions of grace note chords at bottom of keyboard. Rhythms moving around an implied dotted crotchet pulse.

(2) *Andante con moto*. Continuation of two high monodic lines *ppp* from (1). Alternation of pedal and staccato.

(3) *à l'Allemande*. Wide arpeggiated *ff* chords, or angular lines, in differing metrical units.

(4) *Andante cantabile*. Three lines, top line like (3) but here *piano*, with two chordal lines in different registers of the bass. Middle line begins rapid series of notes, leading to:

(5) *Risoluto*. Again three lines. Top line continues middle line of (4), introducing rapid-fire chords. Brutal slurred pairs of chords in extreme bass in other two lines, in differing metres. Registral 'wrenching up' of top line leads to:

(6) *Andante-Allegretto-l'istesso tempo* (Example 2.16). Two lines in each half of the keyboard. Both uneven, with novel experiment in notation, *accelerandos* and *ritardandos* written out as irrational rhythms. Continual shifts between all notes, white notes and black notes at different points in each part, as in *all.fall.down*, resulting in new harmonic fields as a result of different combinations of chromatic, diatonic and pentatonic filters. Overall *stringendo* leads to brief *Allegretto* interruption, hypertrophised version of (1). Increasing disjunction towards end between faster and slower melodic fragments.

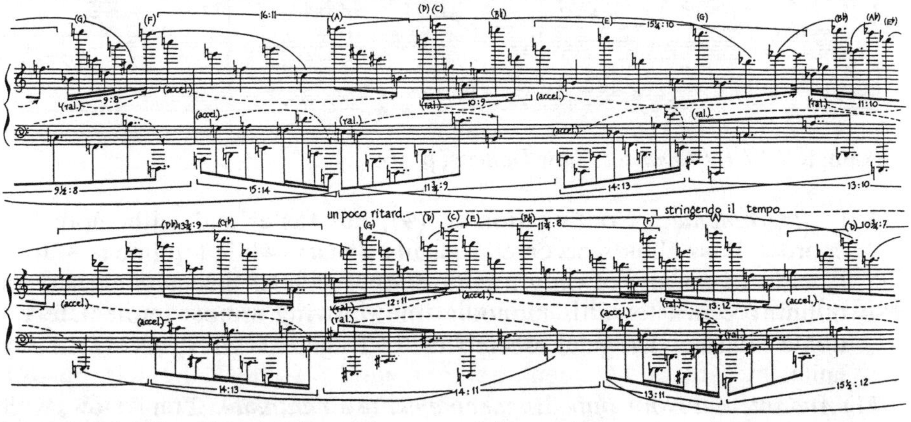

Example 2.16 *Fast Dances, Slow Dances*, p. 8, lines 2-3

(7) *Allegro ma non troppo*. Continuous series of very quick grace notes in both hands, with series separated by long pauses. Lengths of groups within series now seem to follow irregular patterns e.g. in first series have lengths 25-9-14-5-5-9-26-7-3-5-24-2-14-18-14 in right hand, with 20-8-10-5-4-8-24-6-4-5-22-2-13-16-13 in left hand. All in top half of keyboard, dynamics *ppp-mp*.

(8) *Moderato cantabile, molto legato*. Three slow lines in different metrical units. Top line mainly in top three octaves of piano, eventually moving down, middle line ranging widely around middle register, bottom line always in the bass. Bottom line soon introduces chords, as eventually does middle line. Long *crescendo* to:

(9) *Vivace moderato* (Example 2.17). Much longer exposition of idea briefly glimpsed in (5). Here two lower lines have single chords rather than pairs, though still in different metrical units. Rests between chords contain incrementally increasing or decreasing numbers of semiquavers, in the manner of Nancarrow. Further white note/black note filters. Top line utilises a variety of techniques, including rhythmic progression of 7 quavers, 8:7, 9:7, 10:7, etc; palindromic rhythms with increasing/decreasing irrational overlays; reduction from chromatic cluster-like chords to fourths, or whole-tone clusters. All in bass register, with one very high chord during *accelerando* into next section:

Example 2.17 *Fast Dances, Slow Dances*, p. 16

(10) *Allegramente*. Continuation of (9), but faster and with more high chords. Bass chords become gradually denser, while top line is at times filtered to consist of only major/minor seconds, then *diminuendo* and thinning down towards monodic line, moving almost immediately to treble register. Irregular assemblage of fragments with varying metrical units.

(11) *Andante ma non troppo, innocentemente e cantabile*. Long, slow, wide-ranging melody in treble, with occasional low chords in bass.

Both *all.fall.down* and *Fast Dances, Slow Dances,* together with works for other mediums such as *Alongside*, represent the culmination of a phase of Finnissy's compositional development, towards a degree of abstraction not seen since the *Songs*. There is a danger of arid formalism when the external referent does not influence the actual musical material, but if the structure of *Fast Dances, Slow Dances* served some meaningful purpose in the Beethoven work, why should it not be valid in a quite different context?

These works could be said to provide an 'archetypal' example of Finnissy's compositional techniques up to this point, laying bare the technical skeleton of much of his work. Operations upon material are made as clear as possible, though the categorisation of form and content is made problematic by the multi-layering of different developmental progressions. However systematic or random the works might seem in places, Finnissy's decision to write them the way he did is a *human* choice, so their very nature reflects a subjective personality: human characteristics with which a listener may find resonances. One might equally well say that Cage, a composer who Finnissy acknowledges as a major influence, could never completely escape intentionality in his own music, because his intention is manifest in the decision to use the particular procedures that he did, however random they might be. Those who respond to *4'33"* by saying 'I could have done that!' betray a very puritanical streak: that composition is to be judged on the basis of the quantity of labour involved in its production, rather than its inspiration and distinctiveness. I do not wish to propound a completely open-ended pluralist aesthetic, just to point out that the ultimate enigma of the human mind makes it highly unlikely that any other individual would have produced works like these.

The scores define themselves almost as much by what is excluded as included, by their rejection of a too-obvious linearity of development, and the resistance to total systemisation in at least one parameter at any moment. Finnissy is not a dogmatist; all his compositional procedures involve a high degree of intervention in response to his instinctive and personal demands, and the use of random procedures to 'shake up' that which is becoming too predictable. The situation becomes more difficult to grasp philosophically, however, when one considers the similarities between chance and extreme complexity of system, or between chance and human intention, when one considers a human being as itself a complex system. These sorts of questions, to which the works provide one possible answer, would need a whole book in order to be treated in a manner which is even remotely satisfactory. I can merely point out the individuality of these works, even within the highly varied context of Finnissy's output. Some might even consider them to be 'typical Finnissy pieces' but this leads to a contradiction since they are the only works to fit such a category.

However, finding that a structuralist model of the world was not all-inclusive - there were many things which could not be reduced to an agglomeration of binary oppositions - Finnissy soon afterwards made a determined shift in direction, an attempt to engage in a more obvious dialogue with the 'world outside', through the introduction of materials derived from folk music and the work of other composers. He had reached the end of a line in both compositional and personal senses, having become so disillusioned with his native land that he sought work elsewhere. Before considering the subsequent periods of work, however, it is first necessary to look at the other paths which he had begun to pursue simultaneously, and another major work which was completed before the move.

English Country-Tunes

The thorny subject of England and Englishness is one that Finnissy has returned to at various points during his career. Unlike Ferneyhough or some of the younger composers who have benefited from Finnissy's influence and encouragement, he has chosen for the most part to remain in England, yet always remained conscious of his status as an outsider, as a radical artist and homosexual. Although deeply interested at first in East European folk music, Finnissy realised that it would make more sense to investigate the music of his native land. This research explicitly informed works such as *Kemp's Morris, Folk Song Set* and *Tom Fool's Wooing*, but was nonetheless an important factor in the composition of Finnissy's first large scale piano work, the 50 minute virtuoso epic *English Country-Tunes* (1977/82-85), 'written in celebration of the Silver Jubilee of Her Majesty Queen Elizabeth II'.

To consider the title: Does *English Country* refer to the 'country of England' or specifically the rural part therein? *Tunes* rather than *Melodies* - there is surely some irony in an age when composers are reprimanded for their failure to write 'nice tunes' (notwithstanding the fundamental importance of melody to Finnissy). *Country Tunes* - is this a word-play on 'contra-tunes', as in his later work *Contretänze*, or a play on the first syllable of *Country*, suggesting connotations of sex or sexuality? In Shakespeare's *Hamlet*, Act III, Scene 2, II. 120ff:

Hamlet.	Lady, shall I lie in your lap?
Ophelia.	No, my lord.
H.	I mean, my head upon your lap?
O.	Ay, my lord.
H.	Do you think I meant country matters?
O.	I think nothing, my lord.
H.	That's a fair thought to lie between maids' legs.
O.	What is, my lord?
H.	Nothing.

Finnissy has certainly replied in the affirmative to the last of these questions, explaining that he intended the work to be 'about' attitudes in England to sexuality, a culture which attempts to deny or outlaw many aspects of human sexual behaviour, until they return to haunt it with a vengeance. Such considerations go a long way to explaining the instability and underlying psychotic nature of much of the first three movements of the work.

1. *Green Meadows*. Tempestuous yet distant surges of activity all around the keyboard erupting into sudden split-second violence (Example 2.18a). Low rumblings, building to a peak, then calm again. Emergent shimmerings, extremely quiet, using all registers. Sudden cut off. Violent, but exhilarating traversals up and down keyboard, joined by harsh melody in chords at the very top of keyboard, continually under threat of envelopment by the ascending swathes of notes (Example 2.18b). A gap in the texture, appearance of more diatonic melody in middle register. Top line dissolves, bottom line suddenly returns to rumblings. Alternation of more measured and spacious violence, with now monodic diatonic melody, accompanied first by rumblings, then by top register melody (now *ppp*). Long, timeless, exposition of serene but infinitely distant melody (Example 2.18c).

Rumblings again. 'Almost motionless' continuation of melody leading to second movement.

2. *Midsummer Morn*. Very slow, intensely nostalgic but also passionate, folk-inspired melody exclusively using white notes (Example 2.19a). Climax, a few black notes. Murkier textures (Example 2.19b), then sudden violent outburst across whole of keyboard (Example 2.19c). Return to initial type of music, but here tempered by grace notes, simultaneity of melodies, low accompaniment. Outburst again, introduction of clusters. Barest outline of melodic writing, usurped by grace notes. Third outburst (more organically derived from what has gone before), then sudden *diminuendo*. Uneasy calm, with four melodic lines simultaneously.

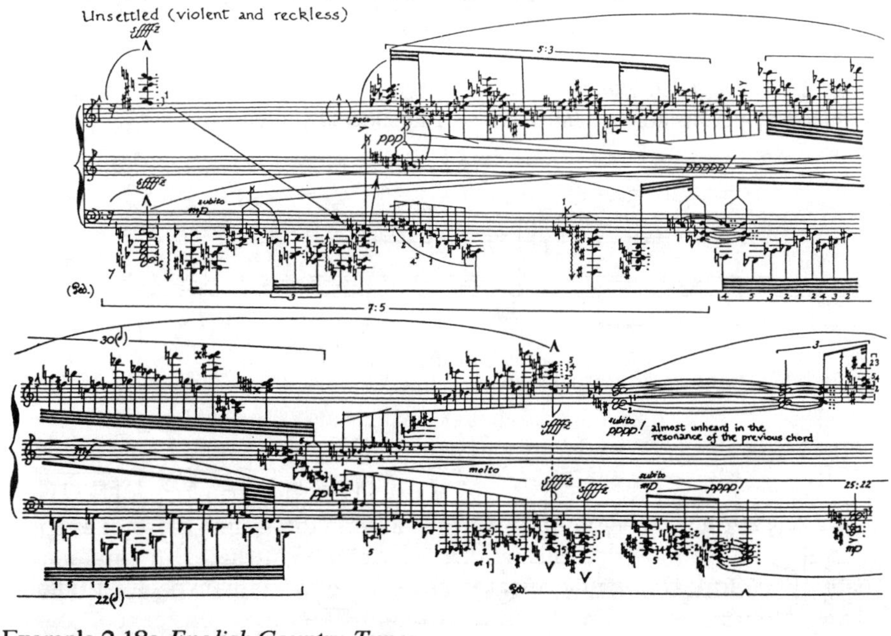

Example 2.18a *English Country-Tunes*

Example 2.18b *English Country-Tunes*

Example 2.18c *English Country-Tunes*
Reproduced by permission of United Music Publishers Limited

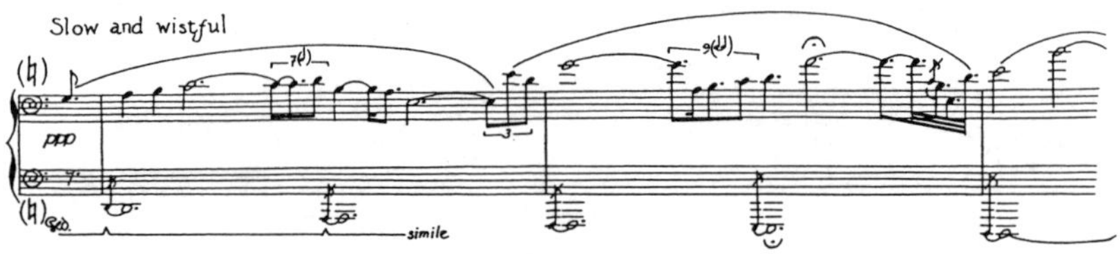

Example 2.19a *English Country-Tunes*

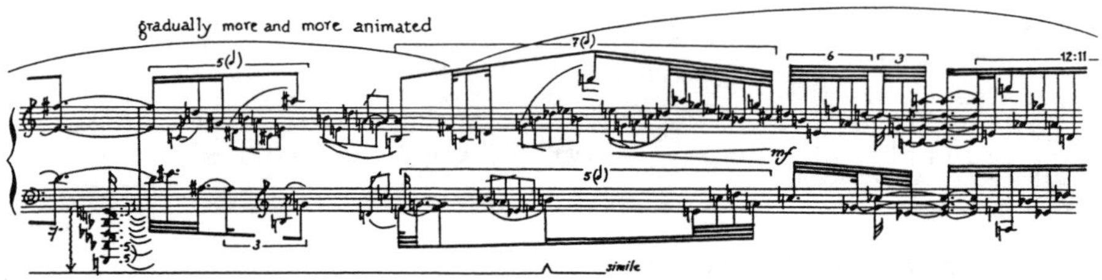

Example 2.19b *English Country-Tunes*

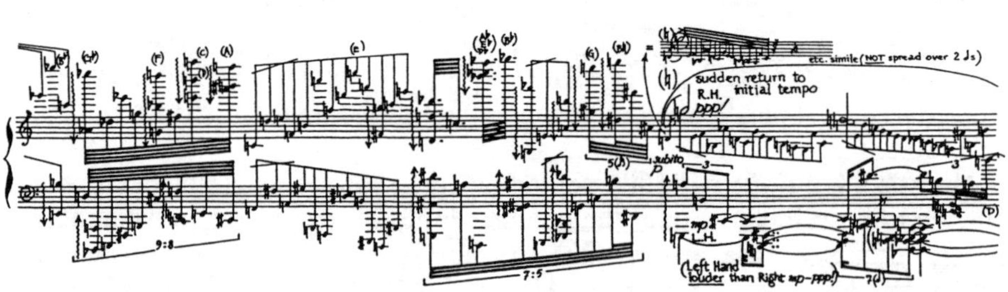

Example 2.19c *English Country-Tunes*
Reproduced by permission of United Music Publishers Limited

3. *I'll give my love a garland.* Continuation of end of *Midsummer Morn.* Increasing stability and tranquillity. Silence. Further continuation. Silence. Single melodic line in centre of keyboard, surrounded by macabre *ppp* sounds, buzzings, wailings, distant mutilated echoes. Silence. Melody alone, now in diatonic intervals. Surroundings again, now more hectic. Bass line suddenly breaks out. Rapid burst of notes, louder and softer with increasing rate of change. Swarm of grace notes in upper register, eventually quietening to *mormorato*, but still at top speed, with occasional clusters producing sensation of immanency (Example 2.20a). Crazed outburst all over keyboard, similar to that in *Midsummer Morn.* Sudden return to *piano* grace notes, moving straight back up to top of keyboard and *forte*. *Crescendo*, quick snatch of breath, then two more violent outbursts. Quick calmings, re-appearance of diatonic melody similar to end of *Green Meadows*, but accompanied by rumblings. Silence. Final melody, *molto sostenuto*, is most paradisiacal moment in whole work, yet uncertain conclusion (Example 2.20b). Brief pause.

Example 2.20a *English Country-Tunes*

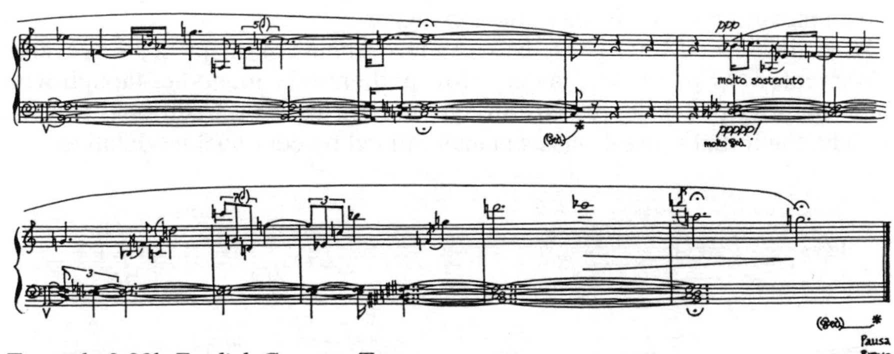

Example 2.20b *English Country-Tunes*
Reproduced by permission of United Music Publishers Limited

Rather than continue with this degree of detail for the whole piece, it should suffice to describe how over the course of the following five movements the music attains both a greater stability and a greater polarisation between extremes. The fourth movement, *May and December*, forms a pivot between the two 'halves' of the work, retaining some of the instability that was a feature of the preceding three, yet with a long murmuring passage in the central register. The fifth, *Lies and Marvels*, is in two parts, the first a type of macho posturing at the bottom of the keyboard, which dissolves to a series of ghostly whispers, the second a brilliant series of ascending arpeggio-like figures in the left hand, with an equally rapid line in the right which is nevertheless more fixed in register:

Example 2.21 *English Country-Tunes*, p. 42
Reproduced by permission of United Music Publishers Limited

The apotheosis of the violence inherent in the work is reached in the sixth movement, *The Seeds of Love*. For the most part a series of psychotic, fragmented gestures, which become more continuous before reaching a manic progression of out-of-phase *staccato* chords in both hands, finally dissolving into an indistinct shimmering in the top register.

After the second brief pause between movements in the piece, the seventh movement, *My Bonny Boy*, is very slow and entirely monodic, though with the sustaining pedal depressed throughout. Based on a traditional English melody, the initial sense of stasis is undermined by continual modulation:

Example 2.22 *English Country-Tunes*, p. 53
Reproduced by permission of United Music Publishers Limited

The last movement, *Come beat the drums and sound the fifes*, might be a reflection on the para-military nature of the English marching band and could hardly stand in greater contrast to *My Bonny Boy*. Exclusively in the outer extremes of the piano, it is a long *Totentanz* (as one might describe the whole work), involving pounding chords in the bass, with a much more rhythmically irregular concatenation of fragments in the treble:

Example 2.23 *English Country-Tunes*, p. 58
Reproduced by permission of United Music Publishers Limited

After the first *fortissimo*, further developments include the introduction of trills first in the treble line, then in the bass, and a more rapid rate of change of dynamic, bringing the work to its mind-blowing conclusion.

English Country-Tunes is a work which moves from an uneasy dialogue between extremes to complete polarisation. It presents both immense rage and nostalgia for a lost world, the latter of which is evoked by the particular utilisation of modal and diatonic material, producing what was for Finnissy a new colour, though the vision is made unattainable because of its haziness, seen through a gauze of tears. The piece is a culmination point like the 'abstract' works described above, the ultimate expression of extremes of passion and anger, almost like a form of catharsis. Certainly any listener is likely to leave the work feeling emotionally drained.

There is much which is dark and satanic, and a form of post-holocaust bleakness, a frightening landscape barely hospitable to man yet strangely beautiful, in the 'England' that Finnissy presents; the country from which he felt deeply alienated, and which he left for a period soon afterwards. The new colours that had been shown to be possible in *English Country-Tunes*, as well as different modes of synthesis, were to be the basis of the following decade-and-a-half's work.

The Piano Concertos

Finnissy's seven piano concertos date from a relatively short period, from 1975 to 1981. They share many of the harmonic/rhythmic/gestural characteristics of the 'abstract' works mentioned above, but also represent a commentary on the nature of the piano concerto as a medium (perhaps not entirely different from the various ways in which composers as different as Globokar and Carter have explored the interrelationships between groups of players), and as such it would be disingenuous to deny considerations of virtuosity.

The relationship between soloist and ensemble is at its most conventional in the *Piano Concerto No. 1* (1975/83-84), which has continual dialogue between the piano and the other instrumentalists and a cadenza in the middle. In the *Piano Concerto No. 2* (1975-76), on the other hand, the piano has a long and extremely varied cadenza at the opening, then is gradually integrated into the ensemble, before ending with another, smoother cadenza, as if the piano has been 'cleansed' by its interaction with others. The *Piano Concerto No. 3* (1978) once more places the piano centre stage, with one of the most brilliant pieces of writing Finnissy has ever created, inspired by the playing of Cecil Taylor:

Example 2.24 *Piano Concerto No. 3*

The ensemble, an unusual combination of oboe, clarinet, two tenor trombones, cello and double bass, is overshadowed by the piano for much of the piece, but the players have correspondingly 'free-jazz'-like parts, with especially imaginative *pizzicato* writing in the two strings. The integration of the piano (whose part includes two extended cadenzas) occurs only towards the very end.

But the *Piano Concerto No. 4* (1978/96) goes a stage further in its demands on the performer, veering towards the impossible. Inspired by Alkan's *Concerto for Solo Piano*, Finnissy has the performer adopt both solo and *tutti* roles, with corresponding changes of texture. There is absolutely no let-up for the pianist, who has to plough heroically through a seemingly endless series of whirling semiquavers, manage a five-part canon (with five different time signatures) in the closing section, and somehow negotiate the most hysterical of fugues:

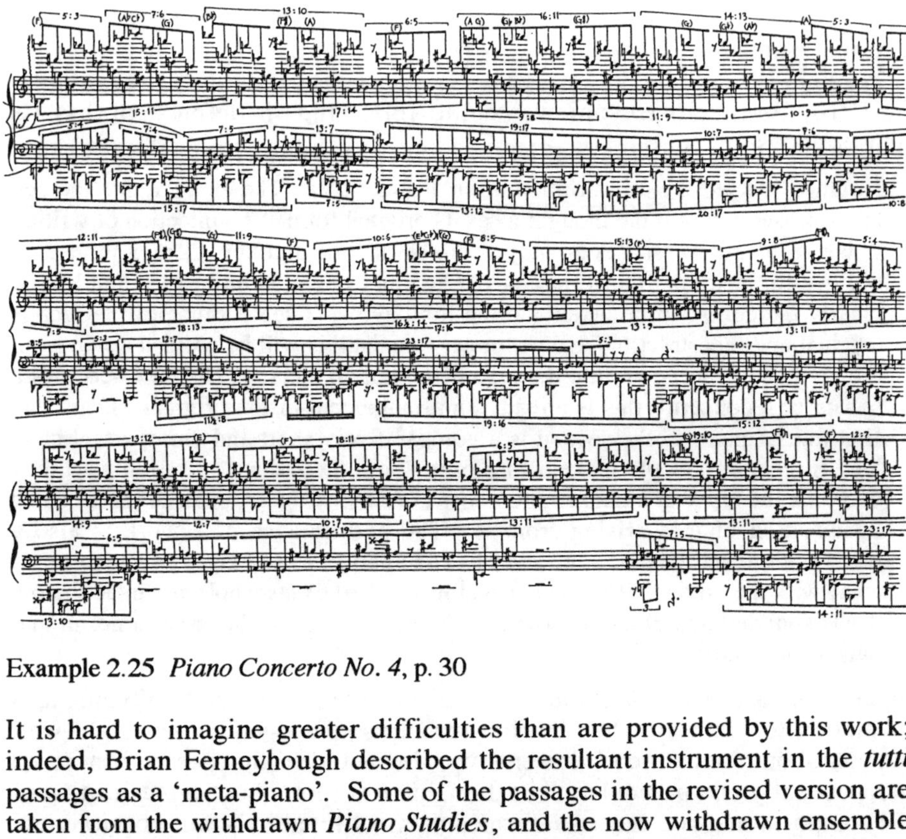

Example 2.25 *Piano Concerto No. 4*, p. 30

It is hard to imagine greater difficulties than are provided by this work; indeed, Brian Ferneyhough described the resultant instrument in the *tutti* passages as a 'meta-piano'. Some of the passages in the revised version are taken from the withdrawn *Piano Studies*, and the now withdrawn ensemble piece *Long Distance* provides the canon at the end.

Both the *Piano Concerto No. 5* (1980) and the *Piano Concerto No. 7* (1981) dispense with a full score, supplying instead a set of parts whose vertical co-ordination is approximate. They both continue explorations of degrees of interaction and integration between soloist and ensemble. In the fifth concerto Finnissy takes the novel step of introducing a wordless voice part; this work operates a process of 'transference', whereby the ensemble is eventually 'infected' by some of the characteristics of the opening of the piano part, while the piano part itself becomes integrated into the ensemble, a form of 'counter-transference'!

The *Piano Concerto No. 6* (1980-81) is like the fourth, for solo piano, and also inspired by the Alkan work. It is an exceptionally strange and eerie work, containing unexpectedly long *spettrale* passages in the outer registers. The writing only becomes more animated and voluminous at a few places other than the beginning, as if the 'orchestra' is only occasionally able to interrupt the 'inner world' of the 'soloist'. The coda congeals what has gone before into a long series of changing trills in both hands. Its rejection of conventions of taste and proportions enables types of material that have been evidenced earlier in Finnissy's output to be seen in a radically new light.

Transcription

In 1910, Ferruccio Busoni wrote the following in defence of Liszt's transcriptions:

> Notation is itself the transcription of an abstract idea. The moment that the pen takes possession of it the thought loses its original form. The intention of writing down an idea necessitates already a choice of time and key. The composer is obliged to decide on the form and the key and they determine more and more clearly the course to be taken and the limitations. Even if much of the idea is original and indestructible and continues to exist this will be pressed down from the moment of decision, into the type belonging to a class. The idea becomes a sonata or a concerto; this is already an arrangement of the original. From this first transcription to the second is a comparatively short and unimportant step. Yet, in general, people make a fuss only about the second. In doing so they overlook the fact that a transcription does not destroy the original; so there can be no question of loss arising from it. The performance of a work is also a transcription, and this too - however free the performance may be - can never do away with the original. For the musical work of art exists whole and intact before it has sounded and after the sound is finished. It is, at the same time, in and outside of Time.[4]

Such a conception of *all* composition as a form of 'transcription' came as a revelation to Finnissy when he first read Busoni's essay. One might well wonder about the nature of this elusive 'abstract idea' that can be conceived independently of a particular realisation, but this form of conceptualisation of the compositional process has informed many of Finnissy's transcriptions and composer tributes. He attempts in these works to make clear his own particular aesthetic and technical priorities by applying them to something pre-existent, with the intention to remove one degree of unfamiliarity from the listening process.

Of course there is nothing particularly new about this approach (except in the degree to which the composer is conscious of it); think of Bach's transcriptions, Mozart and Beethoven's innumerable sets of variations, Debussy's ironic cribs of Wagner, Stravinsky's utterly original re-working of Pergolesi; more recently Berio's collage of Mahler, Debussy, Boulez and other's in the *Sinfonia*, Kagel's fixation on small elements within received genres, Cage's use of a citation as just another type of sound with no special importance, and, most ominously, the claustrophobia created by the 'closing in' of many voices from different times and places in B.A. Zimmermann's *Requiem für einen Jungen Dichter*.

Finnissy's transcriptions do not clearly fit into any of the above categories, although they are clearly informed by this history. His approach is above all 'critical' - he is uninhibited about modifying or mutating his source material to suit his own ends. Starting from a belief that all composers are dealing with a vocabulary that has both natural and cultural/historic connotations, and thus that an 'original idea' is well nigh impossible, Finnissy has in this strand of his work (which in different manifestations has become his primary concern) dealt with the fundamentally *diachronic* nature of music; to achieve the 'not-yet-heard', one must find new ways of treating that which already exists, emphasising processes rather than material. I would suggest that without a thorough knowledge of what has come before, a composer is in great danger of 're-inventing the wheel'; those who ignore history are in danger of repeating it, and so on.

The first work that might be described as a 'transcription' is a curious affair called *Romeo and Juliet are Drowning* (1967/73). In this piece, Finnissy takes music from the love scene of Berlioz's *Romeo et Juliette*, then gradually submerges it within a series of descending notes and chords derived from the drowning scene in Berg's *Wozzeck*:

Example 2.26 *Romeo and Juliet are Drowning* (two extracts)
Reproduced by permission of Oxford University Press

While the two types of material are not new, the nature of their combination creates a most original piece of music; the different periods and places from which the sources originate serve the purpose of distancing and objectification.

A series of three pieces, *Ives* (1974), *Grainger* (1979) and *Nancarrow* (1979-80), each written on the occasion of anniversaries of the respective composer's birth or death, pays tribute to those aspects of the composers' work which Finnissy believed to have been integral to his own musical language. Each of these composers, despite all the historical evidence of their influence, has all too often been dismissed as 'eccentric' (as has Finnissy himself), because each pursued a direction tangential to the hegemony of the primarily Austro-German canonical tradition.

Example 2.27 *Ives*. Reproduced by permission of Edition Modern

Yet none of these pieces merely pastiche the respective composer's style. The explosive opening of *Ives* (Example 2.27) may have something in common with the opening of 'Hawthorne' from the *Concord Sonata* (a piece which has never ceased to fascinate Finnissy, since the age of eleven), and the unusual use of ragtime rhythms might also relate to similar passages in the *First Sonata*, yet the piece could not have been written by anyone other than Finnissy himself.

The inspiration for *Grainger* came as much from his ideas as his music. In a letter Grainger described his experience lying on a boat on Lake Melbourne. The sheer variegation and unpredictability of the sounds of the water and nature that he heard heightened his awareness of how strait-jacketed and un-free much 'classical' music actually was. This was to lead to his composition of 'free music', with the use of irrational rhythms, continual metre changes, overlapping *glissandi* and much more in some of his less popular works. *Grainger* is exclusively at the outer ends of the keyboard, consisting of two outer melodic lines, and two inner lines of trills, an attempt to evoke the sound of Grainger's proposed 'kangaroo machine':

Example 2.28 *Grainger*

Nancarrow bears a superficial resemblance to some of the *Studies for Player Piano*, with a canon between the two hands, in different tempos and metres (Example 2.29), with one hand playing flourishes of notes of equal durations, while the other has palindromic rhythms, followed by an anticipatory series of irregularly spaced single *staccato* notes, before the situation of the two hands is reversed. The ways in which such material is developed bears some relation to those in *Fast Dances, Slow Dances*.

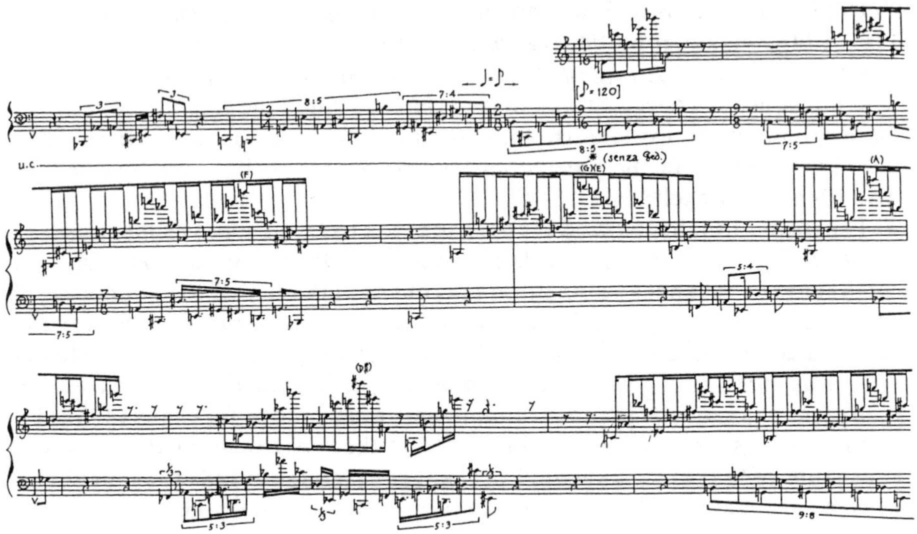

Example 2.29 *Nancarrow*

It is now worth considering a work derived from a specific source, to understand precisely how this source is transformed into the finished piece. While there is no 'super-formula' into which any source can be fed to produce an instant transcription - Finnissy's compositional processes are continually altered in accordance with the needs of each particular work - nonetheless *G.F.H.* (1985) (Example 2.30) provides a relatively typical example of how he creates a work of transcription.

Written to celebrate the tercentenary of Handel's birth (whose transparency and seemingly endless facility for creating line is much admired by Finnissy), the work takes the opening of the *Trio Sonata Op. 1 No. 1* as its point of departure (Example 2.31a). This appears in the third voice at the beginning. Finnissy splits the melody into seven pitch cells, each of three notes, then inverts them to produce a further seven cells (Example 2.31b). The pitches for other voices are then derived by transposing combinations of these cells. The top voice is a random permutation of retrogrades of the cells, while the second voice consists of the inversions in order. After finishing the initial exposition of the melody, the third part also uses a random permutation of the pitch cells (Example 2.31c,d,e). Each line was composed separately; when Finnissy came to put them together, some pitches were modified to prevent contrapuntal overlap and unwanted harmonic combinations.

Finnissy also created a vocabulary of rhythmic cells, probably derived from just a few, some of whose possible relationships are shown in Example 2.31f. The method by which the actual rhythms are determined is a little more complex than that for pitch. Finnissy takes *two* randomly derived series of rhythmic cells, then intuitively finds ways of containing cells in the first series in the time of subsections of the second (Example 2.31g).

The melody is passed around the four voices in successively modified forms (the process described above is particularly evident in the rhythm), in voice order three, two, one, four, while the other parts continue the processes of transformation and re-transformation (such that their modification is a 'step ahead' of the main line), while the transpositions gradually work their way down the keyboard (Example 2.31h). Once the line has been passed between all four parts, and before this process becomes too obvious, the *sfffz* chord suddenly interrupts and drags all the voices down an octave.

Example 2.30 *G.F.H.*
Reproduced by permission of Oxford University Press

By this stage they are modified to such a degree that the original melody has ceased to be recognisable, yet something of the 'flavour' remains. It is Finnissy's belief (which I share) that after even the most radical of transformations, a kernel of a source's intrinsic characteristics, however small, will continue to be present in a work which has been created from that source. That his transcriptions do indeed sound so very different, bears this out.

GFH

(a) melody from Trio Sonata op.1 no.1

(b) pitch cells derived from (a)

8-14 are inversions of 1-7. Note also 3=7=11, 4=10=14 in transposition

(c) pitches of first part, beginning

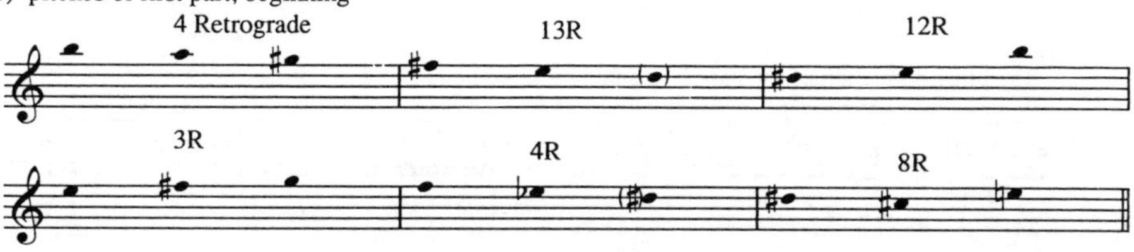

(d) pitches of second part, beginning (original)

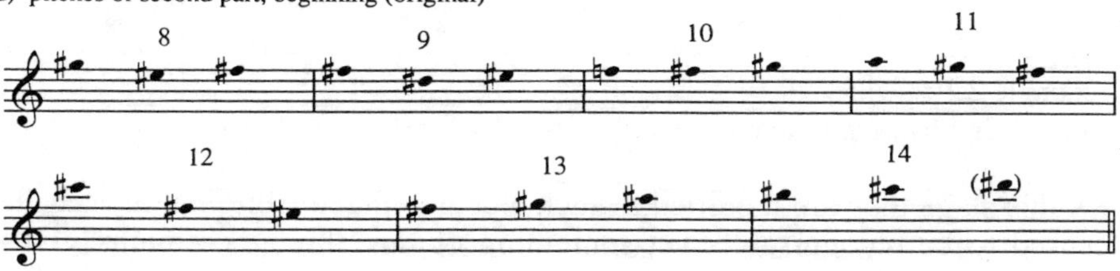

(e) pitches of third part, after initial melody. From random series 2,5,7,11,14,13

(f) Rhythmic cells

5 = retrograde of 2, 16 = topological distortion of 6, 7 = condensed 3, 11 = extraction from 6
20 = 10 + 1 joined with a unit:

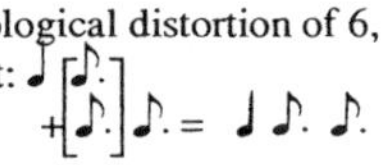

(g) Rhythmic derivation of top part, beginning

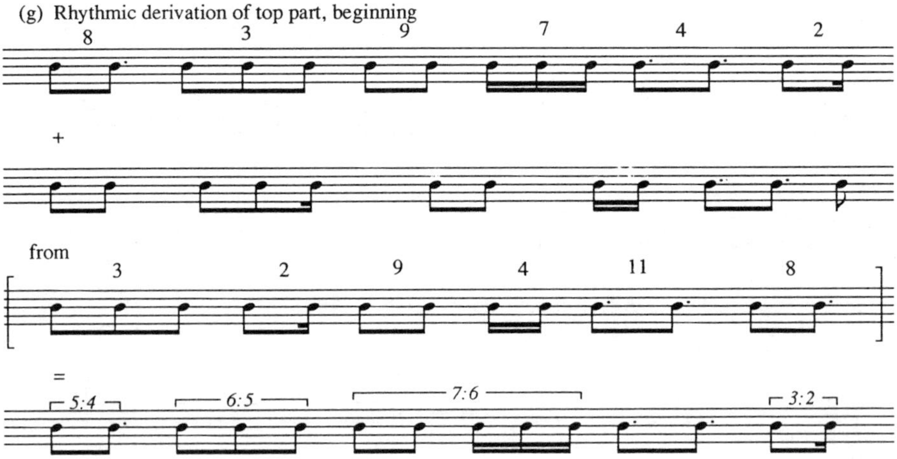

(h) Successive transformations of melody

Example 2.31 *G.F.H.* procedures a-h

In a later work, ***William Billings*** (1990), written while Finnissy was staying in Buffalo, he took a selection of Billings's hymn tunes, performed a 'cut-up' procedure, then re-assembled them interspersed with silences, before expanding upon particular melodic fragments which took his interest:

Example 2.32a Billings sources

Example 2.32b *William Billings*, p. 1

The piece bears a certain resemblance to John Cage's *Apartment House 1776*, which is itself in part based on Billings, though Finnissy's work has a greater element of intention and critique. It presents an evocation of the impossibility of returning to the certainties of the pasts, like a series of distant photographs of lost worlds, tinged with ambivalent nostalgia.

Finnissy's major work of transcription, however, is the series of pieces composed over a long period of time and collected as the *Verdi Transcriptions* (1972-88/95). Inspired by his deep love of 'the energy, passion and wide-rangingly generous humanity of Verdi's operas', and a wish to advocate Verdi against Wagner, who self-styled 'modernists' habitually regarded as a more 'serious' composer (like Mozart or Brahms, to name but two objects of Finnissy's disaffection), he at first intended to write one piece derived from each of Verdi's operas, to be collected in four books. After completing one book of nine pieces, construed as a continuous work, and a collection of six other transcriptions as a second book, Finnissy decided to present these two books, with the inclusion of three fragments in the second collection, as a complete work in eighteen movements.

I	Aria: 'Sciagurata! a questo lido ricercai l'amante infido!' *Oberto* (Act 2)
II	Trio: 'Bella speranza in vero' *Un Giorno di Regno* (Act 1)
III	Chorus: 'Il maledetto non ha fratelli' *Nabucco* (Part 2)
IV	Chorus: 'Fra tante sciagure...' *I Lombardi* (Act 3)
V	Septet with Chorus: 'Vedi come il buon vegliardo...' *Ernani* (Part 1)
VI	Choral Barcarolle: 'Tace il vento, è queta l'onda' *I Due Foscari* (Act 3)
VII	Aria: 'So che per via di triboli' *Giovanna d'Arco* (Act 1)
VIII	Duet: 'Il pianto...l'angoscia...di lena mi priva' *Alzira* (Act 2)
IX	Aria: 'Mentre gonfiarsi l'Anima' *Attila* (Act 1)
X	Romanza: 'Me pellegrina ed orfano' *La Forza del Destino* (Act 1)
XI	Chorus: 'S'allontanarono! N'accozzeremo' *Macbeth* (Act 1)
XII	Duet: 'Vanitosi! Che abbietti e dormenti' *Attila* (Prologue)
	Fragment (a): 'Cielo pietoso, rendila a questo core' *Simon Boccanegra* (Act 2)
	Fragment (b): *La Traviata*
	Fragment (c): 'Vi fu in Palestina' *Aroldo* (Finale Act 1)
XIII	Romanza: 'O cieli azzuri...' *Aïda* (Act 3)
XIV	Duet: 'Qual mare, qual terra...' *I Masnadieri* (Part 3)
XV	Aria: 'Tu che la vantià conoscesti' *Don Carlo* (Act 5)

The total work is much more than a mere ordering of disjunct movements, however; there are several 'running themes' throughout the cycle. During his investigation of Verdi's large output, Finnissy was able to discern a number of recurrent 'archetypal' features, such as a particular type of descending melodic fragment. Indeed, descent per se is the most obvious determinant of the final piece on the cycle, the *Don Carlo* transcription, which ranges from an almost static series of long descending notes derived from the Verdi melody, to a coruscating series of overlapping scales (Example 2.33).

The first piece, the *Oberto* transcription, is literally dredged up from the murkiness of the bottom of the keyboard, after an explosive opening which 'clears the air'. As has been pointed out by Richard Toop,[5] the particular series of tri-chords used here derive from all the possible combinations of intervals in the Verdi melody (Example 2.34).

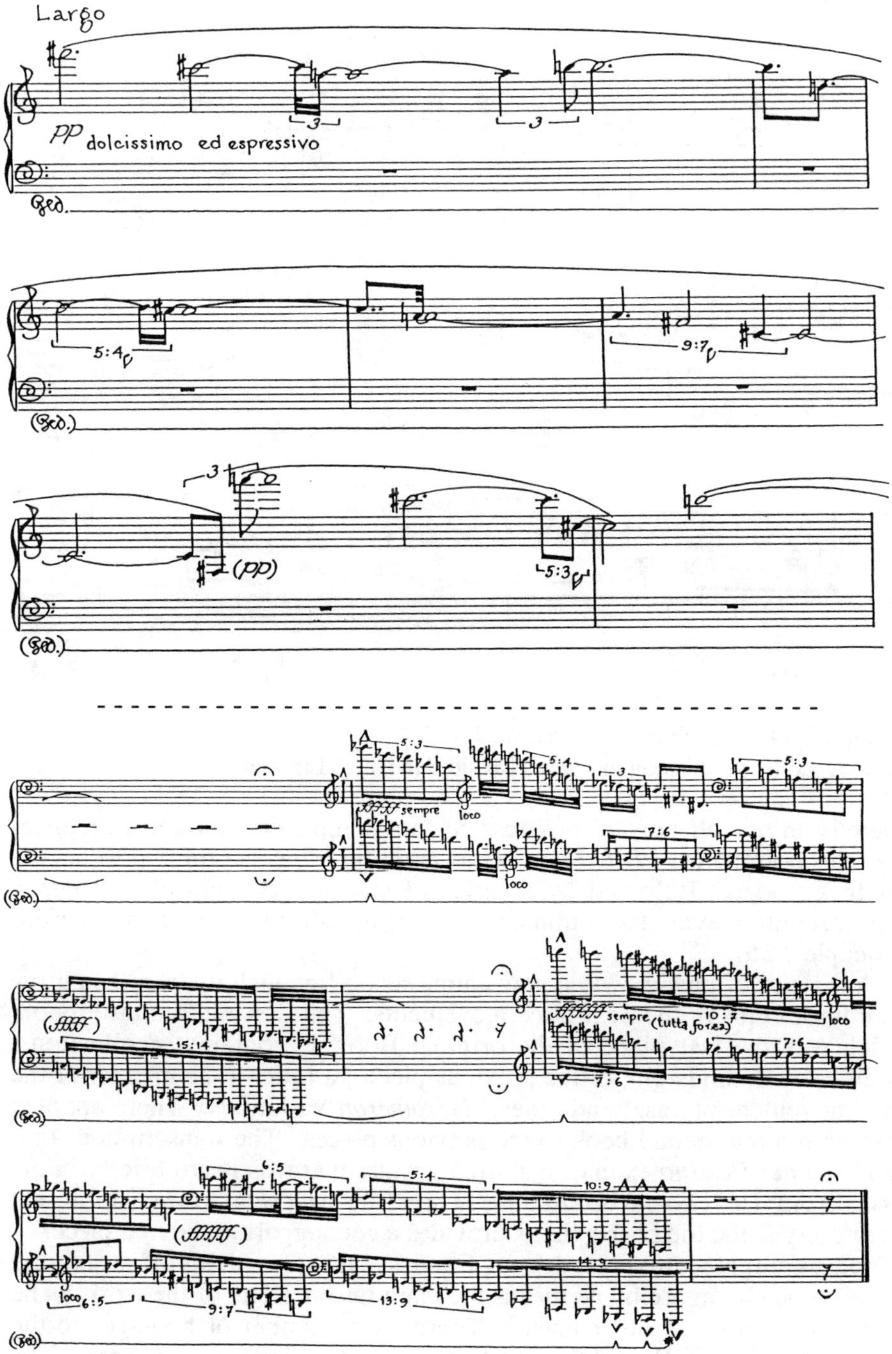

Example 2.33 *Verdi Transcriptions No. 18* (beginning and end)
Reproduced by permission of United Music Publishers Limited

Example 2.34 *Verdi Transcriptions No. 1*, p. 5
Reproduced by permission of United Music Publishers Limited

There is an overall upward progression (not completely smooth) in register from this point to the *I Due Foscari* transcription, which stormily devours the whole keyboard, followed by a series of staccato clusters of a violence unprecedented even for Finnissy, shattering all that has come before (Example 2.35).

New types of music, with a new emphasis on free melody, can then grow from these ruins in the next three movements. The first *Attila* transcription, which was the last piece in the original Book 1, contains recollections, modified with hindsight, of the previous pieces, a little in the manner of the final movement of Liszt and others' *Hexameron* variations. There are also links within the second book to the previous pieces. The transcription from *La Forza del Destino* extends a slurred gesture that was heard briefly in the piece from *Un Giorno di Regno*, while the *Macbeth* transcription, set exclusively at the top of the piano, provides a counterpart to the first piece.

Yet, as might be expected from Finnissy, these methods of sustaining overall momentum are by no means the main raison d'être of the work, as he works on a series of other levels. There are a number of homages to the keyboard styles of Romantic and late-Romantic pianist-composers. The Barcarolle from *Ernani* makes use of a left hand part reminiscent of Godowsky's studies for the left hand alone (Example 2.36).

Example 2.35 *Verdi Transcriptions No. 6*, p. 31
Reproduced by permission of United Music Publishers Limited

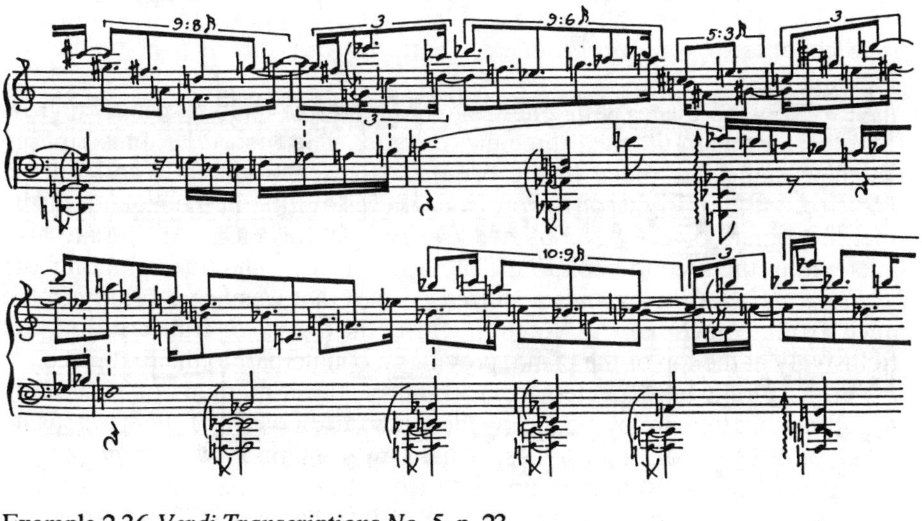

Example 2.36 *Verdi Transcriptions No. 5*, p. 23
Reproduced by permission of United Music Publishers Limited

The Duet from *Alzira* (about the rivalry between a Peruvian Indian chieftain and the Spanish governor), on the other hand, uses as its basic matrix the first piece from Busoni's *Indianisches Tagebuch*:

Example 2.37a Verdi melody *'Il pianto... l'angoscia... di lena mi priva'*

Example 2.37b Busoni *Indianisches Tagebuch* No. 1

Example 2.37c *Verdi Transcriptions No. 8*
Reproduced by permission of United Music Publishers Limited

Distant echoes of Liszt, Schumann, Alkan and others can also be heard from time to time. The method by which Liszt expands a seemingly unimportant ornamental figure in the *Reminiscences de Don Juan*, has a parallel in Finnissy's transcription of *Un Giorno di Regno*, where a dotted rhythm from the original duet keeps threatening to tear the piece apart:

Example 2.38a Verdi *'Bella speranza in vero'*

Example 2.38b Liszt *Reminiscences de Don Juan* (extracts)

Example 2.38c *Verdi Transcriptions No. 2* (extracts)
Reproduced by permission of United Music Publishers Limited

On another, perhaps the most important, level, the whole work stands as Finnissy's first 'Art of Transcription' (a further one was to follow in the *Obrecht Motetten*) and a 'Homage to Busoni', from whose essay the original concept for the work stemmed. The extent of modification of the sources changes in degree between different pieces. In the Romanza from *Aida* and the Duet from *Attila*, the original melodies are clearly recognisable, even though they are presented in a new context:

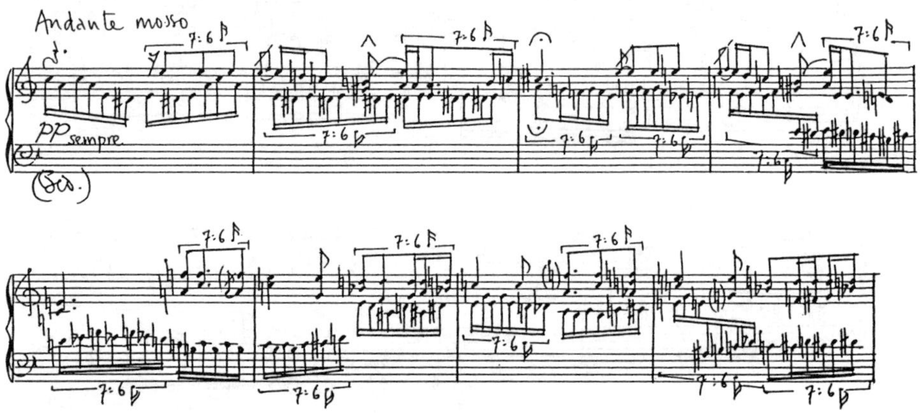

Example 2.39 *Verdi Transcriptions No. 13*, p. 84
Reproduced by permission of United Music Publishers Limited

In the *I Due Foscari* and *Macbeth* pieces, Finnissy is more concerned to re-create his own reactions to the atmosphere and impact of the respective moments in the operas, the materials having been transformed beyond recognition. Other movements inhabit various positions between these two extremes, sometimes submerging the originals within a quite different sort of texture, as in the *Ernani* transcription. In others, such as the *I Lombardi* or *Don Carlo* pieces, Finnissy uses the original as the starting point for his own creative imagination. Finnissy's transcription from *La Traviata* acknowledges the melodic unity of the work, and relates to the whole opera, rather than to any one particular moment, re-working the fundamental melody into an exuberant dance owing perhaps a little to Eastern European folk music (Example 2.40).

Where the *Verdi Transcriptions* are extrovert and highly projected, Finnissy's other large transcription cycle, the *Gershwin Arrangements* (1975-88) and *More Gershwin* (1989-90) present a much more intimate and melancholy sound-world, some of the most personal music Finnissy has ever written. Finnissy had heard Gershwin's songs on his parents' radio as he grew up, so they were for him fused with many memories of childhood. The pieces are also informed by an awareness of the appalling poverty and deprivation in the 1930s, the period from which most of the songs in the first book originate. The songs may have served to divert people's attention from their terrible circumstances, but they also spoke a little of these conditions in the lyrics (although not so explicitly that Gershwin could be branded a dangerous subversive). When writing his arrangement of *Shall we dance?*, Finnissy had in mind the degrading dance contests that many entered in the vain hope of winning a sum that would help them out of their hardship, later immortalised in Sidney Pollack's film *They Shoot Horses, Don't They?* The piece was intended to suggest couples dancing directly on top of a crevice in the earth, which threatens to open up and swallow them (Example 2.41).

Example 2.40 *Verdi Transcriptions Fragment (b)*, p. 80
Reproduced by permission of United Music Publishers Limited

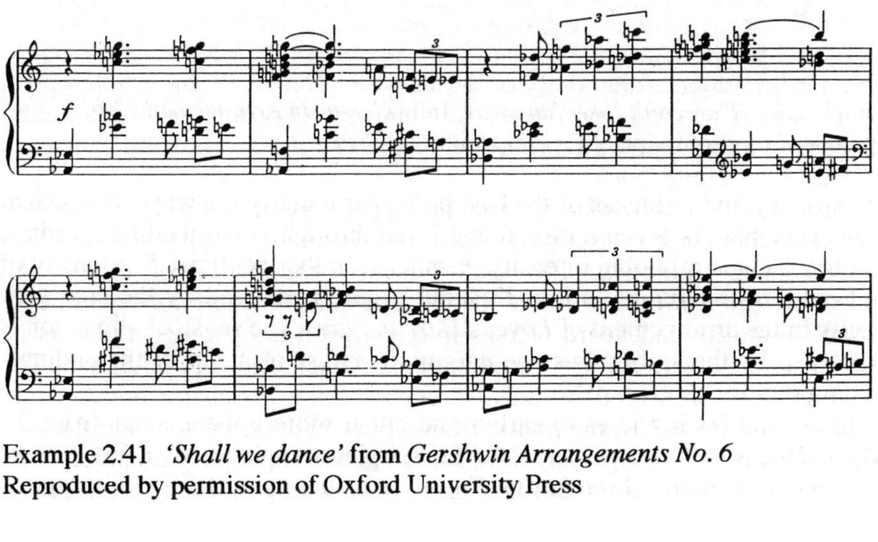

Example 2.41 *'Shall we dance'* from *Gershwin Arrangements No. 6*
Reproduced by permission of Oxford University Press

At the same time as Gershwin was writing his immensely successful music, the Second Viennese School were pioneering atonality and dodecaphony on the other side of the Atlantic. The arrangements attempt to synthesise these musical worlds, which Berg's student Theodor Adorno, amongst others, saw as fundamentally opposed. Gershwin's home-spun brand of chromaticism is pushed to its limits, a narrow melodic tessitura being echoed intervallically in *They can't take that away from me* to produce a form of quasi-expressionism (Example 2.42), providing a transformational parallel to Schoenberg's advancement of Wagner's harmonic experimentalism.

Example 2.42 '*They can't take that away*' from *Gershwin Arrangements No. 5*
Reproduced by permission of Oxford University Press

The intricacy and tightness of the first book, particularly the ways in which at times every note is given a directional force through voice-leading, produce an at times claustrophobic intensity, harsher than the 'poeticised' intensity of the *Verdi Transcriptions*, although some respite is offered by the emergent tonality in the arrangement of *Love is Here to Stay*. The sense of alienation is heightened by the ambiguous and enigmatic nature of many of the endings, resisting rhetorical 'closure'.

The second book relates to earlier and rather more upbeat songs from the early 1920s, with the tautness of the earlier pieces replaced by a freer, more improvisatory feel. *Limehouse Nights* parodies a certain stereotypical portrayal of Chinese music (Limehouse was, at the time the song was written, home to the major Chinese community in London), *I'd rather Charleston* is transformed into a wild stomp, and *Swanee* is given a magical coda:

Example 2.43 *'Swane'* from *More Gershwin No. 6*, last page
Reproduced by permission of Oxford University Press

However, after the bleakness of *Isn't it Wonderful* (note the rhetorical nature of the question), Finnissy ends the cycle with one of his most crushingly angry and defiant statements, *Nashville Nightingale*, written when the dedicatee, Andrew-Worton Steward, was dying from AIDS. The woozy blues of the opening leads to the expropriation of a single line, often an omen of trouble ahead in Finnissy's music (when one dares to assert their individuality, they will soon be crushed by the wrathful masses?), leading to a brazen hammering out of the melody in a ravaging, dissonant environment (Example 2.44).

A similarly 'in your face' approach is also present in Finnissy's subsequent arrangement of Jerome Kern's *Can't Help Lovin' Dat Man* (1990), an ironic comment on the title. Several other more recent pieces attempt either a form of 'meta-transcription' or a synthesis of highly different styles. *Cibavit eos* (1991), written as one of several pieces for the bicentenary of the death of Mozart (a composer who Finnissy does *not* admire) is based on an early choral piece in which Mozart derives his own contrapuntal writing from lines of plainchant which appear alongside. Finnissy takes this process a step further by deriving his own monodic line from the counterpoint (Example 2.45).

Example 2.44 '*Nashville Nightingale*' from *More Gershwin* No. 8, last page
Reproduced by permission of Oxford University Press

Example 2.45 *Cibavit Eos*, p. 1
Reproduced by permission of Oxford University Press

There are several other examples of transcriptions which do not necessarily reflect any particular fondness for the source. Finnissy chose to compose the highly ornate *Strauss-Waltzer* (1967/89) more as a result of his interest in Tausig and Godowsky's own Strauss arrangements than because of any love for Strauss's music.

The use of material from other composers allowed Finnissy to create music that was both accessible yet fresh. In the hands of a lesser composer, such ventures could all too easily result in soggy pastiche or mere eclecticism. However, Finnissy also made use of music from far beyond the boundaries of Western 'art music'.

Folk Music

Finnissy was interested in the folk musics of Eastern Europe from childhood, in part through knowing Polish and Hungarian friends of the family. Later on he was asked to transcribe some records for a Yugoslavian ballet teacher and was immediately struck by the electrifying nature of what he heard. A short piano piece *Svatovac* (1973-74), based on a Macedonian folk melody and a little influenced by Bartók, dates from this period.

When he began to investigate the music of his native land, Finnissy realised that the consciousness of his position as an 'outsider' made that which he discovered no less 'foreign' than the music of Azerbaijan, or Aboriginal Australia. As well as English folk song, he was drawn to Scottish bagpiping, *piobaireachd*, and in particular its types of ornamentational figuration. The ways in which grace notes are used on monophonic instruments, or those lacking dynamic possibilities, provided an ideal tool for retaining a sense of vertical harmony in either monodic or dense polyphonic writing. Always wary of too-obvious linear development, Finnissy replaced the incremental nature of *piobaireachd* with a more circular, or multidirectional, approach. The group of six pieces entitled *Reels* (1980-81) exemplify this:

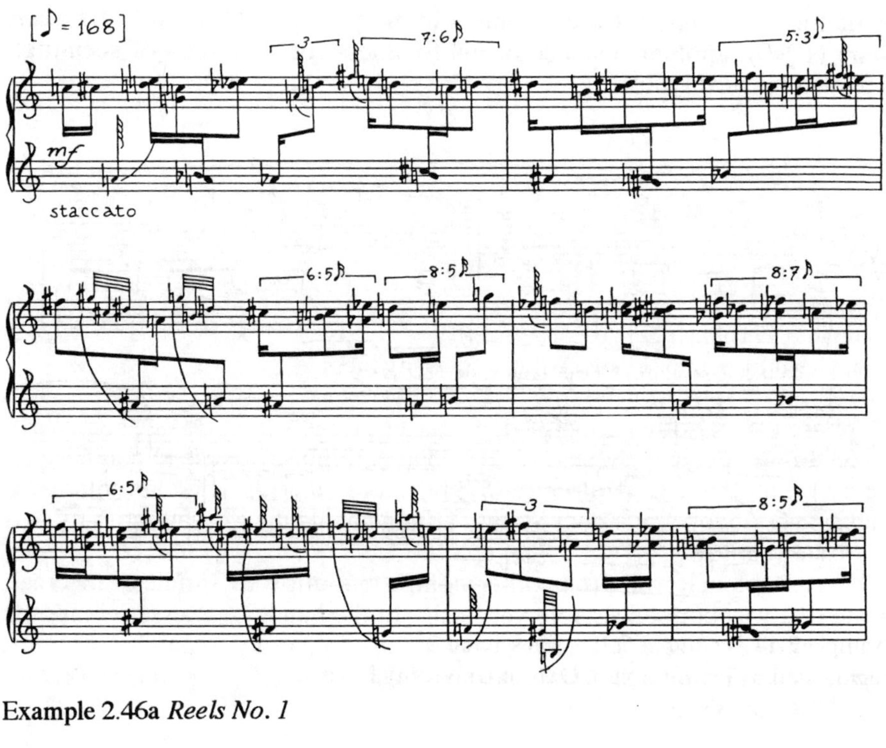

Example 2.46a *Reels No. 1*

Example 2.46b *Reels No 4*
Reproduced by permission of United Music Publishers Limited

It should be clear that, were the grace notes removed, the shifting sense of key would be considerably less audible, and could easily blur into a rather grey unfocusedness.

Piobaireachd remained of great importance to Finnissy; he used its figurations in a quite different context in his setting of Machaut's *De toutes flours* (1990), another instance of his fondness for syntheses of seemingly unrelated musical types:

Example 2.47 *De toutes flours*, lines 1 and 2
Reproduced by permission of Oxford University Press

From the beginning of the 1980s, starting with ***Duru-Duru*** for voice and instruments, Finnissy wrote a long series of pieces based on folk musics from Sardinia, Rumania, Kurdistan, Azerbaijan, Aboriginal Australia and elsewhere. There are obvious pitfalls for a composer from the 'civilised' West when dealing with the music of more 'primitive' cultures. Fetishisation and idealisation serve only to patronise in the manner of the nineteenth-century Orientalists, whereas cheap eclecticism, given a false justification by appropriation of the term 'post-modernism', shows nothing more than an artist's dearth of original ideas. A tendency in politically correct Britain has been to take non-Western musical materials, divest them of all their individual features, then re-construe them within a form of mock-romanticism, presenting the finished products as a shining example of 'Ethno-music'. A white composer who does this will be praised for their 'multiculturalism', or a non-white one for the 'accessibility' of their music; in reality they are committing a form of Uncle-Tommery.

Finnissy was acutely aware of all these dangers, and strove hard to avoid them. His approach was not of pastiche, quotation, or even representation (another thorny area for such a semantically ambiguous medium as music, which semiotics-inspired composers such as Sciarrino have tried hard to address). Rather, Finnissy's folk-inspired works are in essence an attempt to capture in sound his emotional and intellectual reactions upon encountering different cultures, as well as considerations of associated historical and political factors and his attempts to imagine the situation were he himself living under very different circumstances. The later folkloristic works continue the quest to synthesise seemingly irreconcilable cultural differences.

The ways in which the musical materials are treated are not significantly different from those used for the transcriptions, though, as I mentioned earlier, it should not be assumed that Finnissy has some super-algorithm which, when fed any source, will instantly produce a composition. On the contrary, qualities and reflections concerning the sources affect the resultant pieces at all levels, each work a quite particular response to that which is encountered.

It would be disingenuous to deny the existence of similarities as well as differences between the pieces, however. Beyond the obvious fact that each comes from the same composer, all the folk musics are the products of human beings who by definition share some common attributes. The speaker and ensemble work, *Various Nations*, was specifically configured to demonstrate this fact, but it also becomes apparent when different works are compared.

One of the pieces from the first period of Finnissy's folk-inspired work is *Terekkeme* (1981), for piano or harpsichord, whose inspiration comes from the music and culture of Azerbaijan (Example 2.48).

Throughout the piece single lines are alternated with exact doublings at different intervals. Azerbaijanian music is more alluded to than actually quoted, but a number of characteristics can be discerned. The ornamentation is extensive and the melodic lines contrast fluidity with repetition. They attempt to imitate the sounds of the 'zurna' (a type of shawm or oboe), the 'saz' and 'tar' (types of lute), and also demonstrate a greater tonal orientation than in other works such as the strident *Hikkai* (1983). The situation of the Azerbaijanis, living in an area where the tension between Christianity and Islam is at a peak, is another possible conceptual determinant. The extent and means by which any of the musical decisions relate either directly to the sources or the particular degree of compositional mediation will be discussed in more detail when considering *Folklore*, but what should be emphasised is the way in which each of Finnissy's sources generates a rich and distinct palette of colours, possibly more so than when he works in an 'abstract' vein.

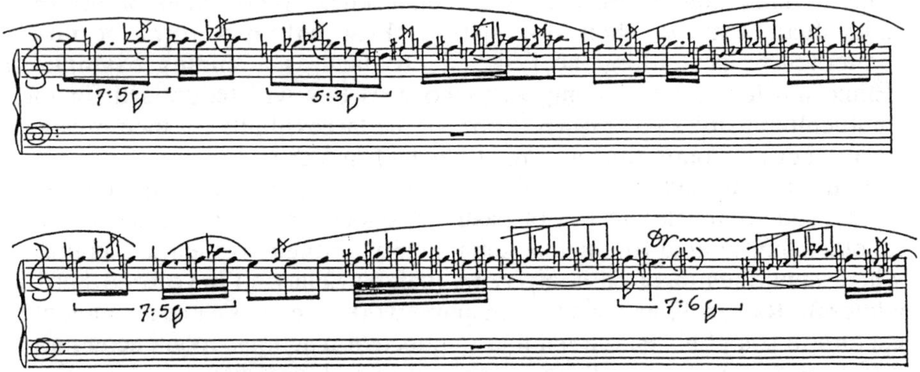

Example 2.48a *Terekkeme*

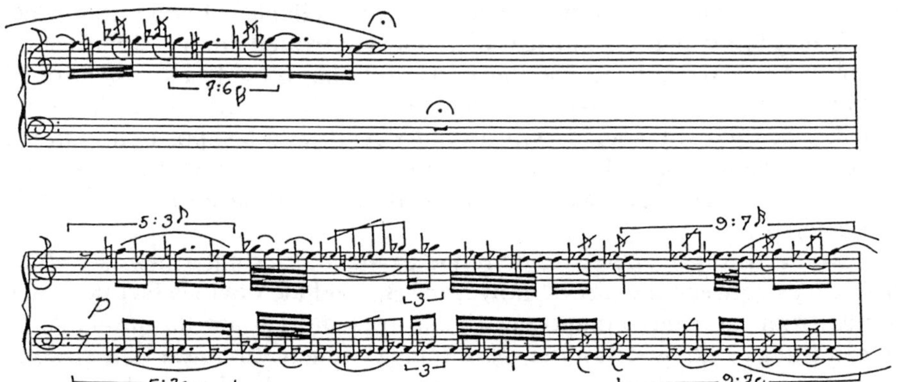

Example 2.48b *Terekkeme*
Reproduced by permission of Oxford University Press

Terekkeme was not in fact derived from any particular instance of Azerbaijani folk music, though some of the other works are. *Taja* (1986) is the last in a cycle of pieces based on a Sardinian melody, together with *Duru-Duru* for voice and small ensemble, *Anninnia* for voice and piano and *Andimironnai* for cello. All of these pieces sound significantly different, yet there are some common underlying factors. The motivation for writing several pieces after this source was analogous to that of a painter who wishes to capture a phenomenon from multiple perspectives. Apprehension of the four pieces' differences can provoke a search for their similarities, and vice versa. What remains an interesting question is the degree to which similarities are a result of either the source materials, the types of treatment they undergo, or simply the fact that they have all been mediated through the mind of the same composer.

Later works, such as *Lylyly li* (1988-89), go a step further in combining folkloristic considerations with other conceptions. The work was inspired by the permanent exhibition of work by Joseph Beuys in the Hessisches Landesmuseum, Darmstadt, which Finnissy described as 'a series of mementos of lost worlds'. He derived much of the material from Rumanian folk-song, but in a highly distorted, out-of-focus, or fragmented manner. This could well be a reflection on another dilemma for an urban composer: is one celebrating qualities of life which advanced capitalist society has lost, or is one perpetuating a form of agrarian myth, a nostalgic view of pre-industrial civilisation, which serves only to keep those in the under-developed world 'in their place'?

The work, entirely *pianissimo*, consists of a journey, through several modes of expression and their combinations:

(A) Melodic line, highly ornamented, with contrasts between sustained pitches and relatively quick activity
(B) Continuous series of trills
(C) Quasi-microtonal lines of dense chords

One might consider the work as being in nine sections, separated by silences in which a fifth in the bass is silently depressed, then the pedal changed, so that the resonance is filtered.

1. Long exposition of (A) (Example 2.49), leading to brief occurrence of (B) then (C), both in two parts.
2. Like 1, but much shorter (A), and slightly longer (C).
3. Again similar, but longer (B) and (C), with top part changing from (B) to (C) considerably before lower part does likewise.
4. Opens with (C), then return to (A). Short (B) in two parts, then much longer exposition of (C), quite blurred. Short return to (A) again.
5. From (A) straight to (C), but here in three parts. Each line less dense and clearer than previously, including monodic fragments.
6. Now (C) in four parts, more blurred. Extraction from this texture of ascending, slowing melody. Music comes almost to a complete halt. (No change of resonance.)
7. Return to four part (C). Almost immediate reduction to three parts; thinning out of individual lines. Brief return to (A).
8. (C) in three parts. Extraction of short fragment of (A), then phrase of two-part (C).
9. Three short fragments of highly blurred, close, two-part (C), separated by changes of resonance.

Example 2.49 *Lylyly Li*, p. 42
Reproduced by permission of Oxford University Press

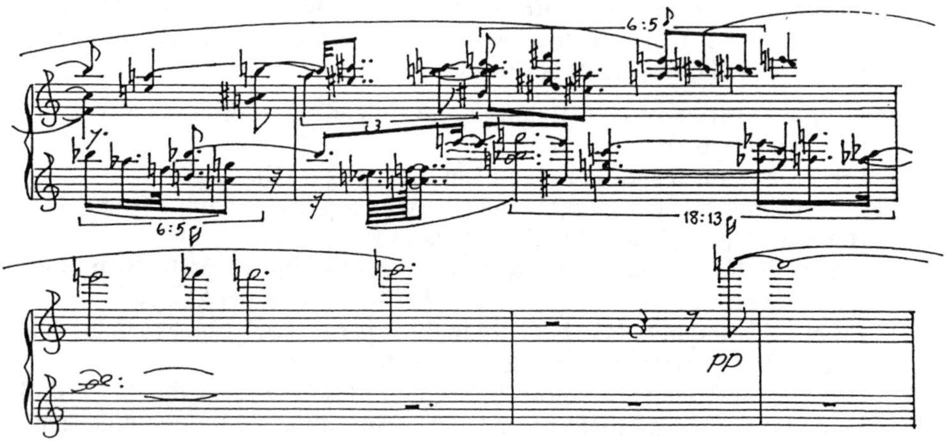

Example 2.50 *Lylyly Li*, p. 46
Reproduced by permission of Oxford University Press

The most obvious line of development is thus a gradual reduction in clarity of line, although, as should be clear from above, this path is not straightforwardly linear. The buzzing of the trills suggests imminent activity and direction, but actually leads to the more blurred combinations of chords.

Lylyly li is a sophisticated and ambiguous work which makes original use of both harmony and density.

Recent Work

The 1990s have been a productive time for Finnissy and the piano, with a more sustained flow of piano pieces than at any time hitherto. Many of the earlier directions, in particular transcriptions, have become integrated into the underlying approach. Pieces have appeared based on the work of composers as different as Machaut, Mozart, Rossini, Mahler and Sibelius. In a response to the hackneyed grouping of Finnissy and others under the label 'New Complexity', and to an issue of *Perspectives of New Music* dedicated to this topic, Finnissy wrote a piece called *New Perspectives on Old Complexity* (1990/92), which moves historically through transcriptions of Dunstable, Bach and Debussy, exemplifying a particular subtext of musical history, which is, as ever, seen through the composer's very personal vision.

Several works have been written as Valentine cards to Finnissy's partner, based on suggested material such as *My love is like a red red rose* (1990) after the Robert Burns poem, or *What the meadow flowers tell me* (1993), a 'cut-up' of fragments from the corresponding movement of Mahler's Third Symphony. These pieces tend to move from one point to another, rather than having a definite beginning and end; an opening up of a camera lens on a continuous flow of activity, rather than on a reified object, and relating once again to the concerns of *Song 9*.

Though most earlier pieces carry a dedication, the need to make 'tribute' pieces which will relate precisely to the interests and enthusiasms of the dedicatees as well as to perceptions of their characters, has also become a central concern. The sad events of composers' and friends' deaths have resulted in numerous pieces in tribute, reflections both on memories and the manner in which these peoples' voices live on beyond their physical passing. *A solis ortus cardine* (1992), written 'to celebrate the life and work of Olivier Messiaen' takes a work of plainsong and transforms it a little in the manner of some of Messiaen's *Quatres Études de Rhythme*, especially the assignation of specific dynamics and durations to individual pitches in *Mode de valeurs et d'intensités* (see Example 2.51a and 2.51b).

Following the tragically early death of the pianist Yvar Mikhashoff, with whom Finnissy performed in the premiere of Cage's *Europera 3*, he wrote a series of five *Yvaroperas*, which mediate between different modes of operatic referentiality, including Cage's own, and also attempt to capture aspects of Mikhashoff's particular style of playing. The second and fourth of these are based respectively on 'The Sun, whose rays...' (Example 2.52a) from Gilbert and Sullivan's *The Mikado*, and 'Je crois entendre encore' from Bizet's *Les Pêcheurs de Perles* (Example 2.52b). The original melodies continue from beginning to end of the pieces, but are at various points joined by more chromatic material, which varies in the extent to which it blends with the main line.

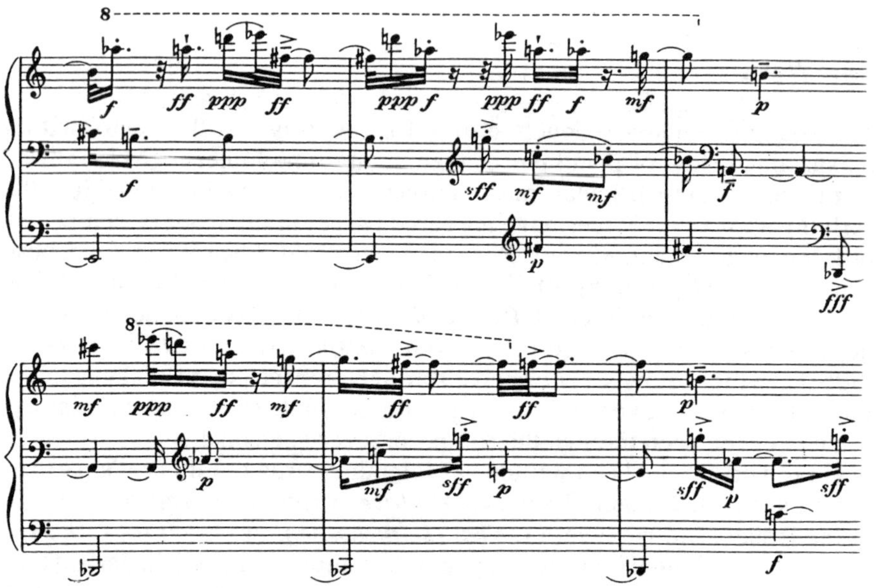

Example 2.51a Olivier Messiaen *Mode de valeurs et intensités*
Reproduced by permission of Editions Durand S.A. (Paris) and United Music Publishers Limited

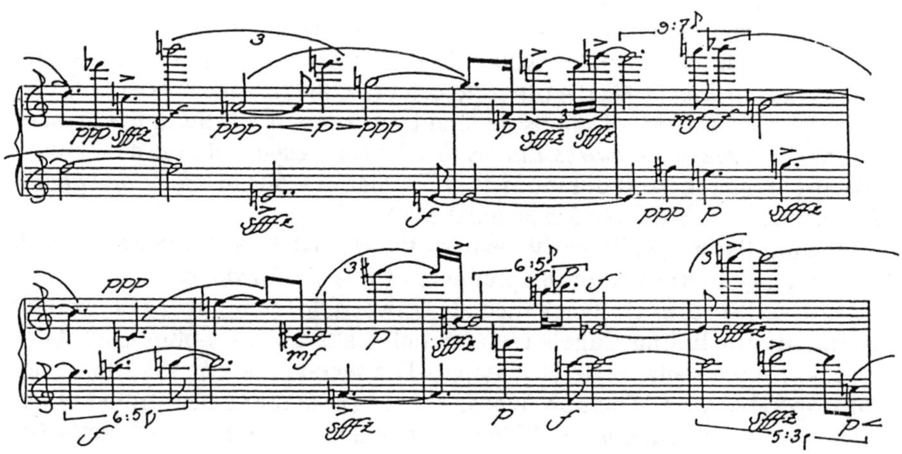

Example 2.51b *A solis ortus cardine*
Reproduced by permission of Oxford University Press

Example 2.52a (a) *Yvaropera 2*

Example 2.52b *Yvaropera 4*
Reproduced by permission of Oxford University Press

The two pieces present different perspectives on a communion with voices from the past. In the second piece, the more chromatic material (which essentially takes the form of a melody with accompaniment) is *ppp* whereas the main line is *pppp*. As both are in the same treble register, the main line seems to appear in gaps within the texture. In the fourth piece, on the other hand, the main line has a more prominent position as it is in the bass, so there is much less overlap in register with the other material. It therefore assumes a more 'solid', foregrounded position. Another memory is that of Finnissy's own earlier operatic transcriptions, in particular the sextet from *Ernani* in the *Verdi Transcriptions*.

The first and third *Yvaroperas* are less clearly directional, making use of a myriad of disfigured fragments from the nineteenth-century operatic repertoire and of their transcriptions by pianist-composers (in the first piece, for example, pairs of ascending scales on alternate beats, with arpeggiated melody, recall Liszt's transcription of Wagner's *Tannhauser Overture*). The Cageian nature of these works is tempered by a quite clear degree of emotional intentionality, broadly melancholy in the first piece, angry in the third. By the fifth piece (written over a year later than the other four), memories have become hazy, one is left with a struggle to recall something ever more distant, impossible to discern behind the fog of time.

As Finnissy gained a greater reputation, he felt a corresponding need to speak out on issues about which he felt deeply, using both words and music. The choice of folk-song to set in his tribute to Cornelius Cardew, *There never were such hard times before* (1991) belies some sympathy with Cardew's analysis of the injustices of modern capitalist society, whereas *Stanley Stokes, East Street 1836* (1989/91) relates to an event in Brighton when a homosexual took his own life in fear of an angry mob who were pursuing him.

However, the most bleak and nihilistic statement that Finnissy has ever delivered in a piano work is contained in the twenty-minute long *Nine Romantics* (1992). The inspiration was an account of the life of the Victorian artist Simeon Solomon, who enjoyed critical and commercial success until he was found in the act of 'cottaging'. Public outrage was fuelled by the homophobia and anti-Semitism endemic in the period, but also by the undermining of the urban bourgeoisie's hopelessly naïve idea of the 'artist' as a type of ultra-refined being to whom natural human desires do not apply. Once the image was shattered, Solomon lived the rest of his life in destitution, reduced to being a pavement artist. Such a glaring example of the wrongs of putting an artist on a pedestal held a particular resonance for Finnissy.

He delineates three types of material: (A) flamboyant, operatic and tempestuous, with voices struggling to break out of a dense texture, (B), a monophonic melody in a middle register, relatively animated, based on Hebrew liturgical chant, as a tribute to Solomon, (C) very slow, quiet but intense chromatic polyphony derived from Wagner's *Tristan und Isolde*, moving slowly upwards in register:

Example 2.53a *Nine Romantics*, material type (A)

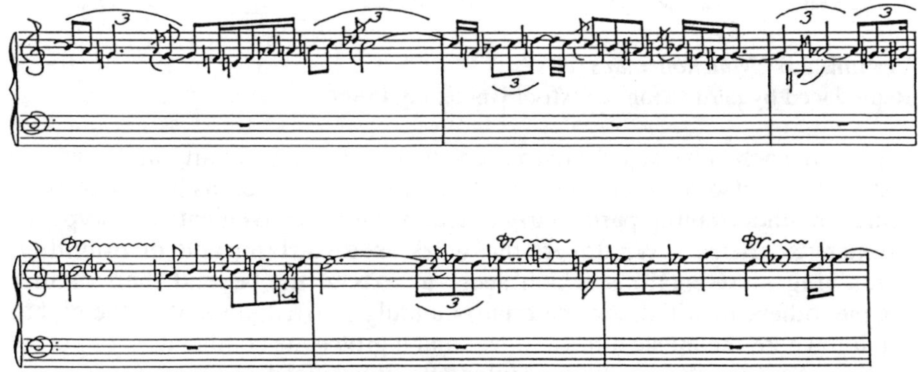

Example 2.53b *Nine Romantics*, material type (B)

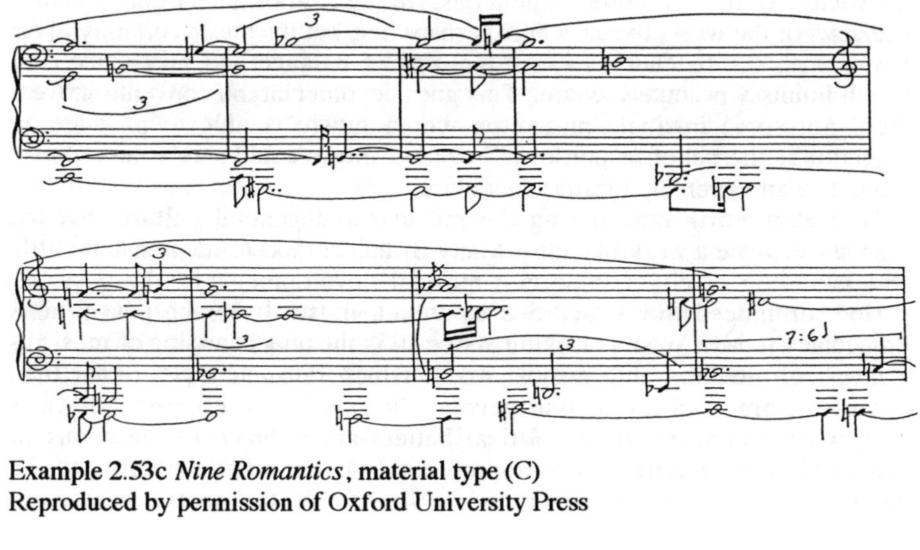

Example 2.53c *Nine Romantics*, material type (C)
Reproduced by permission of Oxford University Press

The first three of the nine sections of the work present each of these material types, after which each is given in the 'guise' of the others (B as A, C as B, B as C, etc.), by combining pitch material from one with another's tempo, density, or other characteristics:

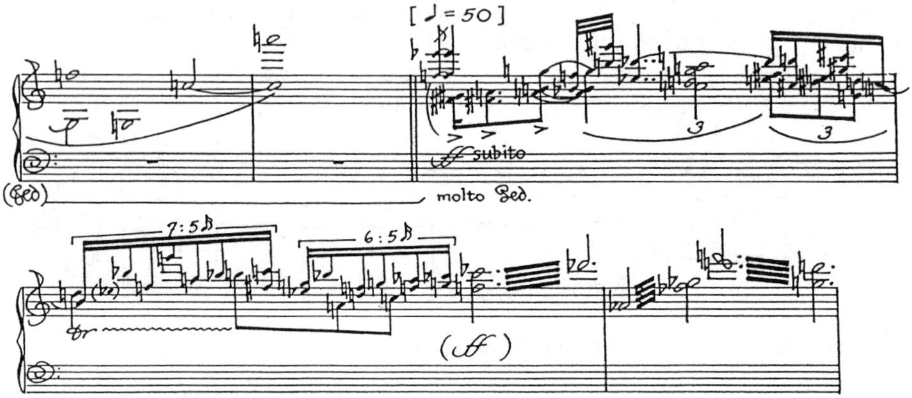

Example 2.54 *Nine Romantics*, p. 17
Reproduced by permission of Oxford University Press

It is as if each 'character' is stripped of its essential identity and made to parade in a false manner. The work could also be seen as an act of self-criticism, undermining particularly character (A), a convenient stereotype for Finnissy's critics. Whatever, the work is disturbing and disorienting, containing slow sections which seem to extend far beyond their natural course, others in which the material is unduly hurried, a point in the eighth section where the music almost 'dies', and a grotesque combination of voices in the last section that seems fundamentally unbalanced.

One might well ask if such a conclusion could be reached without prior knowledge of the composer's intentions. In the case of the particular *modus operandi* of the work, the answer is perhaps not, but the music certainly plays havoc with the listener's natural feelings of balance and proportions, of which Finnissy is acutely aware. This goes beyond cultural convention: were there not some intrinsic means by which music is able to produce an objectifiable kernel of responses in listeners, music could surely never attain more than an extremely localised audience.

It is also worth considering the musical and general culture that led Finnissy to write a work like this. Many British composers demonstrate little understanding of either important musical developments of the post-war period, or indeed those qualities by which music from the past retains immediacy today. What is lacking above all is the understanding of music as a *temporal* medium, and musical works which fetishise style, rather than processes, are unlikely to rise beyond the level of wallpaper. Style is everywhere; people, art or political beliefs are reduced to the status of disposable commodities, to be appropriated or discarded according to the dictates of fashion, reflecting the influence of the worst aspects of

Americanism. Amongst the corresponding inanities of some 'soundbite'-based British musical criticism, one encounters pairings of Finnissy with Ferneyhough, as both of their music happens to contain a greater number of notes than some others, or Lachenmann with Sciarrino, appreciation of either's music rarely progressing beyond the realisation that both use instruments in unconventional manners.

Objectification of musical material or even of musical processes (via such means as dialectic, aura or hyperbole), which is so vital to such different composers as Nicolaus A. Huber, Ivo Malec, Chris Newman, Mathias Spahlinger or Christian Wolff, or for that matter to Beethoven as well, threatens such a shallow point of view, and thus is treated with callous contempt. As I hope to have made clear at various points in this essay, operations upon material and techniques for presenting material in unusual perspectives is of much greater importance to Finnissy than material per se, and so he reacts angrily when patronised by labels such as 'New Complexity', an all too easy categorisation according to superficialities. By the radical objectification procedures he uses in *Nine Romantics*, Finnissy pulls the carpet out from underneath the feet of his critics and offers a form of social critique more devastating than would be possible through a written polemic. *Nine Romantics* may not say what a lot of people would like to hear, but it is a potent statement about our times.

Folklore

The most important of Finnissy's recent piano works is his epic four-part cycle *Folklore* (1993-4), possibly his most ambitious piano work to date and the summation of all his previous work using folk materials. The score is prefaced by the following note:

> *Folklore*. Gramsci's imperative to compile an inventory of the 'infinity of traces' that historical processes leave on 'the self'. Folklore - a distant memory, an assemblage, a critical elaboration, an opposition of conjunctions, an open-ended investigation, a palimpsest, a self-portrait.
>
> *Folklore*. Inherent attitudes. Pretension - the piano (a 'respectable' Victorian mantleshelf, spineless and domesticated) - Grieg (from childhood), another vision of Arcadia (cowherds, and peasants dancing); Grieg's influence on Percy Grainger (dismissed by some as a wayward amateur dishing up folk-tunes for the parlour); Grieg's harmonic innovations (impact on Debussy); John Cage (...Grieg was more interesting than the others...). What else do I remember?

> *Folklore*. England: insular and conservative, institutionalized, de-spiritualized, tawdry and corrupt. Transforming 'angry young men' into embittered, cynical 'couch-potatoes'. Rendering artists impotent through mockery and stereotyping (what is there to be afraid of?). Politics: Capitalism. A *free* country in which censorship is universally rife. Hypocrisy. Bigotry. The cheap laugh. Cardew, Orton, Jarman. 'Deep (Tippett) River'. Heads fall and are swept under the carpet. Nothing behind the eyes. Imperialism is served.
>
> *Folklore*. Travel broadens the mind. (Food broadens the stomach). White men belittle Aboriginals (a member of the music-faculty at Melbourne Uni. asked why I was interested in 'primitive trash'. Do I declare an interest in 'symbols of oppression'?) Power. The Archaeology of Knowledge. Lévi-Strauss, Foucault. Diversity - or the world-culture (e.g. modernism)? Folklore. Untidy - insufficiently selective. Art/Editing/Experience (skill, in itself, potentially obscures icon/essence). A simulacrum. Evocation becomes Provocation.

The title of *Folklore* thus refers to particular instances of folk-culture, to the intrinsic nature of folklore and our perception of it, and to the composer's own personal 'folklore', the many determinants within his musical personality.

The range of reference of *Folklore* is immense, yet it amounts to much more than a mere encyclopaedia. The description which follows shows how the various musical passages relate to their sources, and how the *montage* of different materials takes place. To call up two figures in justification, I would quote Freud's conviction that the essence of a dream lies neither in the plethora of unconscious thoughts that inform the dream, nor in the dream itself, but rather in the 'dream-work', the processes by which the brain converts its subconscious dream-material (modifying, censoring) into the actual dream; and Orson Welles's belief that the truth of a film lies in the editing.

Folklore 1, 'Lovingly and reverently dedicated to the memory of Edvard Grieg', was written for the North Sea Music Festival of Salford, Glasgow and Bergen, and has a distinctly Nordic flavour, making extensive use both of Norwegian folk melodies, as collected by L.M. Lindeman in *Aeldre og Nyere Norske Fjeldmelodier*, and Grieg's folk-arrangements in *Slätter Op. 72*. The ways in which some of the material in *Folklore 1* is derived from these sources is demonstrated in Example 2.55.

Much of the piece is concerned with modulation between different stages of referentiality, a spectrum between exact Lindeman and free Finnissy. The other Nordic determinant is an increasing use of *piobaireachd* ornamentation, which will become a central feature of *Folklore 2* and *3*.

Example 2.55 Lindeman, Grieg

A good deal of the material was created first in long stretches, then edited together to form the finished piece. Here is an outline of the events and their interplay in *Folklore 1*.

1. Bars 1-5. *Allegro con brio.* Introduction, freely from Grieg:

Example 2.56 *Folklore 1*, bars 1-8
Reproduced by permission of Oxford University Press

2. Bars 6-56. *Andante semplice.* Free, from Lindeman, with closer proximity in, for example, bars 14-15. Echoes, *pppp*, in the manner of 'The Alcotts' from Ives' *Concord Sonata*. Violin-like solo, bars 16-18. Contrapuntal insert, bars 28-37. Generally uncertain tonality.
3. Bars 57-63. *Allegretto misterioso*. Bridge passage to:
4. Bars 64-110. *Con brio, animato*. Three more Grieg-derived violin solos in A minor, intercut with counterpoints of two simultaneous Lindeman-derived lines. Insert in F minor. Lindeman and Grieg fragments, six each, presented alternately, always with two or more simultaneous lines from Lindeman. Keyboard configuration variously imitates violin, conventional piano, voice with piano. Insert forms bridge passage into next section.
5. Bars 111-33. *Andante*. Violin solo from Grieg, in C#. Bar 122, referred to as one of 'Later Episodes' in sketches, free Lindeman with accompaniment. Further Grieg.
6. Bars 134-67. *Allegro molto*. After insert of another 'Later Episode' (bars 134-9), free 'pipes and drone' in A. Two more 'Later Episodes' (bars 154-8, 159-64), hybrid of Lindeman and Grieg, then three more bars of 'pipes and drone'.

7. Bars 168-72. *Meno Allegro*. Transition to:
8. Bars 173-268. *Largo moderato, molto tranquillo, luminoso.* Derived from an abandoned tribute to Kaikhosru Shapurji Sorabji, highly ornamented Grieg/Lindeman, in the style of *piobaireachd* (Norwegian/Pibroch), and four inserts, as follows:

Bar 173	Sorabji 1.
Bars 174-5.	'Run-up' to Norwegian/Pibroch.
Bars 176-82	Norwegian/Pibroch 1, G flat (Example 2.57).
Bars 183-4	Insert 1, A flat (Example 2.57).
Bars 185-98	Norwegian/Pibroch 2, G flat (Example 2.57).
Bar 198	(Middle) Sorabji 2.
Bars 198-205	Norwegian/Pibroch 3, G flat.
Bars 206-11	Insert 2, towards A flat.
Bars 212-21	Norwegian/Pibroch 4, G flat.
Bar 221	(End) Insert 3. C with G flat and G minor.
Bars 222-31	Norwegian/Pibroch 5, G flat.
Bar 232	(Beginning) Sorabji 3.
Bars 233-52	Norwegian/Pibroch 6, G flat.
Bars 252-4	Insert 4, around A.
Bars 255-65	Norwegian/Pibroch 7, G flat.
Bar 266	(Beginning) Bridge back to Sorabji.
Bars 266-8	Sorabji 4. Hints of F.

Example 2.57 *Folklore 1*, bars 192-202, p. 14
Reproduced by permission of Oxford University Press

None of the Sorabji fragments presents a clear tonal centre, and within the generally static tonality of the Norwegian/Pibroch, there are several moments where one of the voices briefly changes key, or loses its sense of tonality. The effect of this section could be seen in two different ways, either as a form of phantasmagoria, the illusion being shattered when the music dissolves back into the Sorabji from whence it came, or as a means of giving the tonal music a greater presence, making it more 'real', by objectification. I am inclined towards the latter interpretation of this glorious moment in the work.

Folklore 2 & 3 make use of a wider range of sources. The most obvious of these is a further emphasis on *piobaireachd*. From an earlier and withdrawn piece, *Haen*, which now appears at the end of *Folklore 2* (bars 203-68, Example 2.58a), Finnissy derived four long monodic passages: Haen itself, 'Hinbare', 'Hodrodin', and 'Hintodre', each named after particular ornamental figurations (Example 2.58b).

Example 2.58a *Folklore 2* bars 203-11
Reproduced by permission of Oxford University Press

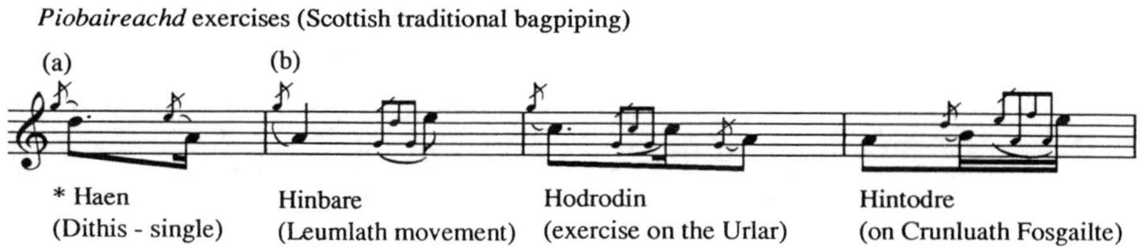

Example 2.58b

Hinbare, Hodrodin and Hintodre were derived quite simply by dividing Haen into 97 fragments, then randomly permutating and transposing them, with the particular ornament placed at the beginning. Hinbare is in the Aeolian mode on F, as is Hodrodin, and Hintodre (which does not appear until *Folklore 3*) in the Dorian mode on G. Such a scheme might seem arbitrary, but it produces both a type of circularity entirely in keeping with the repetitive nature of bagpipe playing, and a series of floating melodies that have no need of direction.

A number of Rumanian folksongs feature in the first half of *Folklore 2*. These come from an anthology 'Cîntecul de Leagăn' (Example 2.59b) and are transposed to various keys, sometimes changing from major to minor, with other alterations. All Rumanian material is referred to in the sketches as 'Rumanian Region':

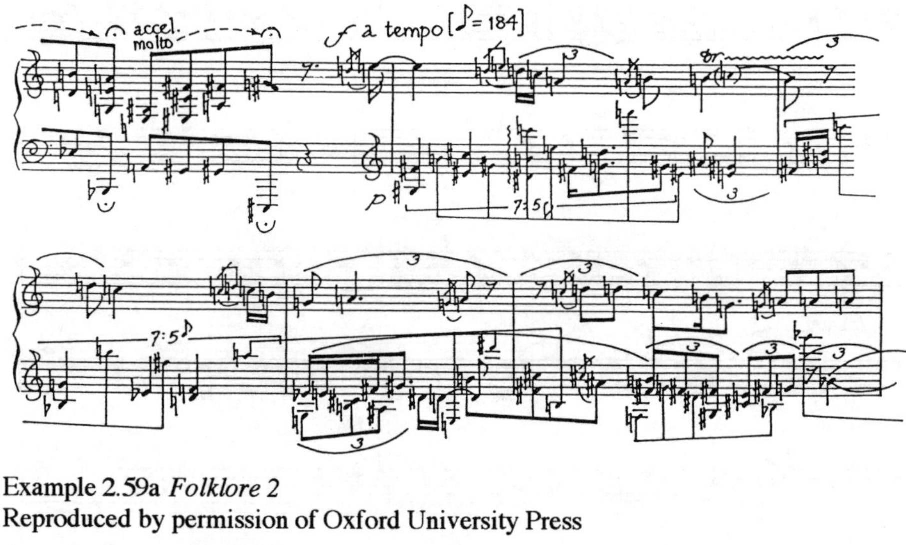

Example 2.59a *Folklore 2*
Reproduced by permission of Oxford University Press

The overlaid random grace notes which appear throughout the movement are in tribute to Cornelius Cardew, after his use of a similar technique in *A Book of Study for Two Pianists*. These reach their apotheosis in a setting of a Chinese folk-song 'The Little Shepherd', in the style of Cardew's own arrangements (Example 2.60).

Some of the folksongs from Cîntecul de Leagăn (note values halved)

Example 2.59b

(a) Ancient Chinese melody "The Little Shepherd", quoted in Oxford History of Ancient and Oriental Music p.116

(b) Example of Cardew's setting of Chinese folk song "Sailing the Seas depends upon the Helmsman"

(c) Cardew/Chinese "The Little Shepherd"

Example 2.60d *Folklore 2*, p. 38
Reproduced by permission of Oxford University Press

Possibly more significant is the dedication of the movement to Sir Michael Tippett, signified musically by the Negro spiritual 'Deep River', as used in Tippett's *A Child of our Time*. There are several meditations and improvisations around this melody, several of which appear before the melody is heard in a relatively simple form towards the end. The other sources are a setting of a Sussex folk-song 'Let Him Answer Yes or No', originally a violin and cello piece written for the 'Brighton Cabaret', two short bursts of activity as a homage to Christian Wolff, which bear a certain resemblance to his piano piece *Hay una Mujer Desparecida*, and a series of extracts from the original version of *Folklore 3*, which I will call Historical/Chronological. *Folklore 2* is organised as follows:

1. *Freely wavering tempo*. Bars 1-10. Hinbare 1, Aeolian on F.
2. Bars 11-42. Rumanian Region (RR) 1.

Faster, capriciously	RR1.1, with pibroch, Aeolian on A.
accel. molto, etc.	Homage to Christian Wolff 1.
a tempo	RR1.2, with Lindeman accompaniment, and Cardew grace note overlays.
poco meno	Homage to Christian Wolff 2.
a tempo	RR 1.3.
lento subito	Meditation on Deep River 1.
a tempo	RR 1.4.
lento subito	Meditation on Deep River 2.
a tempo	RR 1.5.

Example 2.61 *Folklore 2*. Reproduced by permission of Oxford University Press

3.	*Animato*. Bars 43-87.	Rumanian Region 2.
	Bars 43-8	RR 2.1. Lindeman in right hand, Rumanian melody in left, Mixolydian on A. More Cardew grace notes.
	Bars 49-55	RR 2.2. Solo.
	Bars 56-9	RR 2.3. With Lindeman again.
	Bars 60-63	RR 1.6. New melody, continuing RR 1.
	Bars 63-8	RR 1.7. Solo.
	Bars 68-78	RR 1.8. With Lindeman again.
	Bars 79-87	RR 2.4. Return to RR 2. Progressively with 2 Lindemans, 1 Lindeman, solo.
4.	Bars 88-102.	
	Bars 88-90	Historical/Chronological (Hist/Chron) 1.9 (Ex 2.62).
	Bar 91	Hodrodin 1, Aeolian on F (Example 2.62).
	Bars 92-5	Hist/Chron 1.10 (Example 2.62).
	Bar 96	Hodrodin 2 (Example 2.62).
	Bars 96-8	Hist/Chron 1.11 (Example 2.62).
	Bar 98	Hodrodin 3.
	Bars 99-100	Hist/Chron 1.12.
	Bars 101-2	Hodrodin 4.

Example 2.62 *Folklore 2*, bars 90-97
Reproduced by permission of Oxford University Press

5. Bars 103-166. From 2nd part of Historical/Chronological and Hodrodin

Allegro con brio.	Hist/Chron 2.1.
Un poco più ritenuto	Hodrodin 5.
Grave ed appassionato	Hist/Chron 2.2.
Commodo, con delicatezza- più animato	Hist/Chron 2.3. Oblique stylistic references to Roslavets/Scriabin, Brahms, Bussotti
Bars 139-66	Hodrodin 6. Much more extended.

6. Bars 167-268. English Region

Bars 167-70	'Let Him Answer Yes or No', with drones and ornamented accompaniment.
Molto staccato	Cardew/Chinese 'The Little Shepherd'.
Adagio molto espressivo	'Deep River' with Ivesian echoes, followed by blues-like variation, reducing from four voices down to one (from Deep River at end of *Folklore 4*).
Freely wavering tempo	Long exposition of Haen. Initially Dorian on D, progressing through other modes.

So the relatively static music of the bagpipes serve to frame a journey through Rumania and England, the latter of which (through the Cardew motif) impinges upon the consciousness of the former. Conflicting forces appear on the sides of this 'path': shafts of light, culminating in the setting of 'Deep River', then fading away, and finally ominous premonitions of the violence which is to come to the fore in *Folklore 3*. The original version of this part (Historical/Chronological) from which much of the first half of the final version comes, was originally written for a lecture-recital in Taiwan, called 'Brave New Serial World', and also included pieces by Schoenberg, Busoni, Feldman and others. This is the most direct reference to Finnissy's personal 'folklore', describing phases of his development as a composer and a human being (Example 2.63).

The tempestuousness of the opening and beyond are a reflection of Finnissy's memories of student revolt when in Italy in the 1960s:

> This piece probably started when I heard someone glibly dismiss the 1960s as 'part of political folklore'. The 1960s were years of political activism and idealism. In May 1968 I was a student in Rome (sometimes under house arrest, trying to avoid the police in the frequent street riots - they'd spray blue-dye and pick you up later if they couldn't get you at the time - as a student one was always at risk). We talked endlessly and rather naïvely about 'radical social reforms'. 'Liberation' was the byword - friends of mine fought at the barricades in Paris, literally risking their lives for 'values' to believe in. Identifying with 'the oppressed', siding with the proletariat against capitalist exploitation, I began to investigate folk-music: the music of the people and the music of the oppressed. One dubious benefit of the Industrial Revolution was the growth of towns and cities. In the resultant urban sprawl people can lose their identity and contact with fundamental human values. Not surprising then that, during the Nineteenth Century, as this became first apparent, people began to define themselves with 'Nationalism'.

Example 2.63 *Folklore 3*
Reproduced by permission of Oxford University Press

From the eruptive opening gestures, Finnissy works in references to composers who, either as a result of integration or rejection, had a substantial effect on him. This material as a whole provides a chronological account of Finnissy's developing musical mind and, as he says in the note to the piece, the 'infinity of traces that historical processes leave on the self'. Allusions abound to compositional styles, in particular those of Brahms (the 'progressive' as described by Schoenberg, a view that was once shared (but later violently rejected) by Finnissy), Scriabin, Ives and Bussotti.

Within the opening section, Finnissy also inserts four brief fragments referring to the 'elements':

Example 2.64 a 'Water', after Debussy's *Reflets dans l'Eau.*

Example 2.64b 'Earth', after Mahler's *Das Lied von der Erde*;
'Air', an 'air' from Verdi's *Don Carlo*.

Example 2.64c 'Fire', from Scriabin's *Prometheus*. All from *Folklore*
Reproduced by permission of Oxford University Press

Other sections use a setting of a French folk-song 'Hier J'ai Recontré' from Picardie, which was originally a piece for solo violin or violin and piano, in which the piano plays embellishment above drones at the end of each of the violin's verses. This is overlaid by gradually reduced groups of random grace notes, a residue from the Cardew tribute of *Folklore 2*. A section of 'Hintodre' is played twice, identically, at two different points in the movement, a homage to Luis Buñuel's film *The Exterminating Angel*, at one point within which the characters re-enact an earlier scene.

Later sections of the movement refer to traditional Swedish fiddle playing, and are taken from 'Svenska låtar - Jämtland Härjedalen', configured so as to suggest comparison with the earlier mock-Norwegian music, providing another thread through the whole work:

Example 2.65 *Folklore 3*, bars 173-80, p. 66
Reproduced by permission of Oxford University Press

The final reference is to Serbian melodies, as collected in Stevan Mokranjac's 'Song Garlands'. *Folklore 3* runs thus:

1. Bars 1-99. Mostly from Historical/Chronological.

Molto Animato	Hist/Chron 1.1. Three violent gestures, then consolidation.
Marcato e Risoluto	Hist/Chron 1.2. Unstable, continual change of register.
Subito:poco meno mosso	Hist/Chron 1.3. Attempts for voice to come through. Stabilisation, increasing confidence. Submerged tonal elements.

liquido!	'Water' insert.
Bars 33-46	Hist/Chron 1.4.
grossolano!	'Earth' insert.
Bars 50-51	Hist/Chron 1.5.
Bar 52	Insert, anticipating marches in *Folklore 4*.
Bars 53-4	Hist/Chron 1.6.
Bar 54 (*subito*)	Homage to Christian Wolff 3.
Bars 55-8	Hist/Chron 1.7.
quasi arioso!	'Air' insert, F#.
Bars 68-80	Hist/Chron 1.8.
fuocoso!	'Fire' insert.
Bars 83-7	Bridge passage.
Un poco più largamente	Hist/Chron 2.4. Brahms.
Largo sostenuto	Hist/Chron 2.5. Ives.

2. 'European Region'. Bars 100-166. Mostly based on 'Hintodre' and 'Hier J'ai Recontré' (HJR), Inserts are like continuation of elements of Historical/Chronological.

Freely wavering tempo	Hintodre 1. Dorian on G.
quasi Violino	HJR 1. Alternating 'violin' and 'piano', with grace note overlays (though not cut at obvious points).
Freely wavering tempo	Hintodre 2.
quasi Violino	HJR 2.
Bars 107-14	Insert 1, Scriabin/Roslavetz. Brief reference to Rumanian melodies in left hand, bars 113-14.
Bars 114-15	HJR 3 (Example 2.66).
Bars 116-18	Insert 2. Bussotti - Finnissy.
Bar 119	HJR 4.
Bars 120-23	Hintodre 2 (again).
Bars 124-5	Insert 3. Debussy, Renaldo Hahn - *The Orient.*
Bars 126-31	Hintodre 3.
Bars 132-3	Insert 4. Brahms, after Second Piano Concerto.
Bars 133-6	Hintodre 4.
Moderato, Andante	Hist/Chron 2.6. Brahms.
Bars 149-51	Insert 4. 'Bird-music'.
Bars 152-6	Hist/Chron 2.7. Brahms - Scriabin.
Bars 157-9	Hintodre 5.
Bars 160-64	Hist/Chron 2.8 Scriabin - Ives.
Bars 165-6	Bridge to next section.

3. Bars 167-244. As pibroch fades away, other Nordic element returns.

Andante sostenuto	Swedish 1. Includes 'violin' solos.
Moderato con anima	Swedish 2.

Bars 190-96	Swedish 3 (more ornamented).
Bars 196-7	Rumanian melody.
Bars 197-227	Serbian 1.
Bars 227-31	Swedish 4. Solo (like Rumanian melody) then 'chorus'.
Bars 232-3	Hist/Chron 2.9.
Lento, in modo 'notturno'	Swedish 5.
Bar 239	Hist/Chron 2.10 (from third crotchet). Highly enigmatic yet visionary ending.

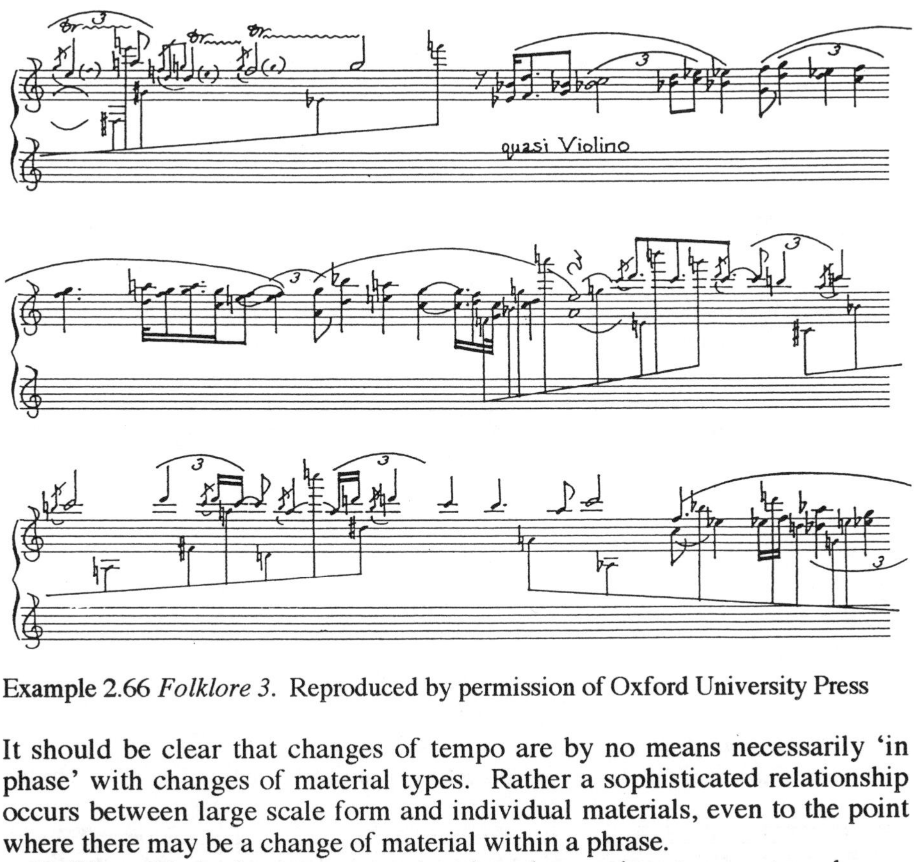

Example 2.66 *Folklore 3*. Reproduced by permission of Oxford University Press

It should be clear that changes of tempo are by no means necessarily 'in phase' with changes of material types. Rather a sophisticated relationship occurs between large scale form and individual materials, even to the point where there may be a change of material within a phrase.

Folklore 3 is both more aggressive than the previous two parts and more equivocal, progressing from rage to bewilderment via many side-routes, some humorous, others ironic. Most of the running threads have at this stage been brought to a conclusion. It is left for *Folklore 4* to attempt some sort of summation.

There is a greater preponderance of music here from the Far East and America, and most of the European elements have died away, though a few traces of *piobaireachd* remain. The sources include music from India: Finnissy selects random bars from 'Folksongs of South Gujarat' by Madhubai Patel, then modifies them to produce a melody in the bass:

Example 2.67 (Patel derivation)

Counterparts are provided by a flute-like melody, derived from the 'Anthology of Korean Traditional Music' (Korean Music Research Institute) and a denser chromatic material ('Chromatic'):

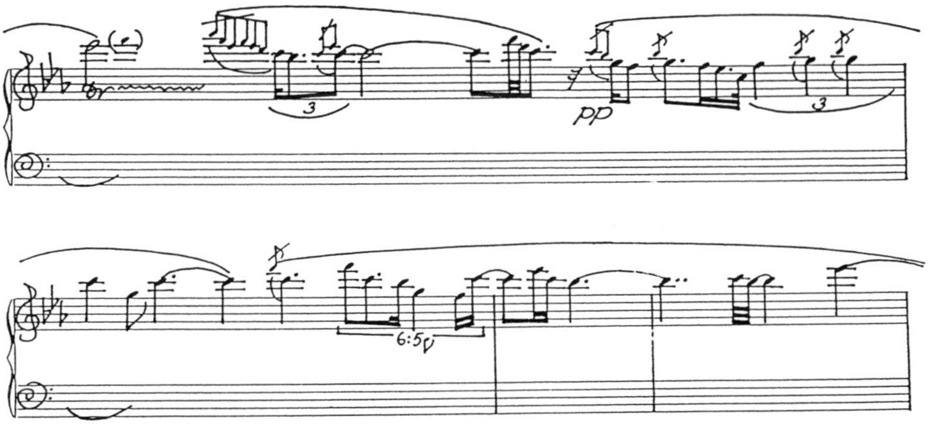

Example 2.68 *Folklore 4*, bars 14-19, p. 73
Reproduced by permission of Oxford University Press

The structure is as follows:

1. *Quite Fast, strong and affirmative.* Bars 1-47.

Bars 1-4	Indian 1. Dorian on C.
Bars 5-17	Korean 1. Aeolian on C.
Bar 18	Chromatic 1.
Bars 19-21	Indian 2.
Bars 22-33	Korean 2.
Bars 34-6	Indian 3.
Bars 37-42	Korean 3.
Bar 43	Chromatic 2.
Bar 44	Korean 4. Aeolian on A.
Bars 45-6	Chromatic 3.
Bars 46-7	Korean 5. Aeolian on C again.

For the second section, Finnissy uses two brief references to a choral work, *The Stones*, by the movement's dedicatee, Rodney Lister, and two much longer melodic lines, in different modes, from a traditional Chinese melody, the second of which includes pibroch-like inserts.

2. *Slowish and Gentle.* Bars 48-53.

Bars 48-9	Lister 1.
Bar 50	Chinese 1, Dorian on F#. Extended (Example 2.69).
Bars 51-2	Lister 2 (Example 2.69).
Bar 53	Chinese 2. Dorian on F. Extended. With pibroch insert (Example 2.69).

Example 2.69 *Folklore 4*, from bar 50, p. 79
Reproduced by permission of Oxford University Press

The next section is a long random 'cut-up', in the manner of William Burroughs, of 70 different fragments. The first 20 of these (though they do not of course appear in this order in the piece) are taken from a volume of Sousa's Marches, whose inclusion in this particular context recalls Ives, while others refer to material from earlier in the piece and elsewhere in the composer's output, and include several silences (their position is thus the result of random rather than strategic processes). Finnissy accommodates these within a series of pre-selected tempos, whose changes again are not configured so as to relate to any particular predominance of material.

3. Bars 54-112. Random cut-up of fragments. Bars 63, 65, 66, 70, 78, and several more from Sousa. Tempo structure: *Allegro moderato; crotchet = 116; Andante; Adagio; Allegro - alla marcia; Più mosso; Allegro -alla marcia; Più mosso*. Pause:

Example 2.70 *Folklore 4*, bars 96-100, p. 85
Reproduced by permission of Oxford University Press

The final two sections are as follows:

4. *tempo libero*. Bar 113. Chinese 3. Highly extended (longest uninterrupted line since 'Haen'), first in Mixolydian on G, then Dorian on B.

5. *Lento, molto sostenuto, quasi sognando*. Bars 114-37. Smudged blues improvisation around 'Deep River'. As at end of *Folklore 2*, but with melody in third voice, quicker accompanying voices and no thinning out of voices. Coda, bars 131-7 (Example 2.71).

We have moved from the Nordic flavour of *Folklore 1*, through the many-faceted European-ness of the following parts, to an upper 'Pacific Rim' of America and the Far East in the last part. What remains is the voice of the oppressed, as exemplified by the Negro spritual, and a polarisation between long interrupted melody and frenetic montage, recalling the similar polarisation in *English Country -Tunes*.

Example 2.71 *Folklore 4*, bars 130-37. Conclusion
Reproduced by permission of Oxford University Press

Folklore is open to many different interpretations, not least because of the diversity of the reference material and conceptual overdetermination[6] of the work. Though the materials were not chosen in order to demonstrate their similarities, as is the case in the earlier work for speaker and ensemble, *Various Nations*, similarities certainly can be discerned, as is inevitable when dealing with 'found' objects which have a history of their own. A sense of unity is perhaps provided by the fact that they are all experienced through the eyes (and ears!) of a singular individual. The work might on another level be seen as a celebration of global intercommunication, revealing both similarity on one level and diversity on another. In another sense, the consistent modifications and distortions reflect the futility of nostalgia or primitivism, as one often encounters it in the more crude manifestations of 'green' politics. Orton's defacing of library books, the impossibility of Jarman's imaginary landscapes, Cage's panoramas (*Roaratorio*, the *Europeras*), Lévi-Strauss's searches for the elemental structures of man, all these spirits hover over this immense and ultimately beguiling work, variously passionate, angry, glorious, mysterious, bleak and disorientating, from a composer who searches far and wide in a quest for the truth and provides at the very least a new level of feeling and understanding. What stays in the mind longest, however, is the love of melody, of the human voice, which sings and goes on singing as the world burns around it, the oral tradition of so much folk music, from a composer who is not afraid of the self, with all its vulnerabilities.

Conclusion

The journey from the *Songs*, through *Fast Dances, Slow Dances*, *English Country -Tunes* and the *Verdi Transcriptions*, to *Nine Romantics, Folklore* and other recent works is long and wide-ranging. Many elements have been explored to their logical conclusion, discarded, re-integrated in a different manner, then synthesised with other new elements. Yet I believe the recent work, in particular *Folklore*, Finnissy's crowning compositional achievement for the piano, to show the necessity of much of what has come before. His utterly un-sentimentalised re-introduction of functional tonality or modality as part of a spectrum which contains at its other extreme the most savage chromatic dissonances or even para-microtonality, allows for the widest possible range of colours and emotions, bringing to mind Charles Ives' bewilderment at the idea that either tonality or atonality should become doctrinaire. Only a few other composers, such as B.A. Zimmermann, Heinz Holliger, Helmut Lachenmann or Christian Wolff have in their different ways been able to achieve such a form of synthetic transcendence. At the time of going to press, Finnissy is engaged on a project that will dwarf even *Folklore*, a projected four-and-a-half hour piano piece *History of Photography in Sound.* There are only a small number of composers who could successfully realise a work of this scale, but Finnissy may well turn out to be one of them.

Notes

1. An opus number does not signify any particular chronology in Finnissy's early work, it is merely part of the title.
2. Robert Kelly - on Stan Brakhage's 'Art of Vision'
3. 'The Piano Music of Michael Finnissy', Brian Ferneyhough.
4. Ferruccio Busoni - *The Essence of Music and other Papers*, translated by Rosamond Ley, Dover 1965/1987.
5. Richard Toop, 'Four Facets of the New Complexity' in Contact 32 (1988).
6. 'Overdetermination' is a term first used by Freud, to indicate when a phenomenon is the product of multiple determinants. A counterpart is 'underdetermination', used to denote a determinant which feeds multiple phenomena.

CHAPTER THREE

The Chamber Music

Roger Redgate

In a postmodern culture where value-free pluralism is the norm and aesthetic values are reduced to the level of circus tricks, it is important to remember that artistic expression is a unique phenomenon which cannot be replaced by the conditions of some other discourse. To adopt any one approach to a body of work as abundant, complex and integrated as Finnissy's must be problematic. It should also be borne in mind that he continues to be prolific, with as much enthusiasm, invention and originality as ever, making any proclaimed overview necessarily incomplete. At the expense of being exhaustive I have decided, therefore, to focus on works which help to illustrate particular aspects of Finnissy's development. Where a number of works belong to a series or to a 'period' the individual examination of each work has been considered unnecessary. Nor have I attempted any detailed analyses, partly because I have never found such documentation particularly illuminating in penetrating the real essence of a work and partly because Finnissy's music is less centred around compositional processes as significant forms of formal cognition than, for example, the music of Brian Ferneyhough.

The expression 'New Complexity'[1] has by now lost what potency it once had as a definition of particular tendencies in recent music, as listeners have discovered that what makes the composers concerned more or less interesting is precisely those elusive qualities and differences which offer resistance to any such categorisation. Superficially, of course, the work of composers like Ferneyhough, Finnissy, James Dillon, Chris Dench and Richard Barrett has seemed to share certain features: notational intricacies, multi-layering of dense textures, extreme uses of instrumental resources in terms of register, dynamics and playing techniques, all combined to articulate formal structures whose complexity extended across every parameter. Brian Ferneyhough and Michael Finnissy were often cited as the patriarchal figures in this notional school, yet in some respects it would be hard to find two composers whose compositional personalities, working methods, structural intentions and influences (not to mention the music itself) could be more different.

Indeed their very differences make for a telling comparison. Fundamental to Ferneyhough's discourse would seem to be the projection of a complex, psycho-philosophical background as an integral component of the compositional and, therefore, musical experience, hence the overriding sense of teleological focus in his work. Finnissy, on the other hand, has embraced an enormous variety of styles and ethnomusicological sources which inform and influence his compositional thought, creating a journey through a rich and varied expressive landscape.

However, the apparent eclecticism of Finnissy's music is not to be confused with some kind of superficial postmodernist posturing, in which various styles or works are cited in the vain hope of establishing meaningful or ironic relationships with the past. Finnissy's concern with tradition goes much deeper, reflecting none of the paucity of imagination, compositional impotence or general lack of critical awareness which is to be found elsewhere, masquerading as some kind of historical alienation. In Finnissy's work one detects a strong sense of empathy with, and a complete integration and appropriation of, the motivating sources fundamental to his musical discourse; their function goes far beyond the banality of exotic quotation often found in other music with similar pretensions. Finnissy himself speaks of the 'on-going process of taking something and treating it, via the realm of one's inner experience'; for him the 'taking of another composer's material is a means of highlighting a musical process'.

This strategy serves not only as a means of structural orientation, but, since the perception of another composer's (often familiar) material is continually subject to contextual shifts, it also allows the articulation of a personalised historico-cultural perspective which is itself a fundamental part of Finnissy's aesthetic. In contrast it would be hard to imagine Ferneyhough ever using borrowed material to highlight a musical process, or even allowing any particular process to appear too close to the surface of his music. Rather the complex interaction between such processes is his central concern, in some cases to the point where the processes themselves become quasi-thematic/motivic elements.

The main thread running through Finnissy's work is perhaps the piano music, which stretches from his earliest writings to the present day and includes some of his most formally ambitious compositions. There is however a significant number of important works for mixed, and very often unusual, ensembles with little or no tendency towards any one preferred or 'conventional' instrumentation. Works such as the *String Quartet* (1984) or *Mississippi Hornpipes* (1982) for violin and piano, both of which are scored for combinations with a long and often daunting classical heritage, radically re-invent their chosen genres, sidestepping any inherited formal obligations.

Works for solo instruments have also formed a major part of the composer's œuvre, although the last decade has seen a significant drop in their production. Apart from the works for solo piano, Finnissy's only solo work composed since 1983 is *Ének* (1990) for solo violin, commissioned by the Carl Flesch Violin Competition, whereas he wrote no fewer than 27 solo works between 1971 and 1983.

It has always been the case that composers have certain stylistic qualities unique to their music which are to a greater or lesser extent inherent in their notation. Finnissy often cites Busoni's belief that the very process of notation involves certain decisions amounting to compromises in the apprehension of a musical image: 'The moment the pen takes possession of it, the thought loses its original form.'[2] As Finnissy points out (via Busoni), notation is a kind of transcription and often involves a transition from a generalised apprehension of sound to a particularisation in some way and this is perhaps especially so in the case of more texturally based music. In this respect Finnissy's own music defies any ready classification: at times textural, at others more gestural, and sometimes so densely gestural as to appear textural. However Finnissy's acute awareness of the relationship between texture, form, harmony, density and melodic line requires that this transcriptive process be radically re-thought in terms of a new formal framework unique, perhaps, to his music. It is this important aspect of Finnissy's musical intuition, so often overlooked by his imitators, that gives his music a uniqueness of purpose and a clear and direct sense of formal intention.

A fundamental part of Finnissy's vision embraces a complex world of temporal relationships:

> ...trying to capture phenomena moving at different rates, to impose a rhythmic grid somehow on different kinds of metric pattern... Things don't move in regular 4/4 or 3/4: they move at all manner of rates - speeding up, slowing down, independently. I wanted to capture that excitement, that dynamic, kinetic quality.[3]

In order to articulate these relationships Finnissy uses a wide and inventive range of notational strategies, pushing more conventional notation to its limits. These range from large groups of grace notes, whose execution is often only spatially defined, to works consisting of temporally independent parts. Often bar-lines are excluded altogether or bear only a tangential relationship to the gestural nature of the music; frequently they are undermined by complex networks of irrational rhythmic groupings. At times they seem to function purely as an aid to co-ordination, rather than indicating precise metric articulations, or they are present simply to define larger scale sectional divisions. Finnissy's choice of any one strategy is, however, specific to each work.

Afar (1966-67) is scored for five instruments and percussion. Despite some very precisely defined rhythmic gestures and the occasional structural division, the work is otherwise devoid of bar lines and time signatures, as if the ensemble were expected to play as one collective consciousness. The music is co-ordinated by an elaborate system of cues (connecting arrows, etc.) which in themselves are necessarily approximations. Particularly interesting is the use of implied anticipatory grace notes to mark the entry of certain gestures (Example 3.1). One has the impression here that such notational strategies may well have been informed by aspects of Finnissy's somewhat extended approach to keyboard writing and textures.

Aside from this comparative rhythmic freedom, however, the music is precise in its gestural outline and in individual detail. It makes use of various types of grace-note notation, from simply 'as fast as possible' to more rhythmically defined groupings (Example 3.2), creating a hierarchy of outside-time temporal relationships, like 'etchings' engraved on the more exact temporal framework of the rest of the music.

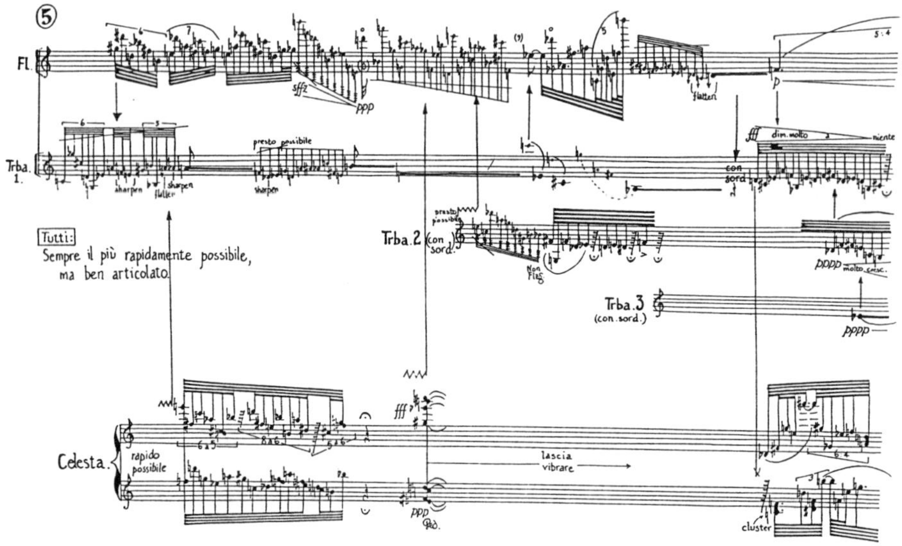

Example 3.1 *Afar*. Reproduced by permission of Edizioni Suvini Zerboni

The gestural nature of the work is characteristically extravagant, using the full range of the instruments with large cross-registral leaps, mixed articulations and extreme dynamics (Example 3.2). Already there is a fastidious attention to the detailed use of articulation and dynamic nuance as both an expressive tool and as a means of establishing a further degree of formal perspective and gestural identity.

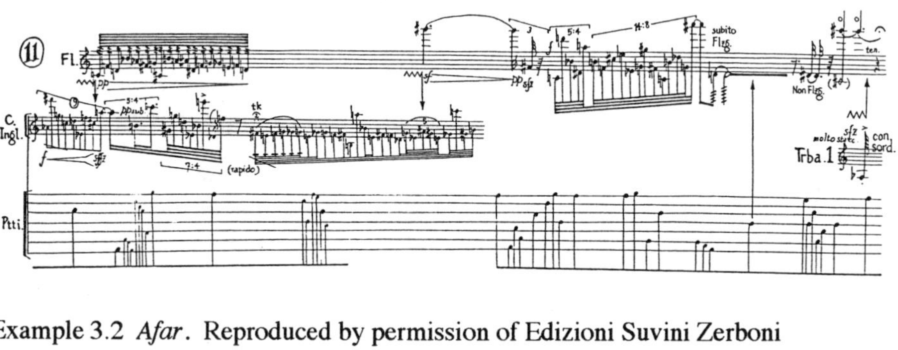

Example 3.2 *Afar*. Reproduced by permission of Edizioni Suvini Zerboni

Significantly absent at this point is any integrated use of microtones, which are here limited to occasional inflections, the players being asked simply to 'sharpen' or 'flatten' indicated pitches. The piece concludes, perhaps rather surprisingly, with a sequence of overlapping harmonic fields (marked *pppp* possibile) which have previously formed a background to the work: here, more harmonically solidified, they are spatially distributed over 50 bars of variable length (each between 6-12 seconds long), like some kind of post-apocalyptic residue:

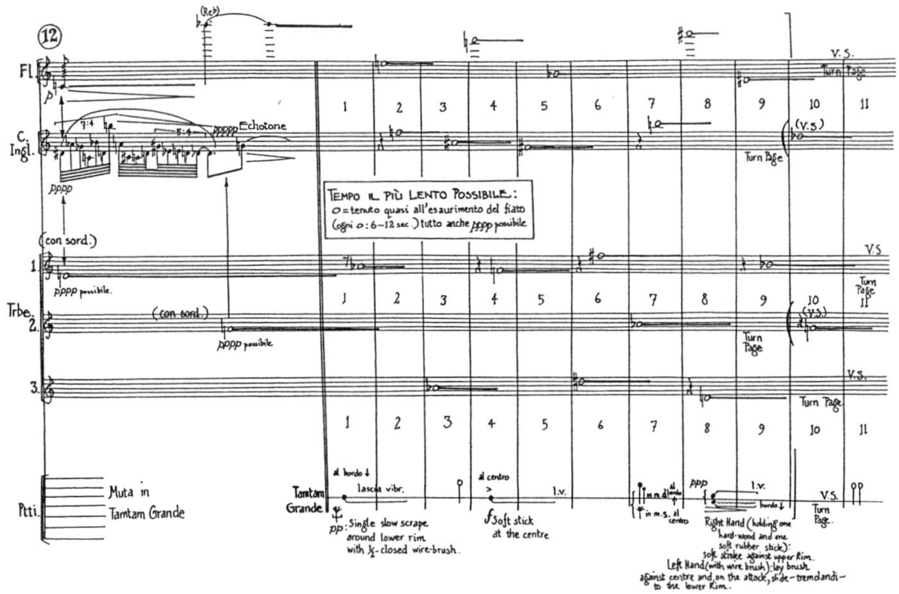

Example 3.3 *Afar*. Reproduced by permission of Edizioni Suvini Zerboni

Nobody's Jig (1980-81) for two violins, viola and cello (so designated by the composer, not a 'string quartet'), on the other hand, is composed of completely independent lines. There is no 'score' of the work and the composer declines to suggest even a possible synchronised version, thus subverting the entire tradition of the string quartet as an ensemble medium! Starting from an initial unison G the players immediately part company (they may synchronise at certain structural points but only if they so desire) and finish independently. The individual parts are composed with as much attention to detail and characteristic virtuosity as might be found in some of Finnissy's solo instrumental works. (An initial glance at the first violin part (Example 3.4) shows a passing resemblance to passages in *Song 13* (1971) and *All the trees they are so high* (1977).) Each part is rhythmically precise and has very specific metronome marks which are to be 'scrupulously observed'.

Despite the degree of independence there is no possibility that this work would ever sound different from the sound-world envisaged by the composer. Neither will it sound radically different to any other work by Michael Finnissy. Each of the individual parts is clearly and precisely defined, at times sharing material with other instruments (though it is unlikely that this would ever occur simultaneously), at others maintaining an individual identity. The implied textures are typical of their composer: extremes of dynamic; the use of the entire range of each instrument, often covered in wide leaps; long passages in harmonics; melodic lines in quarter-tones; an extended use of instrumental timbre and playing techniques. What is distinctive about this work is its particular temporal conception.

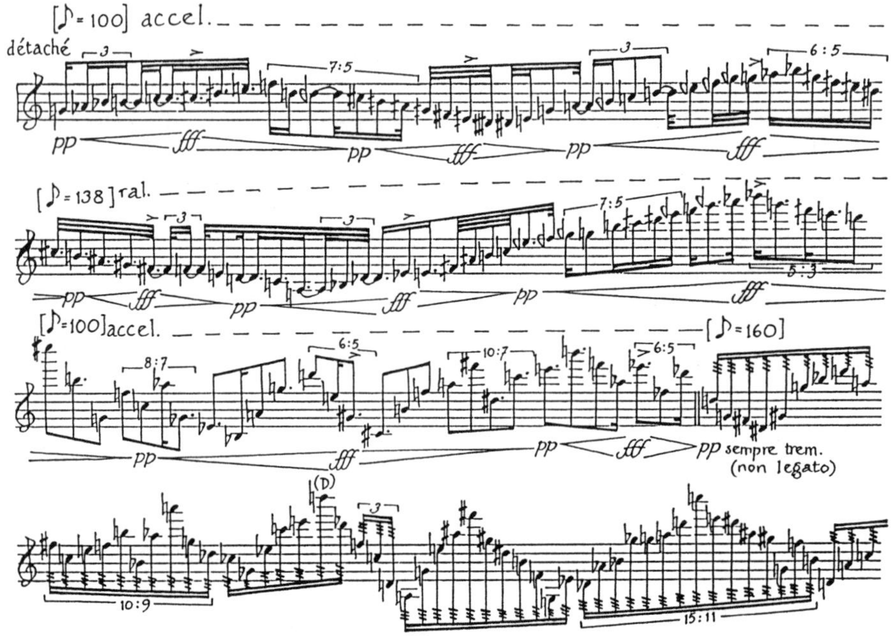

Example 3.4 *Nobody's Jig*

As when upon a trancèd summer night (1966, twice revised in 1968) brings some of Finnissy's temporal preoccupations into sharper focus. Scored for a characteristically unusual ensemble of three celli, piano and two percussion, the work occupies a dark and mysterious sound-world, initially articulated by the three celli in a complex texture of quartertone material, layered in complex, irrational rhythmic figures which continually defy the barline and any sense of metre:

Example 3.5 *As when upon a trancèd summer night*,

The texture is enriched by the entry of the piano at figure 8; initially adding low resonant chords, it later moves to fast staccato lines, contrasting with the legato celli, and so brings the musical image into sharper focus, a process aided by the gradual disappearance of the quartertones (Example 3.6).

After a short cadenza-like senza misura section, the piano is joined again by the celli in a section of clearly defined, superimposed metric layers (5:4, 4:3, and a cross-cutting 5/8), set against irregular irrational layering in the piano. This leads to the first entry of the vibraphone (and the first entry into the treble clef) and, eventually, the second senza misura section in which the piano reaches its extreme high register (where it is later joined by celesta), before finally dissolving into the sound of four suspended cymbals.

Example 3.6 *As when upon a trancèd summer night*

The formal profile of this work is typical of structures that will appear over and over again in Finnissy's subsequent music: the contrast between metrically complex sections and other, freer senza misura writing; transitions through gradual processes such as the elimination of quartertones (often triggered by some other structural event); and on a larger scale, the general transition from very low, rather undefined material, to gesturally more specific material in the high register, and finally to a high spectrum which is once again, defined more by timbre than gestural specificity.

Evening (1974) for seven amplified instruments seems less formally ambitious. Similar structures are at work, especially in the opposition of measured and spatially notated events, which are further emphasised by a more extended exploration of instrumental timbre. Finnissy has always conceived of instrumental writing in terms of the full range of possibilities and the use of amplification here (one of the composer's few ventures in this direction)[4] is specifically intended to enable the extension of these possibilities.

The most complete expression of Finnissy's formal preoccupations during this period is perhaps to be found in *Alongside* (1977) for chamber ensemble, a work which precipitated certain changes in the composer's thinking; indeed it is hard to imagine how this line of thought might practically have been taken any further. The work is extreme in most senses: instrumental virtuosity of a degree previously restricted to solo works, Finnissian leaps across wide intervals for the entire ensemble, dynamic extremes from *pppppp* to *fffff* and an unsurpassed density which seeks to explore new realms of musical experience. The result is a strikingly inventive work of extraordinary power and exuberance.

The work is a remarkable 'explosion' of Finnissy's current technical and expressive resources. Of particular interest is the use of instrumental textures defined not only by playing techniques and instrumental groupings but also by their rhythmic profiles and by the complex layering of dynamics, temporal relationships and densities, in contrasted notational layouts. At first glance the score appears metrically more exact than many of its predecessors, with none of their time-space or senza misura sections. (An early version, however, consisted of 14 unsynchronised strands which were later regulated by a series of numerical chains, creating a complex fabric of irrational rhythmic relationships.) However, in his performance note to the work, Finnissy states, 'Although notated in detail the rhythm is intended to sound free and spontaneous, unmechanical, and without discernible regular pulse'. This reflects an important element of Finnissy's approach to notation and the temporal aspects of music. Inherited notions concerning the significative function of notation in relation to the required musical result must be radically re-evaluated, and further defined by aspects of composer intention. But unlike Brian Ferneyhough, for example, who through his writings and through performance notes in the scores themselves has attempted to define a specific code of practice in which notational complexity is seen as an integral component in the psychology of the performer's learning process, Finnissy has been less inclined to offer guidelines to the performer.

The title, *Alongside*, refers to the juxtaposition and inter-relationship of three fundamental archetypes: melodic lines, harmonic blocks and sharp punctuating attacks. In addition to the already inventive timbral world of the work, notions of balance are re-defined through specific dynamic layouts. Complex relationships between specifically defined textures are created, at times dynamically matched, at others differentiated to create a layered perspective. The opening is one of the few sections in which all the instruments play, each grouped according to a dynamic balance layered thus:

Group I	flute, oboe, clarinet, horn, trumpet, violin 2	***fff***
Group II	trombone, piano, violin 1, double bass	***mp***
Group III	bassoon, viola, cello	***pppp***

Otherwise the section proceeds for 17 bars without dynamic nuance, except for the percussionist who plays crescendi from ***p*** to ***fff***, gradually increasing in length and in the distance between their entries. This is abruptly terminated by two bars of increased density (denser at least in their number of notes) for full ensemble, marked *'subito pppppp senza crescendo'*

(♩ = 90), leading to the first section (without the brass instruments) of more clearly differentiated material (*ffff*, 'harsh, *non legato*').

Example 3.7 *Alongside*

Another important feature of this new section is the introduction of an unstable tempo (governing rhythmically complex and intricate material) which accelerates from ♩ = 66 to ♩ = 104 and then returns to ♩ = 58-66 within seven bars. Similar procedures recur throughout the work and also extend to polymetric relationships: at figure 18 the general metronome mark is ♩ = 96, while the clarinet has a time signature of 3/4, set against the rest of the ensemble's 4/4. Shortly afterwards the piano, and later the percussion too, are instructed to play 'independently', according to their own, individual tempi. The individuation of lines is further emphasised here by a fourfold dynamic layering:

Group I	horn, trumpet, trombone	***ff***
Group II	piano	***pp - ff***
Group III	cello	***p***
Group IV	clarinet	***ppp***

This temporal independence is immediately preceded and prepared by a kind of internal temporal erosion, in the form of an 'outside time' structure (figure 12 in the score), punctuated by the first two silences of the work. Here the main body of material is provided by the strings: the violins play different rates of accelerandi (to some degree determined by the number of notes within each group), while the cello and bass play groups of notes 'freely and irregularly', all played in relation to a series of accelerandi indicated by the conductor (Example 3.7). This is the only point where structural elements are clearly defined by significant temporal transitions, creating mobile and internally complex blocks of sound. It is perhaps ironic that here, where the temporal stability is at its most flexible both in terms of speed and notational practice, that the work's overall temporal nature is given a sense of focus in an otherwise 'free-floating' perceptual environment.

Silence has always been an important structural element in Finnissy's music, not only in defining or being defined by surrounding events, but also as a further extension of musical texture. Its integration into the musical fabric has various functions: the abrupt opposition of sound to (total) silence, in terms of both the macro- and micro-structure of a work; the resonance of analytical aftermath; a space charged with the mounting tension of anticipation; various forms of coloured or otherwise articulated silence (distant resonance, echoes...). In *Alongside*, silences which increase in length punctuate violent outbursts in the brass and percussion, against a distant harmonic backdrop provided by the strings, culminating in the ceremonial brutality of the first of a series of solo drum strokes, marked *'sffffz tutta forza'* and using both sticks simultaneously.

The climactic force of this moment is further emphasised by its structural role, since here the differentiation of the work's main archetypal elements is most clearly delineated: harmonic blocks (*ppp sempre*) in the strings; violent, linearly derived outbursts in the horn, trombone, bassoon and percussion (*ff*) and less frequent, wide-leaping figurations in the flute, oboe and clarinet (*fff*). Only the piano, with its short and irregular percussive attacks, accommodates extreme changes from *ppp* to *ff* and *sffz* (Example 3.8). The multi-layered textures of Japanese *Gagaku* and the gestural intensity of Noh theatre had been a formative influence on *Alongside* and it is at this point that they come closest to the surface of Finnissy's music.

Example 3.8 *Alongside*

Alongside is one of its composer's greatest achievements and a work which captures the 'dynamic, kinetic quality'[5] of phenomena in the world around us. Few other of Finnissy's chamber works attempt this degree of intensity, density, complexity and virtuosity, although that is not to say that they are in any way more simple! Over the next few years his music turned to a new, uniquely charged sound-world, as if his music had imploded under the force of its own gestural intensity, creating a kind of expressive 'black hole'. Before moving on, however, two solo works composed in the same year as *Alongside* merit particular attention. *Sikangnuqa*, for solo flute and *Pavasiya*, for solo oboe doubling oboe d'amore, both have titles derived from Hopi Indian sources. (A third work, *Talawva*, for small ensemble, is also part of this cycle but is at present withdrawn, pending revision.) Both explore realms of formidable virtuosity, as if compressing the timbral potential of an ensemble into a single line (Example 3.9). Perhaps Finnissy was indeed exploring possible dimensions beyond the boundaries of *Alongside* here.

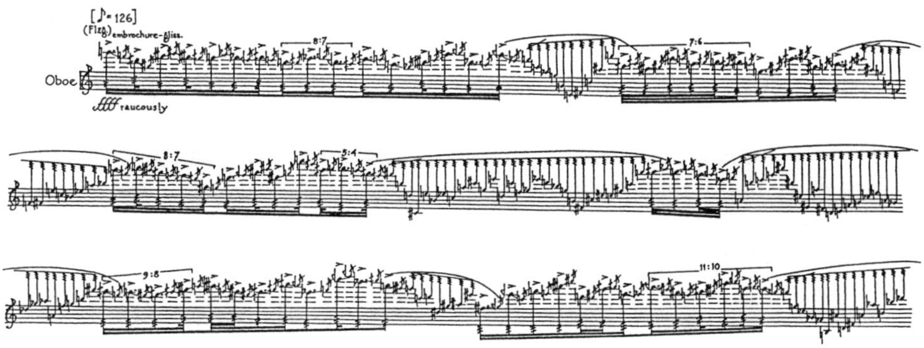

Example 3.9 *Pavasiya*

This earlier period of Finnissy's music seems to represent a kind of musical expedition, a coming to terms with, or perhaps appropriation of, the inadequacies of the notational system in its ability to capture certain important aspects of his particular musical vision. To some degree all composers are faced with this problem and find their own solutions, which in turn form an important (if subliminal) part of their compositional make-up. Indeed it might be argued that the degree to which composers accept inherited notions of the function and possible limits of the notational system is inversely proportional to their critical awareness of notation's structural function as an integral component of the expressive discourse.

The 1980s saw a radical change in the sound-world of Finnissy's music, informed by the consolidation of a new creative agenda: to fashion a new music, as a kind of imaginary folk music, through the search for underlying musical archetypes; the development of new harmonic, melodic and gestural materials, defined by complex microtonal writing within narrow frequency bands and the introduction of ornamental gracenotes, melodic embellishments and glissandi. This change was the result of Finnissy's burgeoning interest in the music of other cultures. Explicit reference to the influence of folk music, and especially English folk music, had been made in a number of Finnissy's works since 1969, such as *Folk Song Set* (1969-70, revised 1975-76), *Doves Figary* (1976-77), *English Country Tunes* (1977) and *Kemp's Morris* (1978). An interest in Japanese music, theatre and art in the 1970s had also surfaced in works like *Tsuru-Kame* (1971-73), *Goro* (1978), *Kagami-Jishi* and *Hinomi* (both 1979) and, less overtly, in *Alongside*. In the 1980s these references extended to include elements of Australian Aboriginal, Azerbaijani, Javanese, Kurdish, Rumanian and Sardinian music and Finnissy adapted and refined many of the formal devices he had developed in earlier works to accommodate this wealth of new possibilities.

A transitional work from this period is *Jisei* (1981) for solo cello and small ensemble (although the cello is neither especially prominent nor is its writing particularly soloistic). While retaining some of the gestural and textural characteristics of *Alongside*, this work introduces many new features, resulting in a compellingly original formal design. As with *Alongside* the underlying influence is Japanese; 'Jisei' is a Japanese word meaning 'aerial spirit'.

The works opens with a typically imaginative texture: the cello plays percussive pizzicati in rhythmically irregular groupings against three tom-toms whose material, although marked at the same dynamic as the cello, is much more rhythmically defined:

Example 3.10 *Jisei*

At figure 1 these instruments are joined by flute and oboe, playing shrill, high glissandi within a narrow range (rarely more than a third apart and often as close as a quartertone) and at a constant dynamic (*f*), marking the beginning of a new kind of textural thinking in Finnissy's music. This entry induces an immediate disintegration of the opening texture. The cello begins to make extreme dynamic transitions (from *f* to *pp*), weaving in and out of the general musical fabric; the more rhythmic definition of the percussion line is eroded by the introduction of irrational rhythmic groupings and rests, breaking up any sense of regularity (Example 3.11).

The ensemble is joined by the viola at figure 4 in the first 'tutti' section (but without the solo cello or the piano, who is assigned an independent role throughout). At first sight this seems a typically dense and complex texture, reminiscent of passages from *Alongside*. The performance direction here, however, is 'always inflexible, no expressive rubato', quite different from the approximate tempo markings and 'free floating' lines of *Alongside* (Example 3.12).

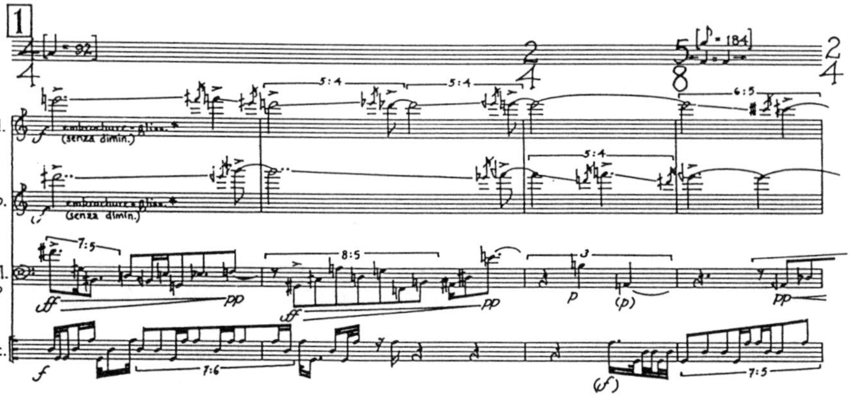

Example 3.11 *Jisei*

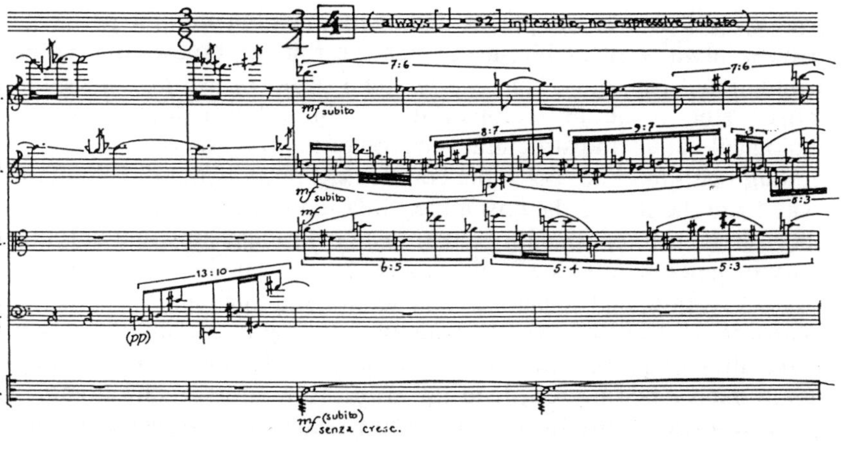

Example 3.12 *Jisei*

This 23 bar long section has a time signature of 3/4, except for one 3/8 bar at its mid-point. Any sense of the bar line, of course, is eradicated by long irrational groupings across them. This rhythmic irregularity is complemented by sequences of superimposed, non-synchronised phrase marks (one in the flute, against two in the oboe and three in the cello, for example), defined by abrupt and extreme changes in dynamics. The effect of this passage is quite remarkable. On the one hand, three temporally independent lines are clearly audible. On the other hand, the global dynamic markings and synchronised phrase groupings create the sense of more unified textures alternating between moments of driving determination, lyrical virtuosity and improvisatory fluidity:

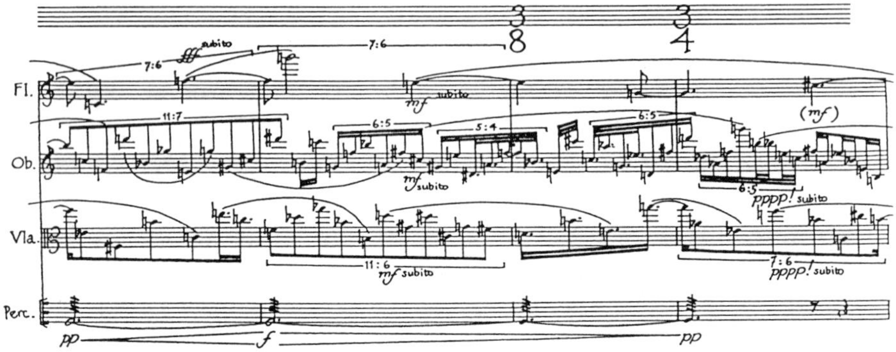

Example 3.13 *Jisei*

This complex layering of irrational rhythmic groupings and phrase structures, unified by a global dynamic profile and in combination with the performance indication, 'always inflexible, no expressive rubato', creates a structurally multi-functional passage. This is a moment of notational brilliance from a composer who is acutely conscious of the relationship between the psychological nature and structural function of his notation.

Although still marked 'solo' the cello's next entry is not differentiated in any way from the rest of the ensemble. In a long, slowly unfolding passage for oboe, viola, solo cello and percussion an ever increasing and unremitting intensity is generated. Once again this process is aided by Finnissy's acute notational perception. The passage has none of the usual nuances of dynamic and phrasing; instead the overall dynamic marking is gradually stepped up, each escalation prepared either by abrupt crescendi for the whole ensemble or by subtle use of percussion, leading to the first entry of the piano. The complete absence of any further expressive nuance contributes to creating a remarkable build-up of tension.

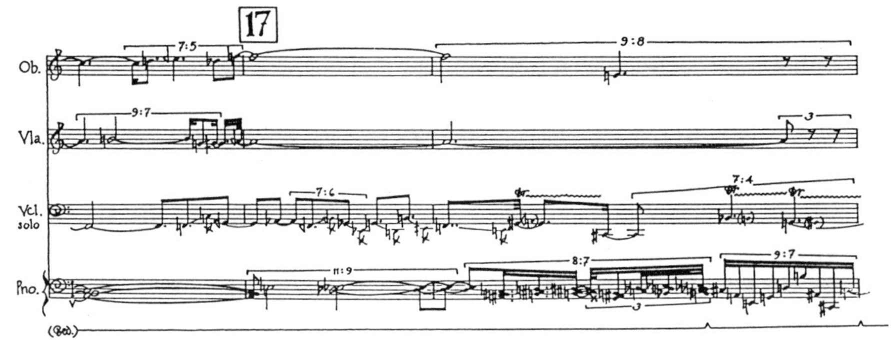

Example 3.14 *Jisei*

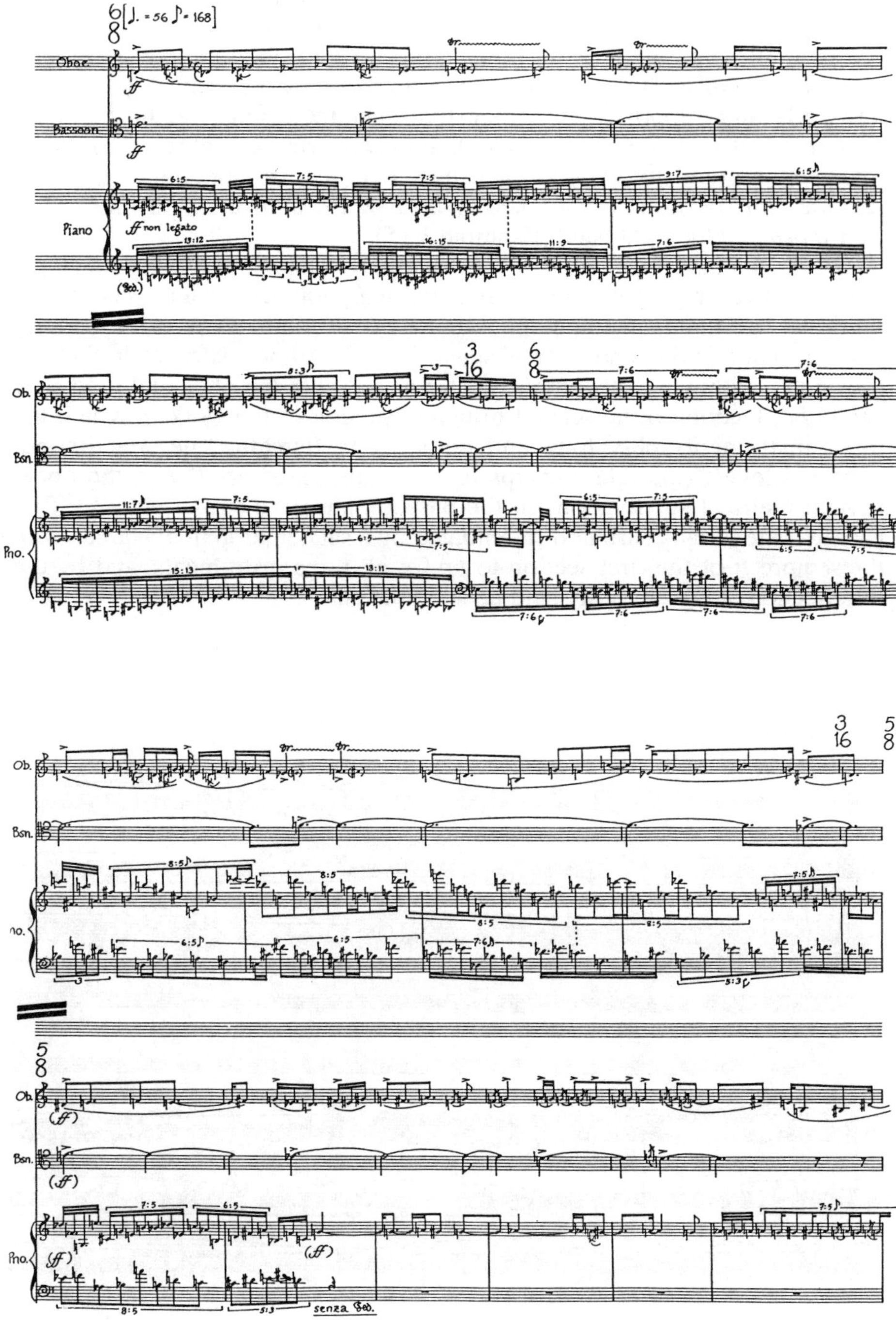

Example 3.15 *Keroiylu*

By the time of ***Keroiylu*** (1981) for oboe, bassoon and piano, the music projects a strong influence from modal folk melody, reflecting the Azerbaijani folk dance of its title. The opening oboe melody is mostly limited to a narrow tessitura, further characterised by ornamental grace notes and trills and supported by drone-like sustained notes in the bassoon. Simultaneously, the piano has two, rhythmically very complex, interlocking lines which gradually widen in tessitura, with a corresponding decrease in textural density (although marked *sempre ped.*), until a single line is left (*senza ped.*) in the right hand (Example 3.15).

For the remainder of the work the piano plays melodic contours in a single line, coloured only by changes in register, temporal density and pedalling, a bold use of the instrument characteristic of Finnissy's extraordinary instrumental thinking and textural sensitivity. This line, restricted initially to four notes within a minor third, is intertwined with the oboe and gradually 'unfolds', leading to the second principal section of the work in which the three instruments play long and complex melismatic lines on distinct temporal levels (the relationships to the main tempo are 9:7 in the oboe, normal metrical subdivisions in the bassoon and 10:7 in the piano). This passage is texturally further differentiated by a sudden drop in dynamic, from the sempre *ff* of the first section to *pp* for all three instruments, and by the introduction of continuously held pedal in the piano.

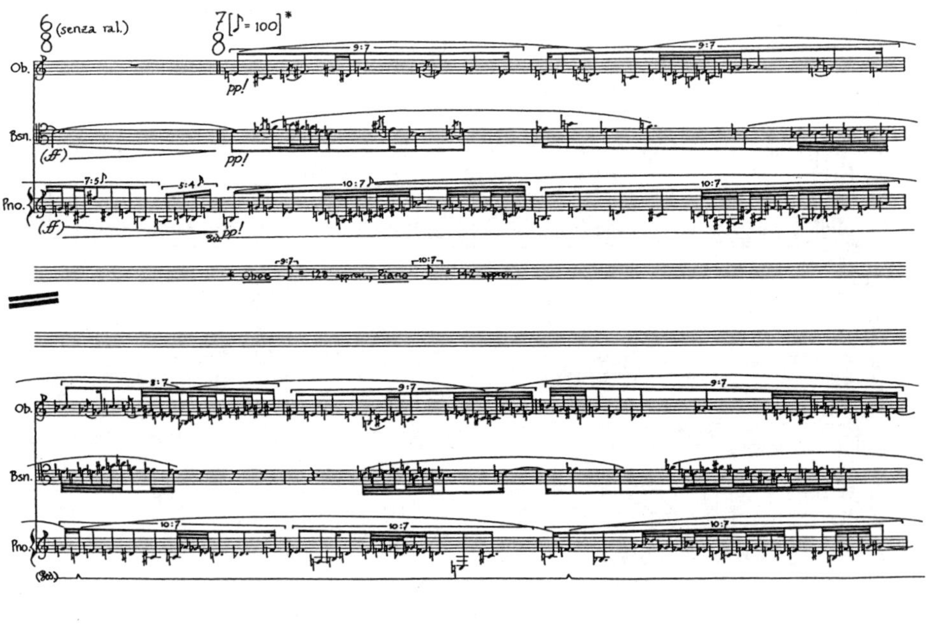

Example 3.16 *Keroiylu*

Example 3.17 *Aijal*

After a short melodic duet for oboe and piano right hand, the oboe is joined by the bassoon in a passage, marked *ff non legato*, which is set against an unusual background resonance created by a dense, sustained *pp legatissimo* line in the piano. The final section of the work is given considerable impact by the sudden use of abrupt changes between opposed dynamics and the unprecedented use of the oboe's high register with the bassoon's low register, the first time in the work that any two lines have not occupied the same registral space.

A surprising absence from *Keroiylu* is the use of quartertones, a feature in so much of Finnissy's instrumental music. Finnissy had rarely used quartertones simply to increase the number of pitches available for his transformational processes. Instead their use was always invested with specific structural and timbral significance and used as a means of highlighting musical perspective and formal differentiation, as in *As when upon a trancèd summer night* they had served to emphasise elements of harmonic focus.

Finnissy's two stays in Australia inevitably inspired an interest in Aboriginal music which in turn resulted in a series of works with Aboriginal Australian titles. The first of these for instruments alone is *Aijal* (1982) for flute, oboe and percussion, which further examines some of the new formal possibilities. The title, meaning 'sky', is perhaps reflected in the continuous use of the high registers of both the flute and oboe, never even descending to the treble stave, for at least half the work!

In contrast to *Keroiylu*, the use of quartertone material is consistent throughout, the texturally defined formal blocks being articulated by abrupt changes of dynamic, timbre and articulation. The opening section juxtaposes high, chirping sounds in the flute and oboe with a whip and, later, a bass drum in the percussion. Here the wind material is at a constant dynamic (*ff*) in blocks whose lengths vary between one and five bars and has a rich, microtonally coloured, harmonic and timbral density. This is emphasised by the use of the whip, whose single timbre undergoes extreme dynamic inflection (from *pp* to *ff*) in blocks of activity whose general tendency is to increase in length (Example 3.17). This interchange is abruptly terminated by the violent entry of two tom-toms, precipitating a transformation of the wind material with shrill, distorting glissandi. Throughout this section successive blocks alternate between *pp* and *fff*, although within each block all the instruments are matched dynamically.

The sudden descent into the middle/lower register and *pp* in the winds introduces melodic lines confined, characteristically, within a narrow range, whose interlocking phrase structures are subtly supported by the resonance of two suspended cymbals. Each section of the work and of the musical materials out of which it is made is defined not only by timbre and specific dynamic markings but also by tempo, all of which are brought into opposition with one another in the concluding section of the work (Example 3.18).

Example 3.18 *Aijal*

In *Jisei*, *Keroiylu* and *Aijal* one can hear the evolution of a new line of compositional thought, whose identifying characteristics are the product of an increasing refinement of technique. All three works present, in their clearest forms, the raw materials of a rich and complex musical language, and each work seems to focus on the exploration of quite specific formal preoccupations, establishing a new phase in Finnissy's instrumental writing. Many of the textures and formal devices undoubtedly echo those found in earlier works but they are being re-discovered and re-defined by their new contexts. One also has a strong sense of formal consolidation in these works; Finnissy had reached a level of technical assuredness on which he would build with startling fluency in the period to come.

It is worth considering for a moment the latent properties of this language which Finnissy's acute musical perception had identified as being useful for further development. The articulation of formal blocks not only by abrupt changes in dynamics, texture and tempo but also by changes in harmonic and gestural content was to become an important feature of Finnissy's handling of larger scale formal architecture. In subsequent works this approach to textural definition was to be extended to the superimposition of materials, enabling a greater differentiation of complex layers of musical information. This is turn has interesting harmonic implications. The temporal nature of Finnissy's music had always meant that functional harmony, in any conventional sense, was all but impossible. From his earliest compositions, however, Finnissy was always aware of a strong relationship between harmony and texture and had used this to re-create a feeling of harmonic direction in his music.

In the more recent pieces this 'harmonic' sense had become fully integrated into his compositional thinking. Even the most microtonal passages have a point of focus, either in the form of a drone, as in *Keroiylu*, or as an unstated point of reference, as in many of the works that followed, so that even the most complex, convoluted melodic lines have a strong sense of direction. Because these lines were generated by the use of random numbers, intended to produce non-recurring pitch sequences, they might otherwise seem to meander. On the other hand, the use of random numbers means that the character of the musical 'material' is identified more by statistical features, rather than by specific thematic or motivic elements.

Of course each pitch system, be it microtonal, chromatic or modal, has unique harmonic and timbral implications and possibilities, which Finnissy had explored in earlier works. These were now to be combined in some of his most fascinating textural and harmonic imaginings. The next work in the Australian series, *Banumbirr* (1982) is shaped by many of the formal strategies outlined above. The opening section, scored for flute, violin, piano and (later) cello, is typically dense and consists of complex, ornamented lines of chromatic material, intertwined within a narrow tessitura marked *pp non legato*. After five bars the other member of the ensemble, a clarinet, is also embedded within this texture; however, while the clarinet shares the same dynamic and registral ambit as the other instruments, it is given a more soloistic role, playing long, *legatissimo* phrases in quartertones:

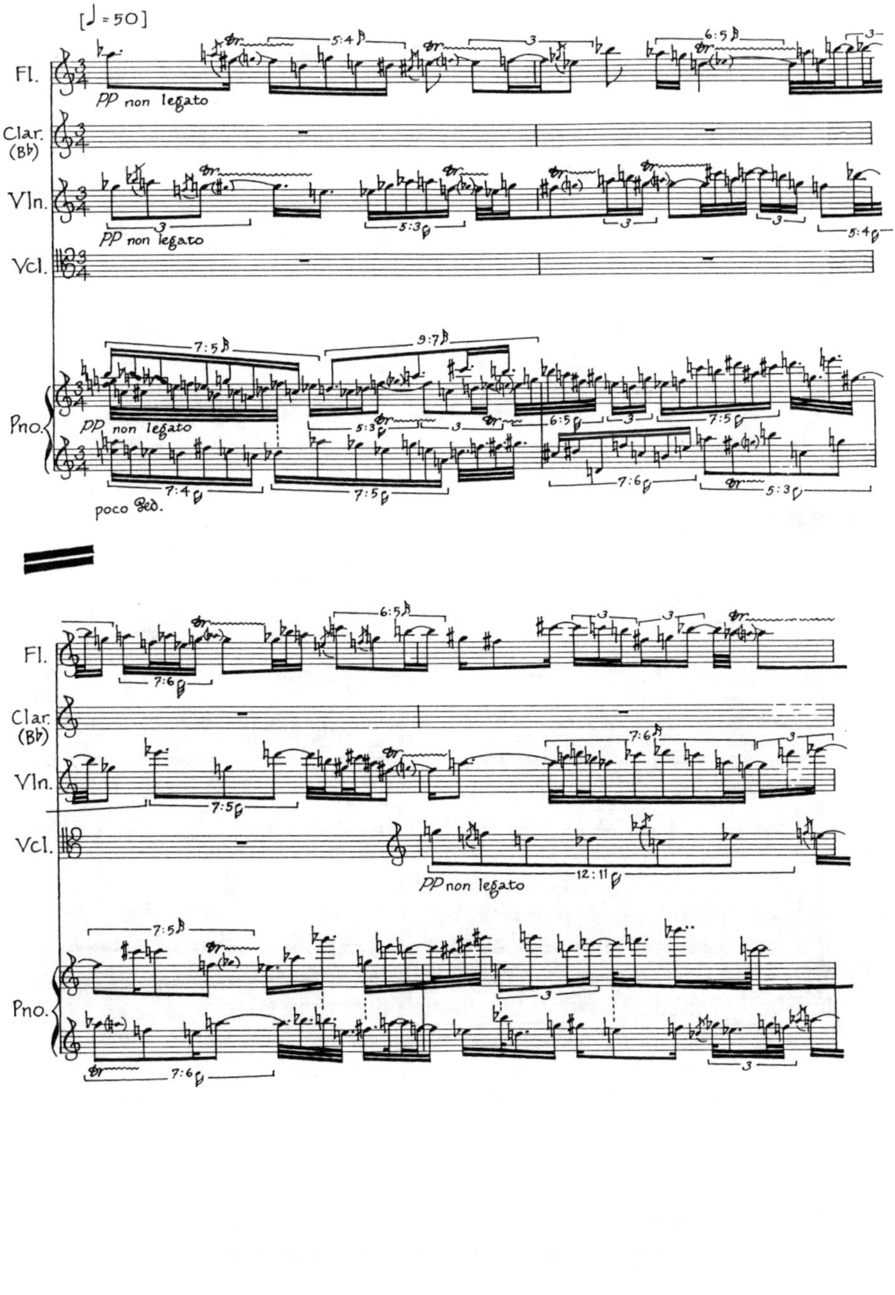
[♩=50]
Fl.
Clar. (B♭)
Vln.
Vcl.
Pno.
pp non legato
pp non legato
pp non legato
poco Ped.
5:4
3
6:5
5:3
5:4
7:5
9:7
6:5
7:5
7:4
7:5
7:6
5:3
7:6
6:5
7:5
7:6
12:11
pp non legato
7:5
7:6

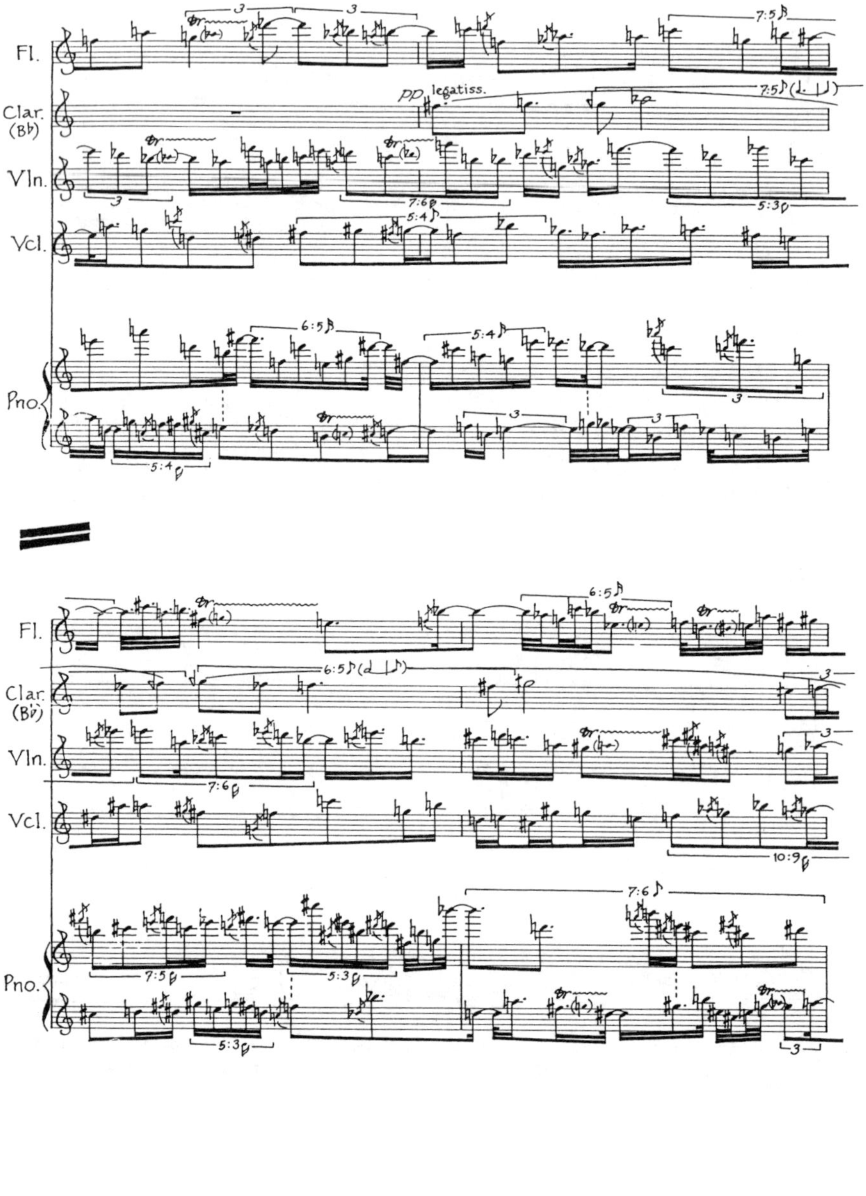

Example 3.19 *Banumbirr*
Reproduced by permission of United Music Publishers Limited

By a process of musical osmosis, these quartertones are allowed to filter through to the other instruments, while the consistently chromatic material in the piano is interrupted by silences of increasing duration:

Example 3.20 *Banumbirr*
Reproduced by permission of United Music Publishers Limited

Subsequently the four monodic instruments' lines develop individual characteristics: the clarinet remains *piu legato (pp sempre)* while the flute plays long detached notes of varying length, shaped by crescendi from *pp* to *mp*; the violin and cello unite in executing long melodic lines, *pp sempre*, with occasional disruptions by *sfp staccatissimo* notes (Example 3.21). Echoes of the opening chromatic material appear in the piano in short bursts at increasingly widely spaced intervals (2, 5, 9 and 11 bars); here, in an otherwise microtonal environment, they sound strangely ethereal.

Example 3.21 *Banumbirr*
Reproduced by permission of United Music Publishers Limited

Two further works for ensemble with Aboriginal titles are *Teangi* (1982) and *Ouraa* (1982-83) in which the principles explored in *Banumbirr* are extended to include the layering of instrumental groups whose material is again differentiated by contrasting use of quartertone and non-quartertone harmony:

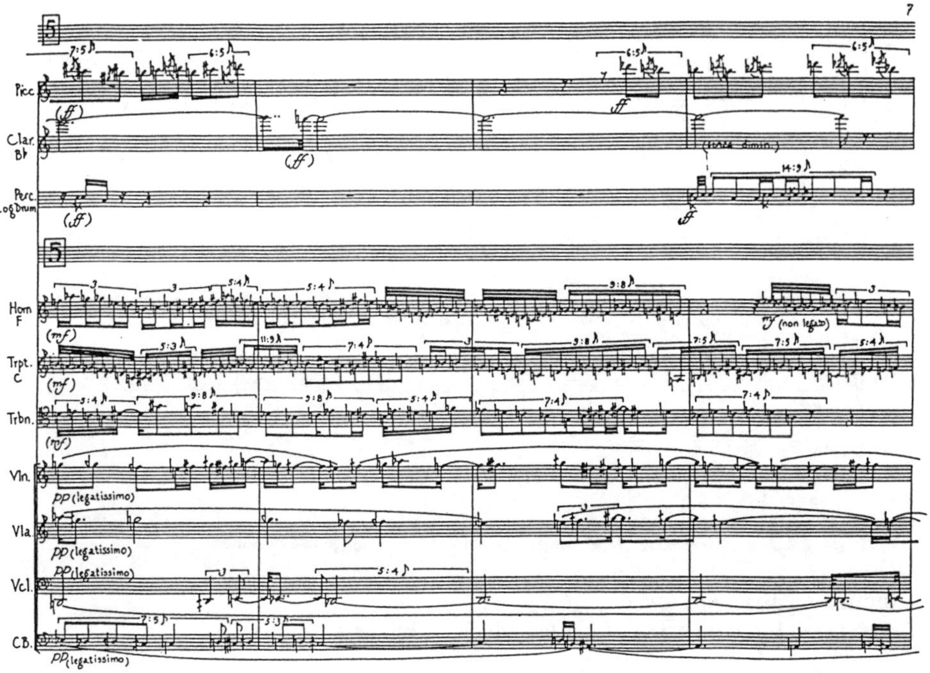

Example 3.22 *Ouraa*

The high point of this technique is exemplified by *Contretänze* (1985, revised 1986), described by the composer as 'Bach turning into Macedonian folk music'. The source material for this work is indeed the music of Bach, so transformed and integrated into Finnissy's musical language as to be barely recognisable.[7] The opening of the work is, perhaps, the point where Bach's music is closest to the surface: the first C major fugue from *Das Wohltemperierte Klavier* Book 1 (Example 3.23a) is just discernible, using different metrical units in each part and also differentiated by dynamic and timbre between wind and strings (the strings play *senza vibrato* and *al ponticello* (Example 3.23b):

Example 3.23a Bach, Fugue in C from *Das Wohltemperierte Klavier*, Book 1

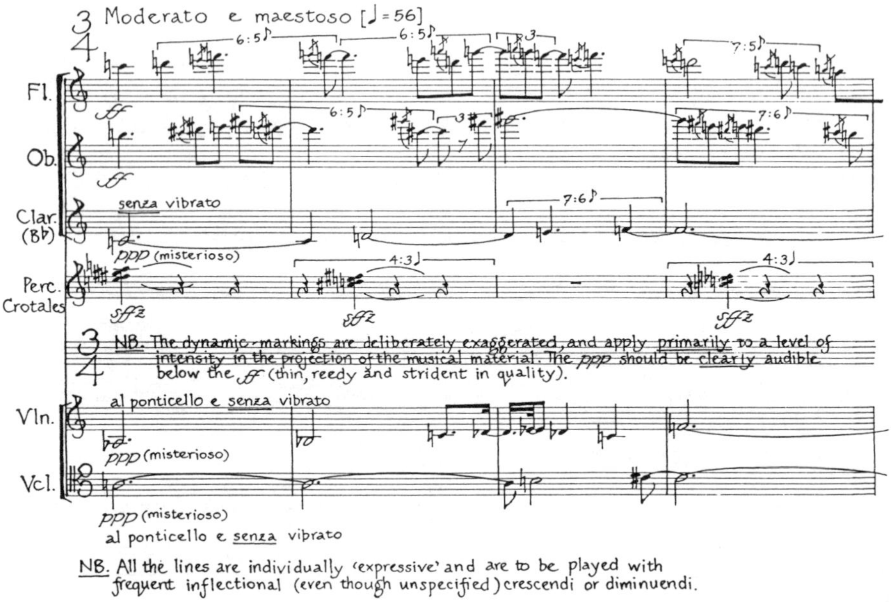

Example 3.23b *Contretänze*
Reproduced by permission of United Music Publishers Limited

Later in the work (at figure 38) this principle is reversed: the winds play *pp* and the strings *ff* marcato, with the strings now further differentiated by the use of quartertone material (Example 3.24).

Throughout the 1980s Finnissy composed a number of works for solo wind instrument with percussion, including *Dilok* (1982 - oboe), *Delal* (1984 - oboe d'amore), *Quabara* (1988 - didjeridu) and *Kulamen Dilan* (1990 - soprano saxophone), each of which strongly reflects Finnissy's interest in a particular folk music (Australian Aboriginal in *Quabara*, Kurdish in the others). In each work Finnissy uses only a few percussion instruments, exploiting them to their full potential. *Quabara* is unusual, not only because the percussionist is asked to use an assortment of trash as instruments (the composer's response to the plight of the Aboriginal peoples in modern Australia), but also because here the composer is writing for an unmodified Aboriginal instrument. As one might expect, sounds associated with Aboriginal traditional music are kept to a minimum and instead the less familiar timbral possibilities of the instrument are explored.

The character of the earlier of these works is a marked influence on the sound world of *Câtana* (1984). Although scored for eight instruments and percussion, the ensemble is divided into three smaller ensembles: a duo (flute and percussion), a trio (oboe, clarinet and piano) and a quartet (violin, viola, cello and harp); within each grouping one instrument has a solo role (flute, oboe and violin, respectively). All these groups are employed in a variety of combinations, at times individually or accompanied by other ensembles, at times in competition with one another. *Câtana* is simpler than some of the other works discussed here, yet it is a remarkable essay in textural inventiveness and colour, qualities enhanced by the clarity of its formal design and gestural function.

Example 3.24 *Contretänze*
Reproduced by permission of United Music Publishers Limited

The majority of Finnissy's pieces have evocative, poetic titles, often linked to the music's ethnic or poetic sources. Two pieces with rather more 'abstract' titles are the *String Quartet* (1984) and the *String Trio* (1986). Both are remarkable for the ambition and complexity of their formal design. They also represent a culmination of certain formal and expressive tendencies in Finnissy's development. The *String Quartet* is a twenty minute work, divided into several sections and played without a break, drawing on techniques from every area of Finnissy's instrumental music. The overall sound-world reflects the influence of folk music, which had by now become an integral part of Finnissy's expressive vocabulary. Constricted melodic lines in quartertones, with a compass of a minor third or less, are contrasted with explosions of more chromatic material. Each new section is characterised by a new notational layout offering divergent formal perspectives. The opening section remains in the upper register for the entire quartet for some fifteen pages. To begin with the music is notated with a fluctuating tempo and no bar lines, the instruments being synchronised by a system of cues reminiscent of that used in *Afar*.

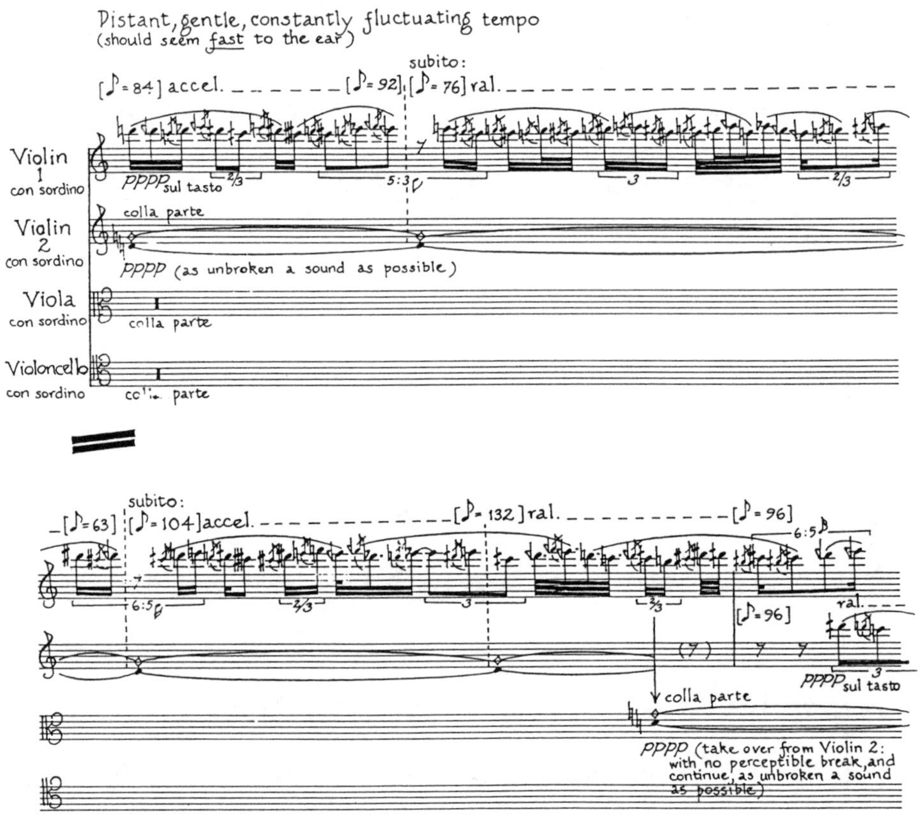

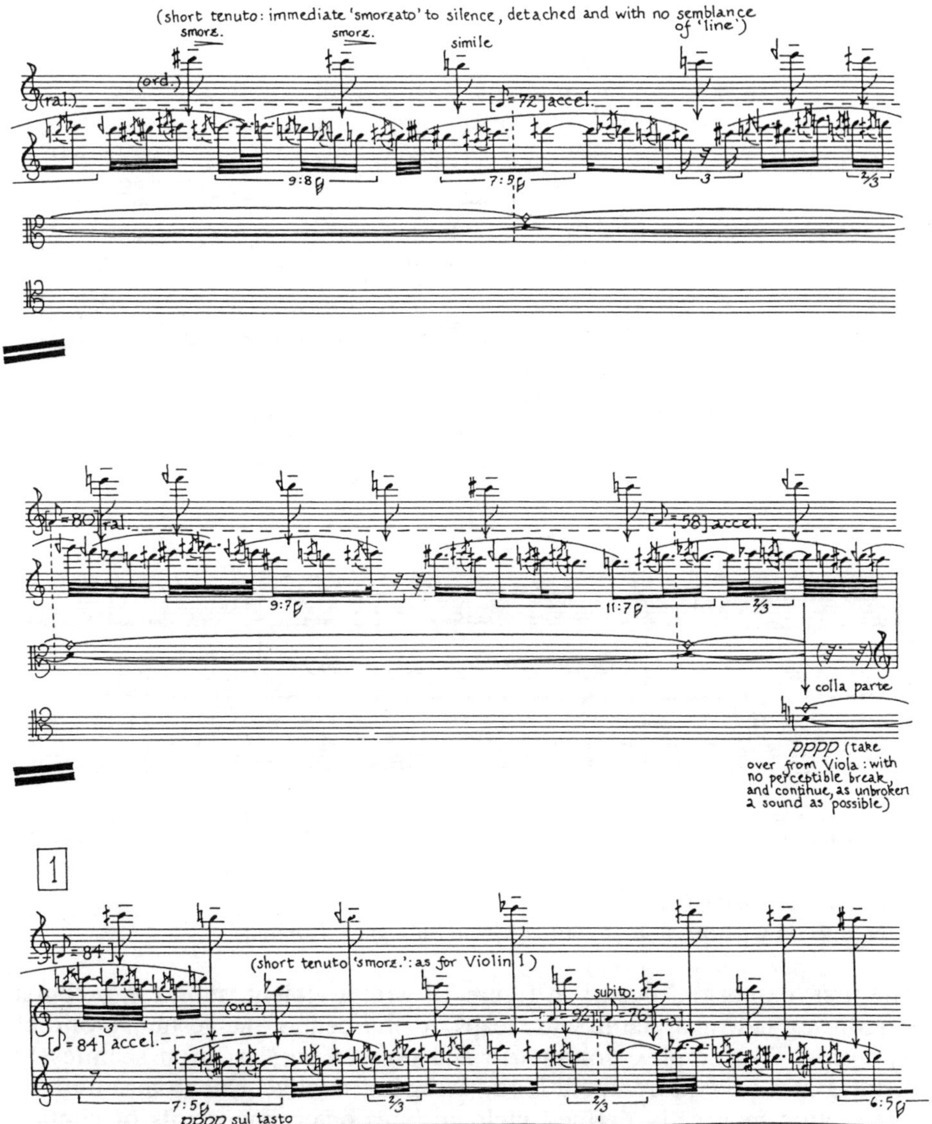

Example 3.25 *String Quartet*
Reproduced by permission of United Music Publishers Limited

By figure 2 a system of bracketed time signatures is introduced, momentarily bringing a feeling of relative temporal stability, articulated by regular figures in the first violin (eighth and sixteenth notes) and viola (7:6 subdivisions). Against this, however, are set free rhythms in the second violin and cello, who are instructed to play 'in an unpredictably irregular rhythm':

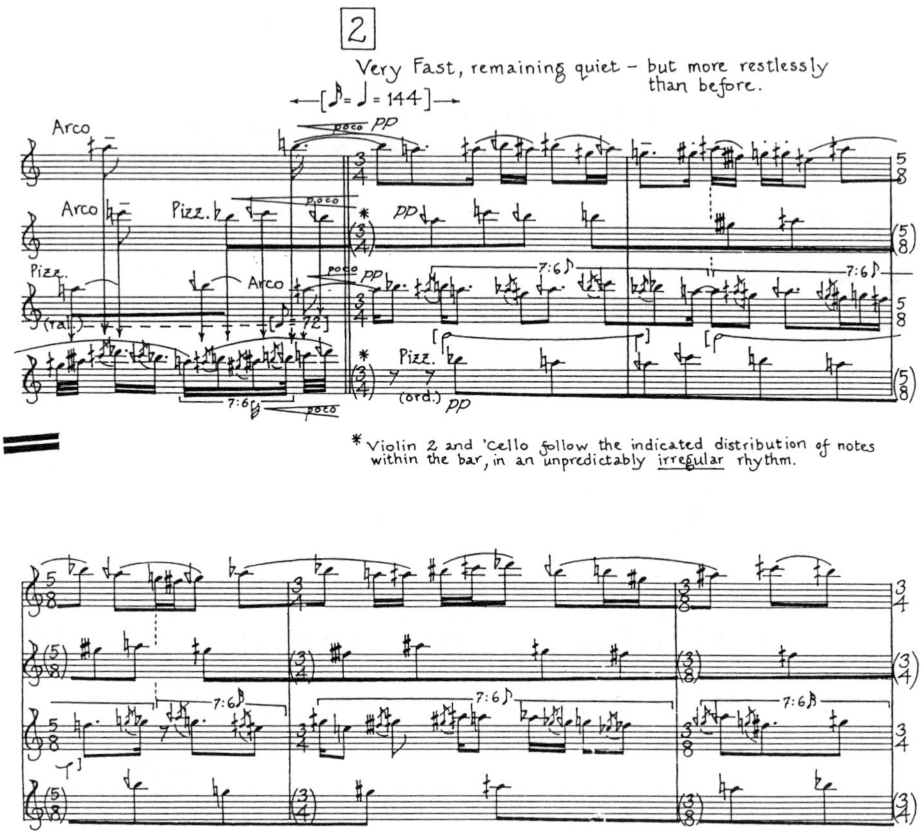

Example 3.26 *String Quartet*, p. 4
Reproduced by permission of United Music Publishers Limited

The first 'explosion' occurs at figure 18 with a violent, subito *ff*, outburst introducing new material in wide leaps, reminiscent of the gestural world of *Alongside*. A complex polymetric and polytemporal section seamlessly disintegrates once more into a long passage of relative synchronisation. In this section metrically defined melodic lines determine points of contact between the other instruments in an accumulation of trills, later developing into freely spaced groups of grace notes.

The *String Quartet* is the culmination of twenty years of musical thought, technique and experience in an explosion of inventiveness and sheer musical exuberance. The early explorations of spatial and metrically complex notation, stratification of temporal levels, wide-leaping gestural figurations and extended instrumental possibilities are successfully brought into a fruitful relationship with the constricted microtonal lines, superimposition and juxtaposition of textures and formal blocks of the more recent works, to form a fully integrated musical language.

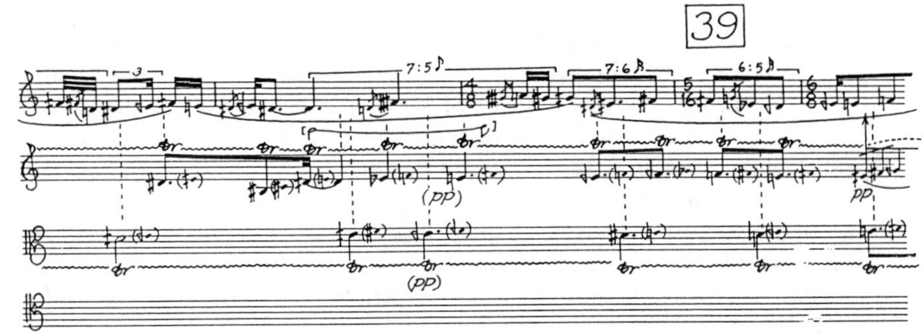

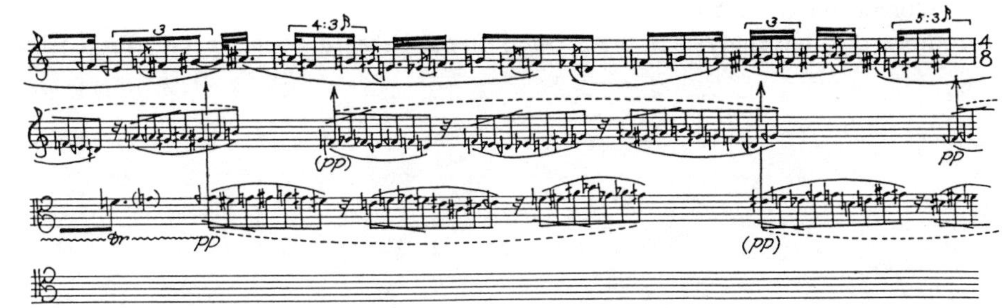

Example 3.27 *String Quartet*, p. 29
Reproduced by permission of United Music Publishers Limited

The *String Trio* is no less an achievement. Played without a break it consists of five main sections, divided into a further 28 sub-sections and lasts half an hour. The starting point for the music is Mahler's Ninth Symphony, reflected at a number of levels within the structure of the music. The tempo markings for the 28 sub-sections are Italian translations of the original German markings in the first movement of the Mahler symphony. More significantly, the opening minor third of the symphony is used in various ways throughout the *Trio* as a structural determinant, while the opening nine notes of the Mahler provide Finnissy with a series of drones which provide important points of harmonic and melodic reference throughout the *Trio*.[8] The intimate and expressive world of this work is unequalled in Finnissy's output; it is chamber music of the highest order, executed with all the integrity, sensitivity, artistic and spiritual insight that distinguish its composer.

Notes

1. The term first found widespread circulation in the late 1980s, in the wake of Richard Toop's article, 'Four Facts of the "New Complexity"', in Contact 32.
2. See the section entitled 'Notation and Transcription', in the fourth part of Busoni's 'Sketch of a New Esthetic of Music', anthologised in *Three Classics in the Aesthetic of Music*, Dover, New York, 1962, p. 85. Busoni first published the essay in 1911.
3. Richard Toop, op. cit.
4. The other notable example for chamber ensemble is *Nowhere else to go* (1989), which extends Finnissy's use of electronics into the instrumental domain itself with the use of a synthesiser alongside clarinet, trumpet, percussion and cello.
5. Richard Toop, op. cit.
6. Ibid.
7. Finnissy created more chamber music with similar processes in the five *Obrecht Motetten* (variously composed between 1988 and 1992) and *In stiller Nacht* (1990), which transform and integrate the music of, respectively, Obrecht and Brahms.
8. For a detailed analysis of the *String Trio* see Richard Toop, op. cit., pp. 15-18.

CHAPTER FOUR

The Orchestral Music

Julian Anderson

In the minds of many people, the name of Michael Finnissy has long been inextricably associated with his large output of music for solo piano, as well as his multifariously scored chamber pieces. We have had ample chance to sample the piano writing under the able hands of the composer himself and increasingly through the advocacy of a number of fine young pianists such as James Clapperton, Rolf Hind, Nicolas Hodges, Joanna MacGregor, Ian Pace and Jonathan Powell. The chamber works have found their way into the repertoires of many new music groups around the world and in this country by ensembles such as Music Projects/London, Exposé, Ixion and the Cambridge New Music Players. But since few orchestras have tackled them, Finnissy's orchestral pieces have not been properly assessed; relatively few people are aware that some of his most beautiful and personal music is actually for large orchestra. It is also remarkable that in an output totalling over two hundred works, only five are for full orchestra. Whatever the reasons for this - and they may reflect economic circumstances as much as personal choice - it remains a curious fact in an output which is not lacking in works written simply from personal need, rather than in response to a commission. By virtue of their scarcity, then, Finnissy's orchestral pieces are special cases, particular and exceptional instances which have demanded and found a variety of musical utterance quite distinct from his other work.

The scarcity of Finnissy's orchestral music is all the more surprising in view of an astonishing piece of juvenilia, rather soberly entitled *Symphony No. 1* (1962-64), which reveals an imagination eager to get to grips with orchestral writing. The innocuous title leads one to expect some mild essay in late-romantic tonal style such as many a sixteen-year-old might have penned around 1962. Not a bit of it: this is a wild, unashamedly sprawling conception, revelling in discontinuity of texture and in harmonic and melodic fragmentation, wilfully disregarding any notions of conventional symphonic form. It has three movements rather than four, with no semblance of conventional formal procedures in them, and uses a harmonic system incorporating twelfth-tones! Astonishingly, many aspects of Finnissy's mature manner are present in this remarkable document. On a purely visual level, the immaculately detailed calligraphy, for which the composer's scores are justly celebrated, is already in startling evidence. Another prominent feature of his early music, which was to remain sporadically characteristic until the end of the seventies, is the juxtaposition of long, tensely static areas - often of long held chords in the extreme bass - with abrupt explosions of scarcely controlled violence, volatile polyrhythmic bundles articulated in great leaps across the entire instrumental range. Readers acquainted with such works as the untitled flute piece written to honour Stravinsky's eighty-fifth birthday, the ensemble pieces *Afar* and *As when upon a trancèd summer night*, the piano piece *Autumnall* (all composed in the late sixties) or indeed *Pathways of Sun and Stars* for large ensemble (1976) will easily recognise their alternation of bursts of activity and stasis in Example 4.1, the opening of the Symphony's last movement (the music is notated in irregular bar-lengths, without time-signatures):

Example 4.1 *Symphony No. 1*

The scoring or the work is as unusual as its musical content. The orchestra is large and strangely constituted: four flutes (all doubling piccolos); four oboes (the last doubling cor anglais); three clarinets (last doubling bass); four bassoons; eight horns and five trombones (but no trumpets); two harps; an odd assortment of tuned percussion - tubular bells, glockenspiel and no fewer than ten timpani (played by five drummers); a guitar, an organ, and a string section without violins. In addition to the main band there are four solo instruments - viola, cello, contrabassoon and a contralto voice - who make sporadic entrances throughout the work, the latter singing extracts from the Fitzgerald/Omar Khayyam *Rubaiyat* and Milton's 'The Passion'. The omissions from the orchestral palette seem as conscious and significant as the chosen forces. The absence of two of the most obviously brilliant and rhetorical sections of the orchestra (trumpets and violins) gives the music a more subtle, agile and jagged sound-world, dominated by the near-expressionist insistence on registral extremes and sharpness of timbre: the fleeting shrillness of piccolos, oboes and high clarinets playing off sombre interventions of the organ, timpani, contrabassoon and divided doublebasses. Such ruthlessly sharp handling of register and timbre has remained characteristic of Finnissy: the scoring of *Red Earth* exemplifies similarly telling restrictions of sound palette.

Although he looks back on it with a certain affection, the composer is the first to admit that his aims in this extraordinarily precocious early attempt were not satisfactorily realised. Several practical problems arise: the multiple leaps onto twelfth-tones, often at great speed and across many octaves in close succession in the string writing, exceed playability even today. Then too, the fifteen-year-old Finnissy - entirely untutored in composition, we should remember, and lacking any practical experience with a real orchestra - assumed that orchestras would have fully chromatic Erard harps at their disposal and wrote for two of them. The organ registration is somewhat eccentric, and the timpani occasionally descend to notes far below those available even on the largest instruments. All of these factors would mitigate against a performance today, let alone in the early sixties. This is a shame for the symphony provides a vivid window into the mind of the teenage Finnissy, and a good deal more besides. But quite specific instrumental textures discovered in this symphony were to re-appear, unconsciously reworked with the hindsight of maturity, when Finnissy finally began to compose for orchestra in the late seventies. The random sprays of woodwind staccati in the symphony's first movement, the long doublebass pedal-tones and the sharp punctuating thuds on timpani, trombones and basses in the second, and especially the remote, almost alienated stillness of the final bar (a sustained cluster of doublebass harmonics and a tremolo on a bell) are all directly parallel with passages in *Offshore* and *Sea and Sky*.

One might well wonder how a composer still in his teens could conceive, let alone notate, such a score. Finnissy's secondary education was fortunate in a number of respects, and provides us with the beginnings of an explanation. He remembers with especial gratitude the luck of having an unusually enlightened English teacher at grammar school named Alan Brownjohn, later to enjoy fame as a poet. Brownjohn seems to have encouraged his pupils to question norms and assumptions, whether artistic, social or psychological, as much as possible. He believed that there should be no separation between life and art, that art should not exist in a social vacuum, and insisted that his pupils explore many unusual areas of political and literary thought. His classes were weaned on far more than the usual diet of Herrick, Thackerary and Walter de la Mare: he gave them the writings of Henry Miller, Mario Praz and Artaud to chew over (still favourites with Finnissy). He also encouraged the students to explore the London theatre and film scenes, then enjoying something of a golden age (Finnissy joined the National Film Theatre in his early teens by lying about his age!). Finnissy vividly remembers attending[1] Theatre-of-Cruelty-style performances of Artaud and of Genet's *The Screens*, as well as the early concerts of Pierre Boulez with the BBC and of AMM with Cornelius Cardew (Finnissy was later an enthusiastic supporter of the Scratch Orchestra's manifestations). Other formative experiences from the early sixties include a performance under Stokowski of Mahler's Second Symphony (then rarely heard) at the Proms, and first encounters with *Die Reihe* as well as scores by Kagel, Stockhausen and Bussotti in the showroom of Universal Edition. All of this radicalised Finnissy's view of the creative act and pushed him towards a view of music as an integral part of life and philosophy.

The texts of the symphony are another symptom of Finnissy's early literary enthusiasms. There are three: two sung by the contralto solo in the first and third movements, the other an inscription at the head of the central movement. All three are distinctly melancholic, bleak, and even confessional in tone, clue-giving devices to the emotional world of the music, and perhaps of much of Finnissy's mature work until the mid-seventies, too. The final quotation, from Milton, reads:

> Mine eye hath found that sad sepulchral rock
> That was the casket of heaven's richest store,
> And here thro' grief my feeble hand up lock,
> Yet on the softened quarry would I score
> My plaining verses...

This set the tone of things to come: in future Finnissy would view his art - in the lineage of, amongst others, William Blake, Charles Ives, Percy Grainger and Michael Tippett - as essentially confessional, personal and self-revelatory. He has always felt close to such figures (another more recent affinity has been with the poetry, visions and music of Hildegard von Bingen), who confront extremes of personal vision and attempt to integrate the 'entire range of experience without excluding anything'.[2] This all-inclusive attitude applies not only to the subject matter of his works, but surely to his exuberant multi-layered textures: a passage such as the concluding outburst of *Sea and Sky*, with fortissimo double-tonguing trumpets, suspended cymbals and piercingly high woodwind to the fore, is fully characteristic of a mind that refuses to hold back or curtail the dictates of its imagination.

Finnissy's first mature orchestral music was written without commission in the mid seventies. It was prompted by a perceptive remark of an early champion of Finnissy's work, the Belgian critic Harry Halbreich, who expressed surprise that, given the flair for controlling and timing rich instrumental textures vividly demonstrated in much of his work at the time (notably the cantata *World* from 1975), Finnissy had never written for orchestra. This remark seems to have struck home for the same year Finnissy began work on *Offshore*, an elegant and fastidious ten minute orchestral tone-poem completed in 1976. Unlike the early symphony, this is scored for standard orchestra: triple woodwind, four horns, three each of trumpets and trombones, tuba, three percussion, two harps, harpsichord, piano and strings. Beneath this apparent 'normality', Finnissy displays idiosyncratic taste in the matter of doublings: there are three cor anglais (two played by the oboists in addition to the standard one), only one bassoon but two contrabassoons, two D-trumpets and only one in C, and two bass trombones with a single tenor. The percussion section - restrained when one remembers many of the more extravagant demands made on this department in much music from the seventies - focuses largely upon high instruments giving grainy, shimmering sonorities rich in unpredictable internal change: maracas, bamboo chimes, tambourine, castanets, suspended cymbals. All of this is symptomatic of a desire to get away from the middle register and strengthen the extremes of high and low, giving a more personally characterised, sharply colourful orchestral sonority. Indeed listening to this work, it is difficult to remember that the composer had still to hear any of his own orchestral writing (and would not for another four years!). *Offshore* sounds remarkably fluent and completely self-confident, and its notation - making elegant but not irresponsible use of space-time and rhythmically free writing alongside the intricate detail of Finnissy's mensural rhythms - exhibits a sense of practicality in the face of the norms of orchestral life, without any stylistic compromise on Finnissy's part.[3] Indeed, at the work's first performance in 1982, when Oliver Knussen brought it to light in the Philharmonia Orchestra's invaluable 'Music of Today' series, it proved eminently amenable to performance on a tight rehearsal schedule (each concert in the series was rehearsed throughout a day and performed the same evening).

Although completed in Eastbourne, *Offshore* is not a seascape. It was composed immediately following the break-up of a relationship and the composer says the trauma of that experience is not unrelated to the encroaching sense of isolation and emotional alienation which is such an unnerving feature of the music and which gave rise to the work's title. It opens with a frenetic buzz of *scherzando* material on strings and percussion, and initially presents an attractively buoyant musical manner. The *scherzando* style is very gradually overtaken by almost glacially calm sustained pitches - at first pedal notes, later dense chords, mainly on the strings - which progressively subdue all other material, stifling the piece into complete silence. The piece unfolds continuously as a succession of more or less contrasted musical panels, each made up of several layers of activity which evolve quite independently of one another in complex juxtapositions. Each layer is quite distinctly orchestrated, and there is no doubling of individual parts, so the layers retain their highly distinctive characters throughout the work. The contents of each layer are as follows:

1. High quasi-random skittering on violins.
2. Very low rumbling (tremolo doublebasses, etc).
3. Short punctuations: a) fluttertongue *crescendi* on 3 flutes and 3 stopped horns; b) cluster-like low doublebass pizzicati.
4. Randomly nested rapid pitch groups (*staccato* or *legato*) on woodwind and brass.
5. Dense explosions of clusters, filigree and glissandi on harps, harpsichord and piano.
6. Lyrical counterpoint on woodwind trios.
7. Sustained single pitches on woodwind or brass.
8. Loud, dense brass or wind chords (medium length).
9. Extremely long-held chords (almost always strings).

Each of these nine layers may also be considered according to its contribution towards one of three fundamental gestural categories from which the music is built: texture, chord and line. Texture - shifting masses of sounds, rather than individually perceived events - is focused on in layers 2, 4 and 5; chords are the principal medium of layers 3, 8, and 9; whilst lines are provided in greater or lesser profusion by layer 1 (dense), layer 6 (thinner) and layer 7 (minimum).

In addition to these nine layers, the three percussionists have a quite independent set of seven rhythmically free mobiles which intervene, regardless of their surroundings, sporadically throughout the piece (there is some evidence from the surviving sketches that these were added to the music just before the fair copy). The effect is startling and quite unusual in Finnissy's output: the percussionists seem like complete strangers to the main musical action, and remain wholly oblivious of it until the substantial coda, where they complement the immobile string chords with occasional trills, bringing *Offshore* to a hushed close.

The layers can be further distinguished by virtue of their changing functions through the work. Some are by their nature elaborate and declamatory, dominating a texture without difficulty. Layers 1, 4, and 6 are good examples: all are typical of material derived from the application of random numbers. Here the random numbers are applied to varying widths of pitch-band: high are relatively narrow in the case of layer 1, more wide-ranging in the case of the floating melodic lines of layer 6, and widest of all in the agitated flourishes of layer 4, the most openly volatile and violent material in the work. These three dominating layers are heard successively, never simultaneously as they would cancel each other out: neither layer 1 nor 4 would be audible beneath a typical outburst of 6, and 1 and 4 would make little sense played together.

Other material is clearly of a normally accompanimental nature, but that does not mean it is used that way in the music. Neither the brief punctuations of layer 3a, the subliminal hum of layer 2, nor indeed the long-held pitches characteristic of layers 7 and 9 are natural candidates for foreground elaboration, as they consist of fairly steady musical states with minimal overall change. At times, Finnissy respects this: the opening of the work, for instance, presents layer 1 (plus the first percussion mobile) for our attention, with no. 2 in a more or less background role underneath the music. Three bars before figure 1, layer 3a enters (the percussion having fallen silent). The three layers then combine to form an almost 'normal' orchestral texture (see Example 4.2): foreground in the highest register and the most prominent timbre (violins), middleground punctuation in the middle register with a more neutral timbre (horns, flutes) and background in the extreme bass. A few bars later the first glimmer of layer 7, also seemingly 'background' music, joins them in the form of a sustained G on the E flat clarinet (later cor anglais). Finnissy tricks us here: we have just become accustomed to this textural counterpoint when the violins cut off abruptly (p.4 of the score) leaving the backgrounds to carry on by themselves. The flute/horn punctuation recurs, now punctuating nothing and therefore assuming quite unexpected prominence, whilst the textural void allows the ear to focus upon both the high cor anglais G and the omnipresent doublebass glissandi for the first time. Such unexpected 'zooming' effects, playing upon or subverting our preconceptions of the roles of 'foreground' articulation and background accompaniment occur fairly constantly throughout the work. The result is frequently - as in the instant just outlined - a Brechtian *Verfremdungseffekt*, a musical alienation posing immediate questions as to the progress of the music, and indeed its purpose.

The most dramatic such effect is the gradual replacement of fast, florid activity by the motionless string chords mentioned earlier. This 'freezing' process is subtly composed into the piece, avoiding over-predictability yet clear enough to prevent a sense of arbitrarily blocked juxtapositions. The following summary of the work's form and the behaviour of the layers within it will illustrate this (note: Fig. 1 (-3) means three bars before Figure 1 in the score, and Fig. 1 (+4) means four bars after Figure 4).

Opening to Fig. 1 (-3)
Layers 1 and 2
Percussion Mobile 1 (medium length)
Fig. 1 (-3) to Fig. 1 (+4)
Layers 1, 2 and 3a
(just before end): *Percussion Mobile 2* (short)
Fig. 1(+4) to Fig. 2
Layers 2, 3a and 7
Fig. 2
Layers 2, 3a, and 6 (3 cor anglais)
(later) *Percussion Mobile 3* (start)

Fig. 3
Layers 2, 7 (strings), and 8 (1 chord)
Percussion Mobile 3 (end)
(later): Layer 4 (low brass and wind, then high wind)
Fig. 4
Layers 5 (short) and 9 (v. long, doublebasses only)
Percussion Mobile 4 (v. long)
Fig. 5
Layer 9 (1 cello, doublebasses, *sub ppp*)
Fig. 6
Layers 4 (wind, brass, v. short), 5, 9 (cello, basses, later violin harmonics)
Percussion Mobile 5 (medium)
Fig. 7
Layer 9 (violins, and violas, harmonics) dissolves to:
Fig. 7 (+5)
Layer 1 (short)
Fig. 8
Layers 4 and 9 (strings, fades)
(later) Layer 8 (1 chord)
Percussion Mobile 6 (short)
Fig. 8(+4)
Layers 4, 5 and 9 (double basses and trombones)
Fig. 9(+2) through 10
Layers 1 (strings), 4 (woodwind), 5 (harpsichord clusters), 7 (woodwind)
9 (trombones, cellos and basses) (later Layer 5 briefly on all instruments)
(Layer 3b at end, single pizz)
Fig. 10(+5)
Layers 3b (single pizz), 4 (longest and most violent occurrences, all brass) and layer 9 (violins, cellos)
Fig. 11(-1)
Layers 3b (single pizz), 4 (single flourish on flutes), 5 (single flourish) and 9 (densely spaced violin and viola harmonics; at 11(+3); this layer transfers entirely to wind and brass for the only time in the work)
Percussion Mobile 7 (longest and loudest)
Fig. 12
Layers 4 (bass clarinet, brief), 6 (3 cor anglais, bassoon and 2 contras)
and 9 (doublebasses)
(*percussion trills accompaniment*)
Fig. 12(+3) to end - CODA
Layer 9 (all strings)
(*percussion trills*)
ENDS

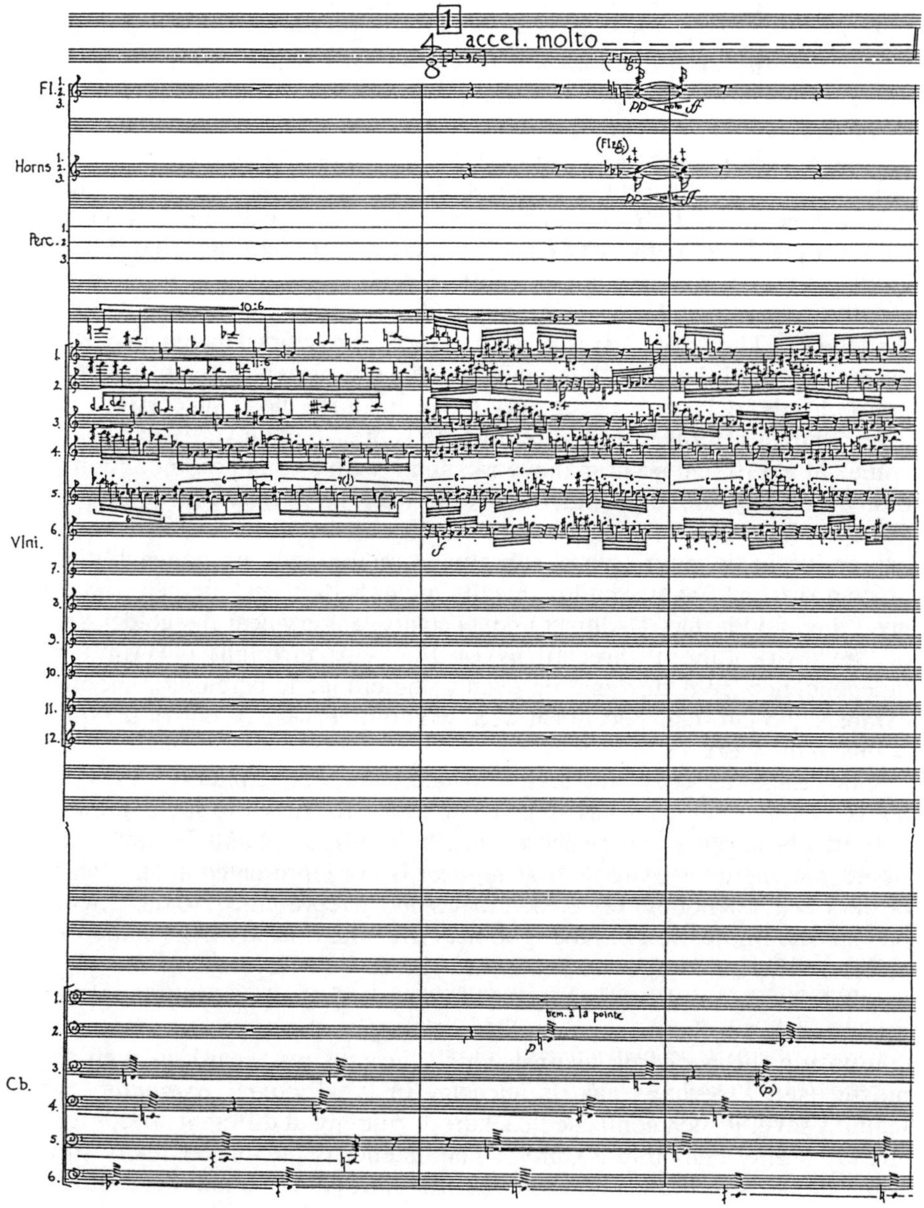

Example 4.2 *Offshore*, p. 3

The boundaries between layers become rather more fluid as the work progresses. The clearest instance is the long, complex texture beginning at Fig. 9(+2), of which Example 4.3 shows an extract. It will be noticed that several instrumental families are assigned more than one layer simultaneously (see form summary). The wind for example play both layers 4 and 7, combining them within single phrases which alternate layer 4's random flourishes with layer 7's single notes. Layer 1 on violins also briefly incorporates this new combination into its own characteristic figuration, so that the overall texture moves towards some sort of homogeneity.

It will be evident from the plan outlined above that layer 9 is by far the most persistent of all. Once it has made its appearance at Fig. 4, it remains a constant presence, with just one short interruption, until the very end of the work. As the other textures die off irregularly, it asserts its dominance steadily. Even the otherwise unintegrated percussion are subsumed into it by the coda. The violin music with which the work opens also returns throughout until the coda, but many layers have a briefer life-span: the dense brass chords of layer 8 occur only twice in fairly close succession, whilst layer 2 never returns after figure 3 in the score. Each layer reaches its own climax at a different point in the work, and it is this counterpoint of climaxes, rather than any single one, that gives the work its elusive formal properties. Thus layer 1 starts the work with its climax, its fullest and most florid expression in the entire work; subsequent recurrences are noticeably muted by comparison. Layer 9 builds steadily towards its climax in the coda, whilst layer 4 explodes into its climax unexpectedly, at very near the golden section of the work (about three-fifths of the way through). With typical independence from surrounding events, the climactic percussion mobile, on cymbals and tam-tams, occurs at what would otherwise be one of the quietest points in the work.

One crucial aspect of the texture which cannot be explicitly shown in the above plan is Finnissy's bass-register writing. Suffice it to say that there are only two brief places in the score - just before figure 4 and for seven bars at figure 7 - where the extreme bass register is not represented at all. For most of the work it is not merely present but heavily represented, to the extent that one has the impression of having to hear the other music across some variety of low, albeit distant, bass humming (be it from layers 2 or 9). This is another device for alienation, a sort of composed aural screen through which the music has to be perceived. The ancestry of this type of orchestration - composing the backdrop against which the music is heard, as well as the music itself - perhaps has its ancestry in Ives' *Fourth Symphony* which features several such composed backdrops running at different speeds against already highly elaborate textures. The listener is thus never really sure, in either the Ives or Finnissy, where the true musical argument lies, as there is always something else to listen to behind the 'main' music being presented.[4]

Example 4.3 *Offshore*

Finnissy had still not heard any of his own orchestration when the London Philharmonic commissioned a large orchestral piece from him in 1978 (*Offshore* was not to be heard for another four years). But it will come as no surprise after the fluency of *Offshore* to see Finnissy building on the achievements of that earlier work and writing for large orchestra with complete confidence and originality. *Sea and Sky*, completed in 1980, shares a number of things in common with other Finnissy works of this period, a period which in retrospect appears an unusual one in Finnissy's output. Finnissy is well known for his readiness to engage explicitly with other music in composing his own, a readiness often amounting to an actual need. His love of folk and traditional musics, his enthusiasm for Handel, Fauré, Verdi, Gershwin, plainsong, Shaker hymns and much else besides have all found prominent expression in major works. Yet it was as a composer of large abstract canvases that Finnissy earned his reputation in the late seventies, most obviously with the ensemble piece *Alongside* (1979) and the present orchestral work. These do not make such explicit use of other music or musical traditions either as source material or as textural/emotional metaphors for the music, and they come closest in this regard to the norms of central European modernist abstractionism. In this respect, if no other, they also come closer in spirit to the work of Ferneyhough than any other Finnissy work, since Finnissy's readiness to paraphrase and recompose other musics is one of the main dividing lines (technical details and emotional differences are others) between his musical world and that of his colleague, with whom he used to be rather fruitlessly grouped. It is interesting to observe that many Finnissy enthusiasts are divided in their opinion of this period: some believe it to contain the composer's finest works,[5] others consider the very lack of extraneous references a weakness in the pieces.[6] The present writer thus feels a bit isolated in enjoying both these works and the less abstract ones.

Like *Offshore* and *Alongside* (to which it is in some ways the orchestral pendant), *Sea and Sky* works primarily with textural and gestural considerations: the modal melodic writing later to be featured in *Eph-phatha* and also present in distorted, microtonal form in *Red Earth* was not yet such an obviously prominent feature in Finnissy's style. That said, the present work can be seen as a journey towards the establishment of a single independent melodic line, followed by its reabsorption into the considerable textural forces that surround it. The work is built upon the confrontation of three fundamental textural types, emphasising respectively the basic categories of *LINE-CHORD-PUNCTUATION*. Generally speaking, these three categories have carefully defined roles throughout the piece which are dependent to a large extent on their ability to hold attention: lines are generally foreground melodic figuration; chords occupy the textural middle-ground; whilst punctuation - percussion strokes or simple blocks chords - is usually background. But by now, the reader will expect Finnissy to question these roles as much as to accept them passively, and such indeed proves the case: each category is given a chance to act as the foreground to a segment of musical time, and to shift in relation to its fellows.

As already stated, melodic foregrounds are the most common of all. The opening and closing pages each present networks of linear foregrounds. In the former instance, nine high wind parts tussle at a variety of speeds within the highest two octaves of the orchestra (incorporating quartertones); in the latter, four trumpets take exuberant random walks in their highest octave (later descending from, then ascending back to this register). The central tutti of the work features a melodic foreground of two heterophonic celesta parts, with many complementary melodic backgrounds (most noticeably a mellifluous horn quartet). The melodic highpoint of the work is a wonderfully extravagant, almost uncontrolledly wide-spanning solo break for clarinet, whose manic energy and verve is reminiscent of such free-jazz clarinettists as the Frenchman Michel Portal. Chords come to the fore in the preceding section, an extremely low chorale for mixed wind and strings which is dealt with in detail below. Two sections highlight punctuation: the first (from page 13 to page 16 of the score) features series of very loud punctuations on the whip, dominating a lengthy section otherwise scored exclusively for the lower instruments in the orchestra. Punctuation - this time in the form of very loud, sharp chords on the lowest brass - comes to the fore again after the clarinet solo has run its course; it is a moment quite similar to *Offshore* - a principal textural element suddenly disappears, leaving what was obviously designed as 'background' material to assume the limelight.

Unlike *Offshore*, there are no fixed manifestations of these phenomena, no fixed set of layers which return through the piece. On the contrary, the work eschews reminiscence and repetition altogether, unfolding in a single dramatic arc of music which has a direct, goal-oriented character unusual in Finnissy's oeuvre.

The inspiration for the work was a watercolour sketch by Turner bearing the same name, a strikingly elemental creation consisting of just two large slabs of scarcely differentiated bluish colour. The representational aspect of the sketch is minimally discernible in the stark confrontation between the two large forms. In Finnissy's work, this is translated into a confrontation between the high and low registers of the orchestra. Much of the piece evolves at the extremes of either register, separately or together, filling in the rest of the sound space steadily right up to the end of the work, where the middle register finally establishes pre-eminence in the form of sustained cymbal rolls.

Writing for large orchestra for the first time, Finnissy planned out a clear sequence of textures of varying sizes of orchestral ensemble, ranging from 5 players to the full compliment of 81, with three tutti sections and a single instrumental solo acting as focal point. The proportions of *Sea and Sky* are determined by the Fibonacci series - the only time that Finnissy has made use of this series in composing.[7] The manner in which the proportional constituents of this series interact with the finished work is fascinatingly ambiguous. Finnissy's initial intention was that it would determine a gradual slowing of events, but his realisation of the work contradicted this plan:

Section no.	**No. of insts.**	**Features**	**Duration**	**Proportion**
1	13	High w.w.	25’	1
2	25	Vns, timps.	25’	1
3	30	Low w.w.	50’	2
4	30	Tuba entry	75’	3
5	10 (later more)	Very low inst.	2’ 05”	5
6	81	Tutti, cel duet	3’ 20”	8
7	18	a) Fls, cel, pizz	1’ 00”)	
	72	b) Tutti chords	4’ 15”) 5’ 15”*	13
8	51	a) Clarinet	4’ 10”)	
	77	b) Tutti	4’ 15”) 8’ 25”*	21

* indicates durations shorter than they should be in strict proportion: the correct reading would be 5’ 25” and 8’ 45’ respectively.

Diagram 4.1 Fibonacci proportions in *Sea and Sky*

Finnissy uses the first few proportions to introduce and develop music in the bass register, as a complement to the extremely high wind shrieks with which the work opens. The bass is introduced with a low tremolo on timpani, followed by the two bass clarinets, two bassoons and contrabassoon. The addition of the strongly accented entry of the tuba (section 4) results in a bass texture whose prominence is equal to that of the high music on wind, and a large ensemble of brass instruments occupy the whole of section 5. Finally all registers combine in the first tutti of the piece, a dense yet delicate texture with a total of 81 separate parts in many superimposed layers.

Thus far the unfolding of events has followed the Fibonacci series in a fairly literal manner. As the sections increase in duration, however, they acquire more and more subsections, so that the listener’s appreciation of the underlying Fibonacci scheme is progressively blurred. Thus the last two sections are rather curiously divided into two parts each, but since the textural and registral contrasts between all of these four parts is considerable, the effect on the listener is of (at least) four different sections following each other at almost regular intervals. The composer’s sketches unambiguously refer to the music between pp. 33 and 38 - section 7 above - as linked subsections filling out a single duration of 5’ 25”. Yet the entry of sections 7b - the second tutti in the work, introducing dense string chords quite unlike anything heard earlier - creates a far greater contrast than that between section 7a and section 6. The contrast between the two final subsections is greater still as the free-jazz break for the lead clarinet is followed by the ferocity of the final tutti with its four concertante trumpet parts. In other words, the Fibonacci proportions are a compositional enabling device, a guideline, for the timing of events which the composer has no hesitation in enriching or even ignoring altogether as his musical needs demand.

For this reason, the above proportions - whilst numerically intriguing - are not an entirely accurate reflection of the music as heard and we shall need to draw up another, quite different, diagram to deal with that. Not shown above, yet just as important to the audible effect of the music, are the textures common to adjacent sections. In general, as the work progresses the music grows in diversity, finally eschewing common material between subsections. This means that the opening 'sections' 1-4 above are likely to be heard as a single larger stretch of music. The addition of numerous transitions and cross-fades render things more complex still, so that the heard form of the work might be closer to the following (the remaining analysis of *Sea and Sky* will follow the section numbering of this second diagram):

Section no.	**Registers**	**Textures**	**Duration**
1	High	w.w. gliss, vls, untuned drums	2' 30"
	Low	Timps, low w.w. and brass	
2	V. low	All low instruments in the orchestra	2' 05"
3	All	Tutti with celesta duet; later thins	4' 20"
4	All	Tutti ('chord exchange' with pebbles)	4' 15"
5	High	Clarinet solo, untuned drums	3' 15"
	Low	Brass, bass drums	
Transition	Low	Building up from bass to	0' 55"
7	All	Tutti with trumpets and cymbals	4' 15'
	Middle	Thins to end (cymbals)	

Diagram 4.2 Alternative form for *Sea and Sky*

Given the paramount importance of texture, density and register in *Sea and Sky*, it comes as no surprise to find from the sketches that many of the more specific details were again determined with the aid of the Moses and Oakford random number tables.[8] First, the range of each instrumental register is decided according to the textural context, and that range divided into either semitones or quartertones. Each pitch is then assigned to a number, and the results read off so that, as a rule, the combination of parts fills out the tessitura concerned without undue emphasis on any individual pitch. Random numbers are also involved in the ordering of rhythmic material. For example, the dramatic interventions on tom-toms between pages 3 and 12 were derived by cutting up a rhythmic sequence (a Boulezian cellular transformation of simple rhythmic cells) into nine discrete segments and reading them in random order, so that the processual feeling of the original sequence is intentionally destroyed and replaced by something much more unpredictable.

Perhaps the most novel technical aspect of the work is its highly personal use of harmonic progression to underpin sections. This is a paradoxical feature of the music, as the chords involved are frequently dense and multi-voiced, deliberately hovering on the border between audible harmonic progression and pure texture. The final tutti (section 7) is a case in point. The dominant sonority is the quartet of ferociously high, double-tonguing trumpets, yet underlying the section and determining its length is a sequence of nine 46-part string chords which, on closer examination, appear to unfold a surprisingly simple series of conjunct voice-leadings. The sheer density, however, prevents any easy discernment of this progression, in context, of course; they sound rather as a static accompaniment, obscured by much louder and more hectic activity elsewhere in the orchestra. The fourth section - marked 'chord exchange' in Diagram 4.2, and named thus in the composer's sketches - offers the nearest resemblance to clear harmonic progression in the whole work. It, too, is underpinned by a slow chorale, but here the chords are far thinner - there are seventeen voices in all - and the overall texture much more transparent. There are two sets of seventeen-part chords played in slow exchange between two mixed groups of instruments: the first consists of 4 horns, tuba, 8 violins and 4 celli; the second features 2 bass clarinets, 4 trumpets, 3 trombones, 4 violas and 4 doublebasses. The progression is shown in Example 4.4, adapted from the composer's sketches. The mixed orchestration and the slow pacing of the harmonic sequence together conspire to make the appearance of each fresh chord a distinct auditory event with its own colour and sonority, whilst maintaining the glacial calm of the section as a whole. Interestingly, the composer says that in *Sea and Sky* such vertical phenomena, like the massive wind and brass chords in *Offshore,* were determined by instinct and ear alone; they are not the product of any predetermined system.

An impressive feature of this score is the ease with which the composer manipulates and transforms every facet of his chosen materials. Particularly noteworthy, and quite without precedent in Finnissy's output, is the degree of sheer spontaneous and lively variation in the details of each type of music. The music abounds in constants which define each section, and each layer within that section: a set of instruments or instrumental registers, a range of speeds, a type of articulation, an average frequency of occurrence. Thanks to the random numbers, these features exhibit an astonishingly rich, non-repetitious range of behaviour which makes for constantly varied and surprising listening. The two sections highlighting punctuation mentioned earlier illustrate this perfectly: if one takes the trouble to listen with care to the exact time distances between each recurrence of the punctuations, one will notice that no two occurrences are ever quite the same space apart or exactly predictable. Neither, on the other hand, are the rhythms completely unpredictable: it is in the skilful drifting around a constant, predictable time-value (or set of values) that the fascination of the textures lies. This is true of the work as a whole: it does not avoid familiar gestural patterns of rise and fall, tension and relaxation, or the clear contrast of speeds and articulations, and there are immediately obvious climactic points. On the detailed level, however, these more familiar behavioural patterns are appropriately complemented by a wealth of unpredictability, so that the listener can shift his focus fruitfully from one level of appreciation to the other, from foreground to background and vice versa, without losing his bearings.

Example 4.4 *Sea and Sky*

There is one other, and most unexpectedly familiar, level of appreciation on which the piece might possibly be grasped, but it is not one to which the composer is so ready to assent. His programme note for the first performance of the piece stated tersely that he would prefer to avoid 'conjuring up a gaudy succession of word images, referring in this case to the pounding of the sea, the shrieking of sea-birds, or the cold and endless azure of the sky' because 'they trivialise my hearing of the actuality and experience which produced musical sound.' At least one critic[9] has agreed wholeheartedly with the composer on this matter stating that 'no more than Debussy's *La Mer* is this a picture drawn from nature... its [textures] seem purely musical phenomena, not requiring explanation.' Of course, the truth of the matter - and this was surely a paradox intended by the critic concerned - is that Debussy's *La Mer is* partly a picture drawn from nature: the first movement, after all, was initially entitled 'Mer Belle aux Iles Sanguinaires', and even if the titles he finally settled on were less wholly specific, they are clearly and deliberately evocative of natural phenomena. Perhaps fearing reprisals similar to Satie's caustic remarks about 'D'Aube à Midi sur la Mer' - 'I particularly like the bit at eleven o'clock in the morning' - most subsequent composers (with the notable exceptions of Richard Strauss and Messiaen) have been at pains to deny any 'programme' behind pieces with suggestively picturesque titles, and that with some vehemence. Finnissy's comment quoted above is wholly typical of this. Yet I do not think it 'trivialises' his achievement to point out that - intentionally or unintentionally - *Sea and Sky* manages to evoke sounds very redolent of the title, albeit composed into a completely autonomous and watertight musical structure which works perfectly successfully as a purely abstract canvas. The opening tangle of piercing woodwind cries is fascinatingly complex in its own right, yet it does (accidentally?) evoke the shrieking of sea-birds. The surging masses of extreme bass a few minutes later, occasionally overwhelmed by tam-tam crescendos, forms a perfect contrast with the preceding music and has plenty of appreciably varied detail to be enjoyed; if it also coincidentally evokes the pounding of the sea, is that a weakness of the music? No more than that the slow sifting of the central chorale, with its endless succession of glistening string chords, is a beautifully timed still centre to the work, and yet possibly also suggestive of the cold and endless azure of the sky. Curiously, each of the 'gaudy word images' that Finnissy in fact *does* cite in his programme note suggests its equivalent in the sounding composition. That is surely a benefit, not a weakness or a triviality; it is another facet of the play between the familiar and the unpredictable, between the immediacy of 'public' statement and the private, detailed contrariness, which make *Sea and Sky* one of its composer's richest achievements.

Sea and Sky marks the culmination of Finnissy's abstract style of the late seventies and was by far the most accomplished piece of orchestral writing by any composer of so-called 'complex' music at that time. Following its successful premiere by the London Philharmonic under Elgar Howarth in 1980, however, the piece disappeared almost without trace, save for a studio performance in 1986 by the BBC Symphony Orchestra. Its revival would be most welcome, for the music has a directness and simplicity of basic utterance (whatever the surface detail) which would surely prove immediate for audiences.

In the early eighties, Finnissy was invited to Melbourne as composer in residence to the Victorian College of Arts for a period of six months. The impact of this visit went far beyond the confines of the usual composer residencies. Quite apart from the associations and friendships set up as a direct result, Finnissy was deeply impressed by the music, art and poetry of Aboriginal Australian culture. Folk musics from many countries had already found a ready response in Finnissy's music. However with the possible exception of English folk music, none aroused such strong feelings of empathy and identification within him as this one. Finnissy has said that the discovery of this culture was like finding 'a new part of myself... almost the discovery of a new personality'. There followed a long sequence of 'Aboriginal' Finnissy pieces, mainly for ensemble: works such as *Ouraa, Banumbirr* (both 1982) and *Warara* (1983 for soprano and ensemble), released a lyricism, warmth and textural delicacy which contrasted sharply with the rebarbative surfaces of the 'constructivist' music of the seventies. This plangent lyricism was to be a prominent feature of all Finnissy's subsequent music; echoes of it can be heard in music whose inspiration is quite separate, like the Venda African chants in *Ngano* (1984), the Rumanian folk inflections of *Catana* (1985) and *Dust in the Road* (1988), or the more generalised folk melismata of *Contretänze* (1983) and the *String Trio* (1985). To draw attention to what are superficially softer edges on the surface of Finnissy's music is not to imply that its meaning had in any way 'softened'; on the contrary, the most typical pieces of this period have an atmosphere which Roger Wright once termed 'a happy melancholia',[10] a curious mixture of exuberance and yearning bitterness in the tortuously winding melodic writing. This is such a common feature of Finnissy's music at this time that it invites some explanation. Speaking of his frequent use of folk or traditional music in his own work, Finnissy has commented that for him 'it symbolizes the origins of music in some way. Or it represents an unconditional response to the act of music-making as a reflection of man's experience, which structured Western concert music certainly often doesn't.'[11] This might account for the celebratory elements, but not the recurrent melancholia. In the television programme, *Dust in the Road*, made in collaboration with Barrie Gavin in 1988 (for which Finnissy's work of the same name was composed), Gavin remarked to the composer that whereas the work had begun life as a celebration of music for a Rumanian wedding ceremony, it had ended up finally sounding more like an intense lament. Finnissy agreed, and commented that the piece had taken on this character 'because my recognition of my inability to form a part of that ceremony made me very sad'.[12] Finnissy's 'folk' period, rather than representing a form of escapism into an idealised past, actively deals with the distance between the traditional and urban cultures, between the raw immediacy of the folk material and its representation in modern Western society. Indeed, another strain in Finnissy's 'Australian' series deals with the traditions of white immigrant culture, most obviously in the series of three books of *Australian Sea Shanties* from the mid to late eighties. And another product of this strain, the piccolo piece *The Eureka Flag* (1983), plays an important role in the shaping of the largest (and so far last) of the Australian pieces, the orchestral work *Red Earth*.

The initial impulse for *Red Earth* came many years before the piece found its final shape. Finnissy takes up the story:

> It has its origins in the Australian landscape. I was flying over the Australian landscape after a visit to Australia in 1982, but the origins of the piece are not only the depiction of the Australian landscape, or... a depiction of my feelings crossing the Australian landscape... it's an attempt to capture an instant in time in which I became aware of what Heidegger has called 'the traces of fugitive gods'. It's a moment... where you suddenly become aware of something - some truth which you can realise as art, or you think you can. And at that moment... of coalescence, I was able to transform 'the view' of that landscape into *sound*, at least in my head, and I was writing a letter at the time to friends I had left behind in Australia in which I had described that landscape in terms of sound... So essentially the piece is a kind of reminiscence of that impression.[13]

More recently, Finnissy remarked that he had needed the distance of several years to digest the immediacy of the initial impression and its attendant emotions. Beginning work on *Red Earth*, Finnissy made an attempt to locate the letter he had written on the flight; on re-reading it he found his feelings had meanwhile changed quite substantially, so that the piece he was about to write had become something quite distinct from the descriptions in the letter. However, on hearing the piece in rehearsal, Finnissy felt that the final work was much closer to the spirit of the letter than he had expected; in particular, he noticed that, as in his other music of the time, a distinct tone of lamentation and loss had come to the fore. The piece emanates a sense of yearning for the Australian landscape and the 'unconditional innocence' of Aboriginal culture; it is the loss of these phenomena - possibly even, as we shall see, their degradation and commercialisation at the hands of Western society - that the piece in effect mourns.

The most immediately obvious factor separating this piece from its orchestral predecessors in Finnissy's output is the spareness of its textures. Even the most dense passages (such as Figure 4, et seq.) do not approach the busier textures of *Sea and Sky* or *Offshore*; there is a deliberate move away from density towards focus and refinement: the strings, for example, are never divided into more than twelve individual parts. The orchestral palette is deliberately restricted, too: from the start Finnissy decided to omit clarinets and horns from his orchestra 'because they are timbrally a particular kind of thing: middle register, rather rich sounding instruments, and I focused instead on the harsher extremes of the woodwind and brass sections.'[14] This choice is the logical consequence of the tendency towards the outer edges of orchestral tessitura which we have already noted every since Finnissy's teenage years. The percussion section is similarly restricted: just untuned drums, maracas, cymbals and a tambourine. One of the most impressive aspects of *Red Earth* is the variety of instrumental colours and textures which Finnissy manages to extract from his self-imposed limited palette; the quality of textural imagination and invention is such that the listener is scarcely aware of 'omissions' as such. Speaking of this in his programme note, Finnissy draws attention to the variety of visual colours he had in mind whilst writing the piece:

> the central desert lands of Australia... a closer resemblance than any other landscape I'd seen to the human body... textures and colours of blood and flesh... a soil, red-ochre in colour when moistened, which the Aboriginal Australians use as a body-paint... 'red' for blood or fire, the colour of the planet Mars, the colour of the sun on the horizon as it rises or sets...[15]

Although the composer once again denies any overtly programmatic or picturesque inspiration in the actual music, the textures are undeniably tactile, even olfactory in their impact: the acrid beating of quartertone oboes, the gently sagging timpani, the sable colours of low drums and pizzicato bass (in regular quavers, uniquely for Finnissy!), the surging brass crescendi, the microtonal wailing of piccolo against viola solo - these things comprise a distinctive, tangy sound world miles away from the composer of (say) *Alongside* or the piano concertos and give this work a subdued, almost claustrophobic intensity of quite specific hue.

The source sets for the pitch and rhythmic material in the piece are the same as for a number of other works in the Australian 'set', such as *Warara*, but are applied in a far more elaborate and broad manner. Because the sketches for *Red Earth* are lost, a detailed analysis of how this happens is not possible. The general character of the material is, however, identifiable from the sketches for *Warara*. These exhibit a preference for drifting permutational figures centred around narrowly focused pitch-ranges, usually replete with microtones and eschewing exact repetition; *Red Earth* too is almost exclusively built out of this type of pitch writing. As in *Sea and Sky*, much play is made on the contrast between stable and unstable use of the bass register. The principally unstable instruments are the timpani, whose low, narrow glissandi are one of the dominant colours of the work: the work opens with a texture prominently featuring this figuration, and in a quasi-reprise very unusual for Finnissy, the timpani glissandi return to close the work, emphasising the circularity and non-directionality of this stylised ritual.

The polar opposite of the timpani glides is the frequent use of sustained drones and pedal points in the bass instruments, heightened by the introduction into the orchestral arena (for the first time anywhere, as far as I know) of two didjeridus (see Example 4.5). The composer is at pains to deny that these instruments have any 'picture postcard' aspect to them: they aren't to be seen as a token attempt at 'sounding Aboriginal', nor do they sound that way - their function is, he insists, the purely structural one of enhancing the use of drones already prevalent in the music. And, indeed, their initial appearance in the score is most carefully prepared. From figure 4, the nearest to an overtly dense texture is developed at some length by the full orchestra - a network of many simultaneous laments in all registers, underpinned by a long sequence of sustained pitches in the extreme treble (oboes) and the extreme bass (trombones and bass trombone). As this subsides, a more strident texture overtakes featuring tremolos in the treble register accompanied by a bass drone F sharp, sustained in a relay between the trombones and timpani rolls (on stable pitches). As the F sharp drone fades, it is continued naturally by the didjeridus. Their appearance is prepared by a progressive focusing of the bass register for several minutes before they are heard.[16] The didjeridus return for the last section, where again they are carefully placed in a coherent context - in this case, low sustained pitches on bassoons and celli - which ensures that they make textural sense and don't stick out as exotica.

Formally, the work unfolds as a series of contrasting and overlapping threnodies. This may seem to recall the sequence of panels which makes up *Sea and Sky*, but there are some significant differences, most importantly in the handling of time. The earlier work eschews repetitions or reprises of any sort: nothing returns. In *Red Earth* things do return and a new section does not necessarily correspond to a total change of texture - many elements are retained across sectional divides, so that the composer has a more refined control over the rate of change in the music (the degree of *newness*, Stockhausen would say) and can sculpt a more complex and ambiguous temporal architecture. Whereas *Sea and Sky* functions as a gradually decelerating curve of events whose duration was, as we have seen, determined by the proportions of the Fibonacci series, the unfolding of events in *Red Earth* is almost uniformly unhurried and gentle. No special proportions are evident from the real time durations of any section relative to any other. This uniformity of time unfolding enhances the trance-like atmosphere of the piece, as does the absence of any build up or pivotal climax - again in strong contrast to the unidirectional, strongly gestural form of *Sea and Sky*.

Dynamics are almost uniformly low in *Red Earth* and the majority of loud dynamics are approached smoothly through crescendi; this allows the listener (and the composer) to concentrate upon the melodic writing which is at the heart of this work. Thus the events that occur two-thirds of the way through the piece are all the more shocking: against a duet of piccolo and viola accompanied by tremolo strings the entire percussion section explodes in a series of four unison drum thuds of deafening ferocity (Example 4.6). The surrounding texture remains oblivious to these enigmatic intrusions and the last of them leads into the very quietest and most lyrical music in the piece (Figure 38 et seq.). The drum thuds appear to be isolated occurrences until the final section, where they return in greater profusion, bringing the work to an unexpectedly brusque end. Several commentators have wondered at the significance of the drum explosions in the context of a work otherwise so dominated by subtlety of texture, timbre and microtonal inflection. Speaking of them, Roger Wright has aptly referred to Finnissy's liking for the presence of an 'audible scream' [17] in all his works, and indeed their impact retrospectively in *Red Earth* seems to be one of suddenly heightening and concentrating the desolation of the work as a whole as much as disrupting it. I feel them to be the product of two additional (and related) factors. Firstly, Finnissy has often spoken of his concern that our expectations of musical form, content and predictability are 'highly culturally and therefore socially determined' and that rather than just carry on regardless, his concern is 'to recognise these factors and if necessary deliberately work against them'.[18] Second, Finnissy may well have been concerned that instead of listening carefully to the intricate details of his melodic writing, listeners might simply be lulled by the slow rate of change, smoothly blended orchestral textures and generally low dynamics, a possible danger had not he inserted a shock of some sort. As Varèse said to Xenakis explaining his attitude towards the general public: 'Alright, you've got to rough 'em up a bit, put a bomb under them sometimes, haven't you?' [19] Sentiments with which Michael Finnissy might well agree.

One further way in which the composer adds variety to the pervading desolation of the textures is through the contrasts of solo, concertante (chamber music) and tutti sections, contrasts which in *Red Earth* are surprisingly numerous and clear (so much so that the piece might be said to be a kind of subdued concerto for orchestra). The following plan illustrates the placing of the solos in relation to the other textures:

I (opening)	Concertante 1	Woodwind, trumpets, violins, timpani.
II (Fig. 4)	Tutti 1	Full orchestra.
III (Fig. 9)	Concertante 2	Flutes, bassoons, trombones, harps, cymbals, maracas, timpani, 4 solo violins, violins, violas.
IV (Fig. 15 -6)	Solo 1 (oboe)	Accompaniment: didjeridus, harps, drums.
V (Fig. 20 - 5)	Concertante 3/ Solo 2 (cello)	Single wind, trombones, drums, pizzicato bass, tremolo violins, violas, celli.
VI (Fig. 27 - 3)	Concertante 3 (continued)	As above minus violins, plus harps.
VII (Fig. 31)	Tutti 2	Full orchestra (overlapping crescendi).
VIII (Fig. 35)	Solos 3 (piccolo, viola)	Tremolo strings.
	DRUMS 1 (Fig. 36 +5)	
IX (Fig. 38)	Concertante 4	Flutes, bassoon, didjeridus, all perc, strings.
X (Fig. 47)	Solos 3 cont. (piccolo, viola)	Accompaniment: 1 flute, 1 oboe, bassoons, timpani, low strings.
	DRUMS 2 (Fig. 52 - END)	

Diagram 4.3

Example 4.5 *Red Earth* - note the combination of stable and unstable bass writing in the didjeridus and timpani respectively.
Reproduced by permission of Oxford University Press

Example 4.6 *Red Earth* (cf. Diagram 4.3, Section VII)
Reproduced by permission of Oxford University Press

Only two tutti passages, then, and those relatively restrained; the piece mainly alternates chamber music, for ever varied ensembles, with expressive solos. There are several more or less sharp textural breaks, the largest between Tutti 2 and Solos 3 (the tutti is literally interrupted in mid flow), and between Solos 3 and the following chamber music. The smoothest join is just before this, between Concertante 3 and Tutti 2: the latter takes on and simply exaggerates elements from the former (notably the sustained single note crescendos). The join between some sections is smoothed over slightly by the use of cinematic *fondue enchainé*: introducing a new texture beneath a previously existing one, as is the case at the end of Solo 1, where the basses' regular pizzicato and the sporadic cello solo of the following section are begun just before the oboe solo fades. The areas of greatest unpredictability in the textural behaviour are therefore placed two-thirds of the way through, leading up to the first drum explosion, and at the very end of the piece, where the drums burst in again.

The drum explosions may have another, more concrete implication, since the two solos against which they are placed are derived from two of Finnissy's earlier Australian pieces. The piccolo solo is derived from transposed and reshuffled quotes from *The Eureka Flag*, a short work written five years before to celebrate an event from Australia's colonial past: a workers' rebellion, in which the newly liberated republicans hoisted a flag with a bold star sign to celebrate their victory. Example 4.7 shows the first few relevant fragments from the earlier work. Against this, the viola solo enunciates similarly reordered and transposed quotes from another, this time Australian aboriginal piece, *Ouraa* for eleven instruments (the title is the Aboriginal for wood, and log drums feature prominently in the work). These two self-quotations always come together in *Red Earth*, returning in the final section of the work and provide one of the few instances in which the composer combined his music from Aboriginal Australia with that from white immigrant Australia. An optimistic gesture, of empathy or of hoped-for reconciliation? Or maybe something more ironic? An uneasy unity, in any case, as the drum explosions all too discomfitingly illustrate.

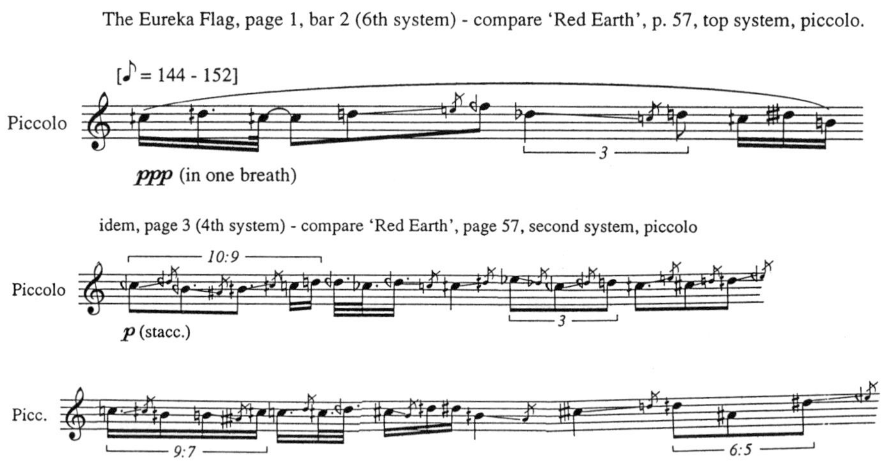

Example 4.7 *The Eureka Flag*, two extracts
(cf. Diagram 4.3, 'Red Earth', Sections VII and X)

Finnissy's next orchestral piece, *Eph-phatha*, built upon the benefits of the spare textures of its predecessor. But whereas *Red Earth* drew a line underneath Finnissy's Australian period, the present work marked a turning point in his style, even perhaps in his choice of subject-matter. *Eph-phatha* was commissioned by the New English Orchestra and their conductor Nigel Swinford for a series of mixed concerts around Britain comprising celebrations of the Evangelical Christian movement. Thus each performance of the piece took place in the context of a fairly heterogeneous combination of events, such as collective religious singing, dance numbers, readings, and so forth. Not at that stage conventionally religious, Finnissy seems to have accepted the commission as an opportunity to examine the nature of religious and revelatory experiences, and their intimate relation to doubt. Finnissy was not about to provide some grand rhetorical affirmation of Christian faith, not least because he is distinctly ambivalent about the rather mixed cultural and social heritage of Christianity in Western civilisation.

The composer was asked to take as his starting point an extract of the New Testament of his own choice. He selected from Chapter 7 of St Mark's gospel, verses 32-5; it's the story of the deaf man whose ears are unstopped by Christ:

> And they bring unto him one that was deaf, and had an impediment in his speech; and they beseech him to put his hand upon him. And he took him aside from the multitude, and put his fingers into his ears, and he spit, and touched his tongue. And looking up to heaven, he sighed and saith unto him, *Eph-phatha*, that is, Be opened. And straightway his ears were opened, and the string of tongue loosened, and he spake plain.

Finnissy's work takes the bare outlines of this extract - 'man freed of deafness' - as trigger for the basic form, and also for aspects of the scoring. The work falls into two parts separated by a (short) general pause. In the first half, the music concentrates upon a succession of textures dominated by meandering oscillations around single pitches (including quartertones). This is 'arrested in mid-flow' (as the composer puts it) by the intervention of three offstage instruments, playing much more diatonic music, without any quartertone inflections or complex irrational rhythms: Finnissy remarks that the sharp contrast between the main orchestra's music and the clarity of the offstage instruments, whose writing has a plainness and linear simplicity reminiscent of plainsong, 'can easily be seen as a musical representation of deaf ears being unstopped. The clean lines correspond to the new world of sensation that must have opened up in an instant in the formerly deaf man.' After a while the on-stage orchestra resumes its music, newly becalmed and with some of the clarity of the offstage trio. An alternation of this music with reminiscences of the fiercer, more rebarbative textures of the first part leads to a final intervention from the offstage trio who conclude the work.

Finnissy admits that the use of three instruments offstage 'has a clear Trinitarian symbolism', a symbolism not restricted to this part of the work. In fact, the whole piece is underpinned by it. The harmonic backbone of the work is a very slow unfolding of a three-voice progression, shown thus in the composer's sketches:

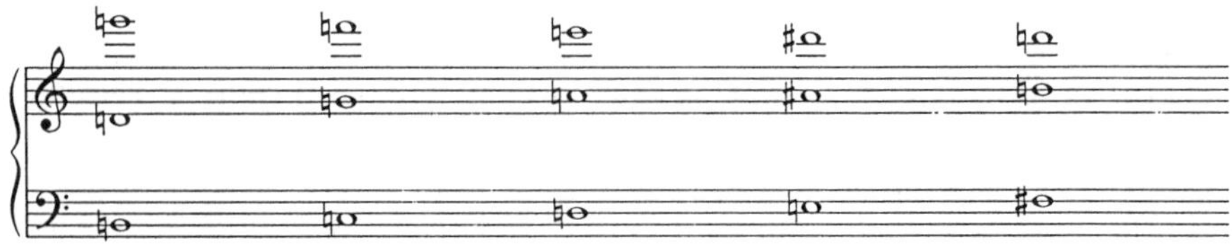

Example 4.8 Harmonic progression from the sketches for *Eph-phatha*

As this example demonstrates, the three voices are placed at great distance from each other, so that each voice represents a different register of the orchestra - high, medium and low. An early sketch also shows that the composer originally identified each voice with a different member of the Trinity: the upper voice is marked 'God the Father', the middle voice 'the Son' and the lowest voice 'the Holy Ghost', although how far this symbolism was followed through in the final work is not clear. Furthermore, the orchestration is also three-dominated: the on-stage orchestra comprises 21 instruments ('=7x3', the sketches note), with a string section consisting, usually, of three each of violins, violas and cellos (there is just one doublebass, however). The rest of the orchestra comprises single wind and brass, a harp, a piano and one percussionist.

The composer's sketches summarise the form of the work in progress as follows:

> 'high/medium/low. GP. short Tutti *ff* OFFSTAGE x2'

Thus the original plan was that the format of the first half of the work (up to and including the first intervention of the offstage instruments) would be reprised in its second half. In fact, things worked out differently: the second half is considerably shorter than the first, lacks a general pause, and the first half itself acquired a whole new section not mentioned in the above plan, which included several extra general pauses in its wake. Nevertheless, the final piece adheres fairly clearly to the triple register progression, shown in Example 4.8 above, in particular to its gradual unfolding of the three voice registers from an initial G major first inversion towards the concluding B minor second inversion chord, so that the work is the result of a single continuously evolving pitch process, and an easily audible one at that. This distinguishes it from Finnissy's other orchestral works which, even if continuous in sound and directional in feel (as *Sea and Sky* was, for example), nevertheless tended towards the overtly sectional. Silence is another factor absent from all *Eph-phatha's* orchestral predecessors and from many of the ensemble pieces.[20]

The use of silence in *Eph-phatha*, limited to the first half of the work alone, is also overtly dramatic, but to different ends. To comment upon it, we have to look closer at the final form of the work. In the sketch, the first half introduces each of the three voice-registers successively in descending order, the bass only entering after three minutes. Perhaps in order to balance the resulting dominance of the highest voice at the opening, Finnissy introduced a corresponding section of about four minutes for middle and low instruments (two each of violas and cellos with low piano and harp), the two violas and piano forming a quasi-soloistic trio with freer flourishes across the texture. This abruptly begins to stutter, and is broken off three times by increasingly lengthy silences. The three registers are then built up in reverse order, from the bottom upwards, in an emphatic passage marked 'jubilant' in the score (Figure 9), and the overriding three-voice progression is resumed. Following the two-second general pause, the whole orchestra combines in the culminating *tutti* outburst, leading in turn to the offstage music. The multiple silences preceding the tutti are obviously present not merely for the sake of variety, but to anticipate and heighten the drama of the approaching revelatory textural 'cleaning' of the offstage music. There is a palpable sense of tension and excitement in these silences: they create the atmosphere of nervous expectancy for the moment of 'unstopping' represented by the offstage music.

Given the strict limitations of the overriding pitch process, it is incumbent upon the composer to provide enough invention in the bar-to-bar detail both to maintain aural attention and to keep the momentum in sight. This assertion need not be seen as a contradiction of the Varèsian aesthetic alluded to above; on the contrary, a composer wishing to play upon the audience's expectations and contradict them must be able to convince them of the validity of his musical ideas in the first place. In *Eph-phatha* Finnissy applies as high a level of imagination in the detailed composition as he does in the gestural realisation of the large scale form, contrasting and superimposing several different types of elaboration around the fundamental harmonic structure:

1. single sustained pitches around the basic pitches
2. tremoli on or around the basic pitches
3. single *glissandi* around the basic pitches
4. melismata around the basic pitches
5. irregular arch-shaped scales away from and back to the basic pitches

Of these five types, the first four all feature random-number permutation of a limited number of pitches; in contrast, the fifth type of material has a clearly predictable character, though this is sometimes disrupted by its irregular rhythmic presentation.

The following extract, taken from the opening of the work, shows that the density and variety which can be obtained from just one pitch - a high G - when the first four types of elaboration are all heard simultaneously is quite sufficient to generate the layered, shifting sound surfaces typical of Finnissy's orchestral work. Type 1 is heard in the wind, 2 on the harp and glockenspiel, 3 in the violas, and 4 in the violins:

Example 4.9 *Eph-phatha* an excerpt from the first section
Reproduced by permission of Oxford University Press

The scalic type 5 is first heard on trumpet and trombone at the entrance of the middle of the work's three main voice-registers at figure 2 in the score, its arch-like forms offering a stark contrast to the unpredictable, irregular contours of its neighbours. Their appearance in the finished piece is an interesting example of Finnissy applying random procedures to apparently predictable material. Example 4.10 shows the relevant page from Finnissy's sketches; there are two sets of nine scalic patterns each - the ascending set, which is played by the trumpet, is on the upper two systems, whilst the descending set, played by the trombone, is on the two lower systems. Each scale ends on the note neighbouring the tonic pitch (middle), so as to lead directly into any other scale. Each scale is provided with an individual number, and the nine scales are then read according to a random-number permutation from Moses and Oakford:

TRUMPET: 9 - 5 - 1 - 8 - 4 - 7 - 2 - 6 - 3
TROMBONE: 9 - 2 - 5 - 3 - 6 - 8 - 1 - 4 - 7
NB: for contextual reasons, the trombone line is transferred to the clarinet after the third scalic statement.

Example 4.10a Trumpet scales from *Eph-phatha*

Example 4.10b Trombone scales from *Eph-phatha*

This sequence of pitches is articulated through rhythmic patterns which drift irregularly around central durations (much as the quartertone writing at the start of the work does around pitches), so that when the two voices are combined any sense of repetitive inevitability is absolutely avoided; the two voices keep returning to the central D, but rarely do so simultaneously, resulting in the desired irregular wavering around the basic tonality. Ex. 4.11 shows a fragment of the two-part polyphony created from these procedures; it should be borne in mind that although this example appears relatively straightforward, it is only one of five simultaneous layers operating on the two voice-registers at this point in the orchestral texture.

Example 4.11 *Eph-phatha* - Trumpet and Trombone polyphonic scales from the first section, orbiting about the pitch 'D'.
Reproduced by permission of Oxford University Press

Perhaps the most distinctly novel element in *Eph-phatha* is its overt harmonic clarity and lucidity, a result of the underlying harmonic progression out of which the music is built. Its slowly gliding melismata around clearly perceptible, sometimes triadically related, central pitches also recall the later music of Giacinto Scelsi (an old enthusiasm of Finnissy), particularly the Fourth String Quartet (1964) and the violin concerto *Anahit* (1966). The rapt intensity of these Scelsi pieces finds a further parallel in many of the more lyrical passages in *Eph-phatha*, such as the orchestra's re-emergence in the work's second part, although the music certainly does not *sound* like Scelsi!

A final word about the music played by the offstage trio and its relevance to the message, if such there be, of the piece as a whole. This was one of the first occasions on which Finnissy employed a style of modal articulation so overtly and intentionally reminiscent of plainchant and medieval music - a facet of his art which was to blossom in a large number of subsequent works from the late eighties and early nineties, often in connection with religious or liturgical texts; the most extreme in this group of pieces is the substantial chamber work, *Cambridge Codex*, for voice and ensemble (composed for Edward Dudley Hughes' Cambridge New Music Players), large sections of which contain no accidentals whatever. I am aware that some of the most ardent supporters of Finnissy's output, especially those who admire the large abstract canvases of the seventies, are unable to appreciate this facet of his music. Perhaps they may mistake the most superficial features of the music for its actual content. There is a world of difference, both in intent and realisation, between this Finnissy and the recent work of (say) Arvo Pärt and John Tavener. For one there is far greater tension in the intervallic writing of the offstage trip of *Eph-phatha* than is characteristic of these other composers, and far more rhythmic inventiveness in the highly wrought rubato rhythms which remain so typical of Finnissy. As can be observed from Example 4.12, an extract from the middle intervention of the offstage trio, the composer has taken extreme care in his choice of colouring accidentals: the diatonicism is caused to fluctuate by the presence of pitches which are modally unstable, such as the pitches A and E in the horn part - both may be either flat or natural according to the melodic inflection required (the E was natural a couple of bars before this extract). Interestingly, the reassertion of A natural arrives just a couple of bars before the arrival of E flat, so that the part is rarely wholly consonant with respect to its neighbours (NB: the score is in C). The cello solo which follows demonstrates the modal destabilisation process in a still clearer fashion: opening with a lengthy melodic phrase entirely in white notes, it quickly develops a number of unpredictable, modally anarchic features such as the rapid alternation between sharps and naturals on the pitches C and F on the last system of the example. The degree of modal and rhythmic emphasis placed upon these changing accidentals - some are treated as passing inflections, others are leant upon as the apex of a melodic phrase - creates a considerable degree of unpredictability and, yes, complexity, which the casual listener, hearing only musical manner rather than matter, might easily pass over.

Example 4.12 *Eph-phatha* - Music of the offstage group
Reproduced by permission of Oxford University Press

Speaking of the use of this cleaner, simpler music coming from offstage, the composer has said that his aim was not merely to evoke some sort of musical 'lost paradise' but to examine the notions and associations that comprise such an ideal, and to do so in a particularly ironic and disruptive way. The modal and rhythms instabilities outlined above are one way of achieving this - there is always something not quite in place in the supposedly 'ideal' music. But as stated earlier, although this offstage music does affect an amelioration of the orchestra's music, it can never wholly cleanse it. The orchestra's re-entrance may be decidedly lyrical and effusive - some of the most delicate orchestral writing Finnissy has composed to date; yet it also resumes the uncertainly drifting pitch-lines of the basic harmonic plan, and the five basic materials which colour it. Before long, moreover, it has re-acquired some of the shrill ferocity of the first half, disrupting the gentler atmosphere introduced by the offstage instruments completely. This uncertain atmosphere is maintained right through to the conclusion, where the re-entry of the offstage group presents the solo trio in reverse order (cello, horn, piccolo) now rather more chromatic, dissonant and modally vague than before. The work fades out on the B minor second inversion at the end of Example 4.12, without any resolution or reconciliation between the two contrasted ensembles. That Finnissy realised his avowed aim to write a piece concerned as much with uncertainty and doubt as with the affirmation of religious faith, was dramatically confirmed after the New English Orchestra's London performance of *Eph-phatha* in 1988. A lady from the audience confronted the composer somewhat accusingly: 'I don't understand. It seems to me that you're not *sure*, you're not *certain*, you won't commit yourself unambiguously, will you?' The composer replied that, on the contrary, she had understood the piece exactly.

Finnissy's next work is a hybrid, neither strictly orchestral nor chamber music, although capable of being played as either. *Plain Harmony*, a commission from COMA (Contemporary Music Making for Amateurs) is a homage to two of Finnissy's mentors - Bernard Stevens and Percy Grainger - and their views on music's role in society. Bernard Stevens was Finnissy's teacher and was a one-time Communist Party member with a long involvement with organisations promoting music making by amateurs in socially disadvantaged communities; indeed he succeeded Alan Bush as director of the Workers' Music Association. He held that music should be part of everyone's experience and should be made available to the whole of society, regardless of income or abilities, views with which Finnissy passionately agrees. His response to COMA's commission is thus a heartfelt contribution to the WMA genre, a picture of the kind of music which he would hope that, in an ideal society, anyone should be able to grasp and take pleasure in performing, in groups of any size desired, a celebration of community music making.

In order to ensure that the work can be played by any size of ensemble of number of instruments, Finnissy omits any indications of instrumentation and notates the work in 'open score' on as many staves as required. This layout immediately recalls the notation of Percy Grainger, who published even his large orchestral works in short score, indicated the instruments required at individual moments by means of arrows, and allowed for innumerable changes, substitutions or omissions of instruments in a performance as long as each part could be clearly heard. He coined the term 'elastic scoring' for this procedure, and his comments about its uses and purpose serve equally well as a commentary of *Plain Harmony* - one of the most elastically scored pieces of music ever composed:

> My music tells its story mainly by means of *intervals* and the liveliness of the part-writing, rather than by means of tone-colour, and is therefore well fitted to be played by almost any small, large or medium-sized combination of instruments, provided a *proper balance of tone* is kept... As long as... the voices that make up the musical texture are clearly heard, one against the other... I do not care whether one of my elastically scored pieces is played by 4 or 40 or 400 players, or any number in between; whether my trumpet parts are played on trumpets or soprano saxophones, whether my French horn parts are played on horns or alto saxophones... whether woodwinds take part or whether a piano is substituted for them... I do not even care whether the players are skilful or unskilful, as long as... they play badly enough to *still enjoy playing*... This 'elastic scoring' is intended to encourage music lovers... to play together in groups... and to promote a more hospitable attitude towards inexperienced music-makers.[21]

The similarities between Grainger's aesthetic credo and the note appended to the score of *Plain Harmony* is striking: Finnissy prescribes that 'the instrumentation throughout is entirely free; it need not, and should not, be of a conventional layout... the more diverse [the timbres] are the better... Each line can be played by any number of instruments... The overall dynamic balance should be as equal as possible.'

The music falls into four distinct parts, separated by a short pause, each scored for a different number of parts and each concentrating upon a different type of texture. An additional source of inspiration in *Plain Harmony* is the Shaker tradition of homophonic hymn singing, most evident in the exuberant first section of the work. Marked 'lustily, as in hymn singing', it is in eight equal parts. A great diversity of part-writing is deployed - parts moved in and out of homophony with each other and there is much parallel or near-parallel writing, but none of these devices is maintained for very long. The resultant harmony is relatively diatonic, even flirting with the conventionally tonal, though with the added peculiarity of the simultaneous combination of tonic, dominant and subdominant chords into cluster-like formations (as at the opening of Example 4.13, the first page of the score), a feature of much folk-band playing in Eastern European traditions. This section breaks off in mid-phrase.

The second section is in four parts and is slower. The harmony is more chromatic, almost bluesy ('rather sentimental' as the score says) and its waywardly sonorous part-writing recalls the rich chromaticism of Finnissy's *Gershwin Arrangements*. The flow of the music is abruptly frozen five times by long pauses on whatever harmony the music has arrived at: 'as though lost in thought', as the composer comments. Like the first, this section cuts off without warning.

Example 4.13 *Plain Harmony*
Reproduced by permission of Oxford University Press

The third section consists of six uncoordinated solo parts played against a double drone on the rest of the orchestra. The solo parts are largely diatonic and are heavily ornamented in the manner of Finnissy's folk-inspired pieces. The drone - F above middle C and the G two octaves lower - was chosen to maintain intervallic tension through the section: the composer experimented with several more consonant combinations before deciding upon this one. This ensures that the music never comes to harmonic repose, even as the six parts drop out, one by one, leaving the drone to end the section alone. To me, the dense heterophony of that section is the texture most overtly reminiscent of other folk music such as the tradition of heterophonic psalm singing found on the Hebridean islands of Lewis and Harris (although this may not be that intended by the composer). The composer himself calls this section 'lyrical, spontaneous and individualistic, a sort of dawn chorus'.

The final section is in twelve parts: two groups of two soli each, plus an eight part ripieno. This is the most complex and layered music in the work: the two solo groups each move at their own speed, whilst the main body of eight parts moves at another speed again. The relationship between the different speeds is not exact: the first solo group moves 'slightly' faster than the main tempo, the second solo group 'slightly' slower - the composer insists that any exact metrical polyrhythm (such as triplets) be deliberately avoided. Paradoxically, the two solo groups are marked *piano*, against the ripieno's *forte* - 'as if in the distance', the score says - and the effect is rather like one of Charles Ives' 'distant choruses' of solo instruments. The part-writing of the solo groups consist mainly of narrow, conjunct intervals, whilst that of the main groups is dense, wide-spanning and often quite rhythmically disjunct. The harmony recalls the polydiatonic formations of the first part, but the parts move faster and there is some swift hocketing of phrases between the two groups later on. This section stops suddenly like its predecessors, but unlike them, the order in which the different layers fall out is left entirely to chance; from the score, it appears that either of the solo groups would probably end the work, as they are given slightly more music than the main one, but the composer does not insist on this.

Finnissy's more recent orchestral work was completed as this article was in progress. *Speak its Name!* was written to a commission from the newly-formed Brunel Ensemble, a small orchestra founded in Bristol by the talented young conductor Christopher Austin to explore new music and revive little-known repertoire. This is a return to the highly personal concerns of Finnissy's early attempted symphony. It is one of a number of pieces in which the composer deals explicitly with aspects of homosexuality; others include the AIDS-inspired song cycle *Unknown Ground* (1989), the opera *Shameful Vice* (1992) and also, it would appear, the large piano work *English Country-Tunes* (1977-84). The title of the new orchestral piece is, or course, a reference to the famous poem by Oscar Wilde's lover, later betrayer, Alfred Lord Douglas - a poem which played an important role in convicting Wilde in the 1891 trial which led to his imprisonment and exile. *Speak its Name!* is Finnissy's longest orchestral piece to date (it lasts about twenty-four minutes), and due to its strong extra-musical inspiration it has the most elusive form of all.

The basic idea is simple enough: the gradual emergence of a single, continuous melodic line played emerging as a unison from a series of multi-layered orchestral textures. Appropriately, the opening presents a veiled welter of melodic figures in which no part can be clearly discerned, whilst the last seven or eight minutes comprise a single lengthy melodic line drawing together all the fragments heard at the start and bringing them 'out into the open', according to the composer. But this fairly straightforward scheme makes a large number of subsidiary sections and events which succeed one another in almost Ivesian exuberance and profusion. Each section deals with a different facet of musical material relating to the work's homosexual subject matter. This happens in many ways: one section transforms material drawn from Italian opera (of which Finnissy is a connoisseur) - an allusion to the 'opera queen' phenomenon; another performs similar transformations upon the music of Schubert, as one of the earliest composers now known to have been homosexual; Tchaikovsky, having had a whole opera to himself, receives less attention, although Finnissy has adopted the composer's favoured device of a throbbing bass to underpin several sections. There are medleys of Finnissy-transformed folk music from Ireland (to represent Wilde) and Spain (to represent Lorca). Most ambitiously, the one real pile-up in the work (page 31) is actually littered with indirect allusions - *not* quotations - to no fewer than six homosexual composers, including some well known contemporaries (at least one of them not yet 'out'); in fact, such allusions are scattered in more or less obvious manners through the whole first part.

This first part is thus full of changing moods, contrasts, disjunctions, things left incomplete. The second half of the work - the final eight minutes - joins together all the threads of the music with the increasingly definite emergence of the continuous melody. Finnissy's melody employs fragments from a wide variety of folk and traditional music, and is played in every section of the orchestra. Here Finnissy employs written-out instrumental doubling for the first time in his orchestral music; hitherto, his liking for layered textures had determined his avoidance of his device, but whilst experimenting with ways in which the scoring of this long melody could be enhanced and diversified, the opportunity to introduce doubling proved apt. On the evidence of the finished score (the first performance is scheduled a few months after this article will be finished) Finnissy has taken to doubling with considerable flair and enthusiasm, from shading individual notes here and there to doubling whole lines for bars at a stretch. [22] Sometimes, instead of straightforward doubling, lines are doubled in fourths or fifths, or irregular combinations of the two producing a kind of false organum. That the work inhabits a quite different sound-world from any other Finnissy is evident in Example 4.14 (p. 52 of the score) which demonstrates all the doubling devices in full flight.

Example 4.14 *Speak its Name!*
Reproduced by permission of Oxford University Press

Even if Finnissy's orchestral works are not numerous, it is clear that each is a major work, occupying distinct and fresh musical territory from any of its fellows. Overall, one discerns a movement away from and back to concerns of an intimate and personal nature, as represented by the early Symphony and *Speak its Name!* The vast *Sea and Sky*, whether its abstract canvas does or does not admit mimetic elements, represents a distinct move, away from the intimate towards mass phenomena of an almost impersonal kind; *Red Earth* marks the beginnings of a retreat from this extreme, combining a structured succession of musical landscape-textures with the distinctly human presences of Aboriginal and colonial evocations into its 'stylised lament'. *Ephphatha's* highly personal, unresolved contemplation of the numinous opened an entire period of Finnissy's oeuvre in which the composer has confronted aspects of the Christian faith. Finally, he deals unsentimentally with facets of his own sexuality, and in so doing firmly reasserts the lyrical impulses which have always been at the heart of his most characteristic work.

Notes

1. For more details, see 'Conversations with Michael Finnissy' elsewhere in this volume.
2. This and all subsequent unattributed quotations draw on a conversation with the present writer in August 1996.
3. It is worth recalling that there was no orchestral precedent for Finnissy as a composer of so-called 'complex' music. Ferneyhough's *Firecycle Beta* (1969-71) had not yet been performed or published, and his mammoth *La Terre est un Homme* would not be completed for another four years. The fluency of *Offshore* is therefore all the more remarkable.
4. In *Offshore* this device is given an added form-bearing dimension by varying the density and stability of its pitch content. On the largest formal scale, the extreme bass writing moves throughout the work from unstable, glissando-ridden textures of considerable density, towards the stable isolated bass pitch at the end of the work. Many varied types of intermediary stages are employed along the way, such as the dense doublebass cluster at Figs. 4/5 - maximum density but complete stability of pitch content (shades of Ligeti here?).
5. See, for example, Roger Redgate's chapter in the present volume.
6. Scc, for example, 'The Panorama of Michael Finnissy (I)' by Ian Pace in *Tempo* 196 (April 1996).
7. I do not know if Finnissy was aware when composing *Sea and Sky* that Debussy also made use of the Fibonacci series to determine the proportions of his seascape, *La Mer* - Roy Howat's research on this topic was not published until 1984 (see *Debussy in Proportion*, Cambridge University Press, 1984).
8. *Tables of Random Numbers* by Lincoln E. Moses and Robert V. Oakford (London 1963).
9. Paul Griffiths reviewing the 1986 Maida Vale revival of the work in *The Times*.

10. Radio 3 Portrait of Michael Finnissy, 2 August 1988.
11. Ibid.
12. Ibid.
13. Portrait of Michael Finnissy, BBC Radio 3, 2 August 1988.
14. Ibid.
15. Programme note for the first performance, BBC Promenade Concerts, Royal Albert Hall, 2 August 1988.
16. In a twist to this process, the appearance of the didjeridus is actually accompanied by the return of glissandi on the timpani, so that a point of maximum stability of pitch-content is contradicted by the reappearance of maximum instability.
17. Portrait of Michael Finnissy, BBC Radio 3, 2 August 1988.
18. Interview in *Dust in the Road*, op. cit.
19. Quoted by Xenakis in the Xenakis promotional booklet published by Boosey and Hawkes in 1966 (ed. Mario Bois).
20. Finnissy's most dramatic and powerful use of silence is probably to be found in the ensemble piece *Alongside* (1979), in which the gradual winding down of a densely polyphonic passage results in the isolation of a single instrument - an untuned drum - which continues its forceful punctuations oblivious of the encroaching void (Finnissy originally intended to end *Alongside* here).
21. Quoted from *A guide to the Music of Percy Grainger*, ed. Thomas P. Lewis, Kahn and Averill, 1991, pp. 272-7.
22. Most performances of *Plain Harmony* will, of course, involve doubling but this is a feature of the work's performance practice rather than its notation.

CHAPTER FIVE

The Vocal Music

Christopher Fox

Music involving voices accounts for more than a third of Michael Finnissy's output, but almost all his music is, at some level, 'vocal' music. The art of transcription lies at the heart of his compositional practice and much of the music he has chosen as the source material for these transcriptions is vocal. The great piano sets, for example, all in some way transform vocal music for Finnissy's own digital 'voice', the keyboard: the *Verdi Transcriptions* take Finnissy's favourite arias as their starting-points; the *Gershwin Arrangements* do the same with Gershwin, often, as Finnissy has said, starting not just with a Gershwin song but with a particular performance of that song in mind;[1] *English Country-Tunes* leaps into its vehemently delineated musical territory from English grounds while *Folklore* attempts a near-global synthesis of folk music.

Amongst the early works, the series of works entitled *Song* are all, by implication, in some way related to the act of singing even if, as Richard Barrett has made clear, the immediate inspiration for the title was not 'song' itself but the *idea* of song as mediated through the work of the American film-maker, Stan Brakhage.[2] More recently, Finnissy's fascination with folk-music has led him to transcribe songs from many different cultures, traces of the originals surviving both in the texture of the music and in the titles of individual pieces: *Botany Bay* has its origins both specifically in the Australian settlers' tune of that name and generally in the musical culture of the early white community in Australia. Elsewhere Finnissy has explored the distinction between vocal and instrumental idioms, a distinction less clear-cut in many cultures than it has been in European art music in the last two centuries: in the *Obrecht Motetten*, for example, he has made instrumental music from Obrecht's settings of the 'Salve Regina' and 'Ave Regina Caelorum' texts.

Finnissy is, as a general rule, *not* interested in what, conventionally, has come to be regarded as 'good' word-setting. As he says elsewhere in this volume, if people want to hear the words then they should buy the book from which they come. In some works texts are used as little more than a ready-made formula for varying vocal timbres, providing a quasi-random set of consonants and vowels. In *Kelir*, for example, the text consists of a series of Javanese ritual invocations - appropriate texts for performance perhaps, since, in their original setting, they preface the performance of shadow-plays, but nonetheless incomprehensible to the sort of audience likely to listen to a concert given by six unaccompanied Western art-music singers. Finnissy's note to the singers at the front of the score confirms this: 'In singing this text the phonetic components of the words simply colour the vocal sound - no attempt should be made to convey its "meaning" or to emphasise the "exotic" quality of the words themselves.'

In other works, where listeners might be expected to pick out words and make some sort of syntactical sense from what they hear, Finnissy provides a musical context in which the words can be heard but he avoids the mimetic approach to text-setting that has been the norm in the art-song for the last 350 years. The conventions of 'good' word-setting require that key words are emphasised by the musical metre and that musical images echo those in the text; Finnissy instead often stresses subsidiary words and ignores opportunities for word-painting unless they can be contained within the larger musical image he is creating. In *Maldon*, for example, high melismata recur on six occasions in the baritone soloist's part but Finnissy almost always displaces them from the most important words or syllables of the lines where they occur, thus:

It **WAS** broken
Tide rising **AF**ter ebb
un**A**fraid, moving
in the **SKY** above
Aelfnoth **AND** Wulfmar

(The use of bold capitals indicates the melismata.)

This may seem perverse, but there is a musical logic at work here since in each phrase the melisma is the central point (Example 5.1a, b and c show three versions of the figure). Only on the last occasion, in the baritone's final phrase, does the melisma move to the end of the phrase,

this game of **WAR**.

The effect is climactic and conclusive: a device which had created a sort of textual suspension in each of its previous appearances, delaying the point at which the sense of each phrase had revealed itself, resolves in its ultimate appearance, onto 'war', the key word of the entire 'Battle of Maldon' poem (Example 5.1d).

Such a view of the composer's relationship to his chosen texts may derive from Finnissy's preoccupation with film-making as a creative model. Just as Derek Jarman's *The Tempest* offers us a transcription, rather than a transposition, of Shakespeare's play into film, so Finnissy will cut or re-order lines or introduce new passages from other sources; the result is a Finnissy work, not a Finnissy setting. Like Michael Tippett, Finnissy is a composer who knows exactly what he wants from a text and he has discovered that the quickest way to find the words he needs is to assemble them himself. It is thus not surprising that there are no Finnissy song-cycles in the tradition which links Schumann to Britten, where the musical work is a duo between poet and composer. This may also explain why almost all the authors of the texts which Finnissy has used in his work are not only dead but also sufficiently dead for there to be no difficulties with publishers or writers' estates over juxtapositions, excisions or transpositions. While Finnissy might be able to find a living writer prepared to accommodate his demands, the guardians of copyright in recently deceased authors are often obstructively protective of textual integrity.

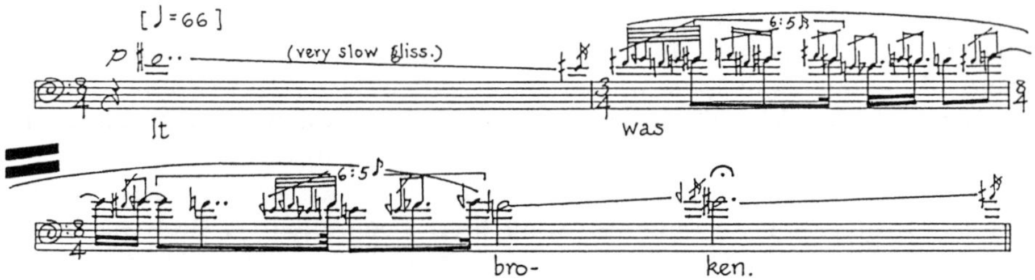

Example 5.1a *Maldon*, baritone part, p. 2

Example 5.1b *Maldon*, p. 13

Example 5.1c *Maldon*, p. 15

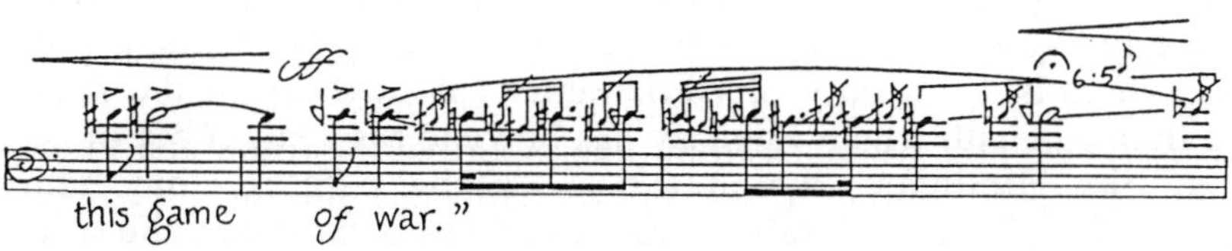

Example 5.1d *Maldon*, p. 33
Reproduced by permission of Oxford University Press

A feature of Finnissy's work as a whole is his fondness for syncretic agglomeration, the drawing together in a single work of ideas from many different sources - different times, different places, different cultures - which nonetheless are shown to have something in common. These ideas may be musical - the drawing together of Dunstable, J.S. Bach and Debussy in *New Perspectives on Old Complexity*, for example - and they may be present either explicitly (those composers' music undergoing Finnissian transcription in the piece) or by inference (the word-play of the title calling up the shades of Babbitt, Wolpe, Carter and other habitués of the pages of *Perspectives of New Music*). Elsewhere the ideas are represented by texts - *Cabaret Vert*, where all the poems in some way relate to 'green-ness', for example - and in most cases the work's title provides a more or less explicit textual indication of the shared subject-matter - *Folklore, Contretänze, World*.

Whatever the form in which different ideas become part of the final work, Finnissy's interest is in demonstrating their commonality, showing how, regardless of circumstance, era or geographical location, people have been susceptible to thoughts and feelings whose congruences are more striking than their disparity. Such a project might seem dangerously close to the colonialist 'anthropology' of men like Pitt-Rivers whose museum in Oxford is stuffed with artefacts from all over the world, arranged not by culture but by type (spoon next to spoon, spear next to spear); it might, as Lynne Williams has suggested in her description of the assembly of the texts for works like *Vaudeville* and *Soda Fountain,* be a 'magpie'-like technique,[3] or it might seem to resemble the early Modernist practice of seeking inspiration in the 'exotic' or 'primitive', rejuvenating tired European vocabularies with oriental or African accents. But Finnissy is neither a Pitt-Rivers nor a Picasso (nor a magpie). While he may propose that, across history and across cultures, certain sorts of archetypal behaviour recur, arising from and eliciting more or less similar responses in different people and peoples to the same sorts of situation, he is always careful to allow differences to remain articulate in the finished work. Indeed in Finnissy's music the celebration of difference at the local level, as section follows section, is often so extreme that it is only by reflecting on the work as a whole, *after* the experience of hearing it is over, that one begins to understand its larger purpose.

Explicit references to the literature and liturgy of Christianity began to appear more frequently in Finnissy's work from 1988 onwards, although a number of earlier works, such as *From the Revelation of Saint John the Divine* and the *Mysteries,* had dealt with Christian subjects. It is interesting to compare the syncretic approach adopted in so much of Finnissy's work with the syncretism not only of Christianity (particularly in the Anglo-Catholic tradition with which Finnissy has become associated) but of other religions, like Hinduism, which thrive on the paradox that human experiences, for all their plurality, can nevertheless be comprehended in terms of divine, universal models. The Bible is itself a spectacular example of a collection of texts whose syncretic reading by Christians through twenty centuries has inspired and validated a range of human endeavours so enormous that considerable theological effort is needed to reconcile them.

Religion (although certainly not religiosity) has been an abiding interest throughout Finnissy's career. The idealist philosophical stance that believes that the same moral and ethical precepts are constant across time and culture is itself a necessary feature of religions. A congruent philosophical position, which is perhaps closer to Finnissy's immediate concerns as a composer, is that advanced by Busoni in his 'Sketch of a New Esthetic of Music'.[4] Busoni's advocacy in his essay of composition as the art of 'transcription' is a recurrent subject throughout the present book; Busoni goes on to argue that 'the performance of a work is also a transcription'[5] and justifies these claims by arguing that

> the musical art-work exists, before its tones resound and after they die away, *complete and intact*. It exists both within and outside of time and through its nature we can obtain a definite conception of the otherwise intangible notion of the Ideality of Time...[6]

Here too is the same conviction that ideas (and, for Busoni, particularly musical ideas) exist in some extra-temporal plane and then take on a specific local form each time they are 'transcribed'.

Finnissy's creation of textual materials for his vocal music is informed by a similar approach. In many works texts are also drawn together from a variety of sources - different times, different places, different cultures. *World*, for example, links William Blake, Myakovsky, Hölderlin, Tennyson, Rimbaud, Hopkins and Dante, with each text excerpted from longer originals. Of other composers with whose work this approach has affinities perhaps the closest is Berio: in works like *Laborintus II*, *Sinfonia* and *A-Ronne* the interconnections between a lattice of texts are explored during the course of the music. Where Finnissy and Berio differ is in the degree of intertextual integration: Berio tends to favour the use of a 'host' text, into which other texts are interpolated, so that all sub-texts are understood in relation to the dominant 'host'; Finnissy generally adopts a less hierarchical approach, where texts co-exist and the relationship between different texts' meanings is more fluid.

Behind this lies Finnissy's preoccupation - recurrent thoughout his work but more obvious since the early 1980s - in making work whose significance is both particular and general. By drawing together texts from a number of different sources Finnissy is able to exploit each text's particularity, providing the local colour on which his invention thrives; by juxtaposing these different texts he is able to draw our attention to larger, transcultural issues. For example, *Maldon* is a site-specific work about a battle around an Essex estuary in the 10th century, described in an eleventh-century poem; on the other hand, Finnissy's decision to set this poem in a modern English translation and his addition of two 13th-century texts as a choral commentary on the older text makes *Maldon* into a piece about *all* battles, *all* conflicts.

There will be those who argue that such a project is fundamentally anti-progressive; after all, if the human experience is a universal constant why try to improve the conditions in which the mass of humanity struggle to survive?

Here, Finnissy would seem to be equivocal - the struggle for change, whether it be material or spiritual, for enlightenment, redemption or transcendence, must be undertaken, but there can be no certainty of fulfilment. Perhaps paradoxically, such equivocation is by no means inconsistent with the Catholic tradition within Christianity, a wing of the church which has accommodated many famous doubters.

Certain other characteristic thematic concerns become apparent when one surveys Finnissy's vocal music as a whole. Love, whether sacred or profane, is perhaps pre-eminent (and transcription is itself a musical act of love). Love-songs abound, from *Horrorzone* (1968-71) onwards ('Amor vuol ch'io sempre ami' ('Love bids me love forever') sings the soprano in *Horrorzone's* setting of Tasso), but love is revealed as an emotion all too easily lost or soured. In *World*, a fragment from Rimbaud's *Les Illuminations* praises 'the lover, neither tormenting nor tormented', but 'the dream crumbles'. In *Unknown Ground* love brings disease and death. Elsewhere, the importance of being true to one's self, of making a principled defence of one's beliefs regardless of the consequences, is paramount. Byrhtnoth in *Maldon*, Tchaikovsky in *Shameful Vice* and Stanley Stokes are all victims in the sense that they died as a consequence of what they represented and because the alternative to death - compromise and its attendant shame - was unacceptable.

Certain characteristics in Finnissy's choice of text also emerge. In the concert vocal music Finnissy is usually uninterested in texts which tell complete stories from start to finish; he is much more likely to choose a text which isolates the emotional intensity of particular moments, particular scenes. As in so much else in his work there are parallels to be drawn with film. As Eisenstein demonstrated, a montage sequence which cuts between faces and actions is read by the viewer as depicting the reactions of those faces to the actions seen. Great film-making is often the art of nuance, an art at its most powerful when a movement of the camera or a cut in the editing room makes us 'see' things which are really not there, drawing the viewer's imagination across the gap between frames of film.

In Michael Finnissy's music a text will, typically, quickly define a scene (the 'establishing' shot) with a description in which adjectival qualification adds emotional weight ('reaction' shots); further observations will be made (a montage of 'cut-aways'); in the shortest pieces, like some of the *Songs*, this suffices, in longer pieces we move on to the next scene. Often (and again one is reminded of Eisenstein's studies in montage) emotion is articulated not directly but through the writer's response to an observed scene: '*Fiercely* the *gaunt* woods to the *grim* soil cling', sings the soprano in *Song 11*; a look is exchanged in 'the *happy* field of hay' [my italics] at the beginning of *Silver Morning*, Finnissy's 'supplement' to Vaughan Williams' Housman settings.

In the general comments above I have avoided any discussion of Finnissy's vocal idiom *per se* for a number of reasons. Most importantly, there is no rigid distinction in his music between the musical vocabularies of voices and instruments beyond obvious practical considerations of range and mobility. This will become particularly clear in the paragraphs on *Mountainfall* and *Ohi! ohi! ohi!*, both of which are virtuoso 'instrumental' pieces for solo voice. Finnissy's vocal writing has changed as his music as a whole has developed: wide leaping lines gave way to much narrower, microtonally inflected figuration which in turn has been succeeded by more obviously modal writing. Because technique is always an expressive consideration in Finnissy's work, his approach to the use of voices and instruments has been modified from piece to piece and within pieces, according to the requirements of each project.

In the popular mythology of performers' gossip about contemporary music Finnissy has often been regarded as 'difficult'. Certainly any soloist considering these works must have complete control, not only of the vocal instrument itself but also of pitch (including the ability to sing microtones at will and not just as an involuntary decoration!), rhythm and dynamics; in fact, all the musicianly qualities of singers like Josephine Nendick, Jane Manning and Richard Jackson with whom Finnissy has chosen to work over the years. Much of Finnissy's vocal music is spectacularly difficult and will remain the exclusive province of such singers, or, as in the case of choral works like *Cipriano* and *Kelir*, of specialist ensembles like the John Alldis Singers or the London Sinfonietta Voices. Recordings of these works demonstrate, however, that for all their difficulty they are supremely *vocal* works which take a visceral delight in this the most physically immediate of musical media.

Finnissy's engagement in composition for amateur musicians[7] has demonstrated that he is capable of creating music which is practicable for less expert singers and which can, without compromise, bear the full weight of his expressive intentions. Indeed, the expressive needs of the composer and the technical capabilities of performers seem to have gone hand in hand. As the drones which had underpinned much of Finnissy's writing since the early 1980s became more stable, and as white-note modes became an increasingly important part of his vocabulary, he found himself writing for singers for whom harmonic reference points and familiar intervals were an invaluable support, enabling them to project themselves wholeheartedly in performance. In a number of these works Finnissy combines professional soloists with amateur chorus; in so doing he is always careful to differentiate the dramatic functions of the different types of singer. In *Maldon*, for example, the solo baritone carries forward the battle narrative while the choir offer a more reflective perspective; in *Anima Christi* the relationship is closer to that of celebrants and congregation in worship.

What follows is a series of more detailed readings of a selection of vocal works from across Finnissy's career. In general I have tried to avoid duplicating those aspects of detailed musical analysis which Ian Pace and Julian Anderson have explored in other chapters; the same techniques for pitch and rhythmic derivation can be found in the vocal music as in all other areas of Finnissy's music. That I have chosen these rather than any number of the other works in the Finnissy catalogue indicates nothing more than a mixture of personal preference (although a number of my favourites are not included) and the need to represent different types of work.

Le Dormeur du Val

Michael Finnissy has often discussed the importance of cinematic thinking in the formation of his creative personality. What is remarkable in *Le Dormeur du Val* (1963-8), his intended 'Opus One', is the audacity with which the composer, still in his teens, carries through his musical film-making. Rimbaud's poem describes a valley, a stream running through it, a young soldier lying by the water; throughout the poem we are told that he is asleep, taking a nap. Only at the end of the poem do we discover that he has 'deux trous rouges' (two red holes) in his left side; suddenly all the clues which Rimbaud had scattered through his description of the young man make sense - his mouth open, his sickly smile: he's dead...

In cinematic terms it is as if we see the figure from a series of different elevations of a single overhead crane shot: at first within the larger landscape, only slowly getting closer. Intercut are a series of close-ups of details, his bare head, his open mouth, the way his feet lie among the flowers; only at the very end do we see the close-up of his wounds. All this we hear from the singer, but the piece contains another, even more audaciously filmic coup, a central section for the instruments alone (but without celesta) which functions as a flashback. As in the flashback/dream sequences of classic Hollywood movies, there are crucial signifiers in both text and imagery. As the mezzo sings 'dort' ('sleeps') the music dissolves into tremolo glissandi in the strings and trills and tremoli in the piano and celesta (see Example 5.2a) and we enter a world in which the arabesques of the first section are replaced by abrupt single events - either individual attacks, or flurries of clusters in the keyboards - which unambiguously represent the sound of gunfire. Ethereal string glissandi return and, as Example 5.2b demonstrates, we come out of this nightmare sequence into the daylight again as the singer continues her description.

The work is scored for mezzo-soprano, piano, harpsichord, celesta and string quartet and, as Richard Barrett has observed, 'it is possible to find echoes of a Boulezian sound-world in the use of three keyboard instruments producing diffuse washes of sound and occasional knotted outbursts.' [8] The vocal writing of *Le Dormeur* also betrays something of the influence of Boulez *chez* Mallarmé (but in early 1960s new music the sound of the female voice in *Pli Selon Pli* was almost all-pervasive) (see Example 5.3). What is quite un-Boulezian, however, is the harmonic density of Finnissy's music. While the timbral world, by turns limpid and scintillating, of Boulez's Mallarmé settings always articulates a fundamentally static harmonic framework, Finnissy's harmonies are in a state of constant evolution and cannot readily be reduced to permutations of a simple harmonic matrix.

Example 5.2a *Le Dormeur du Val*, p. 4, second system

Le Dormeur is also full of early examples of that interpenetration of harmonic and timbral thinking which is perhaps *the* defining characteristic of mature Finnissy. Quartertones and glissandi regularly blur the outline of pitch collections and the harmonic temperature of the music fluctuates dramatically between the densest clusters and the clearest unisons. The spectacular *denouement* of the work's last five bars (see Example 5.4), the music's final shiver of horror, illustrates this perfectly.

Equally un-Boulezian is the bold simplicity of *Le Dormeur*'s formal organisation - two vocal 'scenes' framing the central instrumental 'flashback' - and the literalness of the music's metaphors. In the prevailing aesthetic climate of the carly 1960s avant-garde, a world in which serially-derived formal abstractions were still very much the order of the day, it is hard to imagine a more provocative statement of intent than that offered by the youthful Finnissy, nor one carried off with more bravado.

Example 5.2b *Le Dormeur du Val*, p. 8

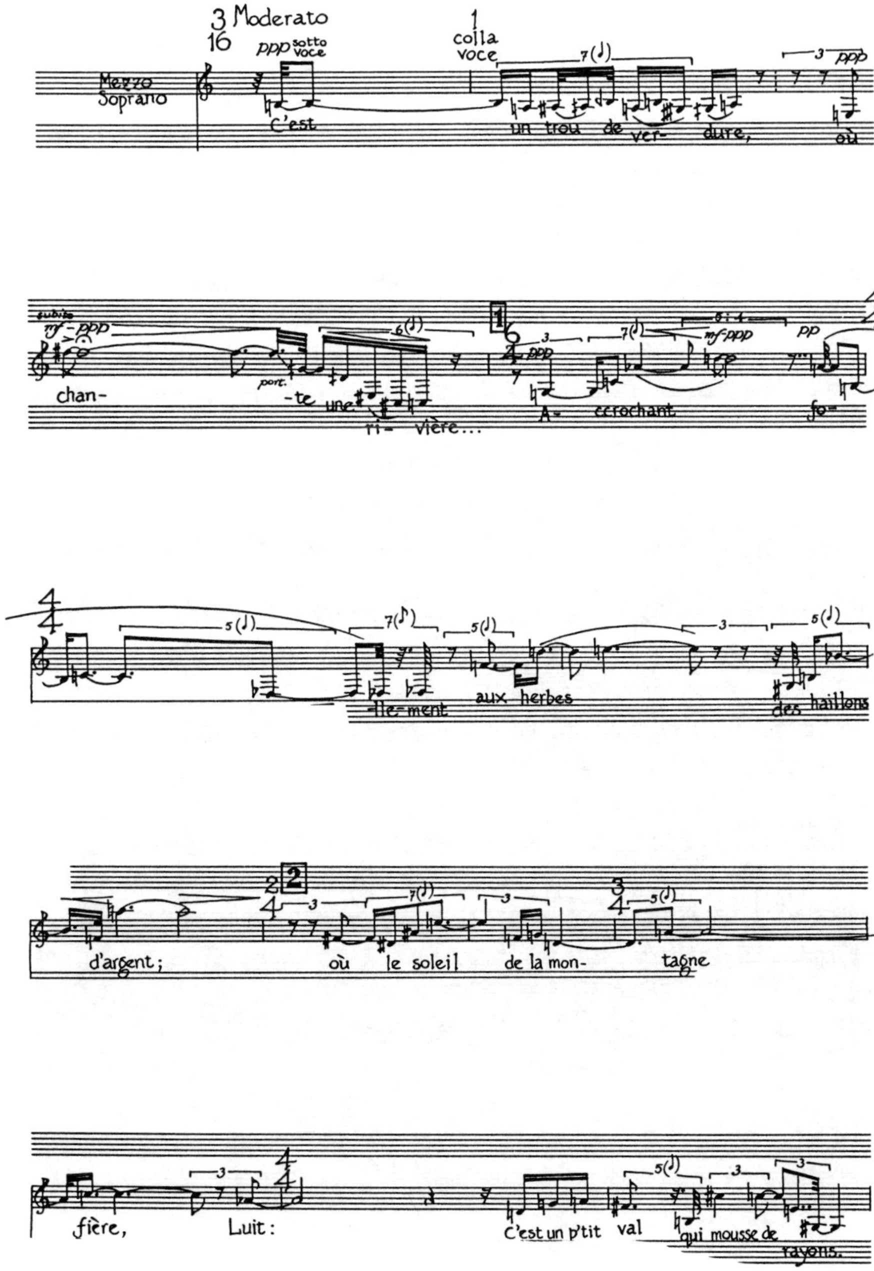

Example 5.3 *Le Dormeur du Val*, voice part, pp. 1-2 ('Accrochant...d'argent')

Example 5.4 *Le Dormeur du Val*, last five bars

Songs

The series of works entitled *Song* consists of eighteen pieces for a variety of media, few of which are 'songs' in the conventional sense. Only six involve a singer: *Song 1* (1966), *Songs 14* and *15* (both 1974) and *Song 16* (1976) are all for solo soprano, *Song 3* (1969) is for soprano, cor anglais, horn, piano and electric organ and *Song 11* (1969-71) is for soprano and clarinet. All of them have the unitary intensity to be found in early cinema, where form was often defined by little more than the number of reels of film to be shot: each scene was timed to fit the length of a single reel and the camera turned until the reel was used up; the action could only change significantly at the end of each reel. In this sense Finnissy's *Songs* are mostly one-reelers: a collection of musical characters are gathered within the frame and the piece consists of a series of exchanges between these characters.

The *Songs* are also full of highly ornate musical imagery. Melodic lines come elaborately dressed in arabesques, with the extravagant instrumental gestures of *Song 3*, for example, coming as close to the high camp of Bussotti as anything in Finnissy's output (see Example 5.5). The language of the text for *Song 11* is similarly extravagant, a fragment from 'On the Cliffs', a poem by the flamboyant master of *fin-de-siècle* decadence, Algernon Charles Swinburne: 'Between the moon dawn and the sun-down here the twilight hangs half starless... Fiercely the gaunt woods to the grim soil cling that bears for all fair fruits wan wild sparse flowers of windy and wintry Spring.'

Example 5.5 *Song 3*, first bar

Elsewhere in this book Ian Pace has drawn attention to the other defining characteristic of all the *Songs*, their preoccupation with extreme opposites - high/low, movement/stasis, long/short. *Song 11* presents us with a number of these. At the simplest level there is the contrast between the first half of the piece, for clarinet alone, and the second half, where the soprano joins the clarinet. Then within the clarinet part there is a host of opposites - very long and very short notes, regular and irregular rhythmic groupings, metric notations 'inside' time and grace note notations 'outside' time, high notes and low notes; Example 5.6a shows the third phrase of the clarinet part which includes all of these oppositions. When the singer enters, her line could be heard as offering a sort of musical mediation - the same contrasts are evident but none is so extreme as in the clarinet part - and after one last flourish (Example 5.6b) the clarinet plays nothing but long notes, each of which anticipates or echoes a neighbouring pitch in the vocal part (see Example 5.6c).

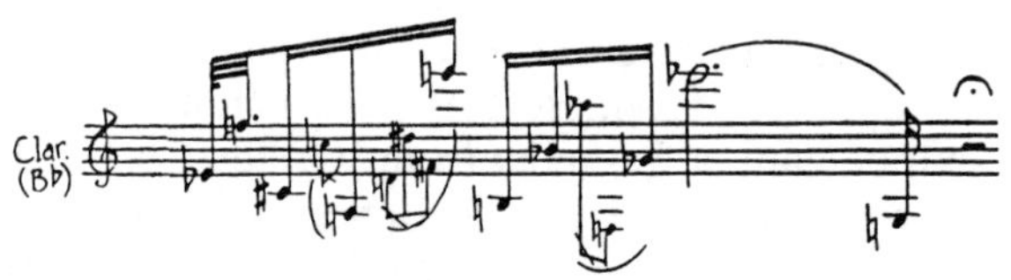

Example 5.6a *Song 11* (clarinet line)

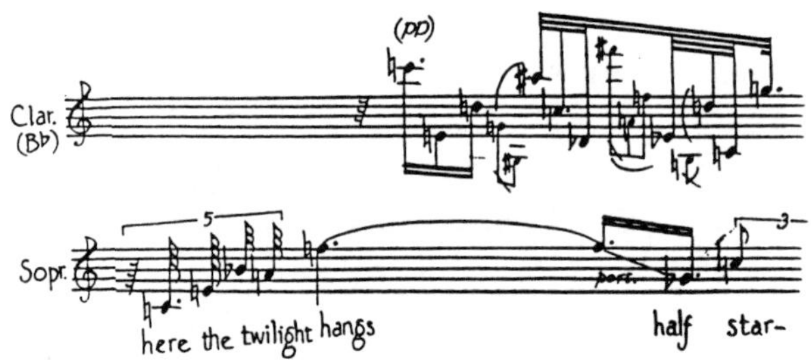

Example 5.6b *Song 11* (clarinet and soprano)

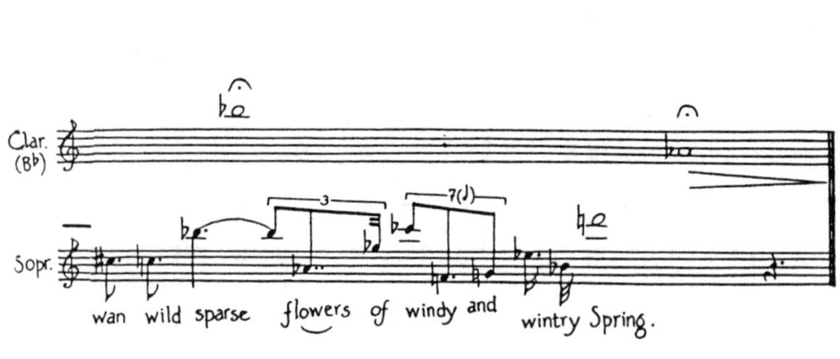

Example 5.6c *Song 11* (clarinet and soprano)

World

As titles go, *World* stakes a big claim, and at the time of its première *World* was Finnissy's most ambitious work: almost 20 minutes of music scored for six amplified singers, singing seven different texts, with an ensemble of 27 instrumentalists, divided into the three groups shown in Example 5.7. Such a disposition of forces might suggest a spectacular *tour de force* cast in the same mould as other works in the avant-garde *cori spezzati* tradition which flourished on the continental European music festival circuit in the 1970s (Ferneyhough's *Firecycle Beta* (1969-71) and *Transit* (1972-75) are notable examples and *Transit* was indeed given its first performance in the 1975 Royan Festival by the same forces who premièred *World*). *World* is, however, resolutely unspectacular, a work of considerable textural complexity which spends much of its time at the quiet end of the dynamic spectrum, only occasionally gathering all its available energies for grand, collective gestures.

1	2	3
2 sopranos	Contralto Tenor	Baritone Bass
Alto flute Tenor saxophone	Oboe/oboe d'amore Clarinet	Flute Oboe/cor anglais
2 trumpets	Horn	Trombone Tuba
Piano	Celesta Cimbalom Harp	Piano
Percussion	Percussion	Percussion
2 violas 2 double basses		2 violins 2 celli

Example 5.7 Instrumentation in *World*

The first performance was given by the London Sinfonietta, directed by Simon Bainbridge, at the 1975 Royan Festival and the incentive to complete the work was provided by a commission from Royan.[9] But Finnissy had begun *World* in 1968 and the choice of texts is indicative of the young composer's fondness for the headily rich imagery of late-19th century poetry (the score betrays another turn-of-the-century enthusiasm: Finnissy's calligraphy on this occasion is obviously borrowed from Charles Rennie Mackintosh!). A scrutiny of the texts - by Blake, Dante, Hölderlin, Hopkins, Mayakovsky, Rimbaud and Tennyson - reveals that the world-view which Finnissy intends to communicate is rich in the paradoxes of subjectivity. Central to each of the texts is the idea of transience, time passing, insights fleetingly gained, the shadowy boundary between the real and the dream. In the words of Mayakovsky, which, like an invocation, are the first to be sung after the start of the work, 'the sea is going away to sleep'; the idea of the endless ebbing and flowing of the tides is elided with the ebb and flow of our own bodies' wakefulness. Later Finnissy turns to Tennyson's *In Memoriam*:

The hills are shadows, and they flow
From form to form and nothing stands;
They melt like mist, the solid lands,
Like clouds they shape themselves and go.

At the core of the *World* ensemble are no fewer than seven keyboard instruments which, together with the harp, spin a web of sound around almost every moment of the music, shrouding it in ambiguity. Finnissy's treatment of his multiple texts is similarly ambiguous: often different texts are overlaid one on another and even single texts are almost always shared between at least two voices, so that the sense of the words is always blurred. The pairing of similar voices in each sub-group of the ensemble further blurs the outline of phrases and the sense of words, as Example 5.8, the first vocal entry, demonstrates. Mayakovsky's Russian sentences are split between the two sopranos who nevertheless share common pitches at the extremes of each phrase.

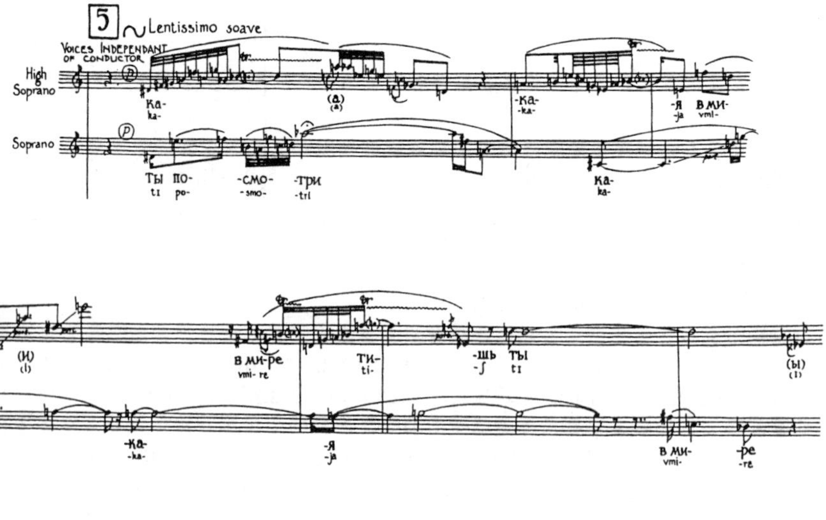

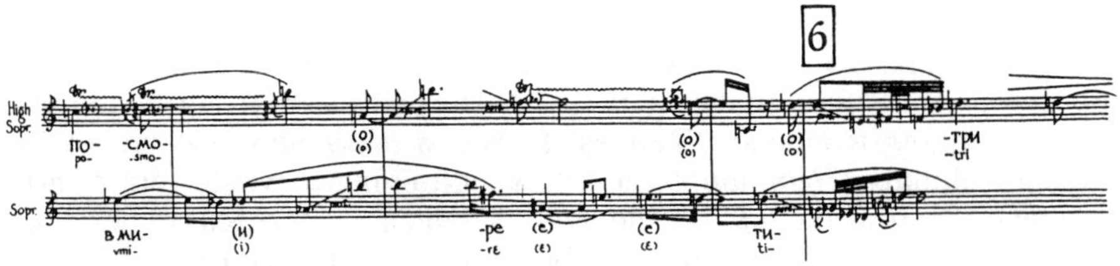

Example 5.8 *World*, pp. 3-4 (voices only)
Reproduced by permission of Edition Modern

The first unambiguous moment does not occur until the end of the work, when for the first time all six voices sing together:

> Love what are love's worthiest, were all known
> World's loveliest - men's selves.
> Self flashes off frame and face. (Hopkins)

But even here the image is clouded by percussion and harp figures playing independently of the main tempo (see Example 5.9 which shows ensemble 2's path through this entire section; ensembles 1 and 3 add similar vocal flourishes for the other voices and trumpets, trombone and percussion to the clarinet attacks).

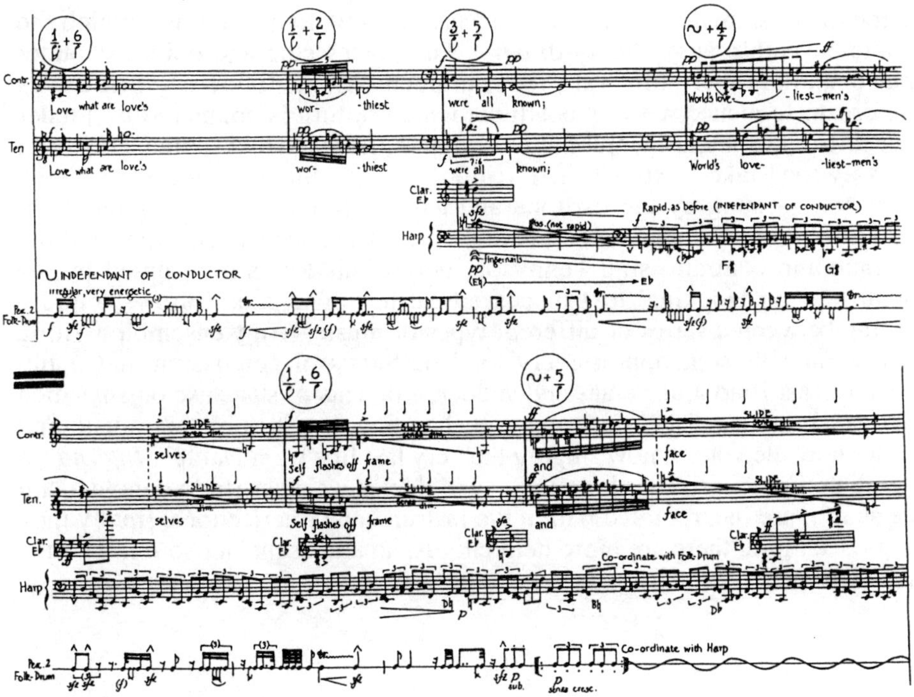

Example 5.9 *World*, pp. 41-2 (ensemble 2 only)
Reproduced by permission of Edition Modern

The densest passage occurs about a third of the way into the score, between rehearsal figures 15 and 16, when the conductor triggers each of the three sub-groups into independent action. First comes sub-group 1, the high soprano singing Rimbaud ('Veilées' from *Les Illuminations*), the soprano singing Hölderlin (*Hyperion* - a text to which Finnissy would return in the tenor and piano work, *...fairest noonday...*, which I will discuss later); then sub-group 3 with both men singing Rimbaud; next sub-group 2, the contralto whispering the entire Hölderlin text, the tenor singing 'O du, mit deinem Göttern, Natur! ich hab ihn ausgeträumt' ('O thou with thy gods, Nature! I have dreamed it') after which he whispers 'von Menschendingen den Traum' ('the dream of human things'). Curiously, at the front of the score Finnissy includes one more line, 'Et le rêve fraîchit' ('and the dream crumbles'), from his Rimbaud extract, which is never sung; the evolution of this passage, however, is a most precise musical translation of the line: the initially extended flurries of instrumental grace notes get shorter and are interspersed with longer notes while each voice eventually lapses into a whisper. As this process approaches its conclusion the music is suddenly overwhelmed by bass drum crescendi from all the percussionists; these too then quickly dissolve into silence and give way to a protracted meditation on this 'dream'-moment.

Like many Finnissy works from the 1970s, *World* is made up of a series of intercut blocks of material. An instrumental introduction, dominated by the sound of the cimbalom, leads to the Mayakovsky invocation into which the whole ensemble is gradually drawn. The voices stop and quicker, louder music, marked 'very forceful', for instruments alone, follows. Then comes the dream sequence with its postlude, which in turn is countered by louder fast instrumental music, 'jubilant - songlike, fierce and ecstatic', preparing the way for Blake - 'Stars of fire rise ... And one Sun each morning, like a New born' - sung by the baritone and bass within an abruptly quieter and slower version of the preceding texture. Just as suddenly this stops and the soprano and contralto sing Tennyson, before this too is interrupted by the vocal tutti on Hopkins' text discussed earlier. The coda follows, rapidly cutting between a series of different types of music - edgy ensemble writing in rhythmic unison, oppressively loud outbursts of percussion and piano clusters, fast fluid arabesques and sudden moments of suspense on sustained chords. Example 5.10 illustrates the changing densities of this music and shows how the voices, now singing the very last line from Dante's *Inferno* ('e quindi uscimmo a riveder le stelle' - 'and thence we emerged to behold again the stars'), are incorporated within the instrumental interjections; finally they sing once more, there are more held chords, an arabesque, a chord ... and the work is over.

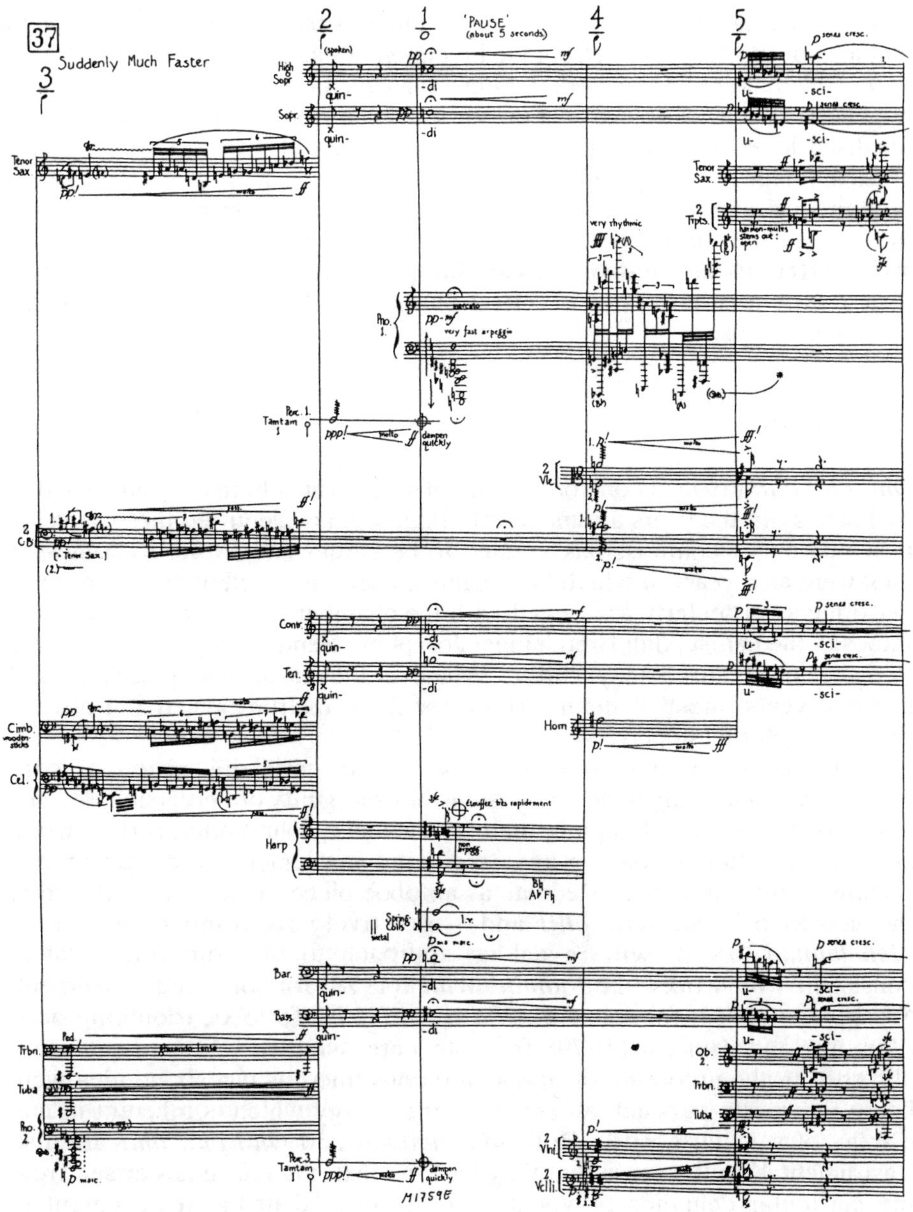

Example 5.10 *World,* p. 46
Reproduced by permission of Edition Modern

World is full of incident and invention, tantalising its listeners with glimpses of so many things. Indeed Finnissy has hinted that, buried in the section which I describe as the dream sequence, there are brief allusions to every piece he had then written. (For example, the bass part in Ensemble 3 on page eighteen of the score is a retrograde inversion of part of *Le Dormeur du Val*.) A possible reading of the work, taking advantage of clues in the texts chosen, might hear the *whole* piece as a dream sequence whose climax is a vision of idealised love. Certainly the formal organisation of *World*, with so many musical images flashing before our ears only to be so swiftly snatched away, is akin to dreaming. But the myriad images of dreaming usually form themselves into narratives, however bizarre; in just 20 minutes of music *World* offers us the stuff of a dream but perhaps not the space in which to form our own narratives or to reflect on the relationship between our inner and outer worlds.

Ohi! ohi! ohi!

Ohi! ohi! ohi! (1978) is one of a group of works for solo instruments written by Finnissy in the years around 1980. Finnissy has identified these as years in which major commissions seemed to be harder and harder to come by; they were also years in which he became closely involved with the group of performers particularly associated with the chamber ensembles Suoraan and Exposé - the cellist Alan Brett, singer Josephine Nendick, oboist Christopher Redgate and flautist Nancy Ruffer. Whatever the reason, solo pieces abound in these years, most of them written for these instruments, if not always specifically for these players.

If it seems perverse to link a vocal piece with discussion of solo instrumental music, then the composer is himself guilty of perversity: *Moon's goin' down* (1980), although written for the tenor, John Potter, is designated as being for 'tenor solo or any solo wind instrument' and was indeed premièred by Christopher Redgate as an oboe piece. However, a glance at the scores of *Ohi! ohi! ohi!* and - effectively its companion piece - *Mountainfall* (1978) will reveal an approach to the solo form that is consistent with works like *Runnin' Wild* (1978) for solo reed instrument, *Sikangnuqa* (1979) for solo flute, *Pavasiya* (1979) for oboe (doubling oboe d'amore) and *Hinomi* (1979) for solo percussionist. All are intensely absorbed in the unfolding of near-continuous lines, as if a single idea were being rigorously pursued; all celebrate the energy which is inherent in any display of solo virtuosity. Both *Mountainfall* and *Ohi! ohi! ohi!* are also 'instrumental' in the sense that they have no text; the music has arisen from the particular demands of vocal writing rather than the requirement to articulate a particular set of words.

Mountainfall borrows quite heavily from the technical resources developed by Cathy Berberian and used most famously in Berio's *Sequenza III*. There are passages involving the extremely rapid articulation of consonants to create an effect akin to a wind-player's triple tonguing (see Example 5.11);

there are 'dental tremoli', where the lower jaw trembles to create a sort of amplitude vibrato; there is extensive use of glissandi, coupled with the alternation of in- and out-breaths, so that the last two and a half minutes of the piece run continuously (Berio does the same in the latter part of *Sequenza V* for trombone).

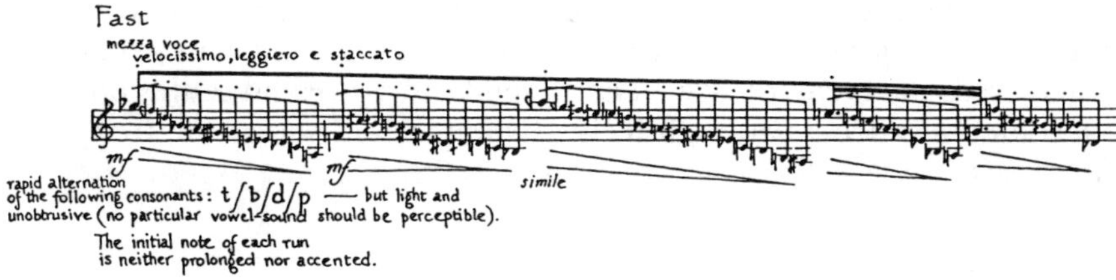

Example 5.11 *Mountainfall*, opening line

But this is not another in the legions of look-alike *Sequenzas* that have filled singers' programmes and publishers' catalogues since the mid-60s. The fundamental distinction between *Mountainfall* and the Berio turns on the role assigned to the performer. In *Sequenza III* (and indeed in *Sequenza V*) the performer represents 'the performer', engaged in some sort of struggle to fashion material which may or may not prove satisfactory either to the audience or to 'the performer'. In *Mountainfall* and *Ohi! ohi! ohi!* the performer *is* the music, her virtuosity deployed unironically to realise the performance text provided by the composer. In *Mountainfall* Finnissy goes so far as to produce a work whose formal dynamic might be heard as representing the singer's own waning energy. The rapid articulations of the opening page, each followed by a 'very long pause' allowing the singer literally to get her breath back, give way to progressively slower music in a narrower tessitura on open vowels. Then humming is introduced and for the latter part of the piece continuous glissandi are performed on alternate in- and out-breaths (Example 5.12 shows the transition between the middle and final sections). It as if the singer has begun in a state of manic hyperactivity and ended in a near stupor, but unlike the *Songs*, whose extremes were also opposed within single musical forms, *Mountainfall* spends as much time in the middle of the continuum as at the extremes.

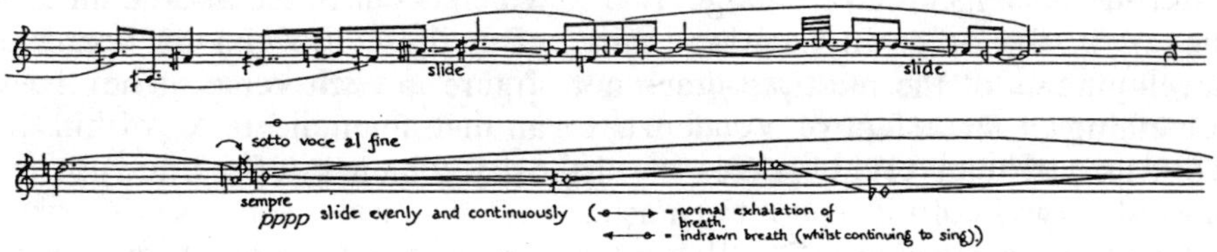

Example 5.12 *Mountainfall*, p. 6, first two lines

Ohi! ohi! ohi! is one of the early examples of the new Finnissy manner that emerged at the end of the 1970s. Whereas *Mountainfall* is derived from abstract musical conceptions - rapid-slow, wide-narrow, broken-continuous, sound-silence - *Ohi! ohi! ohi!* has its roots in a particular musical tradition, made explicit at the head of the score where Finnissy asks for a 'vibrant, rather harsh tone (as in Eastern European folk singing)'. It is possible also to trace the vestigial traces of a strophic form beneath the vocal extravagance of the work's surface. Each 'verse' begins with a narrow, microtonally-inflected,[10] turning phrase around G^1 and goes on to a phrase in which rapid glissandi cross the break between chest- and head-voice and settles on longer notes, sometimes decorated with trills. Example 5.13 shows the first two of these 'verses'.

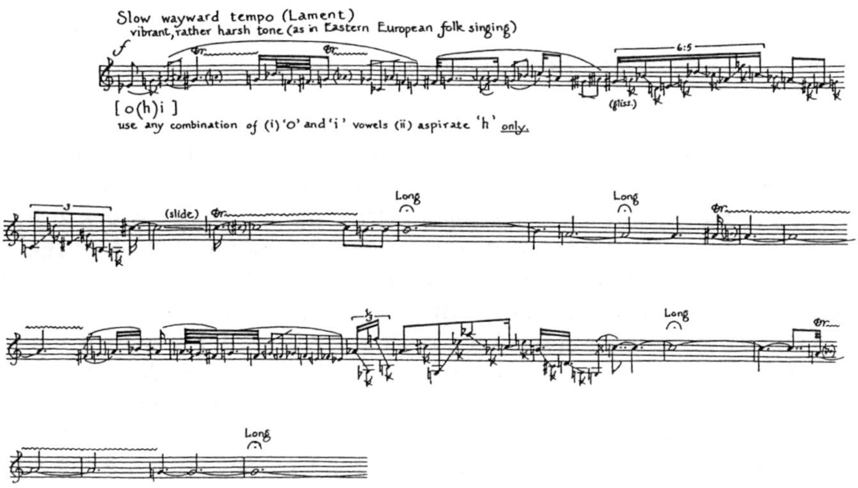

Example 5.13 *Ohi! ohi! ohi!*, p. 1

Almost everything in the work can be traced back to the morphology of the various gestures out of which these verses are made. The exceptions are two chorus-like passages which occur roughly one-third and two-thirds of the way through the piece. The pitch contour of these passages is, however, rather like a stretched version of the glissandi figure *without* the glissandi. There are also three spectacular series of continuous sixty-fourth notes, each covering the singer's entire range, two of which occur in the middle third of the work, the other in the final third. But these too can be heard as developments of the multiple grace note figure in each verse. They have something of the effect of a cadenza, or an instrumental break, within the work as a whole, vivid flashes of virtuosity which briefly interrupt the onward progress of the rest of the music.

The example above also illustrates a recurrent feature of the 'new' Finnissy, the use of tonal centres. These 'centres' are often not visible to the analytical eye if it is searching for the literal predominance of particular pitch classes, because in the Finnissy works of this period they have a tendency to drift higher or lower, often by as much as three-quarters of a tone. The ear, however, becomes aware of particular pitch zones functioning as the centre for the music around them. In Example 5.13 I would suggest that G and C act as central points; indeed these centres remain audible throughout the work. The interval of a perfect fourth is a favourite Finnissy pitch relationship, wide enough to survive a certain amount of the drift described above, narrow enough to be accommodated within a single registral identity on most instruments, and with obvious cadential implications.

Kelir

Of Finnissy's music for voices *Kelir* (1981) is the crowning achievement of his 'eastern/folk' period. Many of the same techniques - long-breathed microtonal lines which stretch out over drones; abrupt timbral changes between successive sections; the use of irrational durational proportions to create metrical fluidity while retaining rhythmic distinction - occur in other pieces from around the same time but are rarely deployed with the same single-minded intensity as in *Kelir*. For 17 minutes Finnissy invents a string of vivid musical images for his six unaccompanied voices, transporting his listeners into an exotic landscape which, while full of resonances from other musical cultures, is specific only to the composer's imagination.

'Kelir' is the name of the curtain onto which Javanese shadow-plays are projected (yet another form of film!) and Nigel Osborne, introducing the first broadcast of *Kelir,* suggested that one might hear the drones which underpin most sections of the work as a musical curtain onto which the figures of Finnissy's music are projected. Osborne went on to point out that the 'kelir' in Finnissy's music is sometimes 'still and diaphanous', at other times 'stormy and billowing', a happy metaphor for Finnissy's use of alternately static and shifting drones. Example 5.14 shows the two types of drones: in 5.14a the sopranos sing extended melodic lines above a constant G sharp_{II} - C sharp_{I} drone which is shared between the four lower voices; in 5.14b contralto and tenor move within a pitch-band between E^{I} and B flat^{I}, while the baritone and bass move within a slightly narrower pitch-band between C_{I} and F quarter-tone flat_{I}.

Example 5.14a *Kelir*, first two systems

Example 5.14b *Kelir,* p. 22, second system and p. 23, top system

Each section of ***Kelir*** is defined by similar distinctions of voice and pitch distribution, as the following table (Example 5.15) demonstrates (the numbering of section is mine, not the composer's):

	Division of voices	Musical characterisation	Tempo	Duration
1	2 sopranos	Microtonal melodies (mostly trills)	= 72	ca. 2' 45" (to figure 6)
	contralto, tenor, baritone, bass	Static drones (G sharp, C sharp)		
2	S, S	Static drones (D, D sharp, eventually E)	= 72	ca. 1' 35" (to one bar before figure 11)
	A, T	Microtonal melodies (mostly trills)		
	Bar, B	Mobile drones, eventually adopting same character as A and T		
3	S, S	Microtonal melodies (scales and arabesques)	= 63	ca. 1' 24" (to figure 15)
	A, T, Bar, B	Static drones (B, E)		
4	S, S, A	Wide-ranging semitonal melodies	= 54	ca. 2' 30" (to five bars before figure 21)
	T, Bar, B	Mobile drones		
5	S1	'Chinese cymbal' interjections	= 54	ca. 1' 51" (to figure 24)
	A, T	Mobile drones		
	Bar, B	Mobile drones		
6	S, S, A, T, Bar, B	Six-part texture - short quick phrases, rhythmic unisons, pauses, longer notes	= 104	ca. 0' 39" (to figure 27)

7	S, S	Mobile drones (first to enter, first to finish)	= 58	ca. 6' 38"
	A, T	Mobile drones (second to enter, A drops out before end)		
	Bar, B	Mobile drones (last to enter, last to finish)		

Example 5.15 Sectional analysis of *Kelir*

That such broad characterisations of the types of music from which *Kelir* is made illustrates the fundamental simplicity of Finnissy's conception, but at the same time this very simplicity makes rich variation possible within each type. As illustration, Example 5.16 shows two passages, both of which I have characterised as 'mobile drones' (Example 5.16a), and two which I have characterised as 'microtonal melodies' (Example 5.16b).

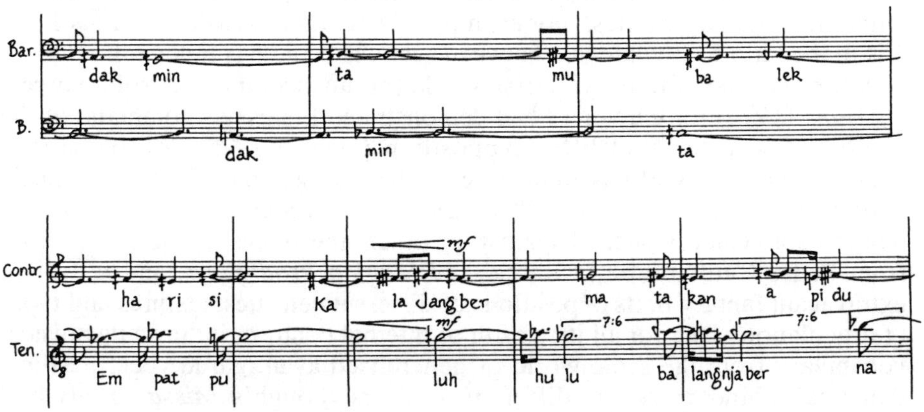

Example 5.16a Mobile drones in *Kelir*

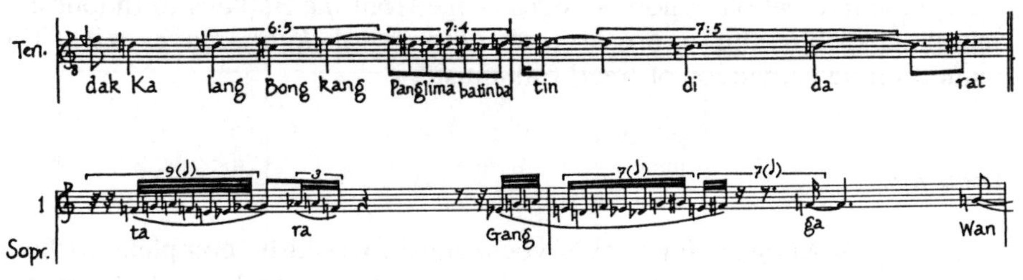

Example 5.16b Microtonal melodies in *Kelir*

But one could also argue that all the material of *Kelir* exists on a continuum from the uninflected long note to rapid figuration. Example 5.17 offers a version of this with material drawn from across the entire work. Particularly striking is the way in which the figure I have described above as 'chinese cymbal', a rapid glissando, is no more than an isolated repeat of the glissando figure which closes each soprano phrase at the start of the piece (see Example 5.14a).

Example 5.17 Evolution of figuration in *Kelir*

Equally simple are the tempo and proportional relationships between the sections of *Kelir*. As the table above shows, tempo relationships are in the approximate ratio 8 : 8 : 7 : 6 : 5 : 10+ : 5+ and many of the proportional relationships can be reduced to even simpler ratios, a number of which fall within the Fibonacci series. For example, the relation between sections 1 and 2 is in the ratio 5 : 3 while that between sections 5 and 6 is in the ratio 8 : 3.

Kelir was not Finnissy's first work for unaccompanied solo voices: *Cipriano* (1974) for ten voices had demonstrated Finnissy's command of the genre and won the Radcliffe composition prize in 1975. A comparison between the two works is indicative of the changes that Finnissy's music underwent at the end of the 1970s. *Cipriano* is a highly dramatic work, in which a solo tenor is pitched against the other nine voices in a setting of texts from Pedro Caldéron de la Barca's *El Mágico Prodigioso*, and is full of extravagant fantasy in its oppositions of different densities, textures and types of articulation. But, for all its wealth of internal contrast, it draws its musical vocabulary from the same world of generalised avant-garde vocal gestures that lies behind works as different as Ferneyhough's *Missa Brevis* and Kagel's *Hallelujah.* Structurally *Kelir* is a much simpler work, but it inhabits a musical world which is, paradoxically, both much more individual and yet also evocative of a much wider range of other musics; Finnissy's 'folk music' is a synthetic creation, whose sources range from the Balkans to Indonesian resonances, but the expressive directness of *Kelir* rings with the unquestioning conviction of 'real' folk music.

Anninnia

No survey of Michael Finnissy's vocal music would be complete without some discussion of those works which combine his own 'voice', the piano, with that of a singer. As was said earlier, there are no *Liederkreise* in the

Schubertian mould in Finnissy's output, although the intense subjectivity of a work like *Winterreise* is to be found in the recent work, *Unknown Ground*. Instead, in a number of works Finnissy makes use of a single text, or a number of texts edited together, sung across a more or less continuous span of music. The piano is never cast in a purely accompanimental role, instead these works are truly contrapuntal duos (paradoxically, nowhere is this clearer than in *Vertue* (1993) for piano and three treble voices in which the piano is almost always monophonic and the voices almost always homophonic!).

The most remarkable of these works is perhaps *Anninnia* (1981-82), dedicated to the soprano Elaine Barry but first performed by Jane Manning in the 1985 Huddersfield Contemporary Music Festival. The text is a Sardinian cradle-song in which derivatives of the nonsense-word 'anninnia' are interspersed within a text (in Sardinian) in which a mother wishes her son - 'whiter than a lily' - to sleep. The sentiment of the words is touching - 'forgive me if I somehow offend you when you grow up', she sings - and the sound of Sardinian itself an attractively exotic variant on Italian but, as with *Kelir*, their sense is bound to be lost on most audiences. Instead Finnissy pulls off a remarkable musical coup, stretching the image of a child, lulled into sleep by his mother's voice, over eleven minutes of music by the audaciously simple device of casting the piano in the role of the child. The piano's music begins loud, with three distinct lines, full of quick movement across the upper half of the piano (see Example 5.18a), and gradually falls, section by section, towards an ever quieter dynamic, to a single line, towards the centre of the pitch range covered by the first section (see Example 5.18b).

The soprano's part in contrast has a relatively consistent density and inhabits the pitch region between the A above middle C and the octave above for most of the piece. Idiomatically the vocal writing recalls *Kelir* and *Ohi! ohi! ohi!* in its use of ornamentation around lines within whose narrow tessitura one or two pitches will often seem to be exerting a particular gravitational attraction. The exceptions are two more wide-ranging, rhythmically more varied passages, marked 'senza rigore', which occur during the extended soprano solo passages (sections N and P in the diagram in Example 5.19).

Finnissy sustains interest across the general trajectory of the piece by alternating the three possible instrumental configurations: voice and piano together, soprano solo, piano solo. Example 5.19 demonstrates this changing distribution, showing the proportions of sections and their instrumental composition, and provides graphic evidence of Finnissy's artful construction. Nowhere does the alternation of different groupings recur more than three times (from E to L), nor do more than two sections of the same approximate length follow one another, but there is a clear background durational unit of about 55 eighth notes which sets up a deep structural pulse around which the whole piece flows. (Numbers in brackets in each section in the diagram express the duration of that section in terms of this unit.)

Example 5.18a *Anninnia*

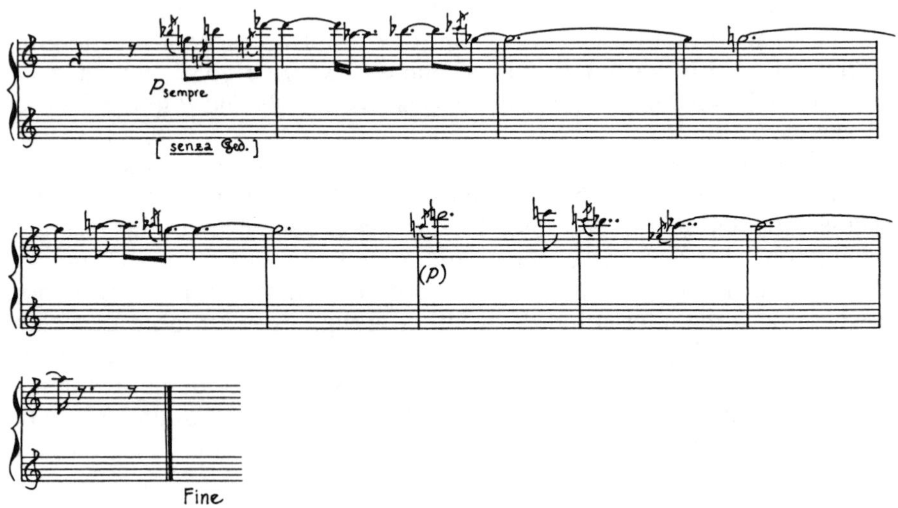

Example 5.18b *Anninnia*

				♪
A		SOPRANO + PIANO		55.5 (1)
B	SOPRANO			55 (1)
C		SOPRANO + PIANO		6 (1/9)
D			PIANO	23.5 (1/2)
E	SOPRANO			80 (1 1/2)
F		SOPRANO + PIANO		2.5 (1/22)
G			PIANO	37 (2/3)
H		SOPRANO + PIANO		38.5 (2/3)
I			PIANO	10 (2/11)
J		SOPRANO + PIANO		48.5 (1-)
K			PIANO	8.5 (2/13)
L		SOPRANO + PIANO		23 (1/2)
M			PIANO	13.5 (1/4)
N	SOPRANO			243.5 (4 1/2)
O			PIANO	21.5 (1/2-)
P	SOPRANO			217.5 (4)
Q			PIANO	23.5 (1/2-)
R		SOPRANO + PIANO		2.5 (1/22)
S	SOPRANO			58 (1+)
T		SOPRANO + PIANO		54 (1)
U			PIANO	3 (1/12)
V		SOPRANO + PIANO		48 (1-)
W	SOPRANO			4.5 (1/12)
X		SOPRANO + PIANO		62.5 (1+)

Example 5.19 Diagrammatic analysis of *Anninnia*

There is an interesting comparison to be made between *Anninnia* and another work for voice and piano from just three years earlier, *...fairest noonday...*(1979). As the dates suggest, these two works lie on either side of one of the great divides in Finnissy's outputs: intervals in the earlier music are generally wider, rhythms more consciously aperiodic (see Example 5.20), there are no immediate idiomatic affinities with musics beyond the European art-music tradition.

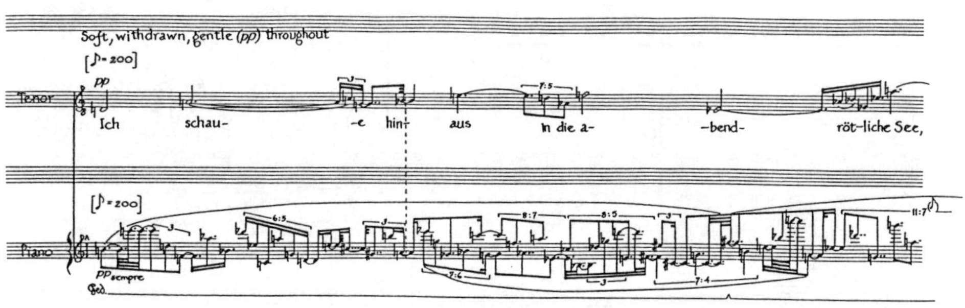

Example 5.20 *...fairest noonday...*, opening line

But *...fairest noonday...* shares with its later counterpart an expressive clarity of formal design which belies any attempt to categorise such music as 'difficult'. As in *Anninnia* the overall form of the work is articulated in terms of instrumental disposition but in *...fairest noonday...* the procedure is rather more complicated. The tenor's music falls into five long sections and one shorter section which overlay a seven-part structure in the piano part. The constituent elements in the piano part are defined registrally - high, middle and low - and the music gradually fills the registral space, as Example 5.21 demonstrates.

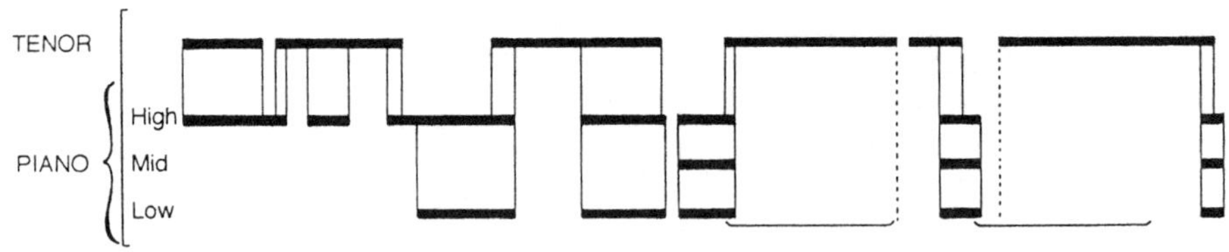

Example 5.21 Registral distribution in *...fairest noonday...*

As is also clear from the example above, much of the vocal part occurs in the gaps between the sections of the piano part. At the beginning these gaps are 'empty', but the penultimate two piano sections ring on into the gaps, the piano sound sustained by the pedal. There is no immediate instrumental mimesis of ideas in the text, nor even much aurally obvious co-ordination of the two parts. Consequently, those points where voice and piano come together are especially telling: the first entry of the low register and una corda pedalling after the tenor's second section ends; the alternation of piano and voice at the end of the work, with each piano section shorter than its predecessor but always saturating the instrument's acoustic space (see Example 5.22).

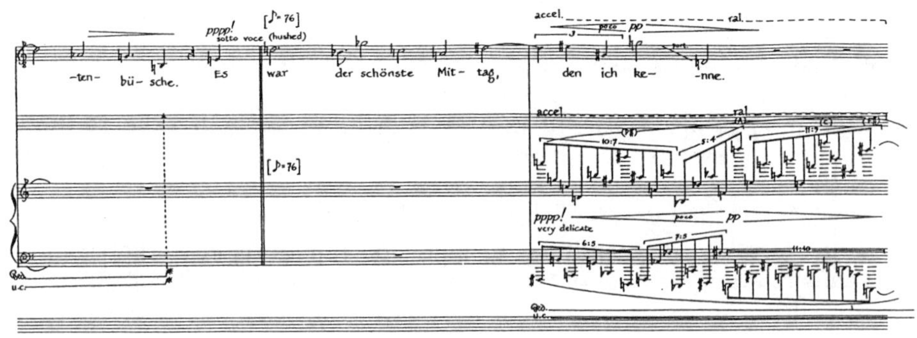

Example 5.22 *...fairest noonday...*

The six sections of the voice part - marked 'soft, withdrawn, gentle (*pp*) throughout' - are notated as continuous spans of music (but the first section, for instance, is almost thirty seconds long, so the tenor is going to breathe somewhere!). Each phrase encompasses the normal tenor range and all but the fifth section settle at some point, usually about two-thirds of the way through, on an ever higher note - B flat^{I}, B^{I}, C^{I}, C sharp^{II}, D sharp^{II}. It is as if the singer is yearning for something lost and ever more distant, a musical equivalent for the images in the German texts which Finnissy has assembled from Hölderlin: 'langsamsterbenden Jugend' ('slowly ebbing youth'), 'Bilder aus hellerer Zeit' ('visions of a brighter time'). Since Finnissy's setting often stretches words beyond the likely limits of sense (even for German speakers) it is through the music that the piece constructs most of its meanings. Crucially, however, the voice's fifth section (see Example 5.17 above), which lies outside the ascending pitch scheme described above, does allow verbal sense to be made of the singer's utterance, as he sings 'Es war der schönste Mittag, den ich kenne' ('it was the fairest noonday I have known'). Music expresses the sense of yearning, words describe its object.

Maldon

Maldon is a small town in north-east Essex, a few miles in from the coast, at the head of the tidal waters of the River Blackwater. In 1991 it commemorated the 1000th anniversary of the most famous event in its history, the battle of Maldon, with a new piece from Michael Finnissy, setting part of the Anglo-Saxon poem which described the events of the battle. Finnissy responded with *Maldon* (1990), a 20 minute work for baritone, two tenor trombones, two percussionists, SATB chorus and organ, which as well as using his own modern English translation of 'The Battle of Maldon' adds sections of anonymous 13th-century poetry as a commentary.

The battle of Maldon was fought in 991 between the men of the region, under Byrhtnoth, ealdorman of Essex, and a marauding Viking army whose fleet had sailed up the estuary Blackwater. The Vikings demanded Danegeld, protection money; Byrhtnoth refused to pay; there was a battle in which the Vikings were eventually beaten off, but only after Byrhtnoth himself had been slain. According to historians the battle, though bloody, was of no great historical importance and did little to stem the growing waves of Viking attacks on the east coast of England. The events of the battle and the figure of Byrhtnoth himself passed into legend, however, and 'The Battle of Maldon', is generally regarded as one of the finest Anglo-Saxon battle poems.

Finnissy's edited version of the original 'battle' poem reduces it to a text of pithy brevity, with all the urgency of late-20th century broadcast journalism. Each element of the original - narration, the Vikings' challenge, Byrhtnoth's response, his call to heaven as he dies, and cries for vengeance from his kinsmen - is present but is radically condensed to produce a series of sharply characterised scenes.[11] Some might regret the loss of the colour and rhythm of Anglo-Saxon, although it is unlikely that there were many in Maldon Church for the Millennium Festivities in 1991 who would have understood the original. It might also be argued that in re-casting the text with the pace of live TV reportage Finnissy has found the contemporary medium closest in tone and intention to 'The Battle of Maldon'.

The beginning of the original text has disappeared from the manuscript sources and it is with this truncated opening - appropriately the words are 'It was broken' - that Finnissy's narrator begins, after a series of screeching exchanges between two trombones, one off-stage right, the other off-stage left, each accompanied by sizzle cymbal tremoli. After his initial melismatic flourish (whose formal function within the work was discussed earlier in this chapter) the baritone declaims the text, syllable by syllable, over a percussion accompaniment, each syllable an emphatically uttered quarter-note separated from its predecessor by between two and five quarter-notes. As the narrative arrives at the end of the first scene in the drama an organ drone is added to the texture, anticipating (and providing a crucial reference pitch for) the first choral entry.[12]

The choir's music never sets any of the translated 'battle' poem; instead, they sing 13th-century texts which Finnissy leaves in medieval English. The majority of these interspersed texts consists of verses taken from an anonymous 13th-century poem, in the 'Ubi sunt' tradition of St Bernard of Clairvaux, in which the transience of earthly life is contrasted with the certainty of the life to come:

1 [16] Where beth they, beforen us weren,
Houndes ladden and havekes beren,
And hadden feld and wode...

[*Where are they who lived before us,
who led hounds and carried hawks,
and owned field and wood?*]

2 [41] They beren hem well swithe heye,
And in a twinkling of an eye,
Hoere soules weren forloren.

[*They carried themselves most proudly,
and, in a twinkling of an eye,
their souls were utterly lost.*]

3 [46] Where is that lawing and that song,
That trailing and that proude yong,
Thos havekes and tho houndes?

[*Where is that laughter and that singing,
that trailing of garments and that proud gait,
those hawks and those hounds?*]

9 [7] Thereinne is day withouten night,
Withouten ende strengthe and might,
And wreche of everich fo...

[*There is day and never night,*
unending strength and might,
and vengeance on all enemies] 13

The original poem consisted of ten six-line stanzas of which Finnissy sets just the four half-stanzas shown above (the numbers in bold indicate from which stanza in the original they come). The numbers in brackets indicate the rehearsal letters in the score of *Maldon* where these texts occur. Once again it is clear that Finnissy's editorial activity has involved both excision and reordering. The choir's music is much simpler than the surrounding music, predominantly modal and often canonic, with the imitation at Finnissy's favoured interval of a perfect fourth, and always underpinned by pedal notes in the organ. Four-part writing is used most sparingly so that its appearance, as in the choir's final phrases (see Example 5.23), with their very 'English' false-relations, is particularly telling.

The anachronistic combination of a central narrative taken from an Anglo-Saxon battle poem with verses reflecting the very different philosophy of medieval Christianity is a fascinating compositional strategy. It enables Finnissy to solve the problem of accommodating two different levels of musical expertise within a single work by casting amateur choral singers in one role (and one historical time) and the professional baritone, trombones and percussionists in another. But it risks the same fate as Britten's *The Rape of Lucretia*, in which Britten[14] frames pre-Christian dramatic action with post-Christian commentaries. In *Lucretia* the result mawkishly sentimentalises both the drama of the opera and the idea of Christian redemption as well as thoroughly confusing the significance of the tragedy. In *Maldon*, however, because the chorus offer their observations *within* the frame of the battle drama and because Finnissy uses different languages - musical and verbal - to differentiate one from the other, we hear them as two separate views of the same events. Finnissy's painstaking equivocation draws us as audience into the ethical debate that the work explores.

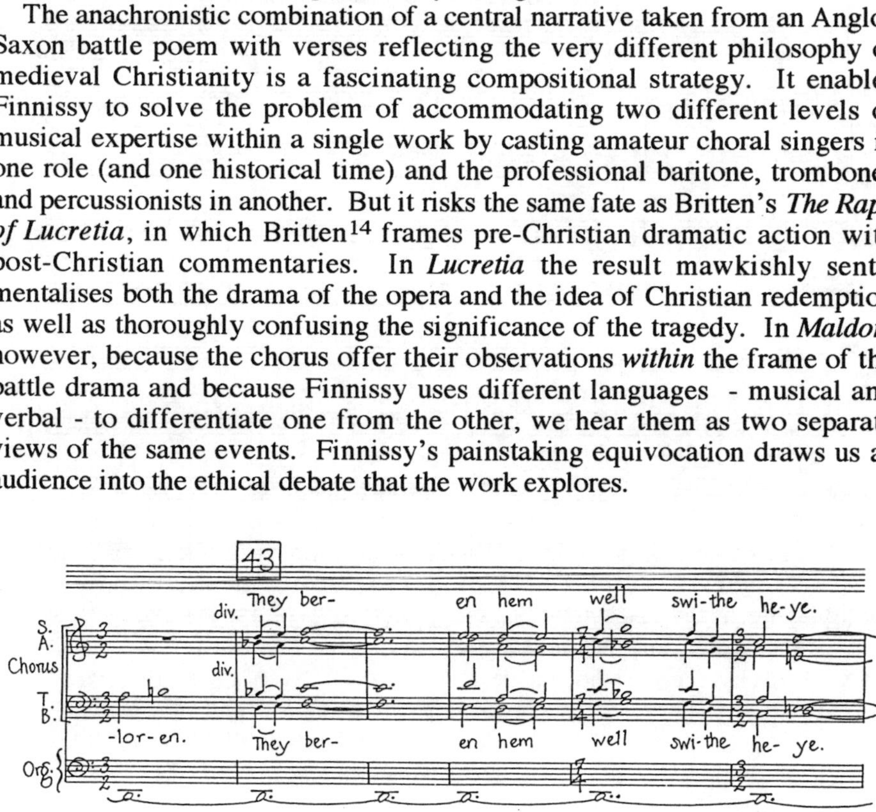

Example 5.23 *Maldon*, pp. 24-5
Reproduced by permission of Oxford University Press

Unknown Ground

Unknown Ground (1989-90) is a work for baritone, violin, cello and piano; it lasts about 28 minutes and is, like the piano piece *Stanley Stokes, East Street 1836* (1989) and the theatre piece, *Shameful Vice*, a work in which Finnissy has dealt explicitly with the suffering of gay men. The published score draws together music that was first performed in the Marlborough Theatre, Brighton in May 1990, when it was interspersed with additional readings, a performance devised by Finnissy in collaboration with the playwright, John Roman Baker. Two types of text are set - extracts from interviews with four men suffering from the effects of AIDS (identified in the score as Nick W., Steve R., Philip X., and Brent T.) and three poetic texts (by Sergei Esenin (1895-1925), Nikolai Kluyev (1887-1937) and Mikhail Kuzmin (1875-1936)) - the former framing the latter. All the texts are written in the first person, but whereas the interviews all deal specifically with aspects of living (or, as Derek Jarman always insisted, 'dying') with AIDS, the poetic texts are particular only in that each in some way touches the subject of love. However the arrangement of the texts, where the general is always preceded and followed by the specific, inevitably favours a reading in which the ambiguities of the love poetry become particular to their present surroundings. Since all the texts are in the first person, sung by a single *male* voice, the different authorial voices are also elided into the single identity of the singer - he is no longer recounting the experiences of seven different people but has himself become the subject of the work.

In the song-cycles of Schubert and Schumann there is a similar location of the singer at the subjective heart of the poetry, but after the high Romantic period this identification of singer with subject has tended, in art-music at any rate, to become the exclusive province of opera; in the art-song, as the form itself has moved from the private to the public domain, the singer has moved slightly off-centre, singing *about* rather than *being* the subject. This centrality of the singer in *Unknown Ground* is emphasised by the way in which Finnissy uses the trio of instruments. The singer appears in each movement and is joined by the instruments thus:

I	cello
II	piano
III	cello, then violin (not together)
IV	cello, later with piano
V	violin and piano, with cello at the end, leading into
VI	violin and cello
VII	violin, cello and piano

In other words, *Unknown Ground* is a work for voice *with* instruments. The instruments alternate between monodies and drones, their parts either imitating or supporting the voice. This is as true of the piano as of the strings: even when the piano plays more than one note the effect is of a noise-rich monodic instrument rather than one which plays chords (see Example 5.24).

Example 5.24 *Unknown Ground*, p.17
Reproduced by permission of Oxford University Press

Idiomatically instruments and voice all set out from the same territory, a sort of *arioso* informed by plainchant and folk song (perhaps particularly pibroch-inflected). They also initially inhabit the same registral territory: in the first movement the cello tessitura covers an octave, from the F below to the F above middle C; the baritone occupies the same range with an additional fourth below. The work as a whole progresses from the smooth, white-note modality of the opening (see Example 5.25a) to a much more irregular, microtonal writing at the end (see Example 5.25b), a progression from tender nostalgia to the ultimate reality of death.

Common to both examples is the predominance of step-wise movement and a rhythmic articulation which alternates longer notes with groups of shorter notes, the former functioning as pitch-centres which are embellished by the latter. However, as the piece progresses, timbres become more complex, rhythms become less metrically stable and pitch-centres tend to drift microtonally. It is interesting to note the way in which *Unknown Ground* anchors the significance of different types of music which, elsewhere in Finnissy's output, have sustained entire pieces. The Dorian/Aeolian modality of the opening has been a particular feature of works for liturgical use (perhaps as much a pragmatic decision as an aesthetic one), while the microtonal writing recalls the earlier folk-inspired works of the 1980s.

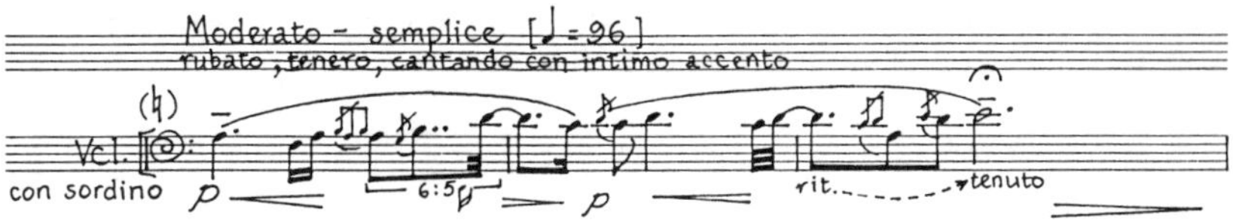

Example 5.25a *Unknown Ground*, p. 1
Reproduced by permission of Oxford University Press

Example 5.25b *Unknown Ground*, p. 35
Reproduced by permission of Oxford University Press

As in any Finnissy work, an exploration of musical and textual sources reveals a richly articulate network of cross-references. A striking feature of the near-contemporary texts is their plainness. Jonathan Cross has said of them that they 'do not, in themselves, suggest a huge musical potential',[15] and certainly they are far less high flown in their utterance than the poems of Rimbaud, Swinburne or Hölderlin which so fascinated the younger Finnissy, but they are surely no less full of 'musical potential' than any other collection of words. As the work of American composers such as Harry Partch and Christian Wolff has demonstrated, any text is potentially 'musical'. In a work like *Barstow,* Partch made music around conversations and letters that he had shared with hobo companions as he travelled across America, while Wolff has shown how anything, from names ('Song' in the *Prose Collection*) to Maoist texts (*Accompaniments*), can be made into music.

Moreover the colloquial plainness of Nick, Steve, Philip and Brent's words makes a direct connection to the Russian poets. Esenin and Kluyev were part of a group of peasant poets who were also associated with Acmeism, a movement in Russian literature in the early years of the 20th century whose aim was to root new writing in the experiences and feelings of ordinary Russian people. Kuzmin had published a manifesto, 'Concerning beautiful clarity', in 1910 in which he had 'urged young poets to cultivate accuracy, conciseness, and economy of language'.[16] The authors of the poems and the interviews are also connected by sexuality. Kuzmin was as openly homosexual, both in his life and in his writing, as was expedient in the Russia of his day, while the evidence of the lives of both Esenin and Kluyev would suggest that their sexuality was, at the least, a 'grey area'. This textual commonality is emphasised by Finnissy's music, which draws the words of poets and interviewees into a single vocal strand. Example 5.26 shows phrases from the third movement (Steve R.) and the sixth (Kuzmin) to demonstrate how consistent the vocal idiom is.

Example 5.26a *Unknown Ground,* p.10, voice only
Reproduced by permission of Oxford University Press

Example 5.26b *Unknown Ground,* p. 25, voice only
Reproduced by permission of Oxford University Press

Unknown Ground is one of the most passionately unequivocal works in the Finnissy catalogue and a work, haunted by death, that cuts across categories. It would be easy to dismiss it as another gay lament, a *pièce d'occasion* that served its purpose as part of the consciousness-raising around AIDS in the early 1990s. It is equally hard to imagine *Unknown Ground* finding its way onto the chamber music concert circuit: it's too raw, too 'political' for an audience to whom music is just a leisure commodity. But *Unknown Ground* deserves many hearings. Musically it is a remarkable achievement, sustaining a single, compelling expressive trajectory across nearly half an hour, and its resonances reach beyond the immediate circumstances of its creation and the catastrophically accelerated mortality of AIDS victims to encompass all our experiences of love and mortality. The final text is an uncanny echo of Dylan Thomas's poem on the death of his father and its cry to 'Rage, rage against the dying of the light': 'I am nearly blind. Everything is starting to get very dark... But I cannot give up... I'll just keep fighting. I'll just keep fighting.' As Peter Garland wrote of Partch's work, 'we should be talking about our own beings, in fact we should be doing less talking and a little more... action...'.[17]

Anima Christi

The literary heritage of Christianity has been a recurrent strand in Finnissy's work since his second acknowledged work, *From the Revelations of Saint John the Divine*, written in 1965, but since 1989 his preoccupation with the living work of the church has intensified and has resulted in a series of works intended either for liturgical use in church, or for performance by church musicians, particularly choirs. Alongside these works have been others, like *Vertue*, which set texts by writers associated with Christian worship (the words of *Vertue* are by George Herbert, whose poetry was a great favourite with the composers of hymn-tunes) and yet others with a less direct, but no less explicit connection to Christianity. The use of an 'Ubi sunt' derivative as a choral text in *Maldon* connects that work to the doctrines espoused by St Bernard of Clairvaux; the 14-part structure of *Shameful Vice* is a parody of the Catholic iconography of the Stations of the Cross,[18] the orchestral work, *Eph-phatha*, takes a Gospel story as its starting point.[19]

When these works started to appear there were those amongst his audience who speculated about the influence of his deeper engagement with Christianity, which Finnissy himself discusses in the earlier chapter, 'Conversations with Michael Finnissy'. These suspicions were encouraged by what seemed at first to be a change in style: Finnissy's harmony had become more obviously modal, his rhythmic invention favoured greater regularity, textures seemed more transparent, even the notation looked 'whiter' as half- and whole-notes replaced sixteenth- and thirty-second-notes In the style-obsessed world of British new music, Finnissy appeared to have shifted camp; his work was no longer so readily labelled as part of the 'new complexity' (a term whose minting was still quite fresh at the end of the eighties) and seemed closer to the 'faith minimalism' of Tavener and Gorecki (another grouping that had rather more to do with music-marketing's fondness for bandwagons than with composers' aspirations for their work).

As each chapter in this book demonstrates, such a view of Finnissy's development is a crass over-simplification. Nevertheless, there were changes. Finnissy's partner, Philip Adams, directs the music in their local church and the sudden increase in church music is a natural response to the composer's wish to share in his partner's work. Few church musicians offer the range of virtuosic skills which Finnissy's earlier vocal music had so extensively exploited, so his linear and harmonic thinking and even his notation had to adjust to a fresh creative challenge. The enthusiastic response of amateur singers to works like the *Seven Sacred Motets* (1991) is an indication of the success with which Finnissy has responded to these new circumstancess.

On the other hand many of the characteristic features of Finnissy's work in the 1980s - linearity, the use of narrow rather than wide melodic intervals, modality, drones - required only a little adjustment to be suitable for amateur singers, to whom a stable intervallic vocabulary and harmonic reference points are reassuring guarantees of musical security which enable the singers to project themselves into the music with much greater expressive confidence. The first entry of the upper voices in 'Hymnos sacrae quos virgini', the first of the *Seven Sacred Motets* is a typically ornate Finnissy melody, supported by a drone (see Example 5.27); one could find many equivalent passages in *Kelir,* for example. In *Kelir* Finnissy achieved rhythmic fluidity by using irrationals to notate precisely each ebb and flow of the line around the main pulse, in 'Hymnos sacrae quos virgini' rhythmic fluidity is a by-product of the plainsong idiom to which the music alludes; in *Kelir* Finnissy invented microtonal modes, in 'Hymnos sacrae quos virgini' he is writing in the Dorian mode; perhaps most importantly of all, in *Kelir* the text was an exotic collection of sounds whose meaning was of no direct significance to either performers or audience, while the 'Hymnos sacrae quos virgini' is a hymn whose meaning is immediately connected to the ethical framework of the culture within which the music was created.

Example 5.27 'Hymnos sacrae quos virgini', *Seven Sacred Motets*, p.1
Reproduced by permission of Oxford University Press

Elsewhere in the *Seven Sacred Motets* there are examples of the textural and textual complexity found in earlier Finnissy. The texts of the *Motets* are alternately Marian hymns or prayers (the odd-numbered movements) and Gospel narratives (the even-numbered movements). The fourth movement is consistently contrapuntal, each voice presenting a different part of St Luke's account (in Chapter 2 of his Gospel) of the young Jesus astonishing the temple clergy in Jerusalem with his wisdom (the soprano begins in verse 48, the alto in verse 42, the tenor in verse 46 and the bass in verse 49). While all the parts are in the Aeolian mode, their rhythmic and motivic independence and the overlapping of their tessitura creates the densest music in the work (see Example 5.28), appropriately so since the text for this movement presents the most complex narrative.

Example 5.28 'Et cum factus esset', *Seven Sacred Motets*, p. 21
Reproduced by permission of Oxford University Press

That the relative simplicity of the musical means of a work like the *Seven Sacred Motets* was the result of Finnissy suiting his musical means to the forces available rather than a major creative *volte face* is demonstrated when one compares it with a work like the *Liturgy of St Paul* (1992-5), written for the superb singers of the Hilliard Ensemble. The *Liturgy* is scored for four singers - counter-tenor, two tenors and baritone - with an occasionally elaborate keyboard part for chamber organ, and takes its form from the order of Mass at St Paul's, West Street in Brighton, a sequence of seven movements interspersing Greek scriptural passages with the Latin Ordinary. Much of the music is as simple as that in the *Seven Sacred Motets* - indeed the plainsong settings of the Mass movements would appear to be quite suitable for a church choir - but elsewhere there is music of considerable complexity, as when in the final 'Communio' movement the voices exhort the faithful to '*Go unto this people and say*, Hearing ye shall hear, and shall not understand; and seeing ye shall see, and not perceive' (see Example 5.29; only the passage marked by my italics is shown). The drama of St Paul's life is superimposed on the drama of the Mass itself. At the beginning of the *Liturgy* he enters, in the guise of the first tenor, from off-stage and the scriptural narrative follows him from his conversion on the road to Damascus to his execution in Rome. In a typically Finnissian elision the singers are celebrants, narrators, congregation and Paul himself.

In *Anima Christi* (1991) Finnissy makes use of different levels of musical ability in much the same way as he did in *Maldon,* with quite straightforward music for the choir, often in only two parts and always supported by organ drones, but exuberantly florid parts for alto and tenor soloists. Here though, the relationship between the two types involves none of the chronological complexities of *Maldon,* but is based instead on the model of celebrant and congregation in worship. Like *Maldon*, *Anima Christi* makes telling use of on-stage/off-stage effects: in *Maldon* the work began off-stage, the sounds of the battle invading the church, while in *Anima Christi* the final section alternates between on-stage music in three-part counterpoint for the altos, tenors and basses of the choir and off-stage music for the sopranos, an angelic chorus singing in three part canon (see Example 5.30). The Trinitarian symbolism is clear, as is the implication that only in the heavenly domain will we understand the mystery of the three-in-one deity. As in all the best Finnissy, the composer's subtlety of thought, his ability to form musical meanings and his apparently irrepressible capacity to invent new music of extraordinary beauty are inextricably bound together.

Example 5.29 *Liturgy of St Paul*, pp. 45-6
Reproduced by permission of Oxford University Press

Example 5.30 *Anima Christi*, p. 24

Notes

1. Finnissy, private conversations with the author.
2. Richard Barrett, 'Michael Finnissy - An Overview', *Aspects of Complexity in Recent British Music, Contemporary Music Review,* Vol. 13, Part 1, p. 38.
3. Lynne Williams, 'Reinstating 'The Spiritual Quest'", *Aspects of Complexity in Recent British Music, Contemporary Music Review,* Vol. 13, Part 1, p. 59.
4. Ferrucio Busoni, 'Sketch of a New Esthetic of Music' (1911), reprinted in *Three Aesthetics in the Aesthetic of Music*, (Dover, New York, 1962), pp. 73-97.
5. Ibid, p. 85.
6. Ibid, p. 86.
7. See Finnissy's discussion of his work with amateur choirs in the opening 'Conversations' chapter (pp. 31-2); see also Julian Anderson's account of *Plain Harmony*, written for amateur instrumentalists.
8. Barrett, op. cit., p. 24.
9. The dedication of the score to the Belgian critic and musicologist, Harry Halbreich, acknowledges the considerable support that Halbreich lent to the advocacy not only of the music of Finnissy but also of Ferneyhough and, rather later, of James Dillon, Chris Dench and Richard Barrett. Halbreich's enthusiasms also embraced the music of Scelsi, Murail, Grisey, Radulescu; his persuasive influence on the artistic direction of a number of major continental European music festivals in the 1970s and 1980s was instrumental in the prominence given during this period to the tendencies in new European composition known as 'spectral music' and 'new complexity'.
10. An interesting feature of *Ohi!ohi!ohi!* is that Finnissy only uses quartertones when the music's tessitura is at its narrowest; elsewhere the music is consistently in semitones.
11. It should be noted, however, that although Finnissy uses less than a quarter of the 'Battle' poem, the urgent quality of his translation is closer to the original Anglo-Saxon than, for example, the rather more elaborate version by Kevin Crossley-Holland, published in *The Battle of Maldon and Other Old English Poems* (ed. Bruce Mitchell, Macmillan, London, 1965).
12. Running the sound of the next scene under the end of the present scene is, of course, a familiar device in film editing.
13. The translation here is taken from 'Contempt of the World', *Medieval English Lyrics,* ed. R.T. Davies (Faber, London, 1963), pp. 56-9.
14. Ronald Duncan, Britten's librettist for *The Rape of Lucretia,* always claimed that the use of the Chorus was Britten's invention rather than his own.
15. Jonathan Cross, 'Vive la différence', *Musical Times* (March 1996), p. 13.
16. Dimitri Obolensky, *The Penguin Book of Russian Verse* (London, 1962), p. xlv.
17. Peter Garland, *Americas: Essays on American Music and Culture, 1973-1980* (Soundings Press, Santa Fe, 1982), p. 59.
18. Cf. Ian Pace's account of this work in Chapter 6.
19. Cf. Julian Anderson's account of this in Chapter 4.

CHAPTER SIX

The Theatrical Works

Ian Pace

The twentieth century has been a rich and fruitful time for the theatre. Craig's radical rethinking of the relationship between theatre's various elements, Brecht's estrangement devices, Artaud's evocation of a primitive spectacle, the concentration and intensity achieved with the most pared-down resources by Grotowski, Beckett's infinitely beautiful yet fatally bleak offerings, Peter Brook's attempts to reintroduce forms of ritual into the modern world, the experimental forms and narratives of such figures as Heiner Müller or Tadeusz Kantor: all have shown the vast potential implicit in the theatrical medium, although much of this work and its underlying ideas remains unexplored territory for British theatrical practitioners. For composers working in the field of music-theatre, both the abovementioned work and the equally fascinating innovations in such a field by Mauricio Kagel, Sylvano Bussotti, Hans Otte, Dieter Schnebel or Hans-Joachim Hespos, are too often ignored in favour of bland forms of narrative theatre, in which the music serves merely to amplify what is already obvious, spoon-feeding the audience.

Michael Finnissy's theatre works, on the other hand, show an awareness of contemporary developments, and a willingness to build on their foundations. His early work looks beyond narrative and conventions towards new, more urgent and direct forms of communication, drawing variously on ancient, medieval, popular or oriental theatrical traditions, whilst maintaining a contemporary perspective. More recently, he has moved closer to a form of opera (though he would still prefer the term 'stage work') subverting in subtle ways the limitations of the genre for which his works have been requested.

Finnissy's relationship with operatic traditions has expressed itself most obviously in his numerous operatic transcriptions for the piano, in particular the long set of *Verdi Transcriptions*. The work was written in part as an attempt to stand up for Verdi as against the more fashionable (in 'modernist' circles) Wagner; to promote a form of opera that not only privileges melody, but is also more stylised and sectional, allowing the possibility of original creation which is not wilfully obscure, by entering into a dialectical interaction with generic conventions, rather than an opera of more 'organic' forms and the one-to-one correspondence of elements that characterise Wagner's ultimate conceptions. Today Finnissy is inclined to be more ambivalent in taking sides between these two traditions, but the explicitly sectional nature of Italianate opera, closer to popular forms such as the variety show, would seem to have informed such works as *Vaudeville* and *Soda Fountain*.

As several of these works have not to date received a performance, and productions of the others have been few and far between, I will give a detailed and graphic description of as many of these unfamiliar works as possible, rather than embarking on a highly analytic study of just a few. I believe them to be amongst Finnissy's most interesting, not least because of their wholly original and utterly idiomatic uses of the voice and voices.

Ritual Theatre

The earliest of Finnissy's theatrical works stand as a continuation of some of the most radical elements of contemporary theatre, involving a renunciation both of story-telling and of an excessive dependence on dialogue, in favour of a focus on ritual and a communion with the elemental, pre-rational aspects of the mind - their intentions (if not necessarily their results) have more than a little in common with Peter Brook's forms of 'ritual theatre' in the 1960s, one of the last occasions when innovative theatre in Britain could be presented outside of a fringe environment. Finnissy made use of sources that suggested timeless forms of ceremonial activity, rites that perform some essential function for mankind.

His first acknowledged work involving a theatrical dimension was derived from an earlier form of music-theatre. *Tsuru-Kame* (1971-73), meaning 'The Crane - The Tortoise', is a setting of a recital/concert type of dramatic ballad (*naga-uta*: an extended poem or song, a particular variety of *shamisen* music). The title comes from a *Noh* play 'Gekkyuden' by Kineya Rokuzaemon X, and the structure and emphasis use concepts both from the aristocratic *Noh* and more popular *kabuki* forms:

Introduction - *Jo*
I. 'Oki' - Introductory song to set the mood and scene
II. 'Ageuta' - A song (usually of high pitch) from that section of a *Noh* play where the principal actor makes his entrance.

Exposition - *Ha*
III. 'Mondõ' - A dialogue (in the *Noh*)
IV. 'Chu No Mai' - The transference of a dance, originally belonging to a *Noh* play, to a *naga-uta*.
V. 'Odoriji' - A dance (also used in the *kabuki*)
VI. 'Gaku' - *Noh*-dance: used in *nagauta*, usually purely instrumental.

Denouement - *Kyu*
VII. 'Kiri' - Commentary, sometimes the final part of the Denouement, sung by the chorus.
VIII. 'Chirashi-Dangire' - The final section and final cadence in *nagauta*.

As is often the case when Finnissy makes reference to other materials, he freely mixes and alters elements, while retaining the large scale form.

The text, which Finnissy sets in Japanese, consists entirely of a narration of events, rather than words in the mouths of characters, telling of the two magical animals of the title who teach an emperor a dance which will ensure his longevity. Its beauty and simplicity make it worth quoting here in full (in English translation):

> At the banquet held each year to celebrate the awakening of spring, the emperor watches as the sun and the moon shine through the gate of eternal youth.
>
> The emperor's garden: its pathways gleaming gold and silver. Arches of lapis lazuli and brocade, agate and mother-of-pearl. The pond's edge - where the crane and the tortoise rest - is like Mount Hōrai. Praise the emperor for his many graces.
>
> Dialogue: A courtier tells the emperor that it is usual, on such happy occasions, for the sacred crane and tortoise to be seen dancing: after which the court-dances are performed in the palace. Let this happen now.
>
> The tortoise and the crane have been living for many years...
>
> ...For centuries, like the pine-trees, like the grove of bamboo by the side of the pond...the tortoise in the water, the crane, with its feathery sleeve-like wings, dance in honour of the emperor's peaceful reign. The emperor delightedly watches them, and then begins to...
>
> ...dance with them.
>
> The emperor's robes: like the temple-of-the-moon robes of the palace...containing all the colours of the autumn, flowers like the edges of maple-leaves in the rain. The long sleeves - as white as fresh winter-snow - flutter, as the courtiers sing.
>
> The emperor now dances to bring prosperity to his country for all of eternity. The courtiers swiftly carry the shrine away as the emperor returns to the place of longevity.

Traditionally, *naga-uta* would involve an ensemble of voices, a *shamisen* (three-stringed lute), *nokan* (transverse bamboo flute with seven holes), *kotsuzumi* (shoulder-held hourglass drum) and *ōtsuzumi* (side-held hourglass drum). Finnissy's instrumentation has some similarities; a solo female voice, a small female chorus of 3-6 singers, a flute, a viola and two percussionists, who play a celesta, chime bars and a vibraphone, as well as a selection of drums, temple blocks, maracas and chimes (bamboo, etc.). There are also three dancers, representing the emperor, the crane and the tortoise. The staging is shown in Example 6.1.

Finnissy avoids the mere stylistic trappings of Japanese theatre, which might turn the work into a form of costume drama; rather the 'Japanese' element originates from the language and the more deep-seated structural processes.

Musically, the work retains certain stylistic characteristics of traditional Japanese music, without resorting to crude 'naïve' stereotypes. A degree of passivity is realised through the extensive use of monophony, with the important addition of a mode of singing derived from *gagaku*, a sort of imitative counterpoint in identical register which Finnissy indicates by instructing the chorus to sing in independent rhythms (Example 6.2).

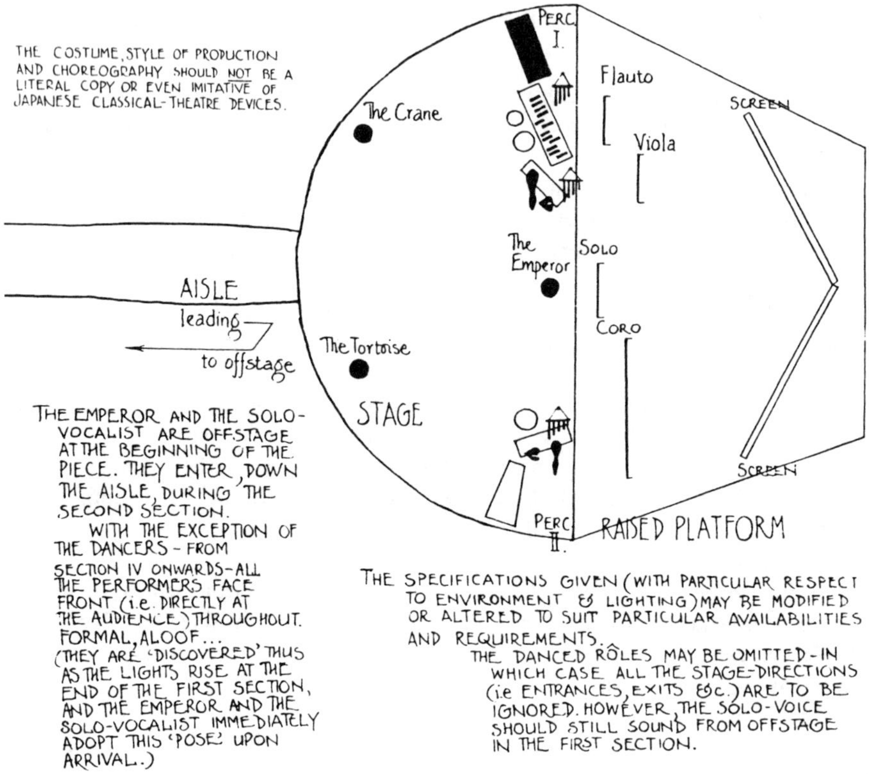

Example 6.1 Staging for *Tsuru-Kame*

As the work progresses, Finnissy notates a slightly less literal version of this type of counterpoint, including the use of echoes of the singers' lines in some of the instruments. *Gagaku*-style counterpoint was to become an important part of Finnissy's compositional armoury, which he later used in works with no explicit Japanese connection, such as *Alongside* for chamber orchestra or the *Seven Sacred Motets* for unaccompanied voices.

Yet the opening song is arresting and even passionate, before subsiding into a state of tranquillity, and has a counterpart in the long flute solo at the end of the work, which opens with a procession-like series of sustained notes, then intersperses a long, relatively steady melodic line with occasional flurries of activity, eventually coming to rest on a repeated pitch. It is almost as if the voice has transferred its magical powers to the flute, paralleling the relationship between the animals and the emperor.

Example 6.2 *Tsuru-Kame*, p. 4. From *Ageuta*

Elsewhere, Finnissy alternates the timeless serenity of the *gagaku*-voices with the death-rattle of temple blocks, maracas and bamboo chimes. The use of various bells to 'cue' the singers serves almost as an alienation device, to contextualise this particular form of phantasmagoria. Spellbinding textures initiate the dance of the crane and the tortoise; when they are joined by the emperor in *Gaku*, the music achieves an almost impossible stillness, only to be broken by the lively and declamatory *Kiri*.

Example 6.3 *Tsuru-Kame* p. 21. From *Kiri*

A mystical effect is achieved at the beginning of the last section by the use of the vibraphone playing random *glissandi* with the fingertips only. As the work is likely to be heard most often by listeners without knowledge of Japanese, Finnissy eschews word-painting in favour of a concentration upon the sound of the language, with numerous spoken phrases.

Tsuru-Kame is a profoundly beautiful work, the first in a cycle of Japanese-inspired pieces (the others being *Gorõ, Kagami-Jishi, Hinomi* and *Jisei*). Finnissy describes it as 'a celebratory kind of ritual and the music fleshes that out. In a way, the music is the justification for it - it couldn't exist any more than it could in Japan without the music - the music is the whole point'.[1] Its immediacy and translucence stand beyond rational or narrative explanation (even in the sense of particular relationships between music, text and theatre), instead stemming from, and appealing to, that which is beneath consciousness.

The work which followed, *Circle, Chorus and Formal Act* (1973), is even more concerned with forms of ritualistic experience. The text and scenario, derived by Finnissy and Fergus Early from a variety of folk-sources, is about the passing of the old and its replacement by the young, 'The kind of rhetorical text in which an old king is replaced annually by a young one is, of course symbolic. Symbolic of new crops and of eventually harvesting them. The 'planting' is then humanised - human seed substituted for grain.'[2] Text only plays a role in the first section, however, as an introduction to a series of sword dances and other forms of 'primitive' theatrical activity. Finnissy uses a small group of players consisting of an oboe/cor anglais, two horns and a percussionist, whilst the stage roles consist of an Old Fool, played by a baritone, two choruses of ten voices each, another on-stage chorus of nine percussionists, collectively playing pebbles, maracas or chime-bars, and an assortment of silent roles.

The Fool introduces six youths, who could well be seen as six 'archetypes' of youth: the first 'a handsome lad - brother to the blazing sun', the second 'a shy young man - brother to the pale moon - but don't be tricked he drives bold and hard!', the third 'a lad swift as the golden hawk', the fourth 'joyful as a strong necked stallion, rolling in the sweet night-grasses', the fifth 'son of the whispering sea, his kisses quiet in the soft hair of the reeds', and the sixth the 'fair son of moist and fertile earth'. Musically, the voice of the Fool is echoed or accompanied in an ethereal manner by the choruses, creating the impression that his words and character delineation resonate in a collective subconscious, whilst the oboe and horns provide colouration and commentary, and the percussion chorus serves to provide punctuation (Example 6.4).

The six youths perform the first sword-dance, which is unaccompanied, then bring on a heavily pregnant old woman, to the sound of a grotesque series of oboe trills, interrupted by high *staccato* notes. She gives birth to a doll, which grows into a second (young) Fool, who is raised aloft by the youths. A second sword-dance follows, accompanied by the percussion chorus playing pebbles in 12/8 rhythms (regular rhythms having been foreshadowed by the ensemble percussionist during the introduction of the youths, Example 6.5).

Example 6.4 *Circle, Chorus and Formal Act*, p. 3

The youths then bring on the spring-bride, to whom is assigned a lyrical cor-anglais solo. The old and young Fools compete for the love of the spring-bride with a clumsy duet for the horns, at one point fixated around a few pitches, which is interrupted twice by cor-anglais solos. As a series of precipatory, ecstatic ascending gestures from the first horn overcome the blustering *glissandi* of the second, the young Fool gains the upper hand and is acclaimed by the spring bride. The old Fool, defeated, falls to the ground, with a 'moan from the bass drum. Then follows the third sword-dance, this time in 4/4, with pebbles, snare drum and maracas, during which the old Fool is slaughtered by the youths; a hobby-horse appears and tramples the dead Fool underfoot.

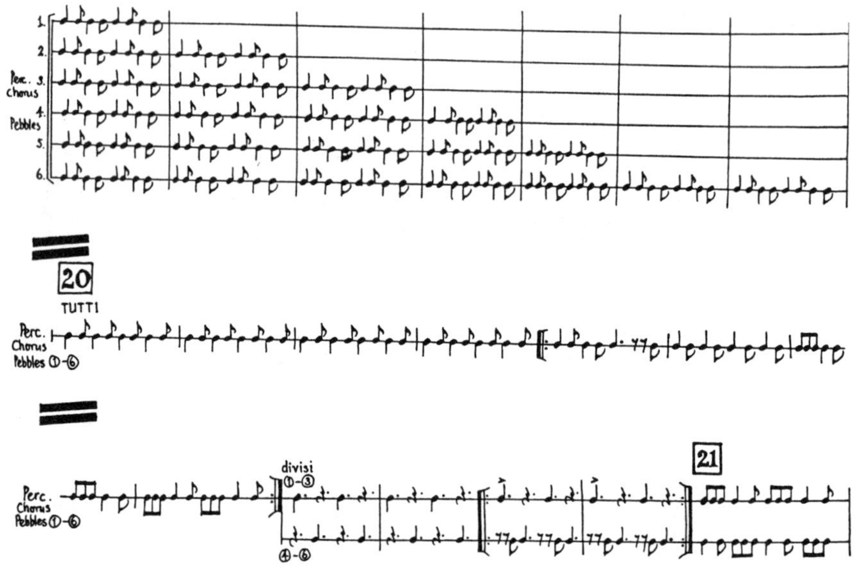

Example 6.5 *Circle, Chorus and Formal Act*, p. 20

The young Fool and the spring-bride copulate to the sound of a long cor anglais solo, climaxing with tremolos and *glissandi* on the vibraphone. The whole crowd then dance together, with a increasingly energetic percussion accompaniment in 3+3+2 quaver rhythms. The old Fool, old woman, young Fool, spring-bride and hobby horse re-appear from the crowd during this dance, emphasising the artificiality of the scenario. The ensemble percussionist beats a repeated rhythm on the snare drum and walks off during the final dance, 'Quête', with a subdued counterpoint in the cor anglais and horns. From off-stage, a distant echo of the first part is heard, as the old Fool introduces another youth.

As can be seen, the work is less a form of narrative than a formalised enactment. It is particularly unusual within Finnissy's output because of its emphasis on repeated, regular rhythms, which the other, more characteristic, types of music serve to 'frame'. Its success in performance probably depends on an appropriate production and choreography; excessive stylisation or some form of period authenticity would probably dilute the sense of an 'outside-time' ceremonial, described by the composer as 'like a religious service'.[3] Whether or not an average concert- or theatre-goer will respond to the work as such is debatable, but this does not necessarily negate the validity of such an attempt to find new ways of relating to that which is most fundamental in human beings.

The third work in this category is the as yet unperformed *Tom Fool's Wooing* (1975-78) which deals with another, equally fundamental, aspect of people and society: the ritual of marriage, as enacted in the traditional 'Wooing' folk-play. The central section of the work is of this type, taken from Alan Brody's *The English Mummers and their Plays: Traces of Ancient Mystery,*[4] but Finnissy frames this with a plethora of folk-poems, magical spells and incantations in Rumanian and Greek, and two passages from Edmund Spenser's *Epithalamion*. The work is scored for 14 solo voices, whose parts involve an almost unprecedented degree of difficulty, with the use of many simultaneous wide-ranging lines requiring exceptional stamina and versatility over the whole vocal register. This work's difficulty exceeds in some senses even that of the works for massed solo voices by such composers as Holliger, Kagel, Schnebel and Ferneyhough, relying as it does on a hyper-acute sense of pitch, and a uniquely musical approach to phrasing and melody, rather than particular expertise in extended vocal techniques. As I have opined elsewhere in this book, Finnissy, like Nono, is one of the few contemporary composers who remains prepared to write for the voice (or, for that matter, for instruments) without doctrinaire use of desiccation and fragmentation; his love for expansive and glorious lines reflects immense generosity and love for humankind.

The poems and spells are combined in the opening section to form a type of narrative of the various stages of the wooing ritual, though the languages are used as much for their sound as for semantic purposes, adding a degree of mystification and defamiliarisation. A series of vociferous cries in the sopranos, almost like forms of mating calls, make extensive use of *portamento*, quartertones and trills and whispered endings to phrases.

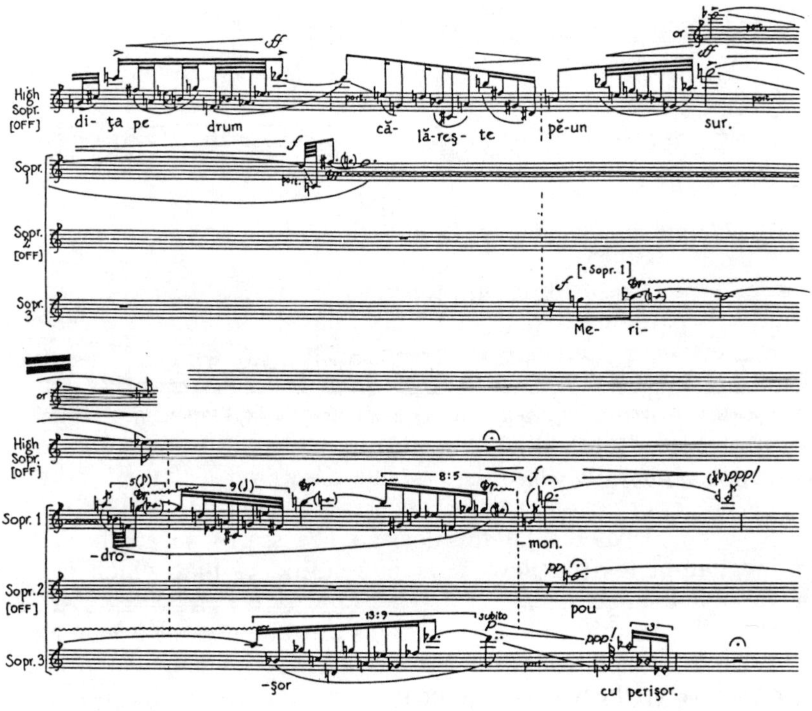

Example 6.6 *Tom Fool's Wooing*, p. 3

This leads to a mysterious *sotto voce* tapestry of sound for female voices, buzzings, rustlings, highly sexually-charged and tantalising undulations, before four of the men burst on with raucous shouts. They are immediately integrated into the women's texture, all now singing on the vowel sounds *a* and *e*, above which the mezzo-soprano sings an evocative setting of the first passage from Spenser ('This day for ever to me holy is...'). Her *glissandi* resonate amongst other of the voices, when suddenly voices are lowered and most speak in an unpitched chant. A few distant echoes of the opening lead to a 'dissolve' into the main play, slow lines in a soprano, contralto and counter-tenor, ('How can I praise you, my love? Thy soul's likeness could nowhere be found...') while others of the singers play drums, as an upbeat to the coming scene .

The play is a bawdy affair, as in turn Tom Fool and his sons attempt to win the affections of Lady Jane (mezzo-soprano) with promises of money or land, or declarations of self-worth, which she immediately sees through. The jaunty music is in complete contrast to that which preceded it and each of the characters has distinct types of melodic contours for their *quasi recitativo* delivery, downward curves for Tom Fool's eldest son (Bass 1), a concatenation of descending intervals for the youngest son (Baritone 1) and upwards curves for Tom Fool himself (Tenor 1):

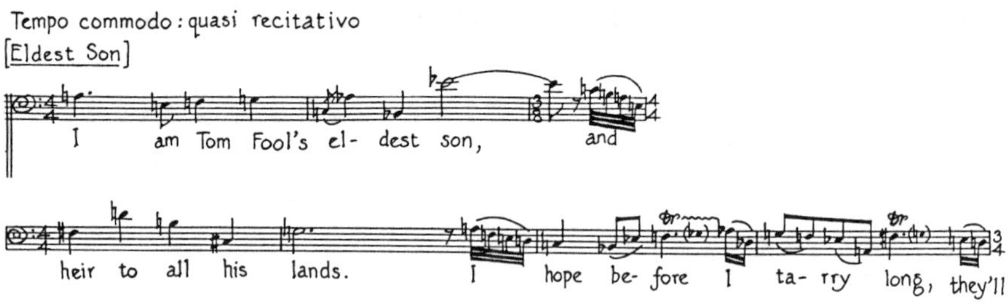

Example 6.7a *Tom Fool's Wooing*, p. 15

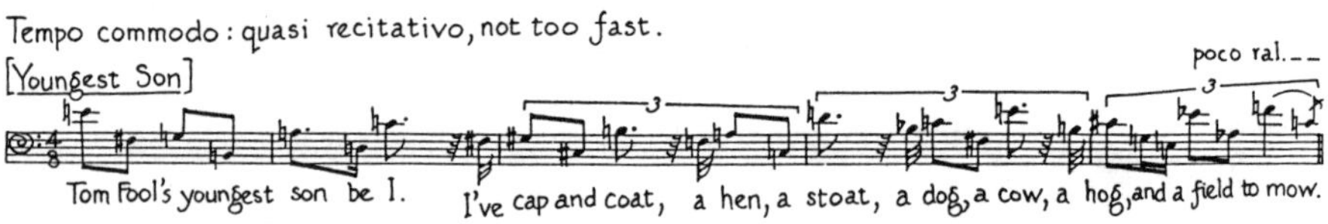

Example 6.7b *Tom Fool's Wooing*, p. 17

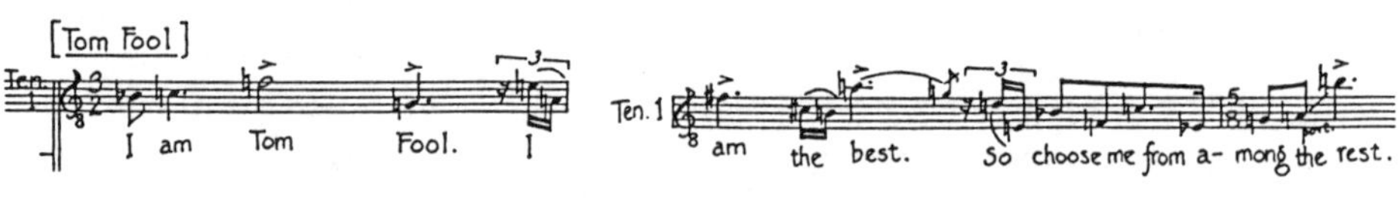

Example 6.7c *Tom Fool's Wooing*, pp. 18-19

Between the wooing attempts, trios of singers, with others playing the drums again, enunciate a commentary, taken again from the Rumanian or Greek poems, the nature of the music serving to clarify the meaning of the texts.

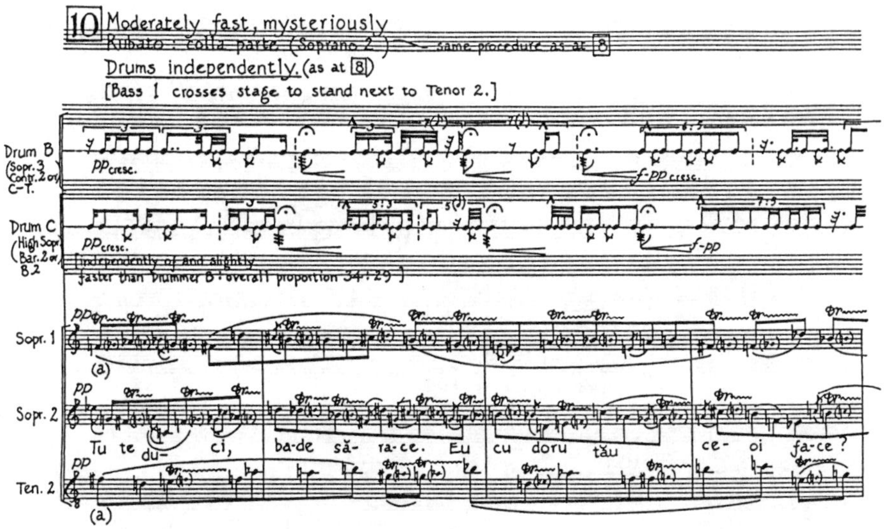

Example 6.8 *Tom Fool's Wooing*, p. 16
Text translates as 'poor boy, you are going away, how can I do without you? You fair maid, will do just fine, There are plenty more lads like me.'

Onto the stage walks Dame Jane (Contralto 1), carrying a baby wrapped in a shawl, which she declares is Tom Fool's bastard son. Tom denies that such a 'valiant hero' as himself could be responsible, but the two sons declare their intention to cut off his head (Example 6.9).

After bemoaning the ingratitude of his children, Tom agrees to submit, but suddenly topples over. Suddenly the other characters are anxious that he be revived, which a speaking doctor (counter-tenor) manages to do. With a series of swaggering *portamenti*, Tom once again offers his wealth to the Lady, but she replies that (in a remarkable about-turn) it is him alone that she wants. Tom cries 'Let us make a jovial wedding!', leading into the final section.

The mezzo-soprano and Tenor 1, who had previously sung the parts of Lady Jane and Tom, sing a long duet in harmoniously imitative counterpoint, the second section from Spenser ('Early before the worlds light-giving lampe, His golden beame upon the hils doth spred...'), surrounded by a mysterious, dreamlike *pppp* texture as the other 12 voices each vocalise more or less independent parts on vowel sounds (Example 6.10).

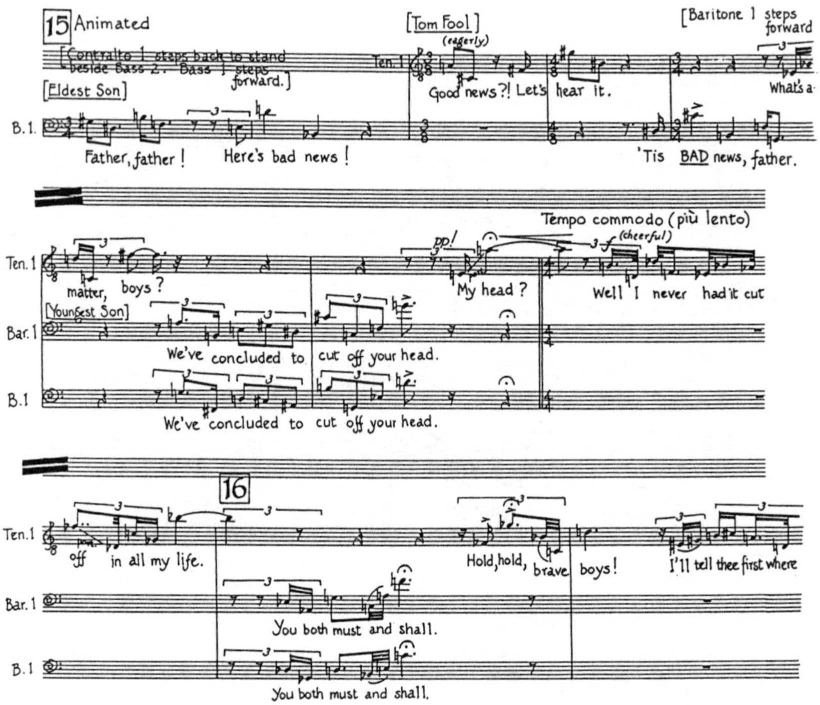

Example 6.9 *Tom Fool's Wooing*, p. 20

With a gradual crescendo, the women work in further folk-sayings and spells, leading to a glorious climax, with the mezzo-soprano singing a solo (Spenser - 'For lo! the wishèd day is come at last'), the women ecstatically undulating, and the men punctuating with chant-like beats on single syllables from their texts. All calms, and the tenor solo (Spenser - 'Now welcome, night!') is accompanied by simultaneous procession-like parts for the women, with much more distant chant-beats from the men.

The use of multiple texts in different languages serves in *Tom Fool's Wooing* to allow for multiple layering of meaning and contextualisation. It is an attempt to demonstrate congruities and resonances between different folk traditions, a panoramic view of the universal rituals of wooing and marriage. The nature of the juxtapositions of types adds to the semantic richness of each. The music is made appropriate to each of the languages being used, allowing their sonic qualities to communicate that which a dictionary could never reveal.

Example 6.10 *Tom Fool's Wooing*, p. 24

The Mysteries

The most substantial body of English medieval 'ritual drama' is to be found in the various cycles of Mystery Plays. Finnissy's settings of eight of these plays remain largely unknown territory, since only the first and fourth of the individual works have been performed complete (at the time of going to press). The individual works are:

1. *The Parting of Darkness from Light* (1975-76)
2. *The Earthly Paradise* (1977-78)
3. *Noah and the Great Flood* (1978)
4. *The Prophecy of Daniel* (1972/79)
5. *The Parliament of Heaven* (1977-78)
6. *The Annunciation* (1978-79)
7. *The Betrayal and Crucifixion of Jesus of Nazareth* (1978-79)
8. *The Deliverance of Souls* (1978-79)

The texts, which Finnissy sets in Middle English, derive in particular from the 'Towneley' or Wakefield cycle, and the 'N-town' cycle, probably East Anglian, but also known as 'Ludus Coventriae' because of the mistaken view that it orginated from Coventry. Within these works, however, are also included excerpts from Gaelic folk-poetry, hymns, the 'Exeter Book' (which Finnissy used later in his *Commedia dell'incomprensible Potere che Alcune Donne hanno sugli Uomini*, discussed below) and other sacred and liturgical texts, providing a socio-historical contextualisation, a montage of sources which interact in a dialectical manner, not wholly unlike Heiner Müller's critical re-workings of *Medea* and *Hamlet*.

There are a number of unifying factors throughout the cycle. Each of the characters in their various nomenclatures (God as Deus, Pater, etc.) are sung by the same voice, and their parts are each derived from a specific gestural vocabulary. The character of God, whose solo opens several of the works, is always assigned a declamatory tenor role, which continually fixes on high notes (Example 6.11), while the son, Jesus, is given a spoken part, until his soul alone (Anima Christi) speaks from beyond the dead.

Other recurrent motives include a series of expanding or decreasing intervals, in either voices or instruments, long sustained chords and forms of widely spaced arpeggiated figuration in the celestas. Some works refer to others in the cycle; for example, the opening of *The Betrayal and Crucifixion of Jesus of Nazareth* is like an instrumental version of the beginning of *The Parting of Darkness from Light.* The generally florid nature of much of the vocal writing was conceived as a reflection of the ecstatic qualities of medieval wall painting and manuscripts.

Finnissy envisaged the *Mysteries* being staged on a pair of carts, like the wooden stalls with wheels that were used in traditional markets, one of which would represent Heaven, with the throne of God, and the other Paradise, featuring the Tree of Knowledge, thus making explicit the fundamental dichotomy. Performers would act both on and off the carts. He also specifies, 'no attempt should be made to disguise the fact that the performance is taking place 'on stage' and 'in concert' - the costumes and props should appear *timeless* and ideally of great simplicity or even crudeness, the pace of the acting ritualistically measured with long and still tableaux'.

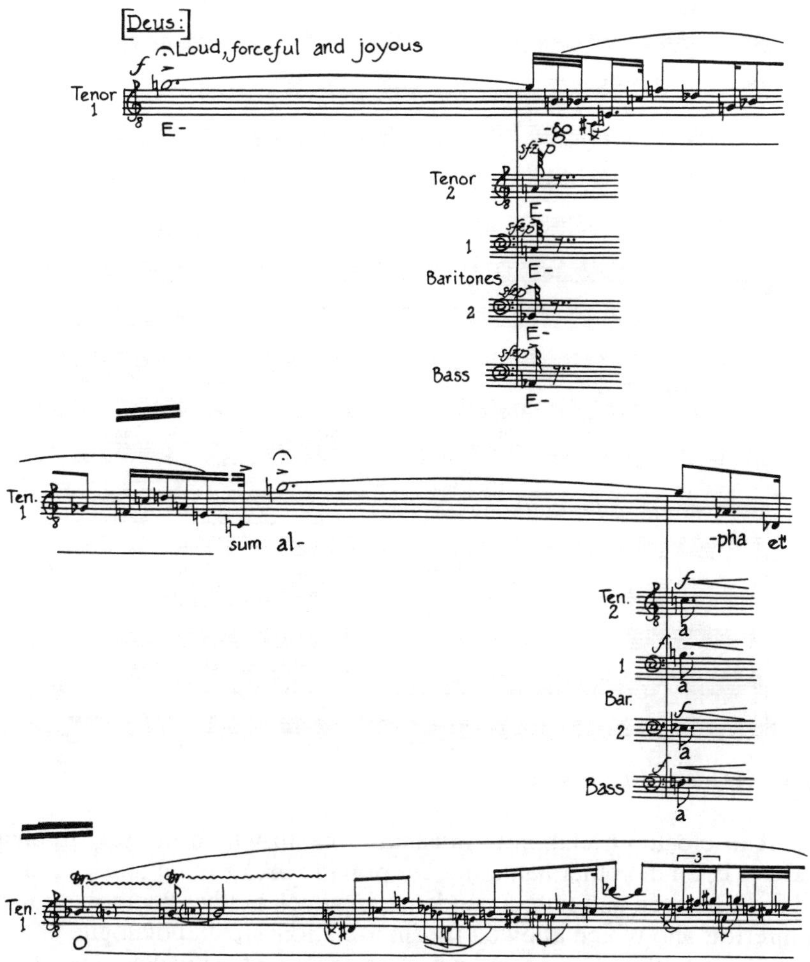

Example 6.11a *The Parting of Darkness from Light*, p. 1

Example 6.11b *The Annunciation*, p. 146

Rather than create an elaborate musical work in which the text is clearly secondary or, on the other hand, merely provide background music, Finnissy aimed for a balance and interdependence in which neither component would seem inferior, and which allowed for interrelationship and dialogue between the two. His combination of and selection from texts is just as important as the music. Long sections of the third and seventh works remain in spoken text, whereas at other points the type of melodisation of the words or their instrumental accompaniment is used to present a particular perspective on what is being said. Long vocal solos tend to assume a form of *arioso* which express overall perceptions of the characters, rather than indulge in over-specific and redundant forms of word painting. Hymns and incantations are often presented in the forms of elaborate motets or sometimes huge, terrifying bodies of sound from combined choirs.

Finnissy's interest was as much in what the plays say about the societies in which they were created, and in how sacred events were represented in terms of situations that could be related to fundamentally human concerns, as in what they say about Christianity. The third work, *Noah and the Great Flood*, a highly pared down version of the third play in the Townley cycle, takes on many of the trappings of a domestic drama. After a long solo, in which the Deus expresses his displeasure with the world he has created and declares his intention to destroy it with the Flood, a spoken scene follows in which the Deus tells the decrepit, self-pitying and rather unctuous character of Noe to build the Ark in preparation for the coming events. Noe communicates this message to his wife and three sons, and they proceed to construct the Ark.

For this section, Finnissy uses three percussionists on a variety of drums and woodblocks, who play from five boxes of repeated material (some of which they include gradually on successive repetitions), using each box for an approximately fixed period of time, then moving to the next.

The modulations between boxes are staggered, so each percussionist changes box at a different point, with the first player acting as 'foreman', leading the way and cueing a series of simultaneous *martellato* beats which bring the section to an end (Example 6.12).

The next scene, also a spoken extraction of key lines from the play, is a hilarious comedy of marital relationships, as Vxor taunts her husband by refusing to obey his orders to follow him into the Ark, telling him instead to 'go cloute thi shone' (go clean your shoes). Notwithstanding protestations from the three daughters, Noe and his wife get into a fight, incurring the disapproval of the three sons (Example 6.13).

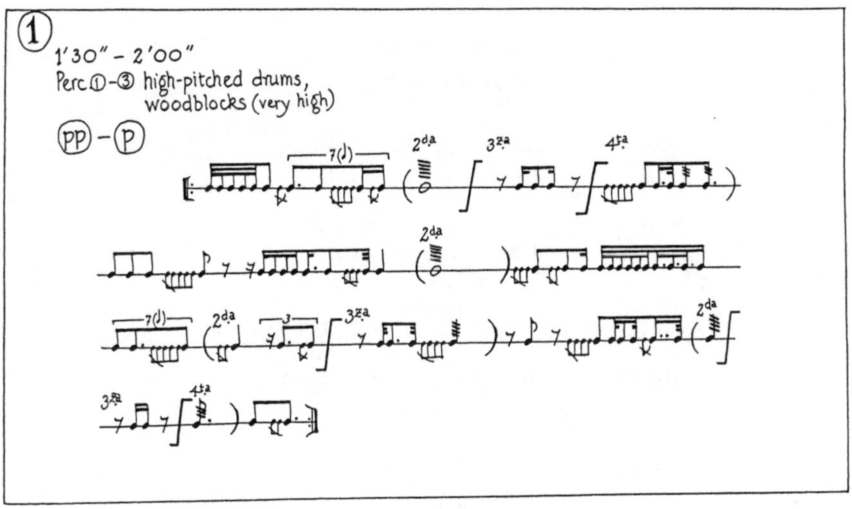

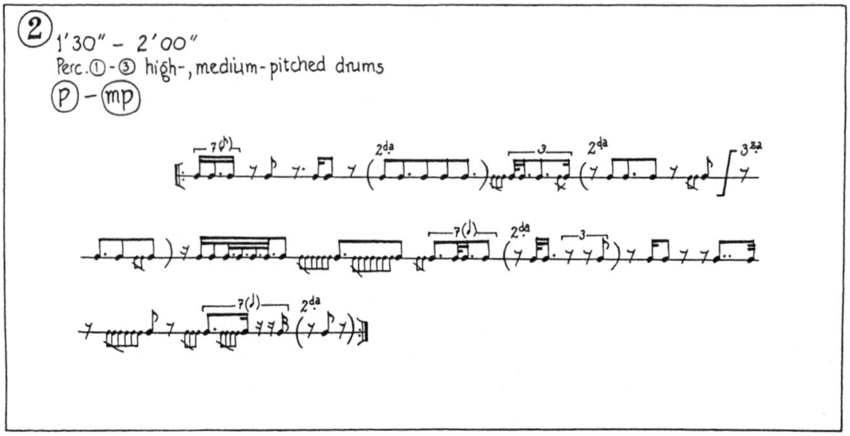

Example 6.12 *Noah and the Great Flood*, p. 61

Vxor: In fath I can not fynd
which is before, which is behynd;
Bot shall we here be pynd,
Noe as haue thou blis?

Noe: Dame, as it is skill
here must vs abide grace;
Therfor, wife, with good will
com into this place.
Behold to the heuen
the cateractes all,
ffull sharp ar thise showers,
that renys aboute;
Therfor, wife, haue done
com into ship fast.

Vxor: Yei, noe, go cloute thi shone
the better will thai last.

Prima mulier: Good moder, com in sone
ffor all is ouer cast,
Both the son and the mone.

Secunda mulier: and many wynd blast ffull sharp;

Vxor: In fayth yit will I spyn;
All in vayn ye carp.

Tercia mulier: Iff ye like ye may spyn
Moder, in the ship.

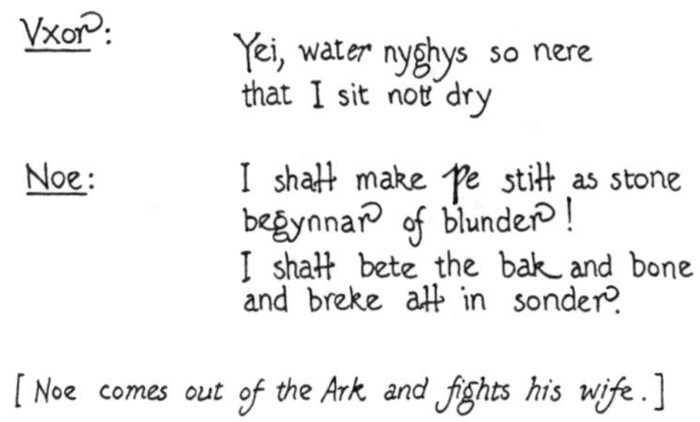

Example 6.13 *Noah and the Great Flood*, p. 64

Finally they enter the Ark together, and the rising of the waters is represented by rolls on cymbals, tam-tam and thundersheet. In scene five, forty days later, Noe sends out the dove and the raven to establish whether dry land remains. The treble recorder and cor anglais play different types of 'bird-music' and walk gradually away from the playing area.

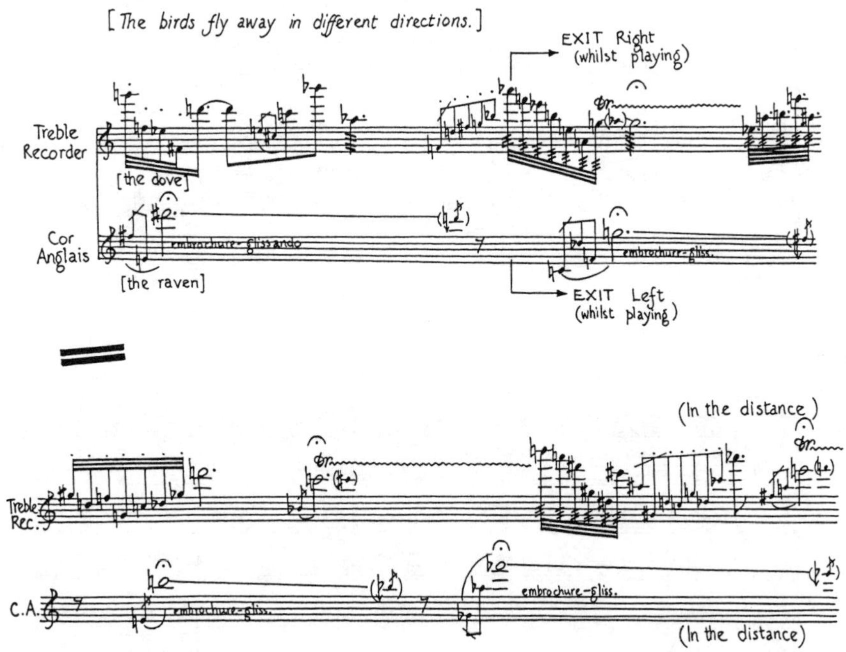

Example 6.14 *Noah and the Great Flood,* p. 67

As the dove returns bearing a leaf from an olive tree, the treble recorder player walks back on, playing an extension of the previous music, and all of the characters give thanks. The sexual politics of *Noah* have their counterpart in Joseph's implied jealousy and fear of redundancy when he discovers Maria's pregnancy in *The Annunciation*.

The fifth work, *The Parliament of Heaven*, is structured in a similar manner to *Tom Fool's Wooing*. The main text, from the N-cycle, is surrounded by a number of hymns and other sequences in Latin, as well as the Gaelic line 'SÙEIL DHÉ MHÓIR' (Eye of the Great God), which had appeared several times in *The Parting of Darkness from Light*. The opening Hymnus is an intricate 21-part motet for three choirs ('Come Creator Spirit, Visit the Souls of Thy People, And Fill with grace from on High, The Hearts which Thou hast Created'), the type of imitative counterpoint bearing a distant relationship to the *gagaku* writing encountered in *Tsuru-Kame*. As this calms, the voice of the Pater emerges, with a solemn stroke on two tam-tams. He is accompanied by a series of decreasing intervals in the four trumpets, from a perfect 11th down to a semitone, which also accelerates and increases in density:

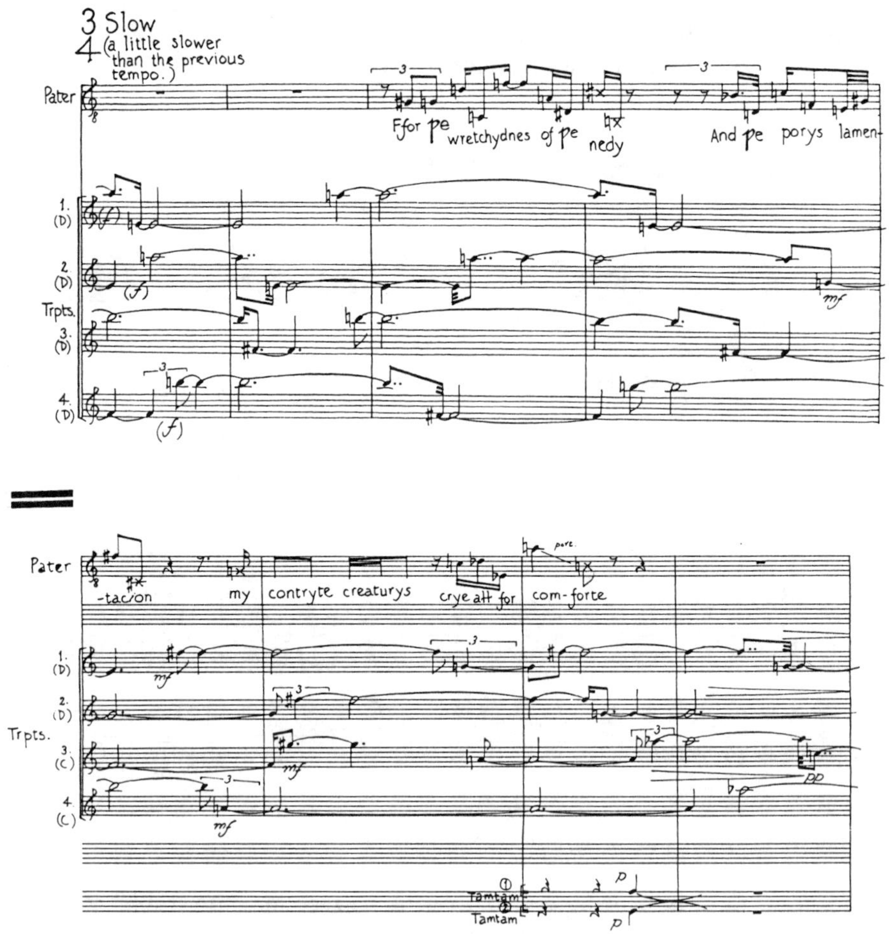

Example 6.15 *The Parliament of Heaven*, pp. 11-12

He speaks of reconciliation and grace to man, but a certain contempt for some of the principles he is supposed to embody is revealed by his inability to sing such words as 'the needy' and 'my contryte creaturys'.

His four daughters, Veritas (Truth), Misericordia (Mercy), Justicia (Righteousness), and Pax (Peace) enter their separate pleas concerning the fate of Adam in the manner of a courtroom drama. Each is associated with a particular instrument, the mezzo, Veritas, with the viola; the soprano, Misericordia, with the oboe; the soprano, Justicia, with the harp; and the extremely high soprano, Pax, with the treble recorder. During their successive initial advocacies, each of these instruments is added to the ensemble, their words coloured cumulatively by what has come before. The viola begins by reinforcing certain key pitches within Veritas's vocal line in the manner of a *cantus firmus*, which continues for Misericordia, with the addition of an oboe embellishment around her part. Different degrees of structural elucidation and ornamentation are progressively introduced (Example 6.16). The manner in which these are utilised suggests Finnissy's particular sympathies.

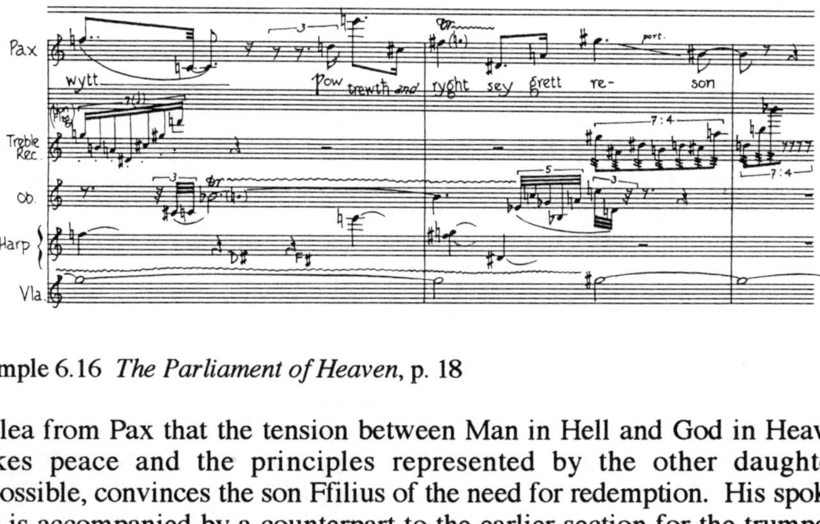

Example 6.16 *The Parliament of Heaven*, p. 18

A plea from Pax that the tension between Man in Hell and God in Heaven makes peace and the principles represented by the other daughters impossible, convinces the son Ffilius of the need for redemption. His spoken part is accompanied by a counterpart to the earlier section for the trumpets: increasing intervals, with oscillating density of attack, this time in the four instruments used for the daughters, with a long cymbal roll and quiet strokes on the tam-tam. Each now with their respective instruments alone, Veritas, Misericordia and Justicia admit the impossibilities of their positions, and Pax informs the company, with a truly spectacular solo (Example 6.17), that only God is capable of enacting the deed that will bring about peace.

Example 6.17 *The Parliament of Heaven*, p. 24

As the Ffilius and the Pater decide that he who redeems Man must be both God *and* Man, the intervals in the trumpets return, here moving in four successive steps from a perfect 12th to a major 7th, a perfect 4th, then a semitone (once again with increasing density), at which point of harmonic tension the Spiritus Sanctus (also a speaking role) declares that he will take on the task of delivering the son to earth.

The three choirs take over the semitone interval, singing 'Eye of the Great God' in sustained and staccato pitches, then begin another Hymnus. A series of long chords, moving at different rates in each choir, are interrupted by an uncoordinated flurry of lines, after which the chords continue, and each choir moves between these two elements independently. As they consolidate upon a pair of perfect 12ths (G-D-A), the trumpets take over the upper interval, and move in two steps down to a semitone, as the Pater instructs the Angel Gabriel to inform the maid married to Joseph that she will give birth to the son of God. The Spiritus Sanctus bids Gabriel tell Mary that he will 'work all this', with a distant echo of the 'Eye of the Great God'.

For the final Hymnus, the three choirs are joined by a children's choir. They all begin with an extension of the type of motet encountered at the beginning of the work, then the adult choirs break off with a whispered Alleluia. The children's choir continues, their parts leading towards an ornate but calm compound of lines from the four daughters, singing Alleluia, with brief outbursts from their associated instruments, and ending with a strident chord from all the instruments:

Example 6.18 *The Parliament of Heaven*, p. 48

The motet continues, with the addition of more elaborate solo parts at the beginning. This time the Alleluia is spoken *mezza voce*. After a second refrain from the daughters, the motet starts for a third time completely in solo voices together with the children, leading directly to the daughters. All the choirs then have a slow crescendo in slow moving chords, towards a massive B flat^{II} - E flat^{I} - F$_{II}$ - $_{I}$ joined by a piercing cluster in the instruments. The trumpets, *piano*, take over the top two pitches from the choirs, who shout the final Alleluia, and crescendo with tam-tams and cymbals to a huge *ffff* ending. The enormity of what is to proceed is rendered in awe-inspiring, frightening terms.

The *Mysteries* anticipate many musical ideas to which Finnissy would return in his series of sacred works over a decade later, particularly in the approach to choral writing. If and when the cycle is heard in its entirety, it should provide an utterly shattering and completely relevant musical and dramatic experience, a modern recreation of the varieties of mysticism, glory, humour, and trepidation that were felt by those who experienced the medieval originals.

Popular and Street Theatre

Finnissy, ever concerned to avoid the pitfalls of either solipsism or hyper-intellectualism, also looked to popular forms of theatre for models, recalling in particular his love for the circus in childhood. By using forms or genres which were accessible and immediate, it then became easier to introduce dangerous, subversive, defamiliarising elements, as Bertold Brecht had realised earlier. In the works that resulted, Finnissy was able to bring about a fusion of the ideas of Artaud, Brecht and Grotowski, creating a form of music-theatre that could be comprehended by an average spectator, whilst dealing with primal emotions, movements and sounds with the utmost economy of (at least theatrical) means.

One of these works is *Bouffe* (1975), for a solo performer on a stage. It is the act of a type of clown, whose neanderthal act is at different points humorous, sad, pathetic and sinister. He dashes on stage, covered in a sheet, then collapses to the floor. Undeterred, he rises grandly to his feet again, then gingerly sticks one hand out from the sheet, moves it about a little, lifts the sheet up a few inches and makes a loud growl. Suddenly he withdraws his arm behind the sheet, then falls to the floor again. As he rises up once more, he emits a loud sniffle and giggles childishly, then holds his arms out (still underneath the sheet), squawks and chews on his saliva. Suddenly he covers his mouth in an attempt to prevent a loud inhaling sound, and turns ashamedly away from the audience. Moving with renewed confidence towards the audience, he pulls the sheet off, stares at them with incomprehension, then looks down at the sheet, closing his eyes and mouth. He moves his head skywards, then emits a concatenation of sobbing, howling, grizzling and self-reprimanding. After looking suspiciously at the audience with one eye, he turns left as if discovering something highly unpleasant there, and emits another amalgamation of coughing, choking, cackling, sighing, smacking of lips and panting. Looking back to the front with an ape-like sound of indecision, he appears to fall asleep then wakes up again immediately. With a sad and pained undulation he attempts to extract a tooth from his mouth, squats on the floor, then takes the sheet in his mouth and falls once again to the floor. Raising his trembling hands, which then fall, he wraps himself in the sheet, begins to crawl off, then after a sudden convulsion falls for the last time to the floor.

Bouffe is music in the sense that the various sounds the performer makes are notated using a form of conventional musical notation. Otherwise it relates both to Grotowski's idea of a 'Poor Theatre' consisting of no more than the performer(s) on stage, whose actions deal with the most primitive of emotions and reactions, and to those of Hans-Joachim Hespos's various works which stand in a no-man's land between theatre and music, and deal with the breakdown of conventional language (and by implication modern society), where only the random pulses, tics, breaths and other forms of pre-linguistic utterance remain, a world that would be further explored in Finnissy's ensemble work *Lost Lands*. Finnissy would seem, however, more open to an element of comedy than Hespos (or other German explorers of music-theatre such as Dieter Schnebel or Gerhard Stäbler); the irony here need not detract from the power of what is being communicated.

One of Finnissy's wittiest works is *Commedia dell'incomprensibile Potere che Alcune Donne hanno sugli Uomini* (1973-75) (Comedy of the incomprehensible power that some women have over men), written for the 'Year of the Woman', a rather camp piece which portrays the primary nature of the interrelationship of the sexes somewhat in the style of the *commedia dell'arte*. The reduction to essentials of characterisation and situations is mirrored in the minimal instrumentation, a cellist (who also plays castanets), a harpsichordist (who also plays a baby-rattle and brass-bell), and a soprano and counter-tenor (who, according to the composer, is by the nature of his voice able to act like a woman). The woman is a Dietrich-like figure, moody, feigning innocence and childishness, able to enact an utterly enfeebling affect on even the most strong-willed of men. The two singers perform their action in five different areas in front of the two instrumentalists. The work is in five sections, changes of scene being signified by a bell:

1. *Il Scontento* (The Discord). The woman manipulates the man's reactions through gazes, mocking, sobbing, causing him to cringe, tremble, squeal and attempt to leave. Hectic trills, arpeggios, *pizzicato* in the instruments. There are no words, emotions are expressed through musical gestures (Example 6.19).

Example 6.19 *Commedia dell'incomprensibile Potere che Alcune Donne hanno sugli Uomini*, p. 4.

2. *Le Maschere* (The Mask). The woman continually sings the word 'love' in a florid, *bel canto* style. By contrast, the man's counterpoint seems pedestrian, reflecting his inability to express emotion in anything but a repressed manner. The harpsichord and cello serve to reinforce the woman's part in the nature of their writing. At the end of each phrase, each stab each other, suggesting the raw hatred lurking underneath the facade that love can be.
3. *Le Lezione* (The Lesson). The man sings the letters of the Greek alphabet, attempting to teach them to the woman, who responds sullenly while shaking a baby rattle in ways which suggest her moods. She mocks her 'teacher' and, by continually mispronouncing the words, lulls him into a false sense of superiority, whilst nevertheless embellishing the rather basic melodic lines which she must imitate. A counterpoint to the woman's rattle is provided by the harpsichord shaking the same instrument. By the end, she makes clear how she can perfectly easily repeat the words parrot-fashion, and can also outdo the man in other respects (Example 6.20).

Example 6.20 *Commedia dell'incomprensible Potere che Alcune Donne hanno sugli Uomini*, p. 15.

4. *La Danza* (The Dance). An extremely rapid duet for harpsichord and castanets. The harpsichordist alternates between wide arpeggios around the keyboard and more close-range lines, as well as clapping their hands and stamping their feet in response to the castanets. Strange silences appear at various points.
5. *Il Giardino* (The Garden). A solo for the woman, singing a text from Genesis B in *The Exeter Book*, a tenth century book of riddles, about the light 'beateous and bountiful' that Eve has received from Heaven, and which she can now teach to Adam.

The piece is very funny, utterly direct, and optimal in its clear dependence on both theatre and music. It demonstrates most penetratingly the incomprehensible power that some music has over words, the immediacy of emotions when couched in terms of sounds and gestures, rather than represented at one remove through a text.

But the most raw, brutal and expressionistic of these works is *Mr Punch* (1976-77/79), described by one critic as an 'immorality play'. Completely different in nature to Birtwistle's psycho-drama *Punch and Judy*, Finnissy's work is an uncompromising piece of street-theatre, intended ideally to be performed with a puppet show. All the roles are played by one singer using different voices, with a seven-member ensemble.

The plot is relatively simple: Mr Punch successively encounters the other characters - Dog Toby, the violinist Scaramuccia, his wife Judy's baby, Judy herself, a Doctor, a police constable, the hangman Jack Catch and finally the Devil - and kills each one either because they annoy him or get in his way, or just for the hell of it. Musically, Finnissy uses materials which serve a leitmotivic purpose but are developed and proportioned in such a way that the work is a coherent musical entity, rather than just a text with a redundant musical accompaniment. The main materials in their initial states are as follows (see Example 6.21):

(a) **Action**. Multiple high trills and tremolos.
(b) **Death**. Very loud blows to the bass drum, perhaps a reference to the killing scene in Berg's *Wozzeck.* Rhythms in morse code, usually spelling DEATH or derivations (MORTE for Scaramuccia, DEATH & DAMNATION for the devil).
(c) **Motion**. Multiple rapid smooth lines in changing irrational rhythms.
(d) **Jig**. Dance in triplets.
(e) **Stillness**. Long sustained notes, parts moving independently.

Example 6.21a *Mr Punch*, p. 1

Example 6.21b *Mr Punch*, p. 3

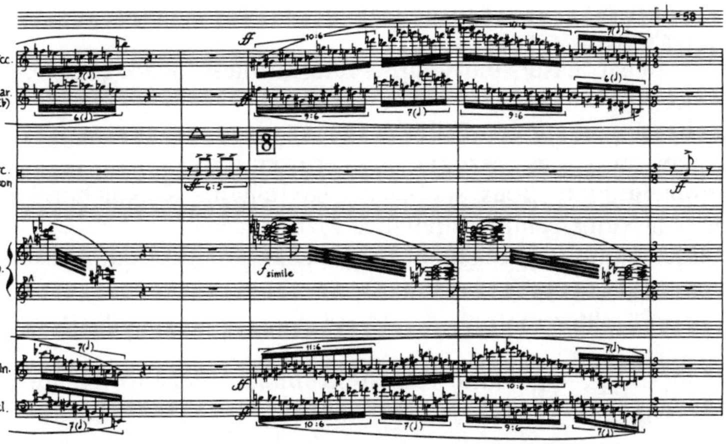

Example 6.21c *Mr Punch*, p. 5

Example 6.21d *Mr Punch*, p. 9

Example 6.21e *Mr Punch*, p. 12

Individual characters then have their own characteristic voice types and instruments.

Punch: squeaky, parrot-like falsetto. Snare drum, bass drum, sometimes other percussion.
Judy: shrewish, nasal, bullying. Flute, Chinese block (one for each side of her character).
Dog Toby: dog imitation. Guiro.
Baby: baby imitation. Flute (taken over from Judy).
Scaramuccia: pretentious, snobbish (fake Italian). Klaxon horn, violin.
Doctor: wheezing, senile, asthmatic. Piano ripples.
Constable: bumbling, obstinate, authoritarian. Pizzicato violin, but lines are mostly unaccompanied.
Jack Catch: thick-witted, matter-of fact, heavy country dialect. Triangle.
Devil: imposing, sepulchral, basso-profundo. Very low piano, flute with tremolos.

The music of the Devil is anticipated at a few points earlier on in the work, suggesting the diabolic features of Punch himself.

The work is divided into seven musical sections with different tempos, which do not necessarily coincide with the exact delineation of the narrative. Here is how it proceeds in both musical and narrative senses (numbers in bold correspond to section numbers in the score, others to rehearsal numbers).

1. *Allegro moderato*

Punch's opening lines, with triangle roll

1-4. **Action 1**. Punch encounters, and is attacked by, dog. Increasing rate of change of trills. Guiro (dog) joined by cheap, tacky sound of klaxon horn (Scaramuccia) towards end.

5. **Death 1**. Punch kills dog. With violin, anticipating next section. A few faint twitches from guiro (dog)
6. Highly virtuosic violin solo from Scaramuccia.
7-8(a). **Motion 1**, interspersed with klaxon horn. Fight between Punch and Scaramuccia.
8(b)-9. **Death 2**, unaccompanied. Punch beats Scaramuccia to death with violin.

The smashing of the violin at this point may be an allusion to Maxwell Davies' *Eight Songs for a Mad King*, first performed by the Fires of London, who commissioned *Mr Punch*.

2. *Adagio ma non troppo e molto espressivo.*

10. **Flute solo 1**. Entrance of Judy.
11. **Fight 1** (Anticipation of fight). Chinese block, to be joined by snare drum. Judy clouts Punch. **Flute solo 2**. Judy fetches Baby. **Fight 2**. Struggle between Judy and Punch for Baby.
12-13. **Fight 3**. Punch knocks Judy offstage. **Flute solo 3**. Punch rocks baby. Interrupted by snare drum roll as baby cries.

3. *Allegro (alla Danza - rhythmic and brutal)*

14. **Jig 1**. Punch jigs Baby.
15-16. **Jig 2**. Rhythm of Jig 1 filtered so that beats become isolated. Low chords in bass, anticipating Devil's music later. Baby cries and Punch hits it.
17. **Jig 3**. Return of triplets.
18. **Death 3**. With low piano tremolo. Punch beats Baby's head against the floor. **Jig 4** - just snare drum.
19. **Stillness 1**, with **Fight 4** (Chinese block (echoing Jig) and snare drum). Enter Judy, who Punch tells about Baby.
20-21(a). **Motion 2** (three rapid gestures, with piano *glissandi*), **Fight 5/Jig 4**. Judy hits Punch with saucepan.
21(b)-23. **Death 4**, unaccompanied. Punch beats Judy to death. **Flute solo 4**. Last gasps of Judy. Punch throws Judy off-stage.
24. **Jig 4**. Punch: 'Lose a wife, and set a man free.. use knife or poison, or little stick.. just like ME', then runs off.
25. **Jig 5**. Snare drum becomes more manic, towards:
26. **Motion 3** (now in tremolos). Punch flung back on stage, lies on ground in pain.

4. *Adagio quasi un poco andante*

27. **Stillness 2**. Enter Doctor.
28-9(a). **Stillness 3**, overlaid with piano ripples. Doctor examines Punch. Anticipation of Constable's and Devil's music.
29(b)-30(a). **Death 5**, joined by Stillness 4. Punch throttles Doctor
30(b)-31(a). **Motion 4**. **Jig 6**, now altered as shown in Example 6.22. Punch runs off.

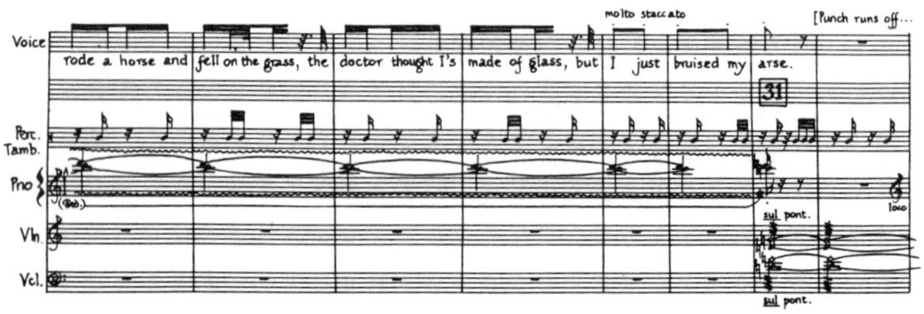

Example 6.22 *Mr Punch*, p. 17

5. *Allegro molto vivace*

31(b). **Stillness 5**, with violin pizzicato. Enter Constable.

colla voce Dialogue. Constable attempts to arrest Punch.

32. **Death 6**, with piano tremoli. Punch beats Constable to death.

33-4. **Jig 7** (further derivative) with **Stillness 6**, introducing ruminating trills. Further rhyme from Punch. **Motion 5** - final phrase.

6. *Andante ma non troppo e molto cantabile*

35-8(a). **Stillness 7**. Very extended, as stage remains empty. Gradual increase in musical activity, with trills, *accelerando* and eventual *crescendo,* suggesting immanent events. Triangle (Jack Catch) enters at climax.

38(b)-39. Triangle roll (like prison bell) remains. Jack Catch enters with gibbet. **Stillness 8**. Like continuation from part way through Stillness 7, eventual *crescendo*.

40-41. Snare drum. Punch enters. Jack Catch explains gibbet. **Stillness 9**. Like snippet from Stillness 7/8. More snare drum and triangle. Further explanation from Jack Catch.

42-3(a). **Hybrid 1**, of previous materials (Action, Stillness, Motion, etc.) with quick montage of themes for previous characters (Scaramuccia's violin solo, Judy's flute solo, etc.), recalling past events. Punch tries unsuccessfully to insert head into noose.

43(b). Third explanation from Jack Catch, who puts head into noose.

44-5. **Death 7**, with accumulating trills and sustained pitches (also like *Wozzeck*). Punch hangs Jack Catch.

46. **Stillness 10**, but in advanced state (as previously) so no longer 'still'. Punch cuts down corpse and exits.

47(a). **Hybrid 2**, without thematic montage.

7. *Presto*

47(b). Triangle roll. Enter Devil, to drag Punch down to Hell.

47(c)-50. *Totentanz.* Three rhythmically accelerating lines of *staccatissimo* chords and notes in piano (Devil), with **Motion 6**, fragments of tremolos in flute, bass drum anticipates Death (Example 6.23). Punch tells Devil he must remain, for he is the best friend Devil has on earth.

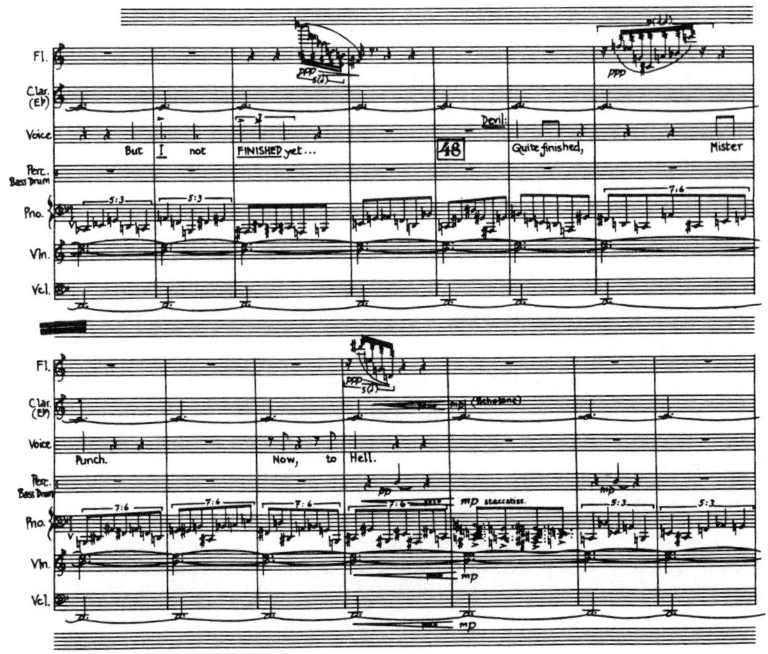

Example 6.23 *Mr Punch*, p. 30

51-2	**Death 8**, unaccompanied, but with *sfz* interruptions from other instruments. Punch beats Devil to death, proclaims misery (and this story) is now over.
53	**Action 2**, bringing music full circle.

As is true of so many of Finnissy's theatrical works, the use of a familiar text enables a more sophisticated yet comprehensible musical work, in which the music can comment upon the events in question. The positive reception that greeted *Mr Punch*, which grabs the audience by the throat and never lets go, would suggest the underlying sadistic tendencies of many people, which has been suggested as the reason for the attraction of a film like von Sternberg's *Der Blaue Engel*,[5] or of many more recent films, not to mention Jacobian Tragedy. For the audience *Mr Punch* acts as a form of catharsis, precisely the aim of Artaud's 'Theatre of Cruelty'. Utterly void of any warmth or hope for humanity, this most cynical of black comedies may also have served a cathartic purpose for the composer. Or perhaps it is a reflection of the amorality of the twentieth century, after world wars and nuclear technology. After completing the revised version, Finnissy was not to return to the theatre for four years, when he would explore much more 'subjective' concerns.

Alienation and Displacement

> Today the Variety Theatre is the crucible in which the elements of an emergent new sensibility are seething. Here you find an ironic decomposition of all the worn-out prototypes of the Beautiful, the grand, the Solemn, the Religious, the ferocious, the Seductive, and the Terrifying, and also the abstract elaboration of the new prototypes that will succeed these.
> (F.T. Marinetti, 'From The Variety Theatre' 1913).[6]

> Our dramatists have no idea at all of the laws of the true theatre. In the Russian theatre of the nineteenth century the old vaudeville was replaced by a flood of plays of brilliant dialectic, plays *à thèse*, plays of manners, plays of mood... [footnote] I mention the old vaudeville not because we must necessarily revive it in the theatre; rather, I quote it as a dramatic form which is linked on the one hand with theatrical - as opposed to literary - traditions, and on the other with the tastes of the people...the vaudeville originated in the art of the folk song and the folk theatre. (From Vsevolod Meyerhold, 'The Fairground Booth' 1911-12).[7]

> American vaudeville produced the cinema's first generation of great comedians, and itself disappeared as a live theatrical genre because of the growing popularity of film as the foremost medium for mass entertainment. 'Although primarily remembered as a vehicle for comedy, the vaudeville show was a very diverse spectacle, incorporating elements of circus (animal acts, trapeze artists), 'serious' theatre (lurid melodramas for the most part), opera (showpiece arias) and other things - such as folk dancing - from the various ethnic traditions that were taken by the emigrants from Europe and Asia to America in the nineteenth century. The average show would contain about a dozen speciality acts, in the bigger cities more, and in the country areas less: the lavishness - and in some cases the wholesomeness - of the spectacle were closely linked to local taste and economics. (Michael Finnissy, programme note to *Vaudeville*.)

Finnissy had been attracted to the variety show since childhood, and its explicitly sectional, non-'organic' nature has more than a little parallel in the ways in which his music is constructed. With *Vaudeville* (1983/87), however, he used the structure of a vaudeville show to deliver a bleak picture of the seven ages of man. To avoid the sentimental pathos that has become something of a cliché since Leoncavallo's *I Pagliacci*, Finnissy specifies that the staging should specify no specific era, and should emphasise 'illusion', stylised, unrealistic performance. The work portrays life as a sequence of 'acts', whereby human beings put on different 'masks' in order to find a role for themselves in a world where their existence is inevitably purposeless. The variety element is played up to the full, but an underlying pessimism seems to inform the generally crude and vulgar music.

The ensemble is essentially the same as that for Stravinsky's *L'Histoire du Soldat* (clarinet, bassoon, flugelhorn (rather than trumpet), trombone, violin and double bass) with a mezzo-soprano, baritone and two dancers. The seven sections are as follows: [8]

1. Birth of four children - their wailing introduced with grand chords and cymbal crashes.
2. Childhood games: Musical chairs, 'Ring a ring o' roses' (Example 6.24), and 'Mother', in which one girl kneels on the floor with her skirt up, and in turns snatches the two boys away from the other girl, who plays 'Mother'. Then the first girl snatches the other girl, the 'Mother', herself, possibly suggesting lesbianism or alternatively an Oedipal complex.

Example 6.24 *Vaudeville*, p. 10
Reproduced by permission of United Music Publishers Limited

3. Romeo and Juliet. Recitativo and Duetto derived in a rather Stravinskyian manner from Bellini's *I Capuleti e i Montecchi*, as the two lovers meet and realise they must escape (Example 6.25). Romeo utterly monopolises the duet, and Juliet can hardly get a word in edgeways.

Example 6.25 *Vaudeville*, p. 28
Reproduced by permission of United Music Publishers Limited

4. Settings of two poems from Walt Whitman's *Leaves of Grass*, 'Cavalry Crossing a Ford' and 'Bivouac on a Mountain Side'.
5. Middle Age. Monologue by aged vaudevillian (see below).
6. Four fast waltzes, getting progressively out of focus and fragmenting. Between first and second waltzes, Flamenco dance, setting of 'El Gran Teatro del Mundo' (The Great Theatre of the World) by Pedro Calderón de la Barca ('Beauty must die! So goes the sad song. Let me not die! Let me blossom as at my first dawning.') in flamenco style, with hand clapping and foot stamping, often out of time, and becoming demented.
7. Old Age. Four characters sit on chairs. One gentleman and one lady dance slow waltz until lights down, while others fall asleep (and possibly die) in their chairs.

The longest and most important section is the fifth. An aged vaudevillian enters, and proceeds to give an imitation of five famous singers, adopting operatic poses, though he does not actually make any sound - his caricatures are enacted in gestural form only. The first four types are shown in Example 6.26.

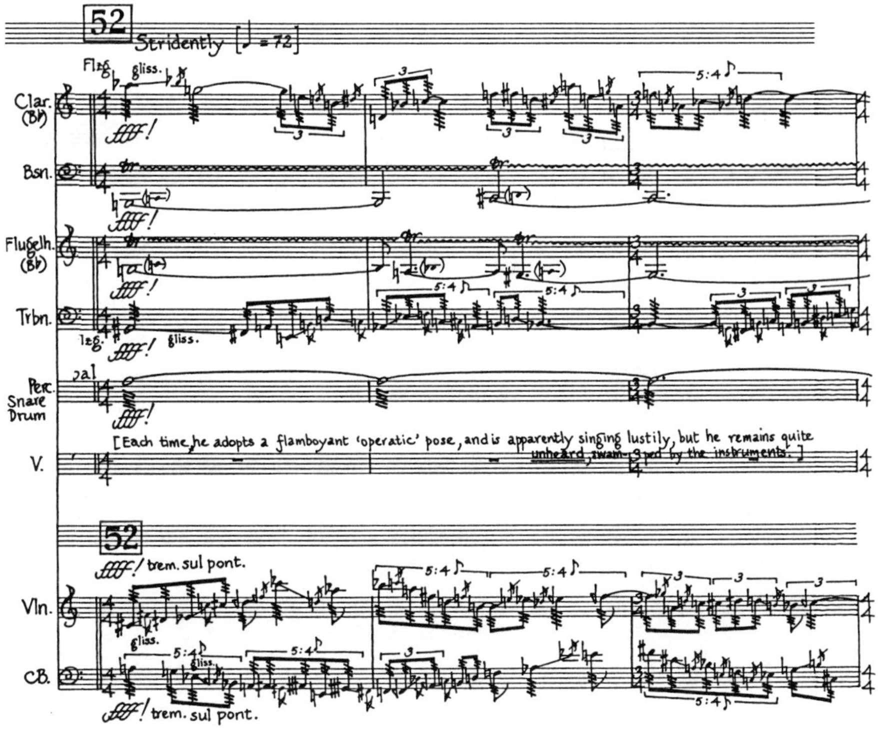

Example 6.26a *Vaudeville*, p. 55

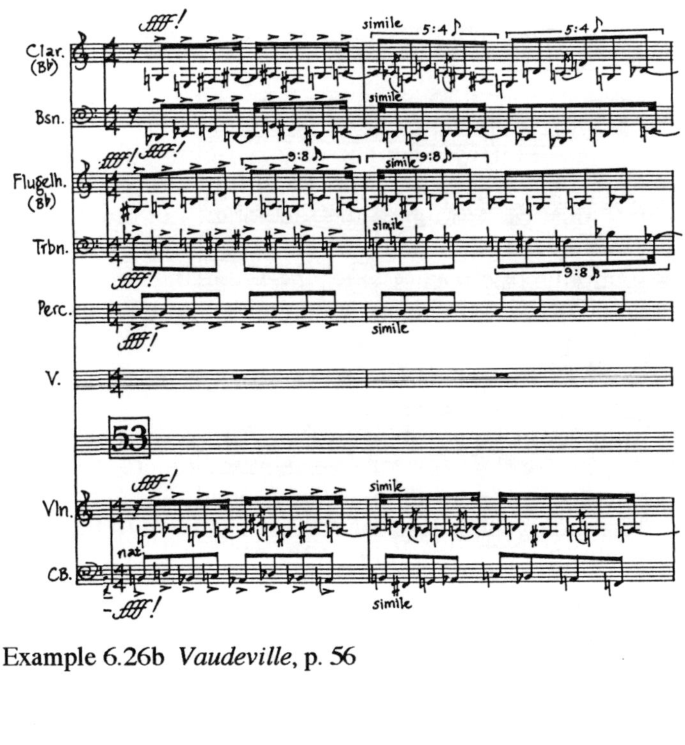

Example 6.26b *Vaudeville*, p. 56

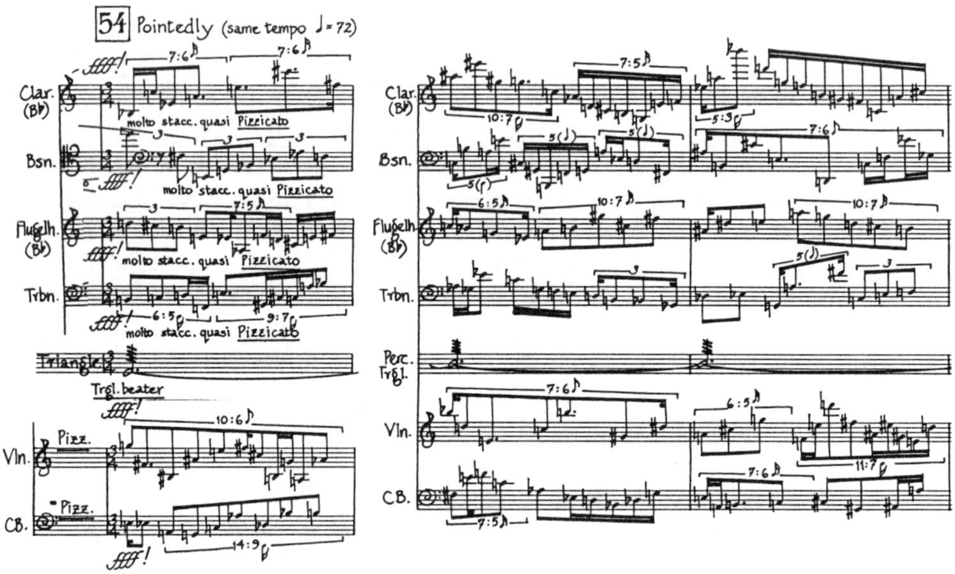

Example 6.26c *Vaudeville,* p. 58

Example 6.26d *Vaudeville,* p. 60

The fifth imitation, which the vaudevillian takes some time in getting round to, consists solely of a coin dropped in a tin, which presumably signifies the poverty that a singer (like this vaudevillian) can eventually find himself in. The vaudevillian repeats some of the imitations, either because he has forgotten which he has already done, or because he (misguidedly) thinks the audience are clamouring to see them again. He also goes on endlessly about the poverty his mother and father lived in (to the accompaniment of a mock-heartbreaking violin solo), then tells the story of his early theatrical days, including an incident where a woman he performed with (and perhaps was deeply in love with, but she would not have him) inadvertently exposed her breasts on stage. A few light moments are provided by musical references to Fred Astaire and the 'Anvil Chorus' (with the clinking coins replacing the anvil). When the audience have finally had quite enough of him, he tunelessly sings the rhyme 'If you've only got a Moustache':

Example 6.27 *Vaudeville*, p. 76
Reproduced by permission of United Music Publishers Limited

The repetitions of the singer imitations, as well as the tedium of the stories, most clearly signify the sense of meaninglessness, and perhaps relate to Finnissy's own searches for categorical 'archetypes'. It may not be too fanciful to suggest an autobiographical element in this scene, a fear of ageing and redundancy. The vaudevillian is like a character from a Beckett or Ionesco play: he searches for some point to his existence, but discovers it is merely a sequence of events, then death. The final musical gesture in the last section recalls this scene. *Vaudeville* lacks the degree of objectivity that can make *Mr Punch* entertaining; its effect is to produce numbness and despair, that need not rely on *verismo* style emotional manipulation to make its point, the sheer awfulness of what is being said requiring no amplification.

The empathy Finnissy shows with the societal 'misfits', who would perform a vaudeville show to an audience who would hate to meet them on the street, is taken further in *Soda Fountain* (1983). This was written in consultation with four singer/actors in Australia, and presents an array of the displaced and marginalised from literary and operatic history. The piece is in fourteen continuous sections, to be performed with minimal costume change, though a few props play a part in distinguishing characters. A chart of the movements, characters, and other details is given in Example 6.28.

As can be seen, each of the four performers has both a spoken and a sung solo, and the ordering of the sections provides for several different symmetries and developments within the whole work.

The displacement is accentuated through the nature of the selections and combinations. In the second part, Mimi, far removed from her Bohemian environment, encounters a Monster from Outer Space. Mimi coughs and sniffles as the Monster moves towards her and attacks her, but all that he achieves is to catch her cold himself. The baffled Mimi, having shed her burden, slinks away (Example 6.29).

In the encounter between Wagner's Brünnhilde and Gounod's Roméo, actual lines are lifted from the two operas (in their original languages), but juxtaposed so as to put both of their words and situations in very different contexts:

Roméo: (hushed but luminous and ecstatic)
Ah! la voilà! c'est elle!
(Ah! There is she!)
Brünnhilde: (frightened and trembling, whisper)
Ein Unhold schwang sich auf jenen Stein!
(A monster has mounted this rock!)
Roméo: (ecstatic)
Viens, funèbre clarté! viens l'offrir à mes yeux.
(Come,... Come and offer yourself to my eyes.)
Brünnhilde: (frightened)
Wer bist du, Schrecklicher? Stammst du von Menschen?
Komm'st du von Hella's nächtlich em Heer?
(Who are you, dread figure? Are you a mortal?
Have you come from Hella's hordes of night?)
Roméo: (enthusiastic)
Ô ma femme! (O my lady!)
Brünnhilde: (horrified)
Weh! (Woe!)

A section from this passage is shown in Example 6.30.

No.	Type	Character	Source	Voices	Props	Actions, Gestures
1.	Solo with Clash Cymbals	Monostatos	Die Zauberflöte - Mozart	Tenor	Lantern, black face-mask	Searching stage.
2.	Duet (sounds)	Mimi, Monster from Outer Space	La Bohème - Puccini	Soprano, Contralto	-	Moves towards each other, transference of cough.
3.	Duet	Brünnhilde, Roméo	Götterdämmerung - Wagner; Roméo et Juliette - Gounod	Mezzo-Soprano, Tenor	Ring	Moving around circle as if on pivot.
4.	Spoken solo	Heathcliff and Cathy	Wuthering Heights - Emily Brontë	Soprano	-	Interruptions - whimpering, scratching.
5.	Solo with Clash Cymbals	Julius Caesar	Giulio Cesare - Händel	Contralto	Roman sword, laurel wreath	Brandishes sward, strikes heroic attitudes.
6.	Spoken solo	Mrs Bennett	Pride and Prejudice - Jane Austen	Mezzo-Soprano	-	Interruptions - sighs, sewing/embroidery.
7.	Trio (notes/sounds)	'Vocal Backing' group	-	Soprano, Contralto, Tenor	-	-
8.	Spoken solo	Sherlock Holmes	The Adventure of the Copper Beeches - Sir Arthur Conan Doyle	Contralto	E.g. pipe, magnifying glass.	Sucking/puffing a pipe, looking at objects through magnifying glass.
9.	Solo with Clash Cymbals	Tatiana	Eugene Onegin - Tchaikovsky	Mezzo-Soprano	Letter, dressing-gown	Reads letter, tears it up.
10.	Spoken solo	Dorian Gray	The Portrait of Dorian Gray - Oscar Wilde	Tenor	E.g. curtain, portrait	Bitter laugh, pulling curtain aside.
11.	Solo with Clash Cymbals	Lakmé	Lakmé - Delibes	Soprano	Anklets of tiny bells, flimsy scarves.	Shaking anklets, playing with scarves.
12.	Trio (spoken)	Hamlet, Lady Macbeth, Carmen	Hamlet - Shakespeare; Macbeth - Verdi; Carmen - Bizet	Soprano, Mezzo-Soprano, Contralto	-	-
13.	Quartet (notes)	Four sheep/four actors	'Baa baa black sheep' - nursery rhyme	All	-	Huddling together, moving to widely spaced positions, running about.
14.	Quartet (sounds)	Tap-dancing contestants in children's Talent Show	-	All	Hard-soled shoes.	Tap-dancing (notated rhythms).

Example 6.28 Overall plan of *Soda Fountain*

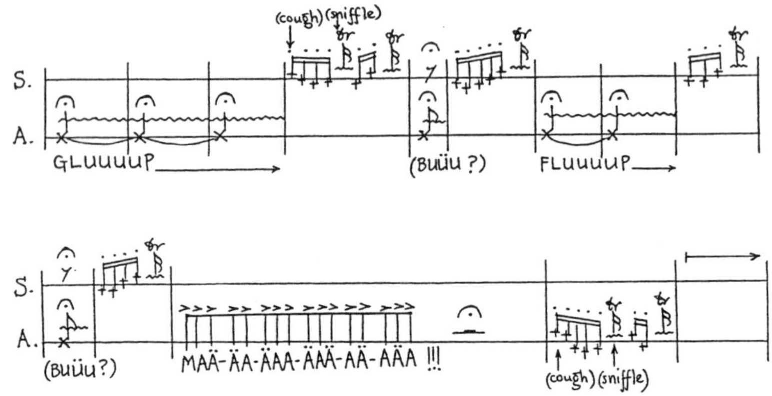

Example 6.29 *Soda Fountain*, p. 8

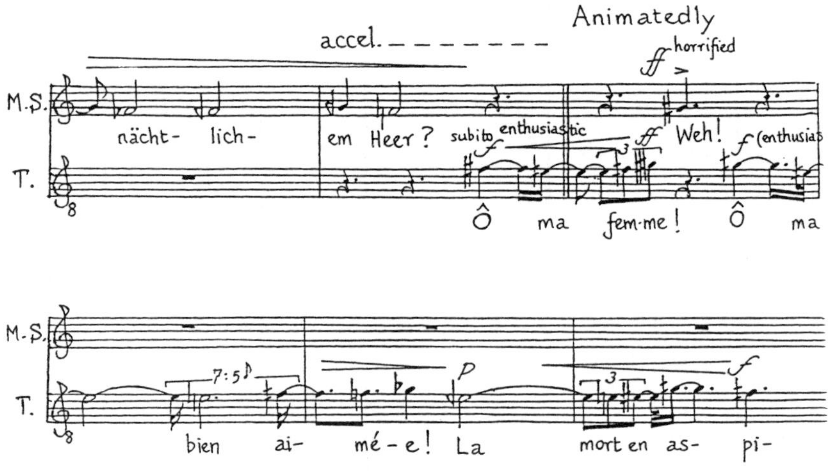

Example 6.30 *Soda Fountain*, p. 11

The manner in which these classic lines are used to construct a dialogue which resonates with aspects of contemporary sexual politics suggests that the seeds of such a world-view are implicit in male-female encounters from any period or place. The language difference serves to add to the effect of this comedy of mutual incomprehension. Both singers wander in a circle, as if attached by a pivot, so they cannot get closer to each other; both also sing in a very similar register, providing for a strained artificial 'heroic tenor' of Roméo contrasting with the more naturalistic register of Brünnhilde. The absurdity of the situation is heightened at the end, when Roméo actually throws his ring at Brünnhilde, whereas in the corresponding part of *Götterdammerung* it was Siegfried who attempted to wrest the ring from Brünnhilde's finger. A set of different narratives is also used in the twelfth section; here they are spoken (though the speech rhythms are notated as a musical score) and almost act as a commentary upon each other, rather than providing for a dialogue.

Each of the sung solo movements is marked 'fast, but constantly fluctuating, tempo: "alla turca"'. They are also unified by the same optional part for two pairs of clashed cymbals in each, which consists of four short gestures which are played at different points during the arias. Finnissy makes use of his characteristic techniques of transcription (dividing a line into short melodic fragments which are then re-arranged, halving intervals, etc.), and intersperses each aria with pauses, during which the singers perform their actions:

Example 6.31 *Soda Fountain*, p. 28 (Tatiana from *Eugene Onegin*)

The solo of Julius Caesar suggests a form of butch lesbianism through the assignment of this role to the contralto, who adopts a heroic attitude, brandishing her sword.

Actions are also used to interrupt the flow of the spoken solos. In the lines of Mrs Bennett from Jane Austen's *Pride and Prejudice* (whose thoughts on marriage belie the servile situation of women in the period), her words are interrupted at random points by a sigh or a gesture of sewing or embroidery, emphasising the permanence and fruitlessness of her situation. The passage from Emily Brontë's *Wuthering Heights* takes words of Heathcliff, telling how he dug up Cathy's grave but crucially omitting his declaration of belief in ghosts, which are interrupted by actions which could be attributed to Cathy, whimpering or scratching at the window to be let in.

The other sections for trio or quartet descend into hilarity and meaninglessness. The 'vocal backing' group perform an atonal, rhythmically irregular trio around the line 'Boo poo pi doo' which metamorphoses into percussive sounds such as hiccups and coughs. Their parts also fragment into single syllables, demonstrating the essential silliness of such vocal sounds by putting them in 'inverted commas':

Example 6.32 *Soda Fountain*, p. 25

Most comical of all is the thirteenth section, in which the performers play four sheep. Using the rhythm of the nursery rhyme 'Baa baa Black Sheep', Finnissy constructs two hockets, using pitched 'sheep-like bleating' in each part. The second of the hockets places the original rhythm simultaneously with its rhythmical augmentation, then diminution. In the third such section, derivatives from these two hockets are used to form a freer 'counterpoint'.

For all the humour, *Soda Fountain* nonetheless leaves a bitter taste in the mouth. The distance created between the audience and the spectacle does not disguise the awful reality of much that is said or represented. Many of the physical gestures, by virtue of their repetitiveness, are like nervous tics, symptoms of the characters' fears and senses of uneasiness. To use a phrase which Finnissy has used to describe his transcription materials, the characters are like 'fish out of water', their hyper-displacement (removed from time and place) serving to counterbalance the ironic stance taken by the composer.

Towards an Operatic Vision

Finnissy dislikes any of his stage works being described as 'operas', because of the plethora of associations conjured up by such a term. Yet his three most recent stage works come closest in conception and realisation to an operatic medium. After finishing the long series of *Verdi Transcriptions* for piano, Finnissy seems to have decided to adopt a less partisan view towards the Verdi/Wagner axis. His subsequent stage works are more organic conceptions and make much use of motivic elements and characteristics.

The first of these works, *The Undivine Comedy* (1985-88, subsequently under revision), which was commissioned by the Almeida Festival, is also the longest and most ambitious of Finnissy's stage works. In discussing this work, I am highly indebted to previous groundwork provided by Finnissy's own programme notes, the essay 'Zygmunt Krasinski and Polish romantic drama' by Maciej Orlos,[9] Lynne Williams' article and interview 'Reinstating The Spiritual Quest'[10] and Andrew Clements' 'Finnissy's Undivine Comedy'.[11]

After exploring several different texts and subject matters, Finnissy decided to set the *Nie-Boska Komedia* (1833) by the Polish playwright, poet and novelist Zygmunt Krasinski (1812-59). Krasinski was born in Paris, the son of Count Wincenty Krasinski, an aristocrat who served as a general under Napoleon. The Count was known and respected for his loyalty, but was actually a terrible opportunist - he switched sides to join Tsar Alexander I's army after Napoleon's defeat. While studying law at the University of Warsaw, Zygmunt was persuaded by his father to break a boycott of lectures organised as a patriotic demonstration (at the time Poland was not an independent state, being variously divided between Germany, Austria and Russia, a situation mirrored in Zygmunt's portrayal of the pull of conflicting forces on his characters). As the only student to continue attending lectures, Zygmunt became the subject of much ill-feeling, and he was forced to leave and continue his studies in Geneva.

In 1830, an insurrection broke out in Poland. Zygmunt at first wished to return to join the insurgents, but was again dissuaded by his father, who portrayed the uprising as mere rabble-rousing from a vociferous minority, not at all the popular movement that it was. Soon afterwards, still in Geneva, Zygmunt wrote *Nie-Boska Komedia*. Poor eyesight prevented his entering a diplomatic career, and he spent most of the rest of his life writing in Italy and France. In 1842 he was forced by his father into an aristocratic marriage which nevertheless survived.

Nie-Boska Komedia is a visionary and apocalyptic play, an incredible achievement for an author who was only 21. It concerns two major characters, a Count who is also a poet, and a Leader of a Revolution. The trichotomy of Art, as represented by the Count's poetry, Life, by marriage and family and Society, by revolutionary upheaval, act as conflicting forces upon the Count. Krasinski does not present easy solutions to this eternal conflict, rather he demonstrates how each ideal is fatally compromised by the flawed nature of human beings. The Count is ultimately unable to realise his artistic vision, and his poetic abilities are challenged by his wife, while the Leader, as is so often true of those who claim to speak for many, is in reality vain, egotistical and potentially despotic.

Finnissy's libretto is a modified adaptation of Krasinski's original play. Krasinski gave his characters names; Finnissy steadfastly avoids any naturalistic or realistic conventions which might make the work seem historically particular, and simply names the characters as the Count, the Countess, their Son, the Leader and the Muse, archetypal figures outside of time and place. The Muse is an interpolation from a vision of an evil Temptress in Krasinski's play, who drives the Count away from family life. In Finnissy's libretto she becomes a much more complex figure who interacts with all the other characters. She often acts as a voice of moral conscience, penetratingly analysing the situations of the peasants who join the Revolution, and in particular their indifference to the plight of women. She remarks on the volatile nature of humanity ('To the errors of former generations they added those that their ancestors never knew - indecision and timidity. And thus they disappeared from the face of the earth, and only a great silence remains after them.'), and incites men to action ('The crowds shout and call for an order. Why do you delay? Issue the order and it will race like a spark, become a flame and then a thunderbolt'). She urges the Count to desert his wife and pursue his poetry, but on the other hand denounces art's 'fake images', recognising the insufficency of art for providing salvation. Her character was also influenced by the work of Alfred Jarry, as Finnissy points out:

> In *L'Amour en Visites* Alfred Jarry writes of the poet's visit to the gardens of the Muse - they are filled with corpses in grandiose tombs. The poet offers the Muse gifts, but she tells him to go away. Taking her rejection as an indication of the inadequacy of his work, he labours to improve - killing himself in the process. As he dies he realizes that the Muse, object of his strongest desires, is blind - emblematic of the irrational way in which she bestows her favours.[12]

As well as freely transforming Krasinski's text to suit the project in question, Finnissy also introduces extracts from two other works which he believed to have areas of congruence with *Nie-Boska Komedia.* To give some actual example of the type of poetry that the Count might write, he paraphrases two speeches from Friedrich Hölderlin's unfinished Trauerspiel, *Der Tod des Empedokles* (second version - 1799), a play Finnissy had considered while he was looking for suitable operatic texts. In the first the Count invokes Nature (the translation is by Michael Hamburger, published in Friedrich Hölderlin *Poems and Fragments*, Anvil Press Poetry Ltd.; 1994):

> O innermost Nature. I have you before my eyes, do you still know your friend? Beloved above all things, do you no longer know me, the poet who offered you living song as a willing sacrifice of votive blood? Into my stillness you quietly stole - deep in the inpenetrable darkness you sought me, and now you are near to me again. By the sacred trees where waters from the veins of the Earth collect, and where the thirsty refresh themselves in the heat of the day - so likewise in me flows the source of life. In me, from the depths of the world it sprang up and merged - and the thirsty came to me. How is it now? Saddened? Am I alone? And is it night out there even by day?

Empedokles is also a poet by whose words crowds are transfixed; he speaks the words of the gods themselves, but after a while begins to believe himself possessed of god-like powers, which angers the 'real' gods. Some of Hölderlin's other lines could equally apply to the Count, or indeed to the very nature of the bourgeois artist, a form of self-conception that remains prevalent today:

> I know him, know his kind, the all too happy,
> Heaven's own spoilt and darling songs
> Aware of nothing else than their own souls.
> If once the moment shakes them out of themselves-
> And those too tender ones are easily shaken-
> Then nothing calms or comforts them, they're driven
> This way and that way by a burning wound,
> Their hearts incurably seething. And he too,
> Calm though he seems; disgusted with the people,
> Deep down he glows now with despotic lust.
> His rule or ours! And we shall do no wrong
> In sacrificing him. His ruin is sure
> In any case.

Finnissy's forms of interaction with musical materials and texts which he did not originate, or indeed random or constructivist devices, have always acted to distance himself from such a self-important view of the artist, solipsistically expecting everyone else to be interested in the closed realms of his 'inner world'.

For the character of the Leader, who Finnissy felt to be weak and undercharacterised in the original, he adapted a section from the fifth dialogue in *La Philosophie dans le boudoir* (1795) by the Marquis Donatien-Alphonse-François de Sade, a section of which - *Yet another effort, Frenchmen, if you would become Republicans* - gained wide circulation as a political pamphlet. These adapted words are equally incendiary:

> The world waits for deliverance from the stink of incense and the vanity of kings. We must do away with impossible morality. We must cultivate beliefs to match the republican character, beliefs to suit our customs and habits, beliefs that elevate the spirit and maintain the liberty that is our goal. We

> must worship only courage, liberty and equality. We must abandon the tyranny, the vulgar mysteries and the dogma of any religion that can confuse or blunt the edge of the republican spirit. We must resist the renewal of that chaos from which we have just emerged. Let us remember...

The ending of the narrative is also considerably changed:

> In the original play, The Leader is defeated by a vision of Christ, which didn't seem to make any sense after the encounter he had earlier, in which he repudiates the Count's ethics and his religion, and so I had him defeated by a much more hedonistic vision. The light that he sees in the sky is symbolic of the light which plays a part in the undermining of all characters - they all have 'insights'; moments of illumination; moments when they can see inside themselves. The Leader sees the sky about to fall in on him. It's a kind of apocalyptic vision - a premonition - and he just wants to be made blind - he doesn't want the reponsibility of seeing.[13]

Finnissy's adaptation has some parallels in the critical re-workings by contemporary Polish directors, as in Jerzy Grzegorzewski's own production of *Nie-Boska Komedia* or Tadeusz Kantor's experimental productions of Witkiewicz, though Finnissy is less averse to narrative than some such figures. The following is a scene-by-scene synopsis.

1. A poet has deserted his Muse to marry another woman. The Muse calls upon the Spirit of Poetry to tempt and delude him - denouncing mankind for its timidity and indecisiveness. The aristocratic poet - a Count - is concerned that his creativity might have deserted him, and when accused of betraying his ideas, he turns his back on his pregnant wife and promises to follow the Muse - his Fate and Fury.
2. Damning his wife for failing to understand his vision or ambitions, the Count leaves her to write the 'poetry of the future'.
3. Seventeen years have passed. Burnt out by their relationship, the Count and the Muse seem unable to go on.
4. The Count returns to his castle to find that his wife has disappeared.
5. The Muse tells the Count that his wife has been taken to an asylum.
6. The Countess reveals that she has now become a poet, the Count's equal, and offers to describe anything that he asks of her. She relates a vision of the end of the world, and collapses as he begs her to be calm - the way she used to be.
7. The Muse asks why the Count's child is unlike other children...perhaps all children were like him before Adam's fall.
8. The Count orders his blind son to pray for his mother's soul. The son's prayers anger the Count, but - when reproached for not loving his mother - the son explains that he can hear the Countess's voice, and it is her words that possess him.
9. The Revolutionary Leader announces the founding of a Republic, while the Muse tests the Count's social conscience. The Count is too preoccupied with his own thwarted ambitions to notice what is happening around him, until the

Muse tells him of the Revolution, whereupon he finds a new resolve and a way to exploit circumstances to his own ends.

10. The Son is lost in his visionary world when the Count tells him of the Revolution. He asks only for his father's protection but the Count's thoughts are elsewhere.
11. The Count has joined the Revolution but his fascination with it has begun to wane. The Muse questions mankind's, and her own, ability to act with honesty and compassion calling for action rather than words. The Revolutionary Leader challenges the Count, and warns his followers of the power invested in him.
12. The Dance of the Revolutionaries. The Muse sings of the new citizens of the Revolution. The Count, suddenly unable to accept the violence and Godlessness of what he hears, turns his back on the Revolution.
13. Neither the Count nor Leader will compromise their visions of the future.
14. The Muse describes the castle at dawn, under imminent attack from the Revolutionaries and hands the Count the venerated sword of Saint Floristan challenging him to defend himself and his values.
15. The Son waylays his father with a vision in which a man stands trial for crimes against humanity. When asked who the accused is, the son tells him 'You, Father, it is you!' Terrified by this outburst, the Count silences his son.
16. The Count prepares for final judgement, claiming that God has appeared to him in the midst of a cloud, like an eternally burning sun, 'ever shining but illuminating nothing'.
17. The Leader asks if the Count has fallen in battle. The Muse hands him the sword. The Leader seems suddenly disturbed by the brightness of the sky. He begs the Muse to blind him, but she cannot. [14]

The text is as much an amplification of contradictions in society and humanity, from which the audience is left to make their own conclusions, as a vision of the future. Elements of Krasinski's own personality and experience can be seen at various points in both the characters of the Count and the Son. As various commentators have pointed out, Karl Marx was only 15 at the time when the play was written, yet it foreshadows not only Marx's ideas, but also those of Lenin (in the character of the Leader) and suggests the possibilities of the forms of totalitarianism masquerading as progress that were to be experienced in the twentieth century. For this reason, the play was banned for a long period in the Soviet Union, where the ruling powers deemed it to be reactionary in nature. Whether this is so, or whether the play stands as a bleak pessimistic, even nihilistic statement, or as an allegory of Christian redemption, are questions beyond the scope of this discussion.

Before considering the music, I should point out that my comments generally apply to the revised version of the score, which has not yet been completed at the time of writing (though the sections still awaiting revision are unlikely to be substantially changed). The original version made use of a nine-part ensemble of flute/alto/piccolo, oboe/cor anglais, clarinet/bass/E flat clarinet, two percussionists, chamber organ/celeste and string trio. Finnissy felt that this ensemble sounded too much like a substitute orchestra, and in the revised version he instead uses two piccolos, two oboes, two percussion and string trio. The density of the ensemble writing in the original also added what was perhaps an unnecessary degree of incomprehensibility to what was already a complicated scenario, and could sometimes crowd out the voices, so this is considerably pared down in the final version.

The symbolic nature of the work is made apparent through the vocal characterisations. The part of the Count is mainly in a comfortable but narrow register between B flat below middle C to the D below. The registral boundaries act as constraints to generate a compressed energy, which bursts out when the Count becomes angry and oversteps the pitch limits. The Countess begins with a form of plainchant, as does the Count though at one derivative remove, exemplifying a greater 'worldliness'. When the Countess later goes insane in Scene 6, she adopts a form of wild jagged coloratura writing, derived from Bellini and Donizetti, extreme even by Finnissy's standards. Her voice is recorded twice on tape, which are played simultaneously. In the 14th scene, her off-stage voice, in a trio with piccolo and oboe, oscillates between this type of florid writing and something a little more like plainchant. The Count's part in turn moves gradually towards a form of expressionistic parlance, mirroring aristocratic decline. These various types of writing are demonstrated in Example 6.33.

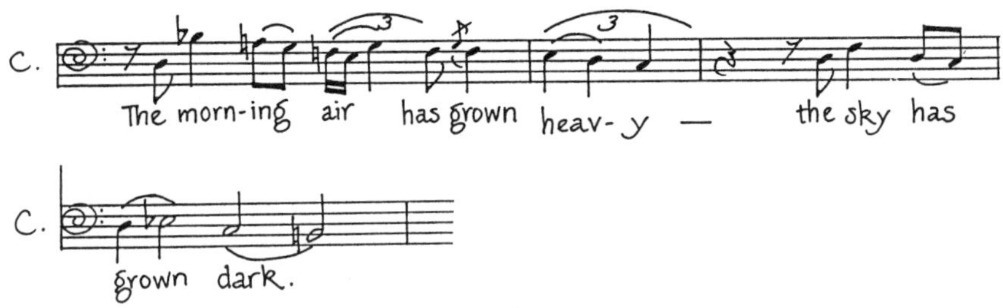

Example 6.33a *The Undivine Comedy,* Scene 1, p. 19

Example 6.33b *The Undivine Comedy*, Scene 16

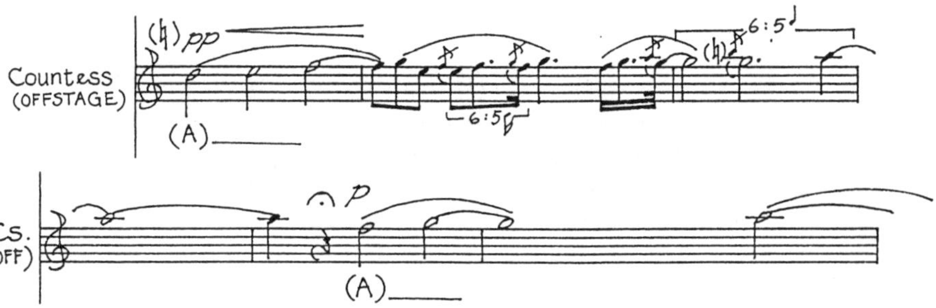

Example 6.33c *The Undivine Comedy*, Scene 1, p. 1

Example 6.33d *The Undivine Comedy*, Scene 6
Reproduced by permission of Oxford University Press

The Son also makes much use of plainchant, in particular the *Veni creator spiritus*, but he also takes over the coloratura from the Countess. Thus it is his mother towards whom he feels closest and is most influenced by, not his father, who deserts him.

The Leader's part shares some melodic characteristics with the Count, but is set almost entirely in a hysterical high voice, mostly falsetto. His impassioned neurosis leads to blood-curdling cries at the end of the work. Most often his part consists of falling contours, reflecting his belief that the wrongs of mankind stem from the 'fall' of Adam:

Example 6.34 *The Undivine Comedy*, from Scene 9
Reproduced by permission of Oxford University Press

The part of the Muse has a 'foreign', extra-European quality compared to the other voices. She plunders the seemingly infinite contoural possibilities within an extremely narrow tessitura, some derived from Near-Eastern incantations and Russian folk-recitation, which Finnissy used because of their 'speech-based' nature. Her part could be said to 'infect' the others, and cuts in to the harmonious world of the aristocrats from the beginning (Example 6.35).

The arch-structure of the music is monolithic in nature and parallels the vocal development of the Count. Each of the four Acts (1: Scenes 1-6; 2: Scenes 7-10; 3: Scenes 11-13; 4: Scenes 14-16) centres around a particular interval: a perfect 5th in the first act, through a 4th and 3rd to a 2nd in the last, which finally achieves a unison in the final bars. Such a scheme reflects dominant ideologies, historically given representation through music, from organum (when the church and the aristocracy were at the height of their powers) to extreme dissonance (expressionism, the crisis of capitalism and bourgeois society) with the glimpse of a form of sonic liberation (Scelsi?), for which a societal equivalent is more difficult to evince (or is this a subtle suggestion of the 'Christian redemption' interpretation I mentioned earlier? - this work ushered in a further series of pieces derived from plainchant). Richard Barrett has suggested that 'the gradual contraction of each act's formative interval from a fifth to a unison, cannot bear the structural weight assigned to it, especially given that the vocal writing sometimes tends to obscure an already complex textual argument'.[15] I believe on the contrary that the bare nature of this musical device is most appropriate so as *not* to obscure the text, though other potential obfuscation between music and text will probably be reduced in the final version.

Musical references, in texture, instrumental utilisation and vocal writing, abound, to Wagner's *Das Rheingold*, Monteverdi, Bellini, Donizetti, Busoni's *Doctor Faustus* in the organ fantasia of the first version, Strauss's *Ariadne auf Naxos*, Berg's *Wozzeck* and Szymanowski's *King Roger*, an opera whose concerns are not dissimilar. In Scene 9, which represents the maximum deviation of the libretto from the original text, Finnissy constructs a Verdian quartet for the Leader (who is making his first appearance), the off-stage voice of the Countess, the Muse and the Count, creating an intricate network of relationships between their different characters and ideas.

Divisions of class are given musical representation too: bells and plainsong for the aristocracy, and an invented folk music for the peasants, based on Rumanian bagpiping, using the E flat clarinet and *rute*, a bass drum played with birch twigs. The music is also used to express emotions and sensations which the text alone could hardly encompass, such as the terrifying interior madness of the Son in Scene 8. The violence of his solitude is demonstrated by merciless blows on the drums.

Example 6.35 *The Undivine Comedy*, from Scene 1, p. 3
Reproduced by permission of Oxford University Press

To see more precisely how Finnissy relates music to text, characters and narrative, I will now look at Scene 12 (the revised version; the original was taken from a Rumanian-based piece written for television, *Dust in the Road*). In this scene, the Count meets several of the revolutionary peasants, presumably one of the first occasions in which he has come into contact with members of the 'lower classes'. It has been suggested by Orlos that the similarity of this scene to that in *The Divine Comedy* in which 'Dante, led through the Inferno by Virgil, encounters the souls of the sinful and damned' was the reason for Krasinski's title. Certainly such a comparison provides ammunition for those who would criticise the play's reactionary nature.

The most prominent musical material in this scene is a Rumanian-based dance, initially *Andante sostenuto*, but getting more animated, which consists of melodies variously in the oboe, piccolo or violin, accompanied by drones and ostinati in the percussion:

Example 6.36 *The Undivine Comedy*, Scene 12
Reproduced by permission of Oxford University Press

A series of characters, about each of which the Muse comments, are 'conjured up' in front of the Count. First is a servant girl, 'She washed dishes and polished forks, and never heard a good word for her efforts. But now it is her turn to eat and dance.' The melody, at first in C, alternates between the oboe and piccolo, and is mainly in 3/4, while the percussion ostinato, on rute and tom-toms, consists of a repeated rhythmic cell lasting five quarter-notes. This changes to a new four crotchet cell, and a lackey enters, who 'has already killed his former master'. The violin joins the piccolo and oboe, playing simultaneously a third apart from each, though the parts begin to go out of phase. A second lackey is greeted with a further diminution of the rhythmic cell to three crotchets' length. During this time, the viola drone also decreases in distance between attacks, from eighteen to seventeen crotchets, and is joined by dissonant drones in whichever of the other instruments is not playing a melody.

After the entry of an escaped prisoner, and implosion of the rhythmic cell, there is a sudden cut into new material, *Molto meno mosso*. The Muse sings 'free men again', referring in an obvious sense to the prisoners, but Finnissy would seem also to be interpreting this as a premonition of the post-revolutionary future, in which *all* men will be 'free'. The hushed melodies and shimmering tremolos in the strings do indeed have a visionary quality (Example 6.37).

Example 6.37 *The Undivine Comedy*, Scene 12, p. 5
Reproduced by permission of Oxford University Press

A modified version of the folk dance returns, with a less clearly defined sense of metre, as a butcher enters, 'It's all the same - butchering cattle or slaughtering aristocrats'.

With the first musical entry in this scene of the Count, Finnissy introduces a new type of material, a march, or stomp, *Poco piu mosso*, in the violin and viola, which has a greater impatience (arrogance?) than what has gone before:

Example 6.38 *The Undivine Comedy*, Scene 12, p. 8
Reproduced by permission of Oxford University Press

Much more irregular, alienated music in the glockenspiel and vibraphone accompanies the entry of a Woman, whom the Count addresses as 'Milady', upon which he is reprimanded by the Muse. ('She is a free woman. She gives her love freely to all men, to all who acknowledge her rights.') The Count replies curtly ('And did they give her those rings and that amethyst chain in return?') with the stomp once again, and the Muse, undermining the 'language' of the Count from within, sings along with the stomp ('Do not mock her, citizen. She tore those trifling things from the man who became her husband, and was also her gaoler, her enemy, and the enemy of freedom'), causing the beats to disappear. The 'alienated' music returns as the Muse tells the Count that this woman has actually killed her husband in the name of the Revolution.

The piccolo leads back to the folk music, now without the drone, but with pizzicato rhythmic cells in the cello and 'military' triplets in the tenor drum, each of which again diminish in length, as a general enters. The Count questions the Muse's faith in this man's ability to successfully engineer the downfall of the castle, whereupon she retorts that the Count is 'his brother in Liberty, but not his equal in strategy'. Very threatened by these remarks, the Count replies 'My advice would be to kill that man quickly. A new aristocracy will begin with his sort.' Finnissy chooses to remain musically a little aloof from these searching questions, mainly continuing the folk dance.

The Muse is offered a way out from the Count's remark by the arrival of a silk weaver. She avows her hatred for the merchants who exploit such a worker to an ominous pulse on the cello, with single beats and shakes on the tenor drum and tambourine:

Example 6.39 *The Undivine Comedy*, Scene 12, p. 18
Reproduced by permission of Oxford University Press

The Count, wishing to tame the Muse's fiery anger, tells her to 'Drain your glass - It will make you feel better', with the melody once again, as if he would prefer her previous state of mind to that which she exhibits now. The Muse, in identification with the silk weaver, replies that 'She lacks the strength even to lift it to her lips. The age of Freedom will not dawn for her'; her sadness is subsequently represented by a short weeping oboe solo, with impassioned strings. As this fades, she returns to lines of hope for the glorious future she envisages, accompanied by a *molto animato* 3/4 beat with oboe melody, though the harsh dissonances suggest the underlying brutality that will be an inevitable part of the upheaval ('Tomorrow the rich will lie dead in the fields like sheaves of corn').

The last character arrives, a builder whose future temples will have only 'one symbol - The Cap of Liberty'; a sudden shift of emphasis is provided by a chorale in the strings, *Largo sostenuto*, punctuated by anvil and bass drum, as the Count realises the Godlessness of the revolutionaries (Example 6.40).

He vows to 'give their God back to them', and the music thins out as a transition to the next scene.

So Finnissy uses a variable degree of correspondence between the music and the characters in this scene, sometimes giving voice to unspoken or unconscious emotions, at others maintaining a distance to allow a more objective form of perception. This form of objectification allows Finnissy to present his own subjective view of the characters, one that is uniquely his; another composer, even if skilled in similar compositional techniques, would almost certainly present a very different picture.

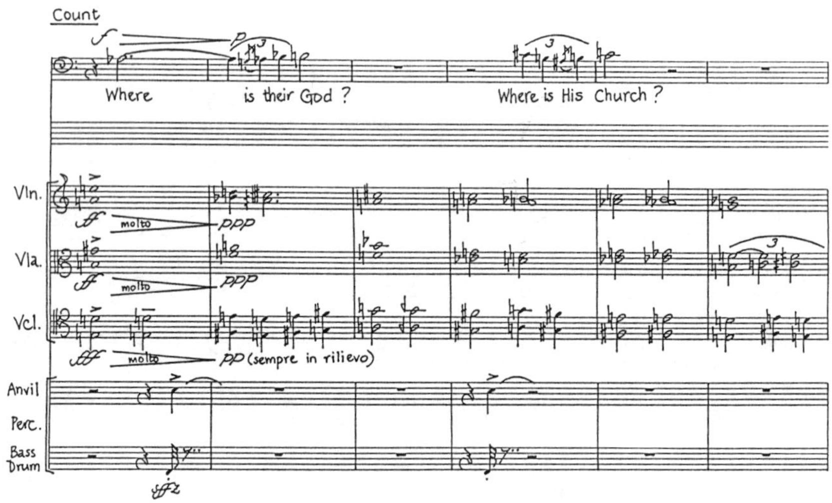

Example 6.40 *The Undivine Comedy*, Scene 12, p. 30
Reproduced by permission of Oxford University Press

The choices with which the Count is faced in *The Undivine Comedy*, between Art and Life, have autobiographical connotations for Finnissy. For most of the 1970s, he spent almost every free hour composing, having little time for a life 'outside'. After reaching a point of despair in 1980, unable to find the recognition he deserved, and unwilling to compromise in the name of easy success, he spent some time working in Australia, from which time onwards his music made more extensive use of materials that were themselves 'outside' of his own intentions. Yet the dilemma that a composer, or indeed any artist, faces in a society where individual integrity and sincerity are usually antithetical to success, remains pertinent. Finnissy has stated:

> I understand 'the artist' to be a person who is trying to get underneath the surface of events, and understand and tell others what life is about. That is his responsibility - 'to see, to hear and to care' - as The Muse puts it. That is why it is such a big responsibility that The Count is turning his back on and why the drama is so apocalyptic. [16]

This quasi-shamanistic view of the artist can become problematic when one is forced to compare the importance of their work with more immediate social concerns, as The Count discovers. It is for these reasons that *The Undivine Comedy* is a thoroughly relevant work for our times. The initial production[17] made use of a set constructed of steel bars, to suggest a medieval dungeon, as well as some historically-derived costumes, which can well damp down the contemporary resonance. One can only hope that future productions resist the temptation to make the work into a 'period piece'.

For his next work, Finnissy chose a much more familiar, but no less universal, text, Zola's *Thérèse Raquin.* He adapted Zola's own play based on the novel to produce an extremely concise libretto, omitting the characters of Grivet, Michaud and Suzanne, to leave only Thérèse, Laurent, Camille and Madame Raquin. The 'opera' he constructed as a result is one of the most intense and claustrophobic works he has ever produced, using a synthesis of Wagnerian, 19th Century Italianate, *verismo* and expressionist genres in a manner which rarely involves slavish imitation of any of them, while retaining a thoroughly modernist perspective.

While much more sparce in terms of density of notes than *The Undivine Comedy*, the formal processes of *Thérèse* could hardly be more complex and intricate; the work operates with superimposed layers of activity, in terms of narrative, characterisation, operatic genre, texture, rhythm, interval, melodic contour and musical reference, between which a multiplicity of dialectical relationships also operates. This is on a compositional level; some of the layers are difficult to perceive consciously, but do affect the total experience. Beyond, as Finnissy uses an extremely large number of 'found' materials, further levels of correspondence and dissimilarity ensue. This is of course the case with any music; even seemingly original musical materials have natural and cultural properties that precede a composer's use of them. By using those materials which can be located elsewhere, and whose properties can thus be more readily apprehended, a composer may stand more chance of controlling them. Such an approach is common to many of Finnissy's recent works, such as *Folklore* for piano or *Glad Day* for ensemble.

To try and understand how these factors are manifest, I will try to summarise and describe the work on several different levels. The synopsis is as follows:

> **Setting**: Paris in the mid-nineteenth century. A dingy, narrow back-street near the Pont Neuf. The parlour room above Madame Raquin's millinery shop. Stuffy, cramped and shabby: a large dining-table, several chairs, bric-à-brac.
>
> A: SUMMER
> **Scene 1:** Thérèse meets Laurent. She tells of her childhood and the unhappiness of her situation, married to the sick Camille. When she questions how much longer she can carry on, Laurent suggests murdering Camille; Thérèse is at first indignant; after a sudden burst of passion she no longer argues.
> **Scene 2:** Each of the four characters is in and out of the room. Camille asks Laurent, who is painting his portrait, about his family and his painting. They both go out to get some champagne. Thérèse complains to Madame Raquin that the 'greedy and lazy' Laurent is practically living in the household. Thérèse, alone, looks at the portrait and moves listlessly about the room. Dark ensues. Camille returns and Thérèse continues to complain about Laurent. Camille is a little frightened and suggests that Thérèse is acting like a ghost; he will wake up and think 'some woman with a white face is creeping round the bed to murder me'. Camille

suggests that Laurent come out with Thérèse and him on Sunday. Madame Raquin, concerned for Camille's health, is alarmed when swimming is suggested, but a little reassured that Laurent will look after him. Laurent and Thérèse suddenly embrace passionately.
Scene 3: Thérèse is alone on stage. Both off-stage, Laurent persuades Camille to go for a swim. Laurent drowns him.

B: AUTUMN THE FOLLOWING YEAR
Scene 4: Madame Raquin mourns her lost son, and speaks of her memories of him. Laurent feigns sympathy. Thérèse is mainly silent, but Laurent speaks with a double-irony of blaming himself; he 'dived in after Camille, but he had disappeared'.

C: THE FOLLOWING WINTER.
Scene 5: Midnight. Laurent, now married to Thérèse, tries to excite her in their new found 'freedom', but she is racked with guilt, saying of Camille 'He's here. In that corner, or that one. Laughing.' then pointing out the portrait. She claims Laurent acted alone, but he claims she is equally guilty. Madame Raquin enters and overhears them. When Thérèse turns to her, 'You forgive me!', she collapses, never to speak again.
Scene 6:With Madame Raquin asleep in the corner, Thérése tells of her fears of betrayal by Laurent, and of her futile wish to escape her predicament.
Scene 7: Madame Raquin watches Thérèse and Laurent's every move. The remorseful Thérèse believes she still loves Camille, to which Laurent replies that he has taken his place, 'I have his wife - I have his bed...These two hands are not mine - they are *his*. *I* am Camille!' Thérèse, remembering her feelings towards Laurent expressed in Scene 2, responds with hatred, defying him to kill her. Provoked, Laurent attacks her, and she stabs him. Thérèse begs forgiveness from Camille, and kisses the portrait, before cutting her own wrists.

Finnissy's rather melodramatic ending is a change to that in Zola's original (a suicide pact). He describes this alternative as more suitable to an operatic/theatrical setting. It also corresponds with his ambivalence towards Zola's conviction that the characters are nothing more than animals, driven by brute forces, unable to make conscious choices. Thérèse's feelings of guilt, though smothered by the volatility of her emotional reactions, nonetheless reflect her sense that choices are and were possible. She deliberately provokes Laurent into attacking her, so that she can then kill him in self-defence, suggesting a more calculating mind than is evident otherwise. I would not agree with those that say this makes her a better person (nor indeed with disproportionate sympathy for her character - her situation is deeply unpleasant, but she is still in some sense an accomplice to the murder); I mention these aspects merely to demonstrate that Finnissy's work is informed by a rather more complex view of the pre-determination/free choice paradigm than was prevalent in the 19th century.

Despite the chronological sequence of events, narrative is not the primary purpose of the work. The story is familiar to many, and for those for whom it is not, the first scene should make subsequent events quite predictable. Rather, the narrative is just one of many threads which hold the work together. Finnissy explores much more complex considerations concerning the characters, their inner motivations, the extent to which they are products of the societies and eras they inhabit, the interdependence of their actions and the sense in which our responses to them are conditioned by musical archetypes and genres, challenging us to rethink many 'natural' responses which are in fact highly indebted to cultural conventions.

The four singers (Thérèse - soprano/mezzo, Camille - counter-tenor, Madame Raquin - mezzo/contralto and Laurent - baritone) are joined by a piano placed on the stage itself; a fifth protagonist who both observes and comments on the others and their situations. It is perhaps not too fanciful to suggest that the pianist, whose presence on-stage acts as a theatrically defamiliarising device, relates to Finnissy himself, representing his experience as a repetiteur and his thoughts and identifications with the many operas and operatic characters he encountered during such work.

For the vocal characterisation, Finnissy attempts to locate the characters in that time and place from which they derive their essential identity. Thérèse's lines derive from Parisian opera of the 1860s, specifically Meyerbeer's *L'Africaine*, demonstrating an affinity between her and Meyerbeer's African girl Inès:

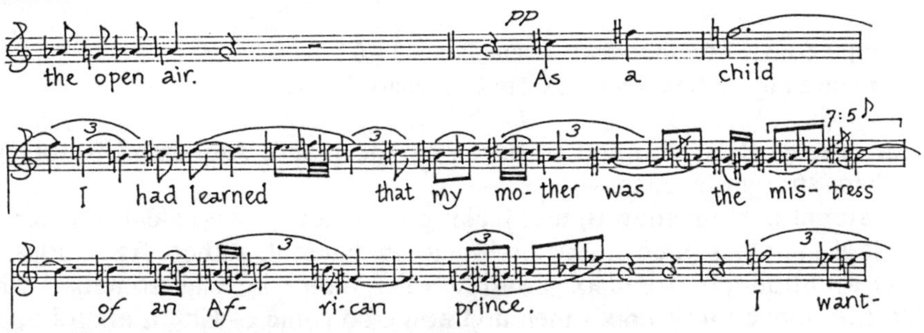

Example 6.41 *Thérèse Raquin*, Scene 1, p. 11
Reproduced by permission of Oxford University Press

The first section of the work to be composed was Thérèse's long aria, or credo, in Scene 6, from which much of her subsequent material is derived. Camille, as a country boy who yearns to return to his birthplace, uses folk-songs from Haut-Normandie or related derived material. Example 6.42 shows a clear arrangement of 'Quand j'étais petit'.

Example 6.42 *Thérèse Raquin*, Scene 2, p. 28
Reproduced by permission of Oxford University Press

His lines generally exhibit a greater smoothness and fluidity than the others, at first suggesting innocence and naïvete. The use of a counter-tenor for his role suggests that he is still a boy, which is certainly the way he is treated both by Thérèse and his mother.

For Madame Raquin, Finnissy uses selections from French opera of around 1800, the time of her birth, by such composers as André Grétry, with more extensive late-baroque ornamentation (when her material is played on the piano) than for the other characters:

Example 6.43 *Thérèse Raquin*, Scene 2, pp. 25-6
Reproduced by permission of Oxford University Press

Her part is often doubled in thirds by the piano, suggesting stability or perhaps straight-lacedness.

Laurent is a Faustian figure, lacking in sincerity, who steals elements of each of the other three characters' melodic material, and configurations. He was a childhood friend of Camille's (or rather he was someone whom Camille looked up to both then and now), so some of Camille's folk-songs infiltrate Laurent's pitches, though their parts are configured in different ways. It is possible that the relationships between their materials could produce an unconscious connection in the mind of a listener (or remind them of this connection which they have gleaned from the text).

Thérèse, Laurent and Camille's parts are divided into short pitch and rhythmic cells, which are usually randomly permutated and modified to produce lines. Multiple levels of derivative are common, as the characters develop according to their experiences, though such procedures can also occur in a non-chronological manner to effect premonitions. Material is sometimes exchanged between characters to reflect the extent of their determination through interactions with others. Vocal devices such as fragmentation of line and angular contours are used at key points in the work to provide emotional immediacy, their effect heightened by their sparing use.

The piano part, when playing together with the singers, is very often monodic and relates to the vocal parts. As well as creating clear 'critical' relationships (sometimes corresponding, at others not), this provides for the extreme sparseness of the work, the tension within the closed room. At some other points, however, it enters into areas of musical referentiality, or provides cross-referencing between different parts of the work to suggest memories, premonitions or other unspoken thoughts. In the interludes, the piano is usually given a more rich and contrapuntal part, allowing for a summary of emotional and intellectual associations with what has gone before and is about to follow.

An outline of the operatic and theatrical structures is shown below. Characters never sing simultaneously, so 'duo' or 'trio' would be inappropriate terms. 'Dialogue' refers to sung exchanges between characters.

Scene 1	Introduction
	Aria - Thérèse
	Dialogue - Thérèse, Laurent (murder)
	Interlude
Scene 2	Introduction
	Dialogue - Madame Raquin, Camille, Laurent, Thérèse
	Dialogue - Camille, Laurent ('portrait' section)
	Dialogue - Thérèse, Madame Raquin (about Laurent)
	Interlude
	Dialogue - Camille (uneasy), Thérèse (Laurent)
	Dialogue - Camille, Madame Raquin, Thérèse, Laurent (plan to go out)
	Interlude
Scene 3	Dialogue - Camille, Laurent (murder)
Scene 4	Introduction
	Dialogue - Laurent, Madame Raquin
	Aria - Madame Raquin ('I haven't counted the days')
	Dialogue - Laurent, Madame Raquin
	Interlude
Scene 5	Dialogue - Laurent, Thérèse - Madame Raquin at end.
	Transition
Scene 6	Introduction
	Aria - Thérèse ('She'll not talk. She'll say nothing. The dream of escape')
	Transition
Scene 7	Dialogue - Thérèse, Laurent (Argument - murder)
	Fragmented attempt at an aria - Thérèse

The boundaries between the delineated sections are sometimes blurred, at others clear. While this outline might imply that the work is a 'number opera', in form it is just as close to a Wagnerian model, as I will show next.

The range of musical reference is immense. Finnissy makes use of a vast number of operatic fragments, many from France in the related periods, though not all (one cannot erase the memory of what has happened in the intervening period, nor ignore historical determinations). Certain types of French operatic archetypes also figure prominently, such as tremoli, diminished sevenths and a particular 'turn':

Example 6.44 *Thérèse Raquin*
Reproduced by permission of Oxford University Press

This referentiality makes its effect through resonance rather than recognition - there is perhaps little for a listener to achieve (other than smug self-satisfaction) through spotting recognised materials. It is not necessary to know the sources in order to appreciate the work; I detail them in order to demonstrate how the work is able to achieve its ends.

In the following analysis, the delineation of sections and nomenclature of materials is my own, although some of my ideas are influenced by conversations with the composer. The material types (the most important of which I will call **Excitement** (buzzing trills or tremolos), **Drowning** (ascending lines, usually in the bass), **Copulation** (wild, ravishing writing in the piano) and **Bach/Passion** (derived from a Chorale Prelude - 'Passion' refers to the emotion brought about by the notion of escape, not the St. Matthew or John Passions!) are usually not static motives; they are given differing representations according to the degree of their presence either in the characters' minds or that of the composer. It is therefore practically impossible to find and illustrate them in some sort of 'essential' form; the extent of development, modification and cross-referencing demonstrated in the sketches makes such a search an impossible task!

Scene 1

A: Piano Introduction: General feeling of claustrophobia; plodding chords, from which melody arises - Thérèse material (from Meyerbeer), shown in Example 6.45.

As Thérèse goes out and returns with Laurent, occasional chords appear within bare melodic line, providing a modicum of warmth.

Example 6.45 *Thérèse Raquin*, Scene 1, p. 1
Reproduced by permission of Oxford University Press

B: Thérèse aria:
B1: *'I've waited so long for you... and set me free.'* Still, rapt writing for Thérèse (pitches from basic material). Piano continues quicker melody, sometimes counterpoint of two lines, occasionally introducing harmonisation of individual notes. The buzzing of the trills or tremolos, **Excitement 1** (with an eye towards Ravel's *Shéhérazade*) are used at the moments when Thérèse enters deeper into her inner sensual world:

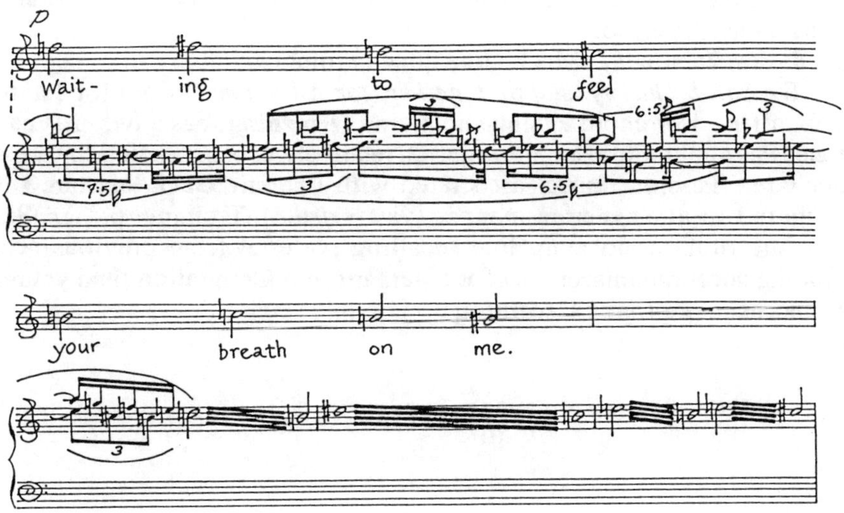

Example 6.46 *Thérèse Raquin*, Scene 1, p. 4
Reproduced by permission of Oxford University Press

'Twice I meant to run away... while I dreamed of hitting and biting.' Piano material to be later used for 'T & C childhood'. Wider intervals for Thérèse with last words leading to:
Copulation 1: *piano*, thoughts of rough, animal-like sex.
B2:*' I can't think now why I ever agreed to marry Camille...I refused to share with him'*. Continuation of main B1 material. More potential 'T & C childhood' material.
Commentary 1: Piano presents elaborate four-voice amalgam of Thérèse material, with many minor 3rds and diminished 7ths.
B3: *'Their house by the river, kept inside when I longed for the open air'*. Trills then tremolos, **Excitement 2**, lead into *Sostenuto, visionario. 'As a child...'*. Most direct reference to *L'Africaine*. Later, Thérèse's 'Staring at the flames...' invokes premonition of particular motive from the Bach Chorale Prelude BWV 646 to be used in Scene 6, **Bach/Passion 1**, also used for 'passion' music associated with Laurent in forthcoming interlude. Such words as 'crushed, dazed' produce fragmentation of Thérèse's melodic line. Section concludes with further tremolos, **Excitement 3**.

C: Thérèse and Laurent:
C1: *'Couldn't we get Camille out of the way...We could enjoy each other all the time.'* Exchange between the two characters, each of whose lines derive from random permutations of cells. Piano line intensifies harmonically, but also gradually slows down.
C2: *'Kill him?'* Very sparse, with slow bare lines in piano, from Thérèse material, as she sings hesistantly, but a little excited. As Laurent suggests ways of disposing of Camille, *Animato*, and appeals to Thérèse's passion, rapid arpeggio and trills, **Excitement 4** (with descending bass anticipating, in inversion, the **Drowning** motif used in the following scene), *'Do what you like with me!'*, leads to:
Copulation 2: Now *fff*. Much more directly implied.
C3: *'We can be happy...happy together, for a lifetime.'* Solo for Laurent. Piano, after a low chord again anticipating **Drowning**, has a two-part canon on the 'Passion' motif, **Bach/Passion 2**, relatively upbeat, leading towards:
Interlude: 'Passion music' associated with Laurent, **Bach/Passion 3**, but configured in a Wagnerian manner (viz. *Tristan*) (Example 6.47). Some short interruptions to main line recalling material from previous scene, including short reminiscences of **Excitement** and **Copulation** (and yet more low chords to pre-figure **Drowning**).

Example 6.47 *Thérèse Raquin*, Scene 1, p. 24
Reproduced by permission of Oxford University Press

Scene 2
Introduction: Camille's music in the piano (monodic). Entry of Madame Raquin (with medicine) introduces ornamentation in her style.

A: All four characters:
A1: Thérèse tries medicine before it is given to Camille. First proper introduction of 'Drowning music', **Drowning 1**, derived from Berg's *Wozzeck* (ascending scales and arpeggios), in piano (Example 6.48):

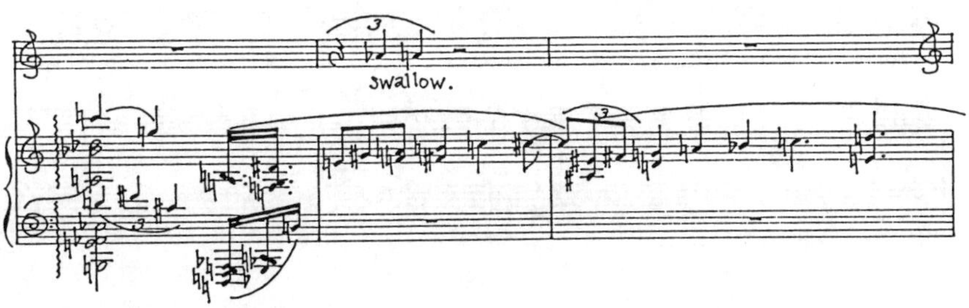

Example 6.48 *Thérèse Raquin*, Scene 2, p. 26
Reproduced by permission of Oxford University Press

A2: *'You have such good health, Laurent'*. Waltz-like 3/4 for Camille. As he asks Thérèse *'we are spoilt, aren't we?'*, sudden shift to sustained chords - her desolation. Thérèse, *'Yes'*, followed by melancholy lines of her music in piano.
A3: *Allegretto.'Do you remember the money my mother gave us when we were children?'* Most immediate 'motif' for Camille - relatively direct reference to Haut-Normandie folk song 'Quand j'étais petit', lyrical, boy-like. Laurent's part is more speech-like, matter of fact, rhythmically;

involves modified permutation of his pitch cells. Piano generally plays Camille-like line, suggesting particular sympathies.
A4: *'It's better than my place'*, preceded by *'On rainy days you'd think this was the cellar'*. As Laurent is reminded of sexual encounters with Thérèse, **Copulation 4** in piano, leading to **Drowning 2**, this time as staccato chords in piano.
A5: *'Poor Camille you are never satisfied'*. Madame Raquin's line recalls 'T & C childhood' material from Scene 1. Her line *'I would have started business in the country again'* to be used in Scene 4. As Camille remembers fondly the trees and the river, buzzing trills and **Drowning 3** in piano indicate his future death.

B: *'The shop bell rings'*. Thérèse couldn't care less about the shop, so Madame Raquin has to go down. Piano plays **Copulation 5**, interrupted by silence and single slur; then bare Thérèse melody again.

C: **Portrait Scene**.
C1: Camille asks Laurent about his father and his work. Both use mainly permutations of their pitch cells. Camille's part is now more 'talkative', adopting Laurent's language in order to endear himself to him. Piano in RH is derived from Fauré's *Le Secret* Op. 23 No.3, with a regular crotchet pulse, and in LH from Berlioz's *Symphonie Fantastique (Episode dans la vie d'un artiste)*, presenting Finnissy's view of Laurent's self-image (Example 6.49).

Example 6.49 *Thérèse Raquin*, Scene 2, p. 39
Reproduced by permission of Oxford University Press

As Laurent's talk ranges back to his own childhood (*'He wanted me to be a lawyer - acting for him in those endless disputes with his neighbours'*), piano shifts momentarily to folk-song material, with short **Drowning 4** in the bass. Note portamento in Laurent's part (*'So I strangled my muse'*).
C2: Piano part much slower. Portrait is finished, Madame Raquin tells Laurent to go with Camille to get champagne.

D: Madame Raquin and Thérèse
D1: Piano only for first three bars. Thérèse attempts to make Madame Raquin believe that she dislikes Laurent (*'Laurent eats and drinks like a wolf...'*) but portamento (as in Laurent's part in C1) belies her real feelings.
D2: Madame Raquin expresses her sympathies for Laurent, with more Berlioz material, though configured in her own way (Example 6.50)

Example 6.50 *Thérèse Raquin*, Scene 2, p. 42
Reproduced by permission of Oxford University Press

Interlude: Thérèse studies Camille's portrait, then moves listlessly around the room. The light fades. A myriadic array of Thérèse's material is configured in two sections, the mid-point provided by two sustained chords, anticipated in previous texture. Second section is clearer (in contradistinction to the increasing uncertainty of both the light and Thérèse's mood). Included are a trill and a tremolo, **Excitement 5**.

The long association in the first scene of the **Excitement** motif with Thérèse should mean that when it appears subsequently, a listener will make the unconscious connection of the piano with Thérèse's thoughts at that time. However, in the second section of Scene 2, she is the only character with whose voice the motif never appears. The association might then be loosened and re-attached in a listener's mind.

For this second section, the piano part consists of a fragmented cut-up of Scene 1, the idea being that the thoughts and words of Scene 1 are determinants for this section, which in turn is a determinant for future scenes.

E: Camille and Thérèse. Camille, frightened by the strange way Thérèse is acting, sings long legato lines, in contrast with Thérèse's hypertrophised and fragmented repetition of Madame Raquin's 'Laurent is like one of the family now'. Piano disappears with Thérèse's 'I'm not joking', returning only at

Camille's 'I shall think that some woman with a white face is creeping round the bed to murder me', with **Drowning 5**, this time descending in chords with increasing numbers of notes.

F: All four characters. Each **Excitement** is a brief interruption of the main line.
F1: Madame Raquin and Laurent enter. Camille tells Laurent that Thérèse frightened him, and about the champagne. Piano generally higher than voices, includes **Excitement 6** (4 crotchets) and **Bach/Passion 4**, and is more continuous. Camille suggests going to the country with Laurent. Piano descends, then tremolo, **Excitement 7** (4 crotchets). Laurent *'jumps ditches full of water and throws stones up to the sky'*, with **Excitement 8** (5 1/3 crotchets).

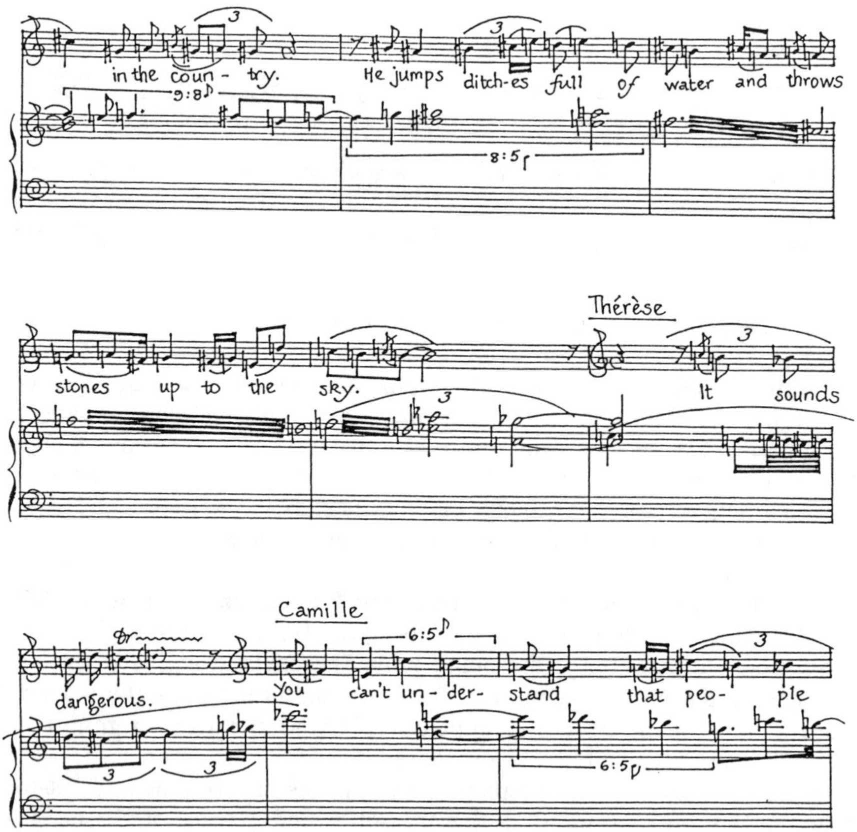

Example 6.51 *Thérèse Raquin*, Scene 2, p. 54
Reproduced by permission of Oxford University Press

Camille is less interested in Thérèse, *'She sits on the ground and stares at things'*, with which comes **Excitement 8** (4 crotchets).

F2: *Molto Animato*. Madame Raquin asks Laurent to take care of Camille. Includes **Excitement 9** (9 crotchets).
F3: *Presto Agitato*. Camille doesn't 'like being treated like a little boy'.
F4: *Molto meno mosso. Calmo*. Camille makes plans, Laurent suggests *'A swim in the river'*; **Excitement 10** (4 crotchets, pause), with **Drowning 6**.
F5: *Più mosso. Agitato*. Madame Raquin is worried. **Excitement 11** (3 crotchets) and Thérèse mentions how frightened Camille is of water, then **Excitement 12** (4 crotchets) and **Drowning 7**. Laurent recalls their swimming at school, with trills in his part and tremolos in the piano, **Excitement 13** (11 crotchets), as well as **Drowning 8**.
F6: *Animato*. Camille is determined to go swimming. **Excitement 14** (4 crotchets, 3 crotchets, 5 crotchets, descending pitches). Madame Raquin tries to stop him.
F7: *Meno mosso*. Camille suggests tea, then tells again of childhood: *'Laurent imitated the horses trotting, and the cracking of the whips'*. As he and Madame Raquin depart, Thérèse repeats Camille's last phrase, leading to:
Interlude: Copulation 6. *Appassionato*. Most prominent, as actual copulation occurs (Example 6.52). Makes use of Laurent's pitches and another multiply-derived set, but intensity of writing probably makes this imperceptible.

Example 6.52 *Thérèse Raquin*, Scene 2, p. 63
Reproduced by permission of Oxford University Press

Piano part thins out (though interrupted towards end with one bar **Copulation 7**), reducing to single slow line of Camille's material.

Scene 3
Thérèse on stage, Camille and Laurent sing from off.

With Camille's first entry, piano stops. As previously, Camille's line is sustained and lyrical, while Laurent's is more urgent and speech-like (Example 6.53a). Thérèse's one line (by which she could be said to become an accomplice) is frightened but with glimmers of the future (Example 6.53b)

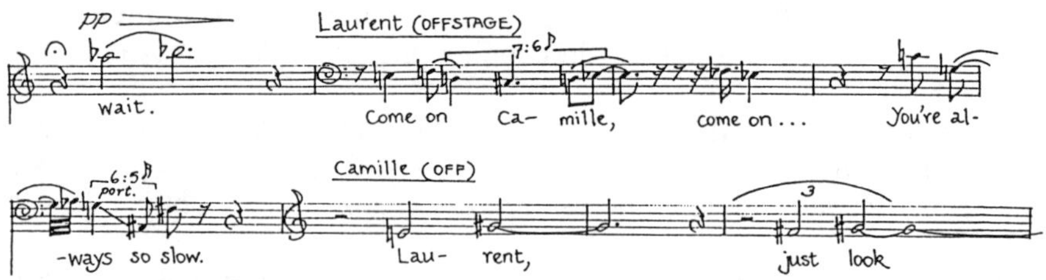

Example 6.53a *Thérèse Raquin*, Scene 3, p. 66

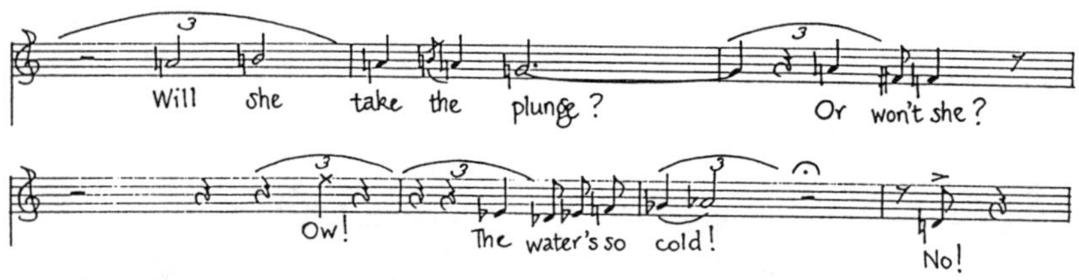

Example 6.53b *Thérèse Raquin*, Scene 3, p. 67
Reproduced by permission of Oxford University Press

The piano returns briefly with Camille's folk music as he emits an unpitched '*Ow*' on feeling the water, then stops again. His line becomes quicker and fragments as it is clear that Laurent is starting to perform his terrible deed. With his death cries, the piano starts again, with a longer line (Example 6.54).

This is the focal point of the narrative, yet it does not coincide with those of theatrical action and musical intensity (the end of Scene 2). The piano line at this point is, however, the longest exposition of Camille's material - the essence of his existence is only graspable at the moment of death. The increased urgency of Camille's part as Laurent is starting to drown him relates to his appropriation of Laurent's manner in the Portrait scene.

For the fourth scene, which centres around Madame Raquin, Finnissy makes use of operatic fragments from the 1760s, earlier than had previously been used for her material. He explains this as wishing to suggest the fact that she has aged beyond her natural years, as a result of the tragedy. The fragments come in pairs and between each successive pair one of the composers (though not the particular opera) remains the same.

Example 6.54 *Thérèse Raquin*, Scene 3, p. 68
Reproduced by permission of Oxford University Press

Scene 4
Laurent, Madame Raquin and Thérèse (who does not sing at all during the scene).
Introduction: **1760s Opera 1**. The two hands of the piano derive from Monsigny (*Le Déserteur*) and Philidor (*Air du Cocher*) for four bars (Example 6.55), then from Grétry (*Lucille*) and Monsigny (*Rose et Colas*). The part thins to one line, then to melodic fragments.

Example 6.55 *Thérèse Raquin*, Scene 4, p. 69
Reproduced by permission of Oxford University Press

A. Laurent and Madame Raquin:
A1: Laurent, unaccompanied, tries to interest the others in cards
1760s Opera 2: From Grétry - *Ariette d'Anacréon* - and Spontini - *Hymne au Soleil (Milton).*
A2: Madame Raquin, a broken woman, in correspondingly broken phrases, still unaccompanied. Her pauses bring short piano phrases derived from the operatic material. Laurent tries to console her, with smoother lines, though **Excitment 15** belies his true feeling.
1760s Opera 3: Spontini - *Oedipe à Colone*, Paër - *Le Maîre de Chapelle.*
A3: Laurent with Madame Raquin again, with more continuous piano line. Includes **Excitement 16**.

B: Madame Raquin's aria. In nine phrases:
B1: *'I haven't counted the days.'*
B2: *'I cry because the tears just come.'*
B3: *'All the time I can see my poor child.'*
B4: *'I see him when he was little.'*
B5: *'It was such an awful death.'*
B6: *'I begged him to give up the notion of going in the water.'*
B7: *'He wanted to show he wasn't afraid.'*
B8: *'If only you knew how I cared for him when he was a baby.'*
B9: *'For three whole weeks, when he had typhoid, I held him in my arms without ever going to bed.'*
Madame Raquin's line, which sometimes refers back to material from Scene 2, begins low (Example 6.56), and is less continuous than the piano, which plays a single line from her material, usually starting a few beats after the beginning of her phrases.

Example 6.56 *Thérèse Raquin*, Scene 4, p. 75
Reproduced by permission of Oxford University Press

In **B4**, the piano starts earlier, and her voice rises, as she recalls her fond memories, but in **B5**, in a similar register, she is 'stranded in mid-air', and the piano line does not start until after her last word. A similar process occurs with the longer **B9**. Overall, Madame Raquin's tessitura rises towards the middle of the aria, then falls again, though this arch is small. **B1**, **B2**, **B3**, **B4** and **B8** end with an allargando; those that don't seem to refer to more directly 'factual' events. **B7** contains a trill, **Excitement 17**.

C. Laurent and Madame Raquin:
C1: *Animato*. Laurent, *'These memories are so painful'*, leads to **Drowning 9** and **Excitement 18**.
Molto Animato. As Laurent pretends to have tried to save Camille, piano refuses to accompany.
1760s Opera 4: *a tempo*. Méhul (who was heavily influenced by Grétry) - *Ariodant*, Nicolo-Isouard - *Joconde*.
C2: *Allegro risoluto*. Madame Raquin decides *'to be sensible. I shan't cry anymore.'*
Thérèse walks out to **Bach/Passion 5** when she tells Laurent *'You're my child and I love you'* - her fake feelings towards Laurent in Scene 2 are now made real. Piano line mainly continuous and monodic, with occasional forays into two- and three-part writing, and more sustained chords. After Madame Raquin's last line, *'She doesn't cry easily'*, the piano plays two lines *agitato subito*, separated by one *calmo*, producing a sensation of unease.
Interlude: 1760s Opera 5. Boïeldieu - *Jean de Paris*, Grétry - *Lucille*. Piano writing progresses towards more florid, arpeggiated style. Low pedal notes anticipate next scene.

Scene 5
The tempo scheme in this scene forms an arch - progressively increasing tempi, with accelerandi at the end of each, then decreasing, with similar rallentando. Laurent and Thérèse each use random permutations of their pitch cells, though modified (or given octave displacement) to produce increasing vocal intensity and hysteria.
A. The piano for the first section alternates bell-like low B flat, A, A flat, A (two bass notes for each subsection).
A1: Crotchet = 63. Laurent tells Thérèse *'The room belongs to us now... We managed to kill Camille and remain free'*, with portamento towards high note for last word (within generally moderate tessitura) suggesting possibility of liberation.
A2: Crotchet = 72. As Thérèse says that Camille's *'corpse is here, between us'*, the durations of her pitches become generally shorter (greater urgency).
A3: Crotchet = 80. Thérèse's voice becomes 'possessed', and uses single grace notes, as opposed to the more casual tones of Laurent:

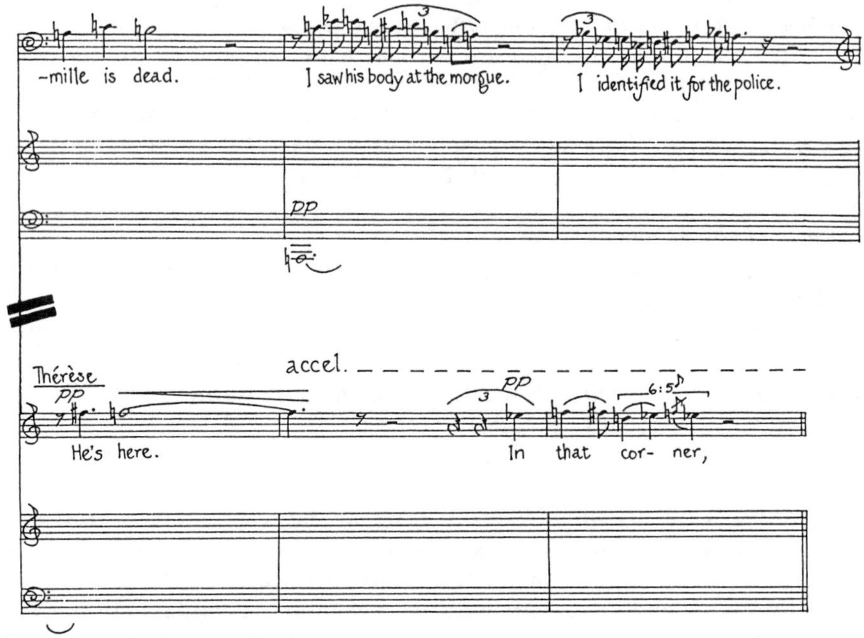

Example 6.57 *Thérèse Raquin*, p. 85
Reproduced by permission of Oxford University Press

A4: Crotchet = 88. Thérèse in shorter phrases, frightened. Laurent more accentuated (impatient), with more 'cavalier' portamenti. As he describes Camille's body at the morgue in explicit detail, he sings more quickly; sadistic excitement has been aroused.
A5: Crotchet = 100. Continuation of **A4**. Laurent calms down a little, but Thérèse will not stop believing that Camille is amongst them.
A6: Crotchet = 112. She gets his portrait (first double grace notes). To Laurent's sarcastic staccato at the end of *'And we'd do it again, wouldn't we?'*, Thérèse now becomes angry and strident in tone, denying any involvement in Camille's murder.
A7: Crotchet = 132. Thérèse continues to protest. Her reference to Laurent as 'you' uses a perfect fifth, whereas the rest of her line in this section is in close tessitura. The second piano knell is a chord instead of a single note, as Madame Raquin appears in the shadow, unseen by the others. This is described by the composer as the beginning of her stroke. Laurent becomes hysterically angry, with detached triplets, *'We killed Camille'*.

B: Laurent and Thérèse suddenly notice Madame Raquin. Their parts do not necessarily mirror the falling tempos.
B1: Crotchet = 152. Madame Raquin's part has a narrow tessitura, in musical response to which Thérèse calms down, though Laurent remains

equally hysterical, *'She didn't love him, said he stank like a sick child'* (detached triplets again). Two more dense chords in piano.
B2: Crotchet = 112. Thérèse alternates angular line with keening high tessitura (Example 6.58). Laurent is more animated (shorter durations).

Example 6.58 *Thérèse Raquin*, Scene 5, p. 91
Reproduced by permission of Oxford University Press

The second of the piano chords begins a series of decreasing note-densities, from four notes down to one.
B3: Crotchet = 88. Thérèse, still with relatively wide or high tessitura, sings to Madame Raquin, begging her mother to take her side. Madame Raquin's collapse is not amplified by any parallel musical interspersion. Thérèse's singing of *'You forgive me!'* as Madame Raquin collapses is one of the most disturbing moments in the whole work.
B4: Crotchet = 63 (no rall). Thérèse, anxious, now sings low, and mainly in triplets. Laurent's impatient reponse pulls these out of shape. Terrified, Thérèse sings *'She must be put in her bed'* in single detached notes.
Transition: Quite direct reference to Bach Chorale Prelude BWV 646, 'Wo soll ich fliehen hin' (How shall I escape?), including **Bach/Passion 6**. Single line, with pedal notes.

Scene 6
This scene consists of a long aria for Thérèse, whose part consists of fragments from Meyerbeer. Piano part from **A** alternates with voice, and is exclusively based on fragments from a Bach chorale prelude, from a phrase of which germinates **Bach/Passion** music. It has three types of phrases: (a) Long notes, (b) Monodic lines, (c) Two part counterpoint, one part moving more quickly than the other.
Introduction: Two part counterpoint, from Bach, a little blurred, coming twice to rest on sustained pitches. Single line continues.
A: All Thérèse's 14 phrases begin on a G.
A1: She speaks of the dream of escaping Camille and starting a new life. Middle register, narrow tessitura (Example 6.59). Piano type (a).

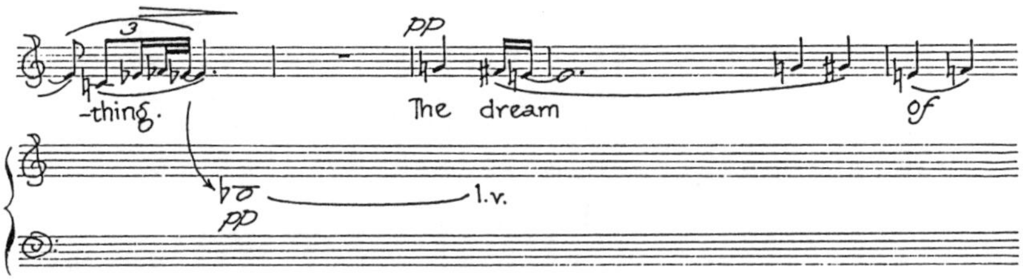

Example 6.59 *Thérèse Raquin*, Scene 6, p. 96
Reproduced by permission of Oxford University Press

A2: Piano type (b) in E flat minor, only at beginning and end. Thérèse sings of how she cannot escape Laurent in an emotional sense, *'We'll end up tearing each other to pieces'*. She begins nervously, *molto animato*, then is resigned, *molto calmo*, while her melodies rise, though a descending portamento is the converse of her passion in Scene 2. Madame Raquin will hear them talk, but *'Say nothing about it'* - she returns to E flat minor for second piano phrase.
A3: She now envisages the physical consequences of a literal escape, *'Filth and squalor'*. Increased resignedness.

B: Now phrases (15 of them), begin on A sharp/B flat.
B1: Narrative continuation of **A3**. In very first phrase, trill signifies **Excitement 19**. Piano has one note, after *'Don't tell anyone anything'*. With *'Silent' 'Cold' 'Threatening'* and *'Doing nothing'*, Thérèse's line almost comes to a halt.
B2: Piano has regular, longer, lines, first type (c), then (b). Thérèse is worried about betrayal by Laurent, *'Not ever happy until the pain drives me mad'*.

C: Phrases begin on C sharp. Increased emotional intensity.
C1: Thérèse's first climax, *'It's a lie'* (preceded by *'That I made him kill Camille?'*). This line *ff*, those before and after *p*. Piano ends with type (b).
C2: Second climax, *'Oh Laurent, your blood seemed to radiate warmth as I passed you'* (interestingly no **Excitement**), dynamics fall from *f* to *ppp*. Appearance in piano of **Bach/Passion 7** (Example 6.60).

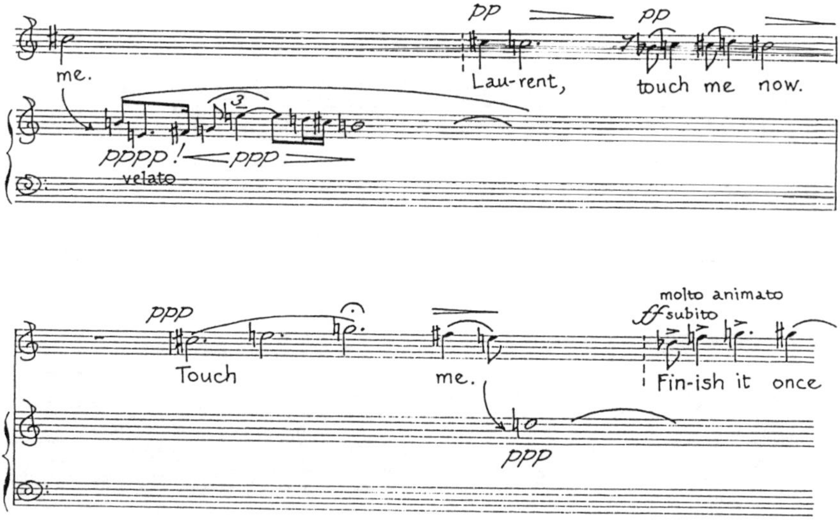

Example 6.60 *Thérèse Raquin*, Scene 6, p. 104
Reproduced by permission of Oxford University Press

C3: Third 'climax', *molto animato 'Finish it once and for all'* - Thérèse wonders if escape really is a possibility, though perhaps the 'escape' she imagines is death. A possibility of hope is expressed through her final line, *'All these people are blind', molto animato*, but the piano continues the Bach material, *calmo*, leading to
Transition: Elaboration of Bach material into denser texture. Hints of **Copulation** and **Excitement**.

Scene 7
During this scene, Laurent and Thérèse are joined on stage by Madame Raquin, 'propped up at the table - stiff, passive, only her eyes watching every movement' and the portrait of Camille (as in the previous scenes). The original version had a derivation of Madame Raquin's music in the piano part; the final version uses the Fauré-derived part of the 'portrait' material from Scene 2. Its characteristic regular beats are here greatly slowed down (at first from one crotchet to seven) and transposed (Example 6.61).

A: Thérèse, remembering the best of Camille, sings a form of lament, while Laurent continues his angular, but rhythmically speech-like material from Scene 5. Word-painting accompanies Thérèse's reminiscence of Camille's 'delicate nature'. With *'now I remember, and I love him'*, her triplets recall Scene 5. A rising portamento accompanies Thérèse's *'I love him and hate you'*, and for *'You are covered with Camille's blood'*, **Excitement 20** (horrible sadism). Thérèse wishes to *'kiss the ground where he lies at rest. That will be my final joy'*, and her line becomes more sedate, anticipating the final section.

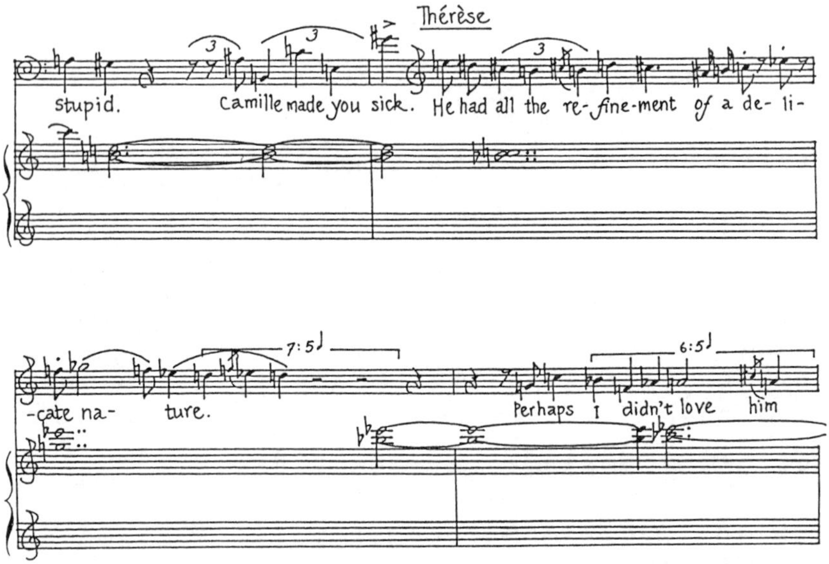

Example 6.61 *Thérèse Raquin*, Scene 7, p. 108
Reproduced by permission of Oxford University Press

B: Laurent becomes more deranged and Thérèse provokes him into attacking her.
B1: After Laurent's tentative *'I have his wife'*, he has a rising portamento for *'I have his bed'*. Falling portamenti then enter his line, for *'My hands don't belong to me anymore'* and *'inside my head. Hammering at it with his fists.'* His encroaching madness is demonstrated by the filtering of his line into short bursts of activity. When he sings *'I am Camille'*, his material is (extremely obliquely) derived from Camille's 'Quand j'étais petit' from Scene 2 (reminding us that he comes from the same place as Camille).
B2: Thérèse berates Laurent for sponging from her and Madame Raquin, leading him to move to strike her. She has falling portamenti for *'Go on - finish it - kill me as you killed him'*, and for her following *'Go on - kill me!!!'* she is almost screaming. She takes the bread-knife, provokes him further with a rising contour, then stabs him as he attacks her. The piano part avoids melodrama; it changes in two respects, larger intervals, and two *sfzp* chords, just before and during the stabbing (Example 6.62).

C: Thérèse's final 'aria' moves towards sedateness and serenity, as in section **A**. The piano part has smaller intervals again, then single pitches. She falls on her knees in front of Madame Raquin, begging her forgiveness. Taking the portrait, *'reverencing it as though it was a religious relic'* and kissing it 'slowly and without passion', her last line *'I kiss...the ground...where you lie...at rest'*, shows that she has attained some sort of peace, before she slits her wrists. The bleakest of endings uses several rising major seconds in the piano, fragmenting.

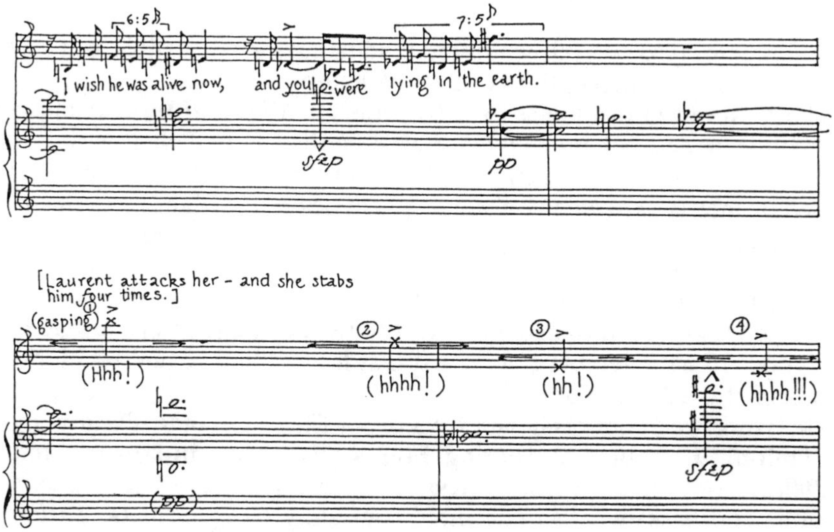

Example 6.62 *Thérèse Raquin*, Scene 7, p. 114
Reproduced by permission of Oxford University Press

I would not for a moment pretend that this analysis represents anything more than a highly particular and subjective view of the work. The choice of 'subtexts' in either text or music (or relation between the two) is my own - doubtless another analyst would give priority to a different set of features. I hope if nothing else to have given some idea of the multi-layered nature of the work, the means of its construction, the particular 'take' on the music-text dialectic (so much more sophisticated than mere word-painting) and the 'paths' taken by several relatively distinctive material types.

For many of the critics at the time of *Thérèse*'s première, the work amounted to little more than a musically redundant salon style accompaniment to a text. Expecting some sort of high-octane grand opera, they were unable to see beyond the deliberate narrow confines of text, set and musical means and to appreciate how Finnissy's work manages to place a certain distance at the outset between the audience and the spectacle, while still conveying with the utmost immediacy the closeted nature of the situation in which the characters find themselves. Certainly anyone will come to this work with pre-conceptions and prejudices, and a 'naïve' listener probably does not exist. However, if one desires exaggerated emotions and subservience of music to textual purposes, or believes objectification and/or 'close-focus' to be inappropriate to an operatic setting, one would do better to listen to *Tosca*.

Thérèse Raquin is of course open to many possible criticisms - the absolute centrality of Thérèse within the later scenes is a little dogmatic and overpowering, whilst Laurent's demonism can seem somewhat one-dimensional. At a few places (particularly in Scene 2), the proximity of some of the types of material can occasionally lead to a degree of greyness, which requires a number of listenings to overcome. However, I believe it to be an immensely powerful, wholly individual and inexhaustible work, which yields up ever new perceptions of a familar story.

The most recent of Finnissy's stage works is *Shameful Vice,* an altogether more didactic and polemical work, based on the life of Tchaikovsky. Since childhood Finnissy had an immense love for Tchaikovsky's music (and had argued its merits vehemently against the advocates of 'high' modernism) and felt empathy towards the marginalisation of another homosexual composer. After scrupulous research into his biographies, letters and music, Finnissy came to believe in the 'kangaroo court' theory of Tchaikovsky's death, in which he was ordered to take his own life by a committee of the 'great' and the 'good' in St Petersburg, appalled that he had had sexual relations with members of the lower classes.[18]

The work was commissioned by Vocem Electric Voice Theatre and the Endymion Ensemble, presenting Finnissy with an interesting musical challenge: to write the work he desired using six voices (3 sopranos, tenor, baritone and bass) with an ensemble consisting of 2 clarinets, 2 trumpets, guitar, harp, 2 violins and double bass. He uses the bass for the role of Tchaikovsky, while the other five singers are unspecified characters, given only a number in the score, who assume different roles within the drama. Their anonymity reflects Tchaikovsky's sense of persecution - all people around are turning against him. He is presented as a sensitive character, maintaining a certain dignity despite the terrible circumstances that befall him, and his vocal line often refers to fragments from the operas.

Bearing in mind Tchaikovsky's intense religiosity, Finnissy structures the work in 14 scenes, relating to the 14 Stations of the Cross:

1. Jesus is condemned to death.	1. Tchaikovsky is condemned by his judges.
2. Jesus receives his cross.	2. He stands accused by the crowd.
3. Jesus falls the first time.	3. In Italy he falls in love with Vittorio.
4. Jesus meets his mother.	4. He recalls his mother.
5. Simon the Cyrene helps Jesus carry the cross.	5. Tchaikovsky and Saint-Saëns dance an impromptu ballet.
6. Jesus and Veronica.	6. Nadezhda von Meck.
7. Jesus falls a second time.	7. Tchaikovsky falls in love withVasya.
8. Jesus comforts the women of Jerusalem.	8. He meets the women of St Petersburg.
9. Jesus falls a third time.	9. He falls in love with his nephew.
10. Jesus is stripped.	10. He is drawn into confession.
11. Jesus is nailed to the cross	11. He is reviled.
12. Jesus dies.	12. He drinks poison.
13. The body is taken and laid in Mary's bosom.	13. He calls upon his mother to lay him to rest.
14. The body is laid in the tomb.	14. Apotheosis.

Tchaikovsky's predicament is made clear in the very first scene, so that most of the subsequent scenes consist of flashbacks to events in his life. The two pivotal scenes are numbers 5 and 12, both purely instrumental. Each consists of an intensely beautiful and melancholy solo for harp, derived from Tchaikovsky's *Fifty Russian Folk-Songs* for piano duet (Example 6.63).

Example 6.63 *Shameful Vice*, Scene 5, p. 32
Reproduced by permission of Oxford University Press

The 12th scene interrupts this type of solo with violent double-bass tremolos, and sets against it staccato quavers and triplets in the violins, derived from *Swan Lake*.

As might be expected, other musical and textual references abound: in Scene 3 to a song *Pimpinella Op. 38 No. 6*, which Tchaikovsky heard from a street urchin with whom he had a sexual encounter, to the *Souvenir de Florence*, in Scene 11 to the piano piece *Mother Op. 39 No. 4* when his mother is recalled; in Scene 6 to the letter scene in *Eugene Onegin*, using texts from letters between Tchaikovsky and Nadezhda von Meck; in Scene 11 to the *Manfred Symphony* , with a re-working of Byron's text; in Scene 13 to Tchaikovsky's verses written in the notebooks of Fanny Dürbach, his governess; to Wagner's *Tannhäuser*, Schumann's *Genoveva* and Meyerbeer's *Robert le Diable* (Example 6.64), which Tchaikovsky saw at the times of his respective encounters with Vittorio, Vasya and his nephew, and the first two of which were major musical influences upon him; in Scene 10 to Delibes' *Coppelia*, in relation to which Tchaikovsky described his own work as 'vastly inferior', and whose scene of girls turned into mechanical dolls by an enamelling process relates to the brothel in which the scene takes place; in Scene 13 to Stravinsky's *Berceuse du chat*. Characteristic features of Tchaikovsky's instrumental and vocal writing also inform the work, such as his continual revoicing of chords (c.f. the last movement of the *Pathetique Symphony*).

Example 6.64a Meyerbeer - Cavatinetta: 'Oh! come è bella' from *Robert le Diable* Act IV (part of grand seduction scene)

Example 6.64b *Shameful Vice*, Scene 9, p. 50
Reproduced by permission of Oxford University Press

Much of the time, several references appear simultaneously, presenting a blurred musical picture, or even a form of pan-Tchaikovsky.

The character of Nadezhda von Meck is not at all that of a generous benefactress; rather she is a harsh, intolerant figure, whose words (all taken from actual documents) show an appalling condescension towards Tchaikovsky ('Perhaps his "illness" is incurable - he doesn't want it to go away', 'You know I think he's scared of *clever* women.'). In the original draft for the libretto, she was to appear in later scenes as a dominatrix, brandishing whips and chains. She is in the final version only referred to explicitly in the 6th scene, while other lines previously attributed to her are given variously to the women of St Petersburg and other characters, so that in Tchaikovsky's eyes her personality is subsumed into all women he encounters. Both Scenes 6 and 8 make use of Tchaikovsky's musical 'signature' (E-E-C-B-A), consisting of all the letters within his name for which an equivalent note can be found, that he wrote in his letters to Madame von Meck (see Example 6.65), as an instrumental backdrop.

Example 6.65 Tchaikovsky's musical signature, used in *Shameful Vice*

The incessant nature of the prejudice that Tchaikovsky encountered is made most explicit in Scene 2, in which the five other characters whisper lines of bigotry ('I know about disgusting perverts like him. They wear women's clothes...It would be no great loss if all such "polluted men" perished utterly'), to the accompaniment of breathy unpitched rhythms in the clarinets and trumpets. Tchaikovsky maintains his dignity in the face of such insidiousness, but with an underlying tone of bitterness, replying 'My good will to those who have taken my life, equally to all those who tried to save it. All are my brothers and sisters now.'

The final scene of *Shameful Vice* is a parody of *The Sleeping Beauty*, in which 'The Lilac Fairy enters with the Prince. In balletic mime she indicates the sleeping Tchaikovsky. The Prince approaches Tchaikovsky...bends over him and gently kisses him - first on the forehead, then on the mouth, then on the right hand...which he then holds as Tchaikovsky rises. The evil spell is broken.' Tchaikovsky transcends the role of tragic hero which he is usually assigned; he returns from the dead both because his music lives on, and to haunt contemporary society in which intolerance is still rampant. Finnissy's music is appropriately brash and 'in your face' (Example 6.66).

For all Finnissy's love for Tchaikovsky, it is immediately clear when listening to the work that he is uninterested in hearkening back to the sort of musical 'emotionality' and consequent view of the autonomous individual that was prominent in Tchaikovsky's class and era. Tchaikovsky's fate came about because he overstepped the dominant ideological assumptions which he inherited; his particular type of music is a reflection of this form of interaction. It is highly unlikely that a composer living in the 1990s could authentically produce a similar response to their own particular circumstances (in an era where the 'self' is known to be a rather more complicated entity); those who attempt to compose mock-Tchaikovsky will either fail (in which case the nature of the disjunctions can be the most revealing aspects) or end up producing glib pastiche, void of all that makes Tchaikovsky's own music special. In *Shameful Vice*, Tchaikovsky's life and work are contextualised, viewed with the benefit of modernist hindsight, and shown to be utterly relevant to modern times in a thoroughly non-nostalgic manner.

Example 6.66 *Shameful Vice*, Scene 14, p. 82
Reproduced by permission of Oxford University Press

Conclusion

It is extremely difficult to generalise about Finnissy's stage works, as they present as diverse a selection as any cross-section of his output. What is revealed is a continually transforming view of the stage and its conventions, the relationships between stage, text and music and music-theatrical predecessors. There are a number of areas which Finnissy has not yet explored, such as a more 'experimental' approach to texts, in which cut-ups and textual montage might be used according to chance or formalist concerns, rather than for the production of meaning. These sort of procedures certainly have precedents in much of Finnissy's musical technique. However, the innate conservatism of many potential theatrical commissioners in Britain militates against such possibilities being realised; one can but live in hope.

What stands to date is an important and neglected body of work that ventures into areas that are certainly unprecedented in British music-theatre (one might mention Birtwistle, but his very much more structurally-based work, where form has a capital letter, is a wholly different concern). Because of the relatively small scale of Finnissy's works (in instrumental and theatrical terms) they have rarely been given the serious consideration they deserve. Works such as *Circle, Chorus and Formal Act*, *Mr Punch*, *Soda Fountain* and *Shameful Vice* are accessible and immediate, but nonetheless explore areas of depth. Others such as *Vaudeville*, *The Undivine Comedy* and *Thérèse Raquin* are altogether more demanding, but do not require specialist powers of cognition to be apprehended. All these and the other works require more frequent (or even first) performances, demonstrating as they do a composer who is willing to take a serious approach to all aspects of the theatrical medium, concerned with the totality of the experience.

Notes

1. Quoted in Lynne Williams, 'Reinstating "The Spiritual Quest"', *Contemporary Music Review* (1995), Vol. 13, Part 1, p. 56.
2. Ibid., p. 56.
3. Ibid.,p. 56.
4. *The English Mummers and their Plays: Traces of Ancient Mystery*, edited Alan Brody (Routledge, 1969).
5. See Siegfried Kracauer' s *From Caligari to Hitler*, (Princeton University Press, 1947), especially pp. 217-18.
6. Reproduced in *Twentieth Century Theatre - A Sourcebook,* edited Richard Drain (Routledge, 1995), pp. 171-4.
7. Ibid., pp. 165-8.
8. All my comments refer to the revised version of the work. The printed copy available at the time of writing is actually the earlier, now withdrawn version. The changes are thus: Replacement of the original third section (Frankenstein) with a new Romeo and Juliet passage, and in the sixth section, cut from 79 to 85, inserting in its place 96-99, then cut 88 to 103, 106 to 110, 112 to 116, 117 to 120. There is also a small cut in the fifth section (between 63 and 65).
9. Reproduced in the programme booklet for the Almeida Festival production. This fascinating booklet also includes provocative quotes from Pier Paolo Pasolini, The Quran, Andre Tarkovsky and William Blake.
10. See note 1.
11. 'Finnissy's Undivine Comedy' in *The Musical Times*, Vol. 129 (1988), pp. 330-32.
12. From the Almeida programme booklet.
13. Quoted in Williams, op. cit., p. 52.
14. By Pierre Audi and Michael Finnissy. First printed in the Almeida programme booklet.

15. Quoted in Richard Barrett, 'Michael Finnissy - An Overview', *Contemporary Music Review* (1995) Vol. 13, Part 1, p. 56.
16. Quoted in Williams, op. cit., p. 53.
17. Discussed further in Williams, op. cit., p. 61-3.
18. This theory is expounded in David Brown's *Tchaikovsky: A Biographical and Critical Study* (4 volumes), (Gollancz, 1978-91).

ABSCONSCION, FOR MICHAEL FINNISSY
by Ken Edwards

Stay
As though astonished
Through the rubric of
"The transformation of love"

In the room
In the rain
How you have been
Many time this way O boy

I don't know if I can
Indure
On the door it says

Use other door
You go through it (the
Turn) and

reels

by Harry Gilonis

affectionately dedicated to
Michael Finnissy on his 50th

unfolding, shimmering sound
seeing with a vigilant eye
listening to restless figuration
the poised necessity of forms
in high light and deep shadow, held
attending with alertness and patience

in the whiteness of snow attending
footprints we saw unfolding
traces held in drift
seeing the value of clarity
history is poised necessity
listening to agile pattern

over unknown ground, listening
attending to the plight of form
poised, dynamic and complex
rapid and headlong unfolding
seeing a tide-textured river
held on the cusp and unwinding

in oblique stasis held
listening to notes in accord
seeing, a labyrinthine dance
attending to the clarity of value
unfolding conjunction of opposites
poised in disrupted flow

an uproar of sound is poised
rapid, tremulous, held
a dialogue with the world unfolding
listening to afar alongside
attending to distant memory
seeing infinite traces

seeing in a field of tension
poised for the bird-like leap
a heron's eye attending
wings, hands, curved and held
listening quite fastidiously
to the music's bright unfolding

Song 9

for Ian Pace

and their hands, the way
they hold their hands,
pianists I mean, in
the pauses, poised, held,
in a way thought
could only default,
still, as a leaf
curled as it dried,
or a crab's shell
upright on shingle

BMIC, London, 6 June 1995

Catalogue of Works

Henrietta Brougham

This catalogue extends and expands 'A Catalogue of the Works of Michael Finnissy' by Tom Morgan published in *Aspects of Complexity in Recent British Music, Contemporary Music Review,* Volume 31, Part 1 (1995). The additions, modifications and re-numberings were made in close consultation with the composer.

Work Numbers

The works are numbered in chronological order or when most of the composition took place. Works such as *English Country-Tunes,* a cycle of shorter pieces which may be performed separately or as a set, are subdivided with a decimal point (eg. 44.01, 44.02).

Withdrawn and Revised Works

Finnissy has on a number of occasions chosen to withdraw or revise works. Withdrawn works which have subsequently been revised and those awaiting revision are included in the main catalogue. Some revisions, such as those to the *Piano Concerto No. 1*, have resulted in works quite different from the original. In all cases, even when there are several versions (as with *Independence Quadrilles,* for example) only the final version is acknowledged by the composer. Some of the withdrawn works have been incorporated (in part or whole) in other pieces. Essential details of these and others are given in the appendix of withdrawn works.

Cycles

Many individual works form part of cycles sharing common material or other characteristics. A list of these cycles and their component works is given as an appendix. The works in each cycle are listed in the order preferred by the composer when the cycle is performed complete, although other orderings are permissible.

Juvenilia

Since Finnissy has allowed some of the earlier works to be published, these and other Juvenilia are included in the main catalogue under the prefix 'J'.

Indexes

Two complete indexes are provided: one arranged alphabetically by title and the other organised by instrumental/vocal categories and chronology. The number refers to the work's entry in the main catalogue.

Abbreviations

Composition dates: a hyphen between two dates indicates the years during which a piece was written. A slash (/) indicates a revision following which is the year(s) in which it was revised. Hence 1982-85/96 means the piece was composed between 1982 and 1985 and revised in 1996. Where a work is withdrawn and currently awaiting revision, the initial composition dates are given and the abbreviation /AR follows. Works awaiting revision cannot be performed.

Instrumentation: 1,1,1,1/1,1,1,1 indicates the numbers of woodwind and brass instruments in the following order: flute, oboe, clarinet, bassoon/horn, trumpet, trombone, tuba. Where a player doubles the second instrument is shown in brackets. Stringed instruments are indicated in the order: first violin, second violin, viola, cello, double bass (1,1,1,1,1).

Full names and abbreviations are used in the catalogue:

afl	alto flute
AR	awaiting revision
arec	alto recorder
asax	alto saxophone
bar	baritone
bcl	bass clarinet
bfl	bass flute
BMIC	British Music Information Centre
bn	bassoon
ca	cor anglais
cbn	contrabassoon
ccl	contra-bass clarinet
cel	celesta
cl	clarinet in A or B flat
ctn	counter-tenor
ctrb	contra-bass trombone
ctu	contra-bass tuba
db	double bass

dir.	director or conductor
ecl	E flat clarinet
fl	flute
fp	first performance
gui	guitar
hn	horn
hp	harp
hpd	harpsichord
mar	marimba or marimbaphone
mez	mezzo-soprano
ob	oboe
oda	oboe d'amore
org	organ
OUP	Oxford University Press
perc	percussion
pf	piano
pic	piccolo flute
ptpt	piccolo trumpet
QEH	Queen Elizabeth Hall
rec	recorder
sax	saxophone
sop	soprano
srec	soprano recorder
timp	timpani
tpt	trumpet
trb	trombone
tu	tuba
UMP	United Music Publishers
va	viola
vc	cello
vib	vibrophone
vn	violin
wb	wood block
xyl	xylophone
/-	composition revised in - (year)

PUBLISHERS

The publisher of each work is show in the main catalogue within brackets [ ].

Boosey and Hawkes
295 Regent Street, London, W1R 8JB;
phone (0171) 580 2060, fax (0171) 436 2850

Composer
can be contacted via Oxford University Press, United Music Publishers (addresses below) or the British Music Information Centre,
10 Stratford Place, London W1N 9AE;
phone (0171) 499 8567, fax (0171) 499 4795

Edition Modern
Amalienstraße 40, D-79133 Karlsruhe, Germany;
phone (0721) 26023, fax (0721) 26044

Oxford University Press
Promotion: 70 Baker Street, London, W1M 1DJ
phone (0171) 616 5900, fax (0171) 616 5901
Sales and hire: Music Department, Walton Street, Oxford OX2 6DP
phone (01865) 56767, fax (01865) 267749

Suvini Zerboni
Via Quintiliano 40, 20138 Milano, Italy (2) 508 4357
in UK via William Elkin Music Services,
Station Road Industrial Estate, Salhouse, Norwich NR13 6NY
phone (01603) 721302, fax (01603) 721801

United Music Publishers
42 Rivington Street, London EC2 3BN
phone (0171) 729 4700, fax (0171) 739 6549

Universal Edition (London)
48 Great Marlborough Street, London W1V 4DU
phone (0171) 437 5203, fax (0171) 437 6115

CATALOGUE OF WORKS

J1 **The Chinese Bridge** (1950) 0' 30"
solo piano. [Composer]
probably lost

J2 **Juvenilia** (1953-58) 5-6'
five pieces: Valse Burlesque, Tambourin, Air and Variation, Preambule, Vêpres [Oxford]
solo piano

J3 **Polskie Tance Op. 32** (1955/62) 1'
Four pieces: Kujawiak-Kozak, Kozak-Drobny, Kujawiak, Zbójnicki [Oxford]
solo piano

J4 **Two Mazurkas Op. 142** (1957) 3'
solo piano [Oxford]

J5 **Two Pasodobles** (1959) 3'
solo piano [Oxford]
No. 1 'In memory of Isaac Albeniz'
Title: Spanish dance in duple tune.

J6 **Forget-me-not** (1959)
voice and ensemble [Composer]
Text: Poem by William McGonagall.
Lost.

J7 **Vieux Nöel Op. 59 No 2** (*c.* 1958-59) 2'
solo piano [Oxford]

J8 **Romance (with Intermezzo)** (1960) 3'
solo piano [Oxford]

J9 **Cantet nunc aula caelitum** (1962)
flute, piano [Composer]
Title: 'Sing we now all our praises'.

J10 **Quem Pastores Laudavere** (1962/65/66)
flute(pic), oboe, piano. Independent parts, no score [Composer]
Title: 'While shepherds gave praise'.

J11 **Symphony No. 1** (1962-64) 20'
soli contralto, va, vc, cbn [Composer]
4(pic)4(ca)3(bcl)4/8hn,5trb/7perc/gui,org,2hp/str(0.0.12.8.6)
fp: unperformed.
Text: Fizgerald/Khayyám 'Rubáiyát', Milton 'The Passion'.

1 **Le Dormeur du Val** (1963-64/66/68) 7'
mezzo-soprano, cel, hpd, pf, 2vn, va, vc [Composer]
fp: 19.11.65. Arts Council Drawing Room, London.
Josephine Nendick, ensemble, dir. John Carewe
fp: (final version) 3.4.68 BBC (studio recording), same performers
Text: from Arthur Rimbaud's poem of same name.
Revision of 1966: minor changes to last section. Revision of 1968: shortened with minor revisions. Formerly published by Universal.

2 **From The Revelations of Saint John the Divine** (1965/1970) 7'
high sop, fl, 2vn, 2va, 2vc [Composer]
fp: 31.10.73. Sheffield University. June Barton (sop),
Graham Mayger (fl), Members of Northern Sinfonia
Text: none.
Some material from earlier work of same title, for sop, chorus and small orchestra.

3 **Horrorzone** (1965-66/1971/1987) 8'
soprano, fl, ca, vib, pf [Composer]
fp: (final version) 8.10.87. BBC Maida Vale (studio recording).
Elaine Barry (sop), Ensemble Exposé, dir. Roger Redgate.
Text: Torquato Tasso
Original version for soprano and piano. 2nd version for soprano and small orchestra. 3rd version for sop or cl, fl, hn or ca, piano 4-hands.

4 **Songs 1-18** (1966-78)
to be performed separately, in groups, or as complete cycle [Composer]
Title: from Stan Brakhage films of same name.
Some *Songs* based on material dating from 1963. Original versions of *Songs 1-4* were conceived as a set.

4.01 **Song 1** (1966/69-70) 4'
solo soprano [Composer]
fp: (final version) 25.8.80. Isle of Man Viola Festival. Jane Manning
Text: Torquato Tasso. Original (withdrawn) version for soprano and piano.
Vocal line the same in both versions. Formerly published by Universal.

4.02 **Song 2** (1968) 4'
2fl, 2ob, 2cl, 2bn, hn, 2 tpt, 3vc [Composer]
fp: 7.9.69 Gaudeamus Festival, Hilversum, Netherlands.
Netherlands Radio CO, dir. Francis Travis.
Performed simultaneously with *Song 5*.
Original (withdrawn) version for soprano and piano.

4.03 **Song 3** (1969) 2'
sop. ca, hn, pf, elec organ [Composer]
Text: Alexander Blok (in Russian).
Original (withdrawn) version was for soprano and piano.

4.04 **Song 4** (1968) 4'
2 solo pf, 2fl, 2ob, 2bn, 2 trp, 3vc [Composer]
fp: 7.9.69 Gaudeamus Festival, Hilversum, Netherlands. Maarten Bon,
Composer (pf), Netherlands Radio CO, dir. Francis Travis.
Original (withdrawn) version was for soprano and piano.
First performance with *Song 2*.

4.05 **Song 5** (1966-67) 7'
solo piano [Composer]
fp: 5.7.68 Acland Burghley School, London. Composer;
choreography: Henrietta Lyons.
Based on material dating from c. 1963.

4.06 **Song 6** (1968/96) 3'
solo piano [Composer]
fp: 5.12.96 (revised version) Conway Hall, London. Ian Pace.
Original version for fl, ob, hp, vc, is unperformed and withdrawn.

4.07 **Song 7** (1968-69) 4'
solo piano [Composer]
fp: 11.4.69 Royal Albert Hall, London. Paul Lowdell (ob), Composer (pf);
choreography: Henrietta Lyons. fp: (final version) 1.1.69
Composer; with same choreography.
Original version was for oboe and piano.

4.08 **Song 8** (1967) 10'
solo piano [Composer]
fp: 9.12.80 BMIC, London.
Based on material from 'Nukterides' (Birds of the Night c. 1963, unfinished).

4.09 **Song 9** (1968) 7'
solo piano [Composer]
'To Ronald Lumsden.'
fp: 17.10.68 Conway Hall, London. Ronald Lumsden.

4.10 **Song 10** (1971) 4'
pic, ob, ca, 2cl, cbn, pf, elec organ, 2 vc [Composer]
fp: 4.6.81 Lisbon, Portugal. Gulbenkian Festival Orchestra, dir. Alvaro Salazar.

4.11 **Song 11** (1969-71) 4'
soprano, clarinet [Composer]
fp: 29.10.81 BMIC, London. Jane Ginsborg (sop), Philip Edwards (cl).
Text: Algernon Charles Swinburne.

4.12 **Song 12** (1972-73) 4'
solo bass clarinet [Suvini Zerboni]
'Voor Harry Sparnaay.'
fp: 28.5.85 BMIC, London. Alastair Logan.

4.13 **Song 13** (1971) 3'
solo violin [Composer]
'To Will Eisma.'
fp: 15.3.82 LIM, Madrid, Spain. Francisco Martin.

4.14 **Song 14** (1974) 4'
solo soprano [Edition Modern]
'For Jane Manning.'
fp: 11.9.74 Flanders Festival, Ghent, Belgium. Jane Manning.
Text: Walt Whitman.

4.15 **Song 15** (1974) 4'
solo soprano [Edition Modern]
fp: 11.9.74 Flanders Festival, Ghent, Belgium. Jane Manning.
Text: none.

4.16 **Song 16** (1976) 3'
solo soprano [Composer]
fp: 25.8.80 Isle of Man Viola Festival. Jane Manning (with *Song 1*).
Text: Petrarch.

4.17 **Song 17** (1976) 4'
solo guitar [Composer]
fp: 4.8.76 Montepulciano, Italy. Roberto Porroni.

4.18 **Song 18** (1976) 3'
solo double bass [Composer]
'To Peter Buckoke.'
fp: 8.8.76 Montepulciano, Italy. Peter Buckoke
(as part of Tradimenti: Theatre piece by Memè Perlini).

5 **Afar** (1966-67) 13'
fl, ca, 3tpt, perc, cel [Suvini Zerboni]
fp: 12.9.71. Utrecht, Netherlands. Netherlands Mobiel Ensemble, dir. Jan Stulen
Title: from Paul Eluard's poem translated Samuel Beckett: 'Out of sight in the direction of my body'.

6 **As when upon a trancèd summer night** (1966/68) 18'
2perc, pf, 3 vc [Universal]
'In memory of my father.'
fp: (final version) 2.11.78. Royal Northern College of Music, Manchester, Park Lane Music Players, dir. Lionel Friend.
fp: 17.7.67. Montreal, Canada. Thomas Igloi, Clive Gillinson, Robert Lay (vc), John Lill (pf), composer (perc). fp: (second version) 21.6.68. Rome, Italy.
Title: from Keats' poem 'Hyperion - A Fragment'.
3rd & final version has longer first section, reinstated from the original plan. Formerly published by IMC.

7 **Untitled piece to honour Igor Stravinsky**
2 versions [Composer]

7.1 **Untitled piece to honour Igor Stravinsky** (1967) 6'
solo flute [Composer]
'For Igor Stravinsky's 85th Birthday.'
fp: 15.7.67 Cheltenham Festival. Douglas Whittaker. fp: (final version) 26.4.78 Musée d'Art Moderne, Paris, France. Pierre-Yves Artaud.
Based on opening chord from Stravinsky's Violin Concerto.
Original version lacks middle secion of the final version.
Published in shortened form in Tempo No. 81, Boosey & Hawkes.

7.2 **Untitled Piece to Honour Igor Stravinsky** (1971) 6'
flute, harp, viola [Composer]
'On the death of Igor Stravinsky.'
Flute part is the same as first version, harp and viola parts added.

8 **Romeo and Juliet are drowning** (1967/73) 4'
solo piano [Oxford]
fp: Unknown. Composer.
Based on love scene from Berlioz's dramatic symphony 'Romeo & Juliet'.

9 **Transformations of the vampire** (1968-71) 14'
cl, 3 perc, vn, va [Universal]
'To Roman Vlad.'
fp: 19.9.73 Hilversum, Netherlands. Ensemble Pro en Contra, dir. Peter Keuschnig.
Title: from Baudelaire's poem 'Pièces condamnées - Fleurs du Mal'.

10 **Autumnall** (1968-71) 5'
solo piano [Oxford]
'For Alexander Abercrombie.'
fp: 6.2.73 Wigmore Hall, London. Alexander Abercrombie.
Title: from Donne's poem 'The Autumnall'.
Original version was for voices and ensemble: 'music drama in the form of a TV script'. 2nd version was an extended version of the 3rd and final version.

11 **n** (1969/1972) 8'
any 1 - 4 players, different ranges. Independent parts, no score. [Universal]
'To Jaap Flier and Willy de la Bije.'
fp: 19.3.70 Cockpit Theatre, London. Students of the Royal College of Music.
fp: (final version) 10.4.78 Wigmore Hall, London.
Members of Peregrine Quintet (fl, ob, cl, hn).

12.1 **Folk Song Set** (1969-70) 13'
version A [Universal]
sop, ca, cl(ecl) flugelhorn, perc, 2vn, va, vc, db
'In memory of Percy Grainger.'
fp: 29.8.76 Venice Biennale, Italy. Joan Logue (sop),
Webern Ensemble, dir. Marcello Panni.
Text: Traditional English, adapted by composer.

12.2 **Folk Song Set** (1969-70/75-76) 13'
version B [Universal]
mezzo, fl, cl, pf, vn, va, vc
'In memory of Percy Grainger.'
fp: 12.1.80 Purcell Room, London. Josephine Nendick (mez),
Capricorn, dir. Lionel Friend.
Text: Traditional English, adapted by composer.
Omits one (high) song from version A: 'If young girls...'

12.3 **Folk Song Set** (1969-70/75-76) 15'
version C [Universal]
mezzo, fl, ob, perc, pf
'In memory of Percy Grainger.'
fp: 19.8.80 Dartington, Devon. Josephine Nendick (mez), Suoraan.
Text: Traditional English adapted by composer.
Omits one (high) song from version A.

13 **Jeanne d'Arc** (1967-71/AR) 18'
high sop, tenor, solo cello, fl(pic), afl, arec, hn, ptpt, bass [Universal]
sax, gui, hp 3vn, va, vc, db
fp: 11.9.72 Hilversum, Netherlands. Gertie Charlent,
Bert van t'Hof, Max Werner, Netherlands Radio CO, dir. Peter Keuschnig.
Text: from The Trial of Joan of Arc.
Currently under revision.

14 **Strauss-Walzer** (1967/1989) 10'
3 pieces based on Waltzes of Johann Strauss [Oxford]
solo piano
fp: (complete) 10.1.90 Purcell Room, London. Jonathan Powell.

14.1 **Wo die Zitronen blühn** 3'
Strauss-Waltzer 1 [Oxford]
solo piano
'For Jonathan Powell.'
fp: 10.1.90 Purcell Room, London. Jonathan Powell.

14.2 **O, schöner Mai** 3'
Strauss-Walzer 2 [Oxford]
solo piano
'For Nic Hodges.'
fp: 28.10.89 University Music School, Cambridge. Nicolas Hodges.

14.3 **Geschichten aus dem Wienerwald** 4'
Strauss-Walzer 3 [Oxford]
solo piano
'For Ben Morison.'
fp: 9.12.89 St John's College, Cambridge. Benjamin Morison.

15 **Alice**
3 versions
Title: from Lewis Carroll 'Alice in Wonderland'
No connection with the withdrawn Incidental Music for Alice (1970).

15.1 **Alice** (1974-75) 6'
version A [Edition Modern]
solo double bass
fp: 26.3.76 Royan Festival, France. Fernando Grillo.

15.2 **Alice** (*c.* 1975) 6'
version B [Universal]
solo cello
fp: date unknown, Holland Festival, Netherlands. Frances-Marie Uitti.

15.3 **Alice** (*c.* 1975) 7'
version C [Universal]
cello, percussion
fp: 15.10.76 Buffalo, NY, USA. Frances-Marie Uitti (vc), Yvar Mikhashoff (perc).

16 **World** (1968-74) 19'
2(2pic:afl)2(oda:ca)2(ecl)0/1.2(2ptpt)1.1/3perc.cimbalom. [Edition Modern]
celesta.2pf.hp/2vn.2va.2vc.2db/6 voices (high sop.sop.mez.ten.bar.bas)
'To Harry Halbreich.'
Commissioned by The London Sinfonietta.
fp: 23.3.75 Royan Festival, France. J. Nelson, M. Thomas, J. Stickland, P. Hall, P. Knapp, W. Mason, London Sinfonietta, dir. Simon Bainbridge.
Text: Mayakovsky, Hölderlin, Rimbaud, Blake, Tennyson, Hopkins, Dante.

17 **Babylon** (1971/AR)
mezzo, ob, ecl, asax, bn, gui, hp, pf, 2perc, 2vc, db [Universal]
fp: 11.9.72 Gaudeamus Music Week, Hilversum, Netherlands.
Kitty Donker (mezzo), Netherlands Radio Chamber Orchestra, dir. P. Keuschnig.
Text: none. Currently under revision.

18 **Snowdrift** (1972) 10'
solo piano [Edition Modern]
fp: 6.2.73 Wigmore Hall, London. Alexander Abercrombie.
Title: from William Sharp 'The White Peacock'.

19 **Irma Cortez** (1970-72/96) 24'
solo baritone, bn, perc, accordion, pf, hp, vn, db. [Composer]
fp: (final version) 25.11.96 Royal Academy of Music, London.
Robert Rice (bar), Manson Ensemble, dir. Composer.
Text: Composer, after 'The Discovery and Conquest of Peru' by Augustin Zarâte.
Original version (unperformed) included actors, no percussion.

20 **Tsuru-Kame** (1971-73) 22'
sop, 3 female voices, fl, 2perc, cel, va, 3 dancers (optional) [Composer]
'To Maurice Weddington.'
fp: 15.9.73 Rotterdam, Netherlands. Kitty Donker (sop);
choregraphy: Richard Alston; ensemble, dir. Hans Neuburger (va).
Title: (Japanese) 'The Crane - The Tortoise'.
Text: Kineya Rokuzaemon X (in Japanese). Based on Noh play 'Gekkyuden'.
Formerly published by Edition Modern.

21 **Circle, Chorus and Formal Act** (1973) 23'
baritone, 2 female choirs, chorus of 9 perc, ob(ca), 2 hn, perc [Composer]
'To the Students of The Place.'
fp: 5.6.73 The Place, London. Students of The Place.
Text: Composer, after traditional English folk-verse.
Formerly published by Universal.

22 **Mysteries** (1972-79) 156'
Parts 1 - 8 [Composer]
Text: Townely and other Mystery Plays, adapted by Composer,
with additional Latin, old English and Gaelic texts.
Based on a project called 'Incidents from the Life of Jesus of Nazareth' performed at The Place, 1974. Copyright formerly belonged to Universal.

22.1 **Mystery 1** (1975-76) 16'
The Parting of Darkness From Light [Composer]
5 voices: 2 tenors, 2 baritones, bass
Commissioned by The Baccholian Singers. fp: 1976 Germany. fp: (final version) 19.10.76 St John's Smith Square, London. Baccholian Singers.

22.2 **Mystery 2** (1977-78) 14'
The Earthly Paradise [Composer]
mezzo, tenor, bass, 2 actors, 2pic, alto recorder, ob/oda, ca,
4 tpt, 2cel, 3perc, 2va, 2vc, db

22.3 **Mystery 3** (1978) 16'
Noah and the Great Flood [Composer]
tenor, 2 actors, alto recorder, ca, 3 perc

22.4 **Mystery 4** (1972/79) 15'
The Prophecy of Daniel [Composer]
4 singers: sop, contralto, tenor, bass
fp: 11.11.84 Huddersfield Festival. R. Hardy (sop),
L. Hirst (mez), M. Hill (ten), S. Varcoe (bar).

22.5 **Mystery 5** (1977-78) 30'
The Parliament of Heaven [Composer]
3 sop, mez, ten, 3 choruses, children's choir, arec,
ob, 4tpt, 3perc, hp, va, 2 actors

22.6 **Mystery 6** (1978-79) 20'
The Annunciation [Composer]
sop, ten, bass, female choir (6S, 6A), speaker, 7tpt,
3tbn, 3perc, 2cel, 4vn, 4va, vc

22.7 **Mystery 7** (1978-79) 20'
The Betrayal and Crucifixion of Jesus of Nazareth [Composer]
2 sop, mez, ten, 6 speakers, 2 srec, pic, pic(afl), oda, ca,
tpt, 3perc, 2cel, hp, 6vn, vc
fp: (section for soprano and trumpet) Washington DC,
date unknown. Phillis Bryn-Julson (sop).

22.8 **Mystery 8** (1978-79) 25'
The Deliverance of Souls [Composer]
8 voices, 4 SATB choruses, children's choir, 5rec, 3fl, 7tpt,
3tbn, perc, strings, church bells

23 **Svatovac** (1973-74) 2'
solo piano [Oxford]
Title: Macedonian dance.
Originally published as an arrangement in The Dancing Times.

24 **Commedia dell'incomprensibile potere che alcune donne hanno sugli uomini** (1973-75) 12'
soprano, counter-tenor, cello, harpsichord [Universal]
'For The Five Centuries Ensemble.'
fp: 30.6.77 Hilversum, Netherlands. Carol Plantamura (sop),
John-Patrick Thomas (ctn), Marijke Verberne (vc), John Whitelaw (hpd).
Title: 'Comedy of the incomprehensible power that some women have over men.'
Text: Composer with early English anon.
Taken from Genesis B: The Fall of Angels.

25 **Medea** (1973-76/AR) 6'
5 voices and orchestra (first version) [Composer]
Some material from 1st version re-used in 'First Sign a Sharp White Moon...'

26 **Wild Flowers** (1974) 10'
2 pianos [Edition Modern]
fp: 26.10.75 ISCM Festival: Paris, France. Katia & Marielle Labèque.
Title: from Blake 'Auguries of Innocence'.

27 **Evening** (1974) 11'
asax, hn, tpt, perc, hp, vc, db [Edition Modern]
fp: (private) 8.4.74 Collegiate Theatre, London.
For the Friends of Covent Garden; choreography: L. Seymour;
London Sinfonietta, dir. A. Lawrence.
fp: (public) 22.10.76 Donaueschigen, Germany. Ensemble 2e2m, dir. P. Méfano.

28 **Cipriano** (1974) 14'
tenor, 9 voice SATB chorus [Edition Modern]
(high sop, 2 sop, mez, ctn, ten, bar, 2bas)
fp: (private) 27.11.75 Birmingham. P. Hall, John Alldis Choir,
dir. J. Alldis. fp: (public) 11.12.75 Wigmore Hall, London.
P. Hall, John Alldis Choir, dir. J. Alldis.
Text: Pedro Calderón de la Barca.

29 **Ives** (1974) 5'
solo piano [Edition Modern]
'In celebration of Ives' 100th Birthday.'
fp: 24.3.76 Royan Festival, France. Jaqueline Méfano.
Part of trilogy *Ives-Grainger-Nancarrow*.

30 **Orfeo** (1974-75/AR) 6'
6 voices, 3 tbn, 2 lute, perc, db (first version), [Composer]
revised for solo mezzo-soprano
Text: Ovid (Book XI of 'Metamorphoses').

31 **Bouffe** (1975) 6'
for a person alone on stage (solo voice) [Composer]
fp: 23.8.86 Three Choirs Festival, Hereford. John Potter (ten).
Text: none.
Formerly published by Universal.

32 **Piano Concerto No. 1** (1975/1983-84) 15'
solo piano, pic, fl, ob, cl, bn, 2hn, 2tbn, cel, 2vn, va, vc, db [Edition Modern]
fp: (first version) 22.3.76 Composer (pf), Nouvelle Orchestre
Philharmonique de Radio France, dir. Farhad Mechkat.
fp: (final version) 6.12.96 Royal College of Music, London.
Ian Pace (pf), 20th Century Ensemble, dir. Edwin Roxburgh.
Substantial revision in 1983-84. Original version had much
larger ensemble and lasted 35 mins.

33 **Offshore** (1975-76) 11'
3(pic)3(3ca)3(ecl,bcl)3(cbn)/4331/3perc/hpd.pf.2hp/str(12.0.10.8.6) [Universal]
fp: 13.9.82 Barbican Centre, London.
Philharmonia Orchestra, dir. Oliver Knussen.

34 **Ru Tchou** (1975) 9'
solo drummer [Composer]
'For Loong-Hsing Wen.'
fp: 9.5.76 Taipei, Tawain. Tetsu Kitano.
Title: Chinese 'The Ascent of The Sun'.
Formerly published by Universal.

35 **Piano Concerto No. 2** (1975-76) 16'
solo piano, 2 alto flutes, strings (3.0.2.2.2) [Edition Modern]
Commande de la Ministère de la Culture et de l'Environnement
fp: 15.7.77 Saintes, France. Jaqueline Méfano (pf),
Ensemble 2e2m, dir. P. Méfano.

36 **First Sign A Sharp White Moon, as if the cause of Snow** (1968/75) 4'
solo alto flute [Composer]
fp: 4.6.88 Brighton Festival. Isabelle Carré.
Title: from John Birtwistle's poem.
Music taken from *Medea.* Original version for piano and 14 instruments.

37 **Pathways of Sun and Stars** (1976) 20'
2(2pic)1(oda)2(ecl:bthn)1(cbn)/3.0.2.0/5perc/2hp/str:(1.0.1.1.1) [Edition Modern]
Commissioned by the BBC.
fp: 15.11.76 Round House, London. BBC SO, dir. Pierre Boulez.
Title: relates to leylines and magic squares.

38 **Jazz** (1976) 5'
solo piano [Composer]
fp: 22.6.78 Middelburg, Netherlands. Geoffrey Douglas Madge.
Part of trilogy with *Boogie-Woogie* & *Fast Dances, Slow Dances*. Structurally based on Beethoven Bagatelles Op. 126. Formerly published by Universal.

39.1 **Mr Punch** (1976-77/79) 21'
Version 1 [Universal]
voice, fl(pic), ecl, 1perc, pf, vn, vc
'To Peter Maxwell Davies.'
Commissioned by The Fires of London
fp: 8.2.78 QEH, London. Mary Thomas (mez),
The Fires of London, dir. Peter Maxwell Davies.
Text: composer, after traditional 18th & 19th century sources.
Original version (25') was presented with Barry Smith's Theatre of Puppets.
Voice takes all nine roles.

39.2 **Mr Punch** (1976-77/79) 21'
Version 2 [Universal]
voice, fl, ob, perc, pf, vn, (vc)
fp: 1979 Suoraan.

40 **All the trees they are so high** (1977) 6'
solo violin [Composer]
fp: 26.4.78 Paris, France. Daniel Rémy.
Title: English folk song.
Formerly published by Universal.

41 **Doves Figary** (1976-77) 7'
(2 versions) [Composer]
solo cello
'For Alan Brett.'
fp: (second version) 11.11.81 Air Gallery, London. Alan Brett.
Based on 'Doves Figary' or 'Chestnut' the 85th tune in
Playford's English Dancing Master.

42 **Lost Lands** (1977) 20'
E flat clarinet, soprano saxophone, piano, guitar, violin [Edition Modern]
'For Klaus Ager and the Oesterreichische Ensemble.'
fp: 13.10.77 Graz, Austria. Oesterreichische Ensemble, dir. Klaus Ager.
Title: from Claude Lévi-Strauss 'Tristes Tropiques'.

43 **Three Dukes went a-Riding** (1977/96) 4'
solo piano [Oxford]
fp: (revised version) 28.6.96 Conway Hall, London. Ian Pace.
Title: derived from several English folk songs.
Originally 3rd of *Piano Studies*.

44 **English Country-Tunes** (1977/1982-85) 43'
8 sections, performable separately. [UMP]
solo piano
fp: First complete performance: 18.12.79 BMIC, London. Composer.
fp: (final version) 13.2.86 BMIC, London. Composer.
Original version written 'in celebration of the Silver Jubilee of Her Majesty Queen Elizabeth II, in 1977'. Revisions in 1982-85 to sections 4 & 6, minor revision to section 1. Formerly published by Universal (first version).

44.1 **Green Meadows** 8'
English Country-Tunes 1 [UMP]
fp: 19.1.78 Leeds Polytechnic. Alexander Abercrombie.
fp: (final version) 13.2.86 BMIC, London

44.2 **Midsummer Morn** 7'
English Country-Tunes 2 [UMP]
fp: 19.1.78 Leeds Polytechnic. Alexander Abercrombie.

44.3 **I'll give my love a garland** 8'
English Country-Tunes 3 [UMP]
fp: 18.12.79 BMIC, London. Composer.

44.4 **May and December** 5'
English Country-Tunes 4 [UMP]
fp: 18.12.79 BMIC, London. Composer.
fp: (final version) 13.2.86 BMIC, London. Composer.
Final version alters first section of original and introduces new central section.

44.5 **Lies and Marvels** (1977/82-85) 3'
English Country-Tunes 5 [UMP]
fp: 18.12.79 BMIC, London. Composer.
fp: (final version) 13.2.86 BMIC, London. Composer.

44.6 **The Seeds of Love** (1977/82-85) 4'
English Country-Tunes 6 [UMP]
fp: 18.12.79 BMIC, London. Composer.
fp: (final version) 13.2.86 BMIC, London. Composer.
Final version uses material from earlier piece *La-di-dah* (withdrawn) and end of first version.

44.7 **My Bonny Boy** 4'
English Country-Tunes 7 [UMP]
fp: 18.12.79 BMIC, London. Composer.

44.8 **Come Beat the Drums and Sound the Fifes** 5'
English Country-Tunes 8 [UMP]
fp: 18.12.79 BMIC, London. Composer.

45 **all.fall.down** (1977) 8'
solo piano [Composer]
'To Klaus Huber; Howard Skempton; Alvin Singleton.'
fp: 10.10.77 Freiburg-im-Breisgau, Germany. Composer.
Title: from nursery rhyme 'Ring-a-ring o' roses'.
all. 'To Klaus Huber'; *fall*. 'To Howard Skempton';
down. 'To Alvin Singleton'. Formerly published by Universal.

46 **Mine Eye Awake** (1977) 6'
lyric soprano, piano [Universal]
'To Elisabeth Lutyens.'
fp: 23.1.78 Harrogate Theatre, Harrogate. Elaine Barry (sop), composer (pf).
Text: William Shakespeare Sonnet 61.

47 **To & Fro** (1978/95) 4'
solo piano [Composer]
fp: 17.2.78 Hilversum, Netherlands. Composer (studio recording), broadcast 7.3.78. fp: (final version) 29.2.96 Conway Hall, London. Ian Pace.
Original version 6th of *Piano Studies*. Final version is different piece.
Formerly published by Universal.

48 **Tom Fool's Wooing** (1975-78) 20'
14 voices: high soprano, 3 sopranos, mezzo-soprano, 2 contraltos, counter-tenor, 2 tenors, 2 baritones, 2 basses [Universal]
Written for the John Alldis Choir.
fp: Unperformed (1996)
Text: English, Rumanian, Turkish & Greek folk poetry, Ibycus, Edmund Spenser.

49 **Piano Studies** (1976-78) 25'
1. Untitled, 2. Hopi, 3. Three Dukes went a-Riding, 4. Huckleberry, 5. We'll get there some day, 6. To and Fro, 7. La-di-dah, 8. Deep down. [Composer]
solo piano
Withdrawn. No. 2 used in revised version of *Piano Concerto No. 4*; Nos. 4 and 8 in *Verdi Transcriptions*, a revised version of No. 7 in *The Seeds of Love* (*English Country-Tunes*).

50 **Ohi! ohi! ohi!** (1978) 5'
solo voice [Composer]
'For Josephine Nendick.'
fp: 21.1.82 Purcell Room, London. J. Nendick (mez).
Text: none.
Formerly published by Universal.

51 **Runnin' Wild** (1978) 8'
solo oboe or saxophone or clarinet or bass clarinet. [Composer]
'To Christopher Redgate.'
fp: 20.7.80 South Hill Park, Bracknell. Christopher Redgate (ob).
Title: Jazz standard.
Formerly published by Universal.

52 **Kemp's Morris** (1978) 5'
solo piano (pianist wearing Morris-bells) [Oxford]
fp: 19.11.81 Oxford University. Composer.
Based on 26th melody of Playford's 'English Dancing Master' (1651) sometimes called 'The cherping of the larke' or 'Muscadin'.

53 **Mountainfall** (1978) 8'
solo mezzo-soprano [Composer]
'To Kris Donovan.'
Commissioned by Josephine Nendick.
fp: 22.1.79 Wigmore Hall, London. J. Nendick (mez).
Text: none.
Formerly published by Universal.

54 **Piano Concerto No. 3** (1978) 25'
solo piano, ob(ca), cl(bcl), 2tbn, vc, db [Universal]
'To Geoffrey Douglas Madge.'
fp: 5.7.79 Middelburg, Netherlands. G. D. Madge (pf), Netherlands Radio CO, dir. Ernest Bour.

55 **Gorõ** (1978) 20'
tenor, afl, cl, hp, vn, va, vc [Universal]
Commissioned by the Bath Festival.
fp: 23.5.79 Bath Festival. Alastair Thomson (ten), Nash Ensemble.
Title: (Japanese) - name.
Text: Kineya Rokuzaemon X.

56 **We'll get there someday** (1978) 3'
solo piano [Composer]
fp: 6.1.79 Amsterdam, Netherlands. Composer.
Originally 5th of 'Piano Studies'. Formerly published by Universal.

57 **Sir Tristran** (1978) 20'
soprano, clarinet, piano, violin, viola, cello [Universal]
Commissioned by the Nash Ensemble.
fp: 15.12.80 St John's Smith Square, London. P. Walmsley-Clark (sop), Circle, dir. Gregory Rose.
Title: after medieval poem.
Text: Malory, Beroul, T. d'Angleterre, M. de France.

58 **Fast Dances, Slow Dances** (1978-79) 18'
solo piano [Composer]
'To Elliott Carter.'
Commissioned by Junction Dance Company.
fp: 23.4.79 North London Polytechnic. Composer.
Part of trilogy with *Jazz* and *Boogie Woogie*. Structurally based on Beethoven Bagatelles Op 119. Formerly published by Universal.

59 **Short but...** (1979) 3'
solo piano [Oxford]
fp: 11.79 North London Polytechnic. Composer.

60 **Alongside** (1979) 19'
1111/1110/perc/pf/str(1.1.1.1.1) [Universal]
Commissioned by the London Sinfonietta.
fp: 19.2.80 St John's Smith Square, London.
London Sinfonietta, dir. Roland Zollman.
Title of printed edition: *alongside* [sic].

61 **Kagami-Jishi** (1979) 11'
flute, harp [Composer]
Commissioned by Marianne Erhardt.
fp: 2.1.80 Purcell Room, London. M. Erhardt (fl), Susan Drake (hp).
Title: (Japanese) - 'Mirror of Lion Spirit'.
Formerly published by Universal.

62 **Piano Concerto No. 4** (1978-80/96) 20'
solo piano [Composer]
(first version) 'To Brian Ferneyhough.' (second version) 'To Ian Pace.'
fp: 30.4.80 Logan Hall, London University. Composer.
fp: (revised version) 4.10.96 Conway Hall, London. Ian Pace.
Final version includes material from *Long Distance* (withdrawn), *Piano Studies No. 2*.

63 **Pavasiya** (1979) 8'
solo oboe and oboe d'amore [Composer]
'For Christopher Redgate.'
fp: 21.2.82 Purcell Room, London. C. Redgate.
Title: (Hopi Indian) - 'Song of creation'.

64 **Talawva** (1979/AR) 8'
mezzo-soprano, fl(pic), ob(oda), perc, pf [Composer]
Title: (Hopi Indian) 'Red light of dawn
(when man fully formed, proudly faced his creator)'

65 **Sikangnuqa** (1979) 8'
solo flute [Composer]
'For Roberto Fabbricciani.'
fp: 7.6.80 Teatro Grande, Brescia, Italy. R. Fabbricciani.
Title: (Hopi Indian) - 'Yellow light of dawn
(in which humankind takes its first breath)'.
Formerly published by Universal.

66 **... fairest noonday ...** (1979) 8'
tenor, piano [Composer]
'To Martyn Hill.'
Commissioned by the BBC.
fp: 5.3.80 Leeds University. Martyn Hill (ten), John Constable (pf).
Text: Friedrich Hölderlin (in German).
Formerly published by Universal.

67 **Hinomi** (1979) 8'
solo percussion [UMP]
Commissioned by Nottingham University for Elizabeth Davis.
fp: 9.6.80 Nottingham University. E. Davis.
Title: (Japanese) - 'The Fire Watch-Tower'.

68 **Grainger** (1979) 4'
solo piano [Composer]
'For Percy Grainger's 97th Birthday.'
fp: 22.7.79 South Hill Park, Bracknell. Composer.
Part of trilogy *Ives-Grainger-Nancarrow*. Formerly published by Universal.

69 **Nancarrow** (1979-80) 4'
solo piano [Composer]
fp: 20.6.80 BMIC, London. Composer.
Part of trilogy *Ives-Grainger-Nancarrow*. Formerly published by Universal.

70 **Sea and Sky** (1979-80) 24'
4(2pic)3.2(2ecl)2(cbn)/4.4(4ptpt)3.1/timp.4perc/ [Universal]
2cel.2hp/str: (10.10.10.8.8)
Commissioned by The London Philharmonic Orchestra.
fp: 16.5.80 RFH, London. London Philharmonic, dir. Elgar Howarth.
Title: after Turner watercolour of same name.

71 **Boogie-Woogie** (1980/81/85/96) 4'
solo piano [Oxford]
'To Roger Wright.'
fp: 16.7.80 Arezzo, Italy. Composer.
fp: (second version) 2.2.81 BMIC, London. Composer.
fp: (third version) 10.4.85 BMIC, London. Composer.
fp: (final version) 29.2.96 Conway Hall, London. Ian Pace.
Part of trilogy with *Jazz* and *Fast Dances, Slow Dances*.

72 **Freightrain Bruise** (1972/80) 3'
solo piano [Oxford]
'For Charlotte Holtzermann.'
fp: 1972 The Place, London. Composer. fp: (final version) 10.5.86 Brighton Festival. Composer.
Substantial revision in 1980.

73 **Piano Concerto No. 5** (1980) 22'
solo piano, mezzo-soprano, fl(afl), ob(oda), vib [Composer]
(separate parts, no score)
Commissioned by Suoraan.
fp: 19.8.80 Dartington, Devon. Composer (pf), Suoraan.
Text: none.

74 **Moon's goin' down** (1980) 4'
any solo wind instrument or voice (range 1.5 octaves) [Composer]
'For John Potter.'
Commissioned by John Potter.
fp: 13.4.81 BMIC, London. Christopher Redgate (oboe).
Title: Jazz standard.
Text: none.
Formerly published by Universal.

75 **Lord Melbourne** (1980) 12'
soprano, clarinet, piano [Universal]
'For the Arioso Trio.'
Commissioned by the Worfield Charity Concert Trust.
fp: 25.9.82 Rudge Hall, Pattingham. Lynda Russell (sop),
David Campbell (cl), Andrew Ball (pf).
Text: none.
Based on English folk-song (as transcribed by Grainger).

76 **Green Bushes** (1980) 12'
contralto, piano [Composer]
Commissioned by Barbara and Alexander Abercrombie.
fp: 17.12.81 BMIC, London. Josephine Nendick (mez), composer (pf).
Title: English folk-song
Text: English traditional, adapted by composer.
Formerly published by Universal.

77 **Piano Concerto No. 6** (1980-81) 15'
solo piano [Composer]
fp: 22.5.81 BMIC, London. Composer.

78 **Nobody's Jig** (1980-81) 20'
string quartet: 2 violins, viola, cello. 4 independent parts: no score. [Composer]
Commissioned by South Hill Arts Centre, Bracknell.
fp: 28.1.81 South Hill Park, Bracknell. Locrian String Quartet.
Title: a melody from Playford's 'English Dancing Master' (1651)

79 **Liz** (1980-81) 1'
solo piano [Oxford]
'Birthday Gift for Elisabeth Lutyens.'
fp: 6.3.81 BMIC, London. Composer.

80 **Piano Concerto No. 7** (1981) 11'
solo piano, wind quintet: flute, oboe, clarinet, bassoon, horn. [Composer]
6 independent parts: no score.
fp: 20.6.81 Greenwich Festival. Composer (pf),
members of Heath Orchestra Wind Ensemble.

81 **Kelir** (1981) 17'
6 voices: 2 sopranos, contralto, tenor, baritone, bass [Composer]
Commissioned by The London Sinfonietta.
fp: 2.11.82 St John's Smith Square, London.
London Sinfonietta Voices, dir. Terry Edwards.
Title: (Javanese) - 'Curtain' (projection-curtain for Wayang shadow-puppet plays).
Text: Javanese traditional.

82 **Free Setting** (1981/95) 8'
solo piano [Composer]
'To Sue Davies.'
Commissioned by London Contemporary Dance Theatre.
fp: 15.10.81 Warwick University. Eleanor Alberga.
fp: (final version) 19.1.96 Holywell Music Room, Oxford. Nicolas Hodges.

83 **Jisei** (1981) 9'
solo cello, flute, oboe, perc, piano, viola [Composer]
fp: 15.9.81 Como, Italy. Alexander Baillie (vc),
Koenig Ensemble, dir. Jan Latham-Koenig.
Title: (Japanese) - 'Aerial spirit'.

84 **Reels** (1980-81/81) 8'
solo piano [UMP]
'To Judith Weir.'
fp: 4.10.81 Guildhall School of Music and Drama, London.
Composer; choreographed and danced by Kris Donovan.
fp: (final version) 30.11.81 composer.
Based on traditional Scottish bagpipe-melodies (piobaireachd).

85 **White Rain** (1981) 5'
solo piano [Composer]
fp: 10.11.88 Surrey University, Guildford. Composer.
Title: from print by Hiroshige.

86 **Duru-Duru** (1981) 9'
mezzo-soprano, flute, perc, piano [Oxford]
'To James and Catia Clarke.'
fp: 21.1.82 Purcell Room, London. Josephine Nendick (mez),
Suoraan, dir. James Clarke.
Title: (Sardinian) - 'Around-around'.
Text: Sardinian folk poem.

87 **Stomp** (1981) 9'
solo piano-accordion [Composer]
'For Mario Conway.'
Commissioned by the Park Lane Group.
fp: 7.1.82 Purcell Room, London. M. Conway.
Title: traditional Jazz term.

88 **Andimironnai** (1981) 9'
solo cello [UMP]
'For Timothy Hugh.'
fp: 24.2.82 St Bartholomew's Festival, London. T. Hugh.
Title: (Sardinian) - one of the formal poetic conventions
of traditional Sardinian verse.

89 **Keroiylu** (1981) 8'
oboe, bassoon, piano [Composer]
Commissioned by the City of London Trio.
fp: 15.1.92 St John's Smith Square, London. City of London Trio:
Gillian Carter (ob), Frances Eustace (bn), Richard Graves (pf).
Title: (Azerbaijan) - heroic folk-dance.

90 **Yalli** (1981) 10'
solo cello [Composer]
fp: 30.3.82 BMIC, London. Alan Brett.
Title: (Kurdish) - folk round-dance.

91 **Terekkeme** (1981/1990) 5'
solo harpsichord or piano [Oxford]
'For Anne de Buck.'
fp: 14.11.91 Purcell Room, London. Jane Chapman (hps).
Title: (Azerbaijan) - lively and impulsive (solo) folk-dance.

92 **Verdi Transcriptions** (1972/92-88/95) 70'
15 Transcriptions and 3 optional fragments, [UMP]
may be performed separately
solo piano
fp: (private) 1.11.86 Finsbury Park, London. Composer (1-9).
fp: (public) 30.6.88 Union Chapel, Almeida Festival, London.
J. Clapperton (1-9, 15); composer (10-14).
fp: (complete with 1995 revisions and fragments)
26.1.96 Conway Hall, London. Ian Pace.
Initially planned in 4 books (one transcription from every Verdi opera).
Book 1: 1-9, Book 2: 10-15. Original versions of 1-7 1972, unperformed, withdrawn. 1982-85: 1-7 reworked; 8 & 9 new (total *c.* 30 mins.).
Book 2 (sketched 1972) 1988 completed 1995 (total *c.* 40 mins.).
Books 3 and 4 never completed. Complete work published in one volume in 1995 with revisions and fragments of 3 further transcriptions.

92.01 **Sciagurata! a questo lido ricercai l'amante infido** (1972/82-85)
Verdi Transcription 1 [UMP]
fp: (private) 1.11.86 Finsbury Park, London. Composer.
fp: (final version) 26.6.87 Middelburg, Netherlands. Composer.
Based on Aria - *Oberto* (Act 2).

92.02 **Bella speranza in vero** (1972/82-85)
Verdi Transcription 2 [UMP]
fp: (private) 1.11.86 Finsbury Park, London. Composer.
Based on Trio - *Un Giorno di Regno* (Act 1).

92.03 **Il maledotto non ha fratelli** (1972/82-85)
Verdi Transcription 3 [UMP]
fp: (private) 1.11.86 Finsbury Park, London. Composer.
Based on Chorus - *Nabucco* (Part 2).

92.04 **Fra tante sciagure...** (1972/82-85)
Verdi Transcription 4 [UMP]
fp: (private) 1.11.86 Finsbury Park, London. Composer.
Based on Chorus - *I Lombardi* (Act 3).

92.05 **Vedi come il buon vegliardo** (1972/82-85)
Verdi Transcription 5 [UMP]
fp: (private) 1.11.86 Finsbury Park, London. Composer.
Based on Septet with Chorus - *Ernani* (Part 1).

92.06 **Tace il vento, e queta l'onda** (1972/82-85)
Verdi Transcription 6 [UMP]
fp: (private) 1.11.86 Finsbury Park, London. Composer.
Based on Choral Barcarolle - *I Due Foscari* (Act 3).

92.07 **So che per via de triboli** (1972/82-85)
Verdi Transcription 7 [UMP]
fp: (private) 1.11.86 Finsbury Park, London. Composer.
Based on Aria - *Giovanna d'Arco* (Act 1).

92.08 **Il pianto...l'angoscia...di lena mi priva** (1982-85)
Verdi Transcription 8 [UMP]
fp: (private) 1.11.86 Finsbury Park, London. Composer.
Based on Aria - *Alzira* (Act 1).

92.09 **Mantre gonfiarsi l'anima** (1982-85)
Verdi Transcription 9 [UMP]
fp: (private) 1.11.86 Finsbury Park, London. Composer.
Based on Aria - *Attila* (Act 1).

92.10 **Me pellegrina ed orfana** (1986-88)
Verdi Transcription 10 [UMP]
fp: 10.11.87 BMIC, London. Composer (with 2 & 3).
Based on Romanza - *La Forza del Destino* (Act 1).

92.11 **S'allontanarno! N'accozzeremo** (1988/95)
Verdi Transcription 11 [UMP]
fp: 30.6.88 Union Chapel, Almeida Festival, London. Composer (with 12-14).
fp: (final version) 26.1.96 Conway Hall, London. Ian Pace.
Based on Chorus - *Macbeth* (Act 1).
Material taken from *Long Distance* (withdrawn).

92.12 **Vanitosi! Che abbietti e dormenti** (1988)
Verdi Transcription 12 [UMP]
fp: 30.6.88 Union Chapel, Almeida Festival, London. Composer (with 11, 13, 14).
Based on Duet - *Attila* (Prologue).

92.12a **Cielo pietoso, rendila a questo core**
Verdi Transcription, fragment a [UMP]
fp: 26.1.96 Conway Hall, London. Ian Pace.
Based on fragment from *Simon Boccanegra* (Act 2).

92.12b **La Traviata**
Verdi Transcription Fragment b [UMP]
fp: 26.1.96 Conway Hall, London. Ian Pace.
Based on music from *La Traviata* (Act 1).

92.12c **Vi fu in Palestina**
Verdi Transcription Fragment c [UMP]
fp: 26.1.96 Conway Hall, London. Ian Pace.
Based on fragment from *Aroldo* (Finale Act 1).

92.13 **O cieli azzuri...** (1988)
Verdi Transcription 13 [UMP]
fp: 30.6.88 Union Chapel, Almeida Festival, London. Composer (with 11, 12, 14).
Based on Romanza - *Aida* (Act 3).

92.14 **Qual mare, qual terra** (1988)
Verdi Transcription 14 [UMP]
fp: 30.6.88 Union Chapel, Almeida Festival, London. Composer (with 11-13).
Based on Duet - *I Masnadieri* (Part 3). Material taken from *Guwark* (withdrawn).

92.15 **Tu che la venita conoscesti** (1981)
Verdi Transcription 15 [UMP]
'To Sally Rettig'
fp: 4.5.82 Oxford Playhouse. Composer.
Based on Aria - *Don Carlo* (Act 5).

92.15 **Rushes** (1981) 18'
Ballet [=Verdi Transcription 15] [UMP]
'To Sally Rettig'
Commissioned by Dance Umbrella.
fp: 4.5.82 Oxford Playhouse. Composer; choreography: Siobhan Davies.

93 **Warara** (1982/91) 9'
soprano, flute, clarinet, percussion, violin, cello [Oxford]
'To Richard and Valérie Hames, Ben, Rachael, Toby and Jessica.'
fp: 29.5.82 Victoria College, Melbourne, Australia.
Victorian Time Machine, dir. Richard David Hames.
[tenor, flute, clarinet, 2 percussion]. fp: (final version) Ixion, dir. Composer.
Title: (Australian Aboriginal) - 'Red Ochre'.
Text: Australian Aboriginal circumcision ritual.

94 **Aijal** (1982) 7'
flute, oboe, percussion [Composer]
'To John Hopkins.'
fp: 18.4.82 Melbourne, Australia. Victoria Time Machine,
dir. Richard David Hames.
Title: (Australian Aboriginal) - 'Sky.'

95 **Banumbirr** (1982/86) 9'
flute, clarinet, piano, violin, cello [UMP]
'To Robert and Merryn Smallwood.'
fp: 16.5.82 University of Melbourne, Australia. K. Duffell (fl), A. Stevenson (cl),
P. Carrington (vn), J. Fletcher (vc), composer (pf), dir. R. Smallwood.
fp: (final version) 22.11.86 Huddersfield Festival. Spectrum, dir. Guy Protheroe.
Title: (Australian Aboriginal) - 'Morning Star'.

96 **Teangi** (1982) 6'
fl(pic), ca, ecl, cl, cbn, 2tpt, perc, vib, cel, vn [Composer]
fp: 28.5.94 Royal Academy of Music, London.
Manson Ensemble, dir. Composer.
Title: (Australian Aboriginal) - 'Flowering Earth'.
Originally entitled *Tya*.

97 **Marrngu** (1982) 8'
solo E flat clarinet [Composer]
'To Lawrence Dobell.'
fp: 28.11.94 Brighton Festival. Andrew Smith.
Title: (Australian Aboriginal) - mythical possum.

98 **Nasiye** (1982/AR) 8'
solo guitar [Composer]
'To Gerald Garcia.'
fp: 22.10.82 Royal Tunbridge Wells, Kent. G. Garcia.
Title: (Kurdish) - folk-dance.

99 **Mississippi Hornpipes** (1982/97) 10'
piano, violin [Composer]
'For Roger Garland.'
fp: 27.1.83 BMIC, London. Roger Garland (vn), composer (pf).
fp (final version): 1.5.97 BMIC, London. Rebecca van der Post (vn), Ian Pace (pf).
Revised version has different first page.

100 **Dilok** (1982) 10'
oboe, percussion [UMP]
'For Christopher Redgate and John Harrod.'
fp: 21.6.83 Melbourne, Australia. C. Redgate (ob), Paul Sarcich (perc).
Title: (Kurdish) - 'dance music' or 'entertainment music'.

101 **Gerhana** (1981-82) 12'
solo percussion [Composer]
'For James Wood.'
fp: 19.11.82 Royal Tunbridge Wells, Kent. James Wood.
Title: (Javanese) - 'Blessed by the Gods'.

102 **Anninnia** (1981-82) 11'
soprano, piano [Composer]
'For Elaine Barry.'
fp: 27.11.85 Huddersfield Festival. Jane Manning (sop), David Mason (pf).
Title: (Sardinian) - 'Lullaby'.Text: Sardinian folk poetry.

103 **Independence Quadrilles** (1982/83/86/88/95) 8'
piano trio: piano, violin, cello. Independent parts. [Composer]
'To Andrew Toovey.'
fp: (1983 version) 1983 Ensemble Exposé ob, pf, vn, vc.
fp: (1986 version) 9.86 Pittsburg USA, fl, ob, pf.
fp: (1988 version) 28.5.88 Brighton Festival. Isabelle Carré (fl), John Rayson (va), James Clapperton (pf).
Original version (1982): pf, vn, vc (not independent parts).
Final version, unperformed (1996).

104 **Cirit** (1982) 8'
solo C clarinet [Composer]
'For Philip Edwards.'
Commisssioned by Philip Edwards.
fp: 6.12.82 Purcell Room, London.
Title: (Kurdish) - dance of warriors.

105 **Whitman** (1980-83/AR)
[Composer]
fp: (1st version) 8.3.93 Purcell Room, London. J Nendick (mez), Suoraan.
fp: (2nd version) 19.5.83 BMIC, London. Jane Ginsburg (sop), George Nicholson (pf).
Two earlier versions (1st for mezzo-soprano, fl(afl), ob(ca,oda), perc; 2nd for voice and piano) withdrawn.

106 **Uzundara** (1983) 9'
solo clarinet [Composer]
'For Robert Schuck.'
fp: 28.4.83 BMIC, London. R. Schuck.

107 **Ouraa** (1982-83) 9'
pic, cl, bsn, hn, tpt, tbn, perc, vn, va, vc, db [Composer]
fp: 2.2.86 Almeida Theatre, London.
Music Projects/London, dir. Richard Bernas.
Title: (Australian Aboriginal) - 'Wood'.

108 **Sepevi** (1982-83) 9'
solo double bass [Composer]
'For Bert Turetzky.'
fp: 1995 or 96, Corrado Canonici.
Title: (Azerbaijan) - folk-dance in triple time.

109.1 **Vaudeville** (1983/87) 45'
Version 1 [UMP]
mezzo, bar, cl, bn, flugelhorn, tbn, perc, vn, db, 2 dancers
'To Oliver Knussen.'
Commissioned by the Vale of Glamorgan Festival.
fp: 30.8.83 Vale of Glamorgan Festival. Mary King (mez), John Rath (bar), Music Projects/London, dir. Richard Bernas.
Text: Walt Whitman, nursery rhymes, H. M. Milner, George Cooper, Pedro Calderón de la Barca.
Published version.

109.2 **Vaudeville** (1983/87) 22'
Version 2 [UMP]
mezzo, bar, cl, bn, flugelhorn, tbn, perc, vn, db
fp: 30.6.87 Almeida Festival. Susan Bickley (mez), Quentin Hayes (bar), Ensemble, dir. Oliver Knussen.
Text: Walt Whitman, nursery rhymes, George Cooper, Pedro Calderón de la Barca..
Shortened version: scene 3 recomposed (Romeo & Juliet - based on Bellini 'I Capuleti e i Montecchi'), and scene 6 trimmed.

110 **Le Lay de la Fonteinne** (1983/90) 22'
Guillaume de Machaut, arranged and edited by Michael Finnissy [Oxford]
soprano, fl(pic), oboe, vib or pf
fp: 29.10.83 Purcell Room, London. Suoraan.
fp: (final version) 9.6.90, Greenwich Festival.
Virginia de Ledesma (sop), Focus, dir. Composer.

111 **Ulpirra** (1982-83) 4'
solo bass flute [Composer]
'For Nancy Ruffer.'
fp: 18.6.83 Purcell Room, London. N. Ruffer.
Title: (Australian Aboriginal) - 'Token of friendship.'

112 **Hikkai** (1982-83) 5'
solo piano [Composer]
fp: 11.9.83 Sydney University, Australia. Composer.
Title: (Australian Aboriginal) - 'Immediately!'

113 **Botany Bay** (1983/89) 4'
mezzo-soprano, flute, oboe or clarinet [Composer]
fp: 1.10.83 Ballarat, Victoria, Australia. Jeannie Marsh (mez), Rachele Skinner (fl), Jane Robertson (cl).
fp: (final version) 18.5.89 BMIC, London. Ixion (version with clarinet).
Text: based on an Australian colonial folk-song.

114.1 **Australian Sea Shanties Set 1** (1983) 9'
Shanties 1, 2 & 3 [UMP]
SAB amateur choir
'For Caulfield City Choir.'
fp: 22.7.84 Copenhagen, Denmark. Pegasus, dir. Richard Crossland.
Text: traditional, arranged by composer.

114.2 **Australian Sea Shanties Set 2** (1983) 6'
Shanties 4 & 1 [Oxford]
solo piano
fp: 20.11.83 Murrumbeena, Victoria, Australia. Composer.

114.3 **Australian Sea Shanties Set 3** (1983) 6'
Shanties 4 & 3 [Composer]
3- and 4-part recorder consort. Unperformed (1996).

115 **The Eureka Flag** (1983) 4'
solo piccolo [Composer]
'For Derek Jones.'
fp: 17.6.84 Melbourne University, Australia. D. Jones.
Title: Australian flag of independence (16th century).

116 **Soda Fountain** (1983) 20'
soprano, mezzo-soprano, contralto, tenor [Composer]
'For Victoria Watson, Sandra Oldis, Jeannie Marsh & Christopher Bogg.'
fp: 23.3.84 Victoria College, Melbourne, Australia.
V. Watson (sop), S. Oldis (mez), J. Marsh (alt), C. Bogg (ten).
Title: O. Wilde, A. C. Doyle, Giesecke, Schikaneder, Illica, Wagner, E. Bronte, Haym, J. Austen, Shilovsky, M. Tchaikovsky, Condinet/Gille, Shakespeare.

117 **Ngano** (1983-84) 18'
mezzo-soprano, tenor, double SATB chorus, flute, 2 percussion [UMP]
Commissioned by the BBC.
fp: 12.6.84 QEH, London. J. Bingham (mez), N. Mackenzie (ten), BBC Singers, S. Bell, J. Holland, D. Johnson, dir. Diego Masson.
Title: (Venda) - evening song. Text: traditional Venda.

118 **Câtana** (1984) 16'
fl, ob, cl, perc, pf, hp, vn, va, vc [UMP]
fp: 8.3.85 Wyndham School, Egremont, Cumbria.
Uroboros Ensemble, dir. Composer.
Title: (Rumanian) - 'Chain'.

119 **Haiyim** (1984) 15'
SATB chorus (minimum 12 voices), 2 cellos [UMP]
fp: 14.11.85 Rosslyn Hill, London. BBC Singers, dir. Simon Joly.
Title: (Hebrew) - 'Peace'.
Text: from Psalms 24, 23, 6, 133, 19, 122 (in Hebrew).

120 **Delal** (1984/88) 9'
oboe d'amore, percussion [Composer]
Commissioned by Jonathan Impett.
fp: 29.11.84 Purcell Room, London. Jonathan Impett (tpt), Michael Blake (pf).
fp: (final version) 12.8.88 Speier Cathedral, Germany.
Christopher Redgate (oboe d'amore), Elizabeth Davis (perc).
Title: (Kurdish) - 'courtly', 'art' or 'beautiful' music.
Original version for trumpet and (closed) piano.
Final version intended to form a pair with *Dilok*.

121 **Lyrics and Limericks** (1982-84) 10'
voice, piano [Composer]
'To Jeannie Marsh.'
fp: 6.6.85 BMIC, London. Sue Anderson (mez), composer (pf).
Title: Ten songs arranged as an acrostic on Edward Lear's name.
(The songs may not be performed separately.)

122 **Two Teaching Pieces** (1984) 2'
solo piano [Oxford]
'For Sally Retting.'
fp: 21.5.91 BMIC, London. Composer.

123 **Celi** (1984/97) 15'
2 sopranos, 2 ecl, trb, 3va [UMP]
original version, 2 high sopranos, flute, oboe, trombone, percussion, double bass
fp: 24.10.85 IRCAM, Paris, France. Penelope Walmsley-Clarke,
Sarah Leonard (sop), Ensemble Intercontemporain, dir. Ronald Zollman.
Title: (Latin) - 'Of Heaven'.
Text: Hildegard of Bingen (in Latin).

124 **String Quartet** (1984) 20'
string quartet: 2 violins, viola, cello [UMP]
'For the Arditti Quartet.'
Commissioned by the Arditti Quartet.
fp: 21.11.85 Huddersfield Festival.

125 **Cabaret Vert** (1985) 10'
mezzo-soprano, flute, cor anglais, percussion [Composer]
fp: 11.5.85 ORTF, Paris, France. J. Nendick (mez), N. Ruffer (fl),
J. Harrod (perc), C. Redgate (ob), dir. Roger Redgate.
Title: from poem by Rimbaud (French) - 'Green Inn Cabaret'.
All poems refer to the colour green. Text: Rumanian folk poetry.

126 **'above earth's shadow...'** (1985) 18'
solo violin, fl/picc, cl, vln, vla, vcl, db [UMP]
fp: 22.11.85 Huddersfield Festival. Irvine Arditti (vn),
Spectrum, dir. Guy Protheroe.
Title: from William Blake 'The Marriage of Heaven and Hell'.
Material taken from *Long Distance* (withdrawn).

127 **East London Heys** (1985-86)
3 Sets (Total of 9 separate pieces) [UMP]

127.1 **East London Heys** (1985-86) 20'
Version 1: 9 pieces [UMP]
strings: nos. 1-5: 2vn, 2vc; nos 6-7 2vn, 2va, 2vc; nos. 8-9: 3vn, 3va, 3vc.
'Written for the East London Late Starters' Orchestra.'
fp: July 1986, Bishop Challoner School, East London.
East London Late Starters' Orchestra (nos. 4 & 8).
In no. 9, 3rd vn, 3 va and 3rd vc play on open strings only.

127.2 **East London Heys** (1985-86) 10'
Version 2: 6 pieces: 1-5 & 8 [UMP]
string quartet: 2 violins, viola, cello
fp: private performance: Sheffield.

127.3 **East London Heys** (1985-86) 12'
Version 3: 4 pieces: 1,2,5 & 8 [UMP]
wind quintet: fl, ob, cl, bn, hn.
fp: 1988, Barbican Foyer, London. including Colin Honour (cl),
Joseph Saunders (ob).

128 **G.F.H./B.S.** (1985-86) 4'
2 pieces: may be performed together or separately [Oxford]
solo piano

128.1 **G.F.H.** (1985) 2'
solo piano [Oxford]
'For the Handel Tercentenary.'
fp: 17.12.85 BMIC, London. Composer.
Title: G[eorge] F[rederick] H[andel].
Based on a quotation from Handel's Trio Sonata Op. 1, no. 1.
For New Music 87 (Oxford, 1987, p.58-9).

128.2 **B.S.** (1985-86) 2'
solo piano [Oxford]
'In memory of Bernard Stevens.'
fp: 3.3.86 BMIC, London. Composer.
Title: B[ernard] S[tevens].

129 **Contretänze** (1985/1986) 17'
fl, ob, cl, perc, vln, vc [UMP]
'To Tom Morgan.'
Commissioned by Elms Concerts for Circle.
fp: 1.2.86 Almeida Theatre, London. Circle, dir. Gregory Rose.
fp: (final version) 18.7.86 Darmstadt, Germany. Ensemble Exposé.
Revised version has an additional Ländler section.

130 **Taja** (1986) 5'
solo piano [Oxford]
fp: 29.1.87 BMIC, London. Robert Keeley.
Title: (Sardinian) - tenor part in Sardinian religious music.

131 **Two Teaching Pieces** (1986) 2'
solo piano [Oxford]
'For Rachel Resnik.'
fp: 21.5.91 BMIC, London. Composer.

132 **String Trio** (1986) 30'
string trio: violin, viola, cello [UMP]
Commissioned by the Gagliano Trio.
fp: 30.10.86 Royal Tunbridge Wells, Kent. Gagliano Trio.
Based on material from Mahler, Symphony No. 9.

133 **Catchpenny Rhymes** (1986/89/AR) [Composer]
fp: (second version) 13.5.89 Brighton Festival. Mary Wiegold (sop), Composers Ensemble, dir. Composer.
Text: Traditional English nursery rhymes.
Two earlier versions (1st: 9 songs for voice and piano; 2nd: songs 2, 3, & 9, for soprano, viola and cello) withdrawn.

134 **Dust in the Road** (1985-88) 12' 30"
fl, ob, cl, 2 perc, vn, va, vc [Oxford]
fp: 11.12.88 BBC TV. Producer: Barrie Gavin.
Material identical to scene 12 of original version of 'The Undivine Comedy'.

135 **The Undivine Comedy** (1985-88/95) 114'
Opera in 17 scenes [Oxford]
sop, mez, ten, 2bar, 2fl(pic,afl), 2ob(ca), cl(ecl,bcl), 2perc, elec org(cel), vn, va, vc
fp: 14.5.88 Theatre de la Bastille, Paris, France. Pauline Vaillancourt, Mary King, Nigel Robson, Richard Jackson, Richard Morris, Ensemble Exposé, dir. Composer.
Text: composer, after the play by Z. Krasinski, with additional material from Hölderlin 'Der Töd des Empedokles' & Marquis de Sade 'La Philosophie dans le boudoir'.
Revised version involves substantial changes to scenes 1, 3, 4, 7, 11, 12, 14 & 16; instrumentation 2pic, 2ob, 2perc, vn, vla, vc. Revised version unperformed (1996).

136 **Gershwin Arrangements** (1975-1988) 40'
13 pieces: may be performed separately [Oxford]
solo piano
fp: first complete performance, 30.6.88 Union Chapel, Almeida Festival, London. Composer (nos. 1,5,7,9-13), James Clapperton (nos. 1-4, 6 & 8).
2 Books: 1-7; 8-13. Based on songs by George Gershwin.

136.01 **How long has this been going on?** (1987) 3'
Gershwin Arrangements 1 [Oxford]
'For John Flinders.'
fp: 26.6.87 Middelburgh Festival, Netherlands. Composer
From *Rosalie* (1928).

136.02 **Things are looking up** (1987) 3'
Gershwin Arrangements 2 [Oxford]
'To John Flinders.'
fp: 1.5.87 The Place, London. Composer (with 3, 5, 7).
From *Damsel in Distress* (1937).

136.03 **A Foggy Day in London Town** (1987) 3'
Gershwin Arrangements 3 [Oxford]
'To John Flinders.'
fp: 1.5.87 The Place, London. Composer (with 2, 5 & 7).
From *Damsel in Distress* (1937).

136.04 **Love is here to stay** (1987) 4'
Gershwin Arrangements 4 [Oxford]
'To John Flinders.'
fp: 10.77 Freiburg-im-Breisgau, Germany. Composer.
fp: (final version) 26.6.87 Middelburg Festival, Netherlands. Composer.
From *Goldwyn Follies* (1938). Original version (*c.* 2 mins.)
was revised by adding an introduction.

136.05 **They can't take that away from me** (1987) 4'
Gershwin Arrangements 5 [Oxford]
'To John Flinders.'
fp: 1.5.87 The Place, London. Composer (with 2, 3 & 7).
From *Shall we Dance?* (1937).

136.06 **Shall we dance?** (1987) 3'
Gershwin Arrangements 6 [Oxford]
'To John Flinders.'
fp: 30.6.88 Union Chapel, Almeida Festival, London. James Clapperton.
From *Shall we Dance?* (1937).

136.07 **They're writing songs of love, but not for me** (1985) 3'
Gershwin Arrangements 7 [Oxford]
'To John Flinders.'
fp: 1.5.87 The Place, London. Composer (with 2, 3 & 5).
From *Girl Crazy* (1930).

136.08 **Fidgety Feet** (1987) 2'
Gershwin Arrangements 8 [Oxford]
'To Philip Adams.'
fp: 10.11.87 BMIC, London. Composer (with 1-7 & 11).
From *Oh, Kay!* (1926).

136.09 **Embraceable You** (1987-88) 3'
Gershwin Arrangements 9 [Oxford]
'To Beatrice Cockburn on her first birthday.'
fp: 30.6.88 Union Chapel, Almeida Festival, London. Composer
(with nos. 1, 5, 7, 10-13).
From *Girl Crazy* (1930).

136.10 **Waiting for the sun to come out** (1987) 3'
Gershwin Arrangements 10 [Oxford]
'To Anne Bolger.'
fp: 30.6.88 Union Chapel, Almeida Festival, London. Composer (with 1, 5, 7, 9, 11-13).
From *The Sweetheart Shop* (1920).

136.11 **Innocent Ingénue Baby** (1987) 4'
Gershwin Arrangements 11 [Oxford]
'To Peter Kite.'
fp: 10.11.87 BMIC, London. Composer (with 1-8).
From *Our Nell* (1922) Gershwin/William Daly.

136.12 **Blah, blah, blah** (1988) 2'
Gershwin Arrangements 12 [Oxford]
'To Pierre Audi.'
fp: 30.6.88 Union Chapel, Almeida Festival, London. Composer (with 1, 5, 7, 9-11, 13).
From *Delicious* (1931).

136.13 **Boy Wanted** (1988) 3'
Gershwin Arrangements 13 [Oxford]
(No dedication)
fp: 30.6.88 Union Chapel, Almeida Festival, London. Composer (with 1, 5, 7, 9-12).
From *A Dangerous Maid* (1921).

137 **Red Earth** (1987-88) 21'
3(pic)303/0330/2didjeridus/4perc, 2timp/2hp/strings [Oxford]
'To Barrie Gavin.'
Commissioned by the BBC.
fp: 2.8.88 Royal Albert Hall, London. BBC SO, dir. Lothar Zagrosek. BBC Henry Wood Promenade Concert.

138 **Quabara** (1988) 9'
didjeridu, percussion [Oxford]
fp: 14.6.88 Holland Festival, Netherlands. Barrie Webb (didjeridu), Elizabeth Davis (perc).
Title: (Australian Aboriginal) - ceremonial chant.

139 **Beuk o'Newcassel Sangs** (1988) 12'
soprano, clarinet in C, piano [Oxford]
Commissioned by Tapestry.
fp: 16.2.89 Newcastle University. Tapestry.
Text: traditional Newcastle folk-songs, from A beuk o'Newcassel Sangs, collected by Joseph Crawhall (1888).

140 **Lylyly li** (1988-89) 8'
solo piano [Oxford]
'For James Clapperton.'
fp: 15.4.89 Buffalo, NY, USA. James Clapperton.
Title: imitated from Joseph Beuys exhibit in the Landsmuseum, Darmstadt..

141 **Wee Saw Footprints** (1986-90) 15'
A set of nine short, easy teaching pieces [Oxford]
solo piano
fp: 21.5.91 BMIC, London. Composer.

142 **Obrecht Motetten**
5 pieces, may be performed separately [Oxford]
'To Richard Toop.'

142.1 **Obrecht Motetten I** (1988-89) 5'
fl, cl, bsn, tpt, tbn, perc, vn, va, vc [Oxford]
fp: 26.2.89 Amsterdam, Netherlands. Delta Ensemble.
Based on Obrecht's Salve Regina.

142.2 **Obrecht Motetten II** (1988) 12'
mandolin, guitar, harp [Oxford]
fp: 12.3.89 Stowmarket. The Penna Trio.
Based on Obrecht's Ave Regina Caelorum.

142.3 **Obrecht Motetten III** (1989) 12'
solo viola, fl, ob, cl, bn, hn, tpt, trb, perc, 2vn, vc, db [Oxford]
fp: 28.1.96 ICA, London. Rachel Stott (va), Cambridge New Music Players.
Based on Obrecht's Salve Regina and Ave Regina Caelorum. Solo viola part performable separately.

142.3 **Obrecht Motetten III** (1989) 12'
viola [Oxford]
fp: 22.5.93 Brighton. John Metcalf.
Solo viola part of Obrecht Motetten III.

142.4 **Obrecht Motetten IV** (1990) 10'
brass quintet: horn, 2 trumpets, trombone, tuba [Oxford]
fp: 17.7.90 Fitzwilliam Museum, Cambridge. Fine Arts Brass Ensemble.
Based on Obrecht's Salve Regina and Ave Regina Caelorum.

142.5 **Obrecht Motetten V** (1991-92) 15'
fl(pic), 3ssax, 3tpts, 3tbn, pf, db [Oxford]
fp: 15.3.92 Utrecht. Orkest de Volharding, dir. Cess van Zeeland.
Based on Obrecht's Salve Regina and Ave Regina Caelorum.

143 **Eph-phatha** (1988-89) 13'
2111/1110/perc/hrp/pf strings (3.3.3.3.1) [Oxford]
Commissioned by the New English Orchestra.
fp: 2.5.89 Northampton. New English Orchestra, dir. Nigel Swinford.
Title: (Greek) - 'Be Opened' (St Mark).

144 **Judith Weir: Songs from the Exotic (on the rocks) 4 songs** (1989) 10'
[Composer]
soprano, clarinet, piano
fp: 4.5.89 Crawford Arts Centre, St Andrews, Fife. Tapestry.
Text: Tradtional Serbian, Spanish and Gaelic.
Composer added clarinet part to an earlier composition by Judith Weir for mezzo-soprano & piano. Also transposed up to soprano range.

145 **Nowhere else to go** (1989/AR) 30'
cl, tpt, perc, synth, cello, tape, electronics [Oxford]
Independent parts, no score
Commissioned by Metanoia.
fp: 29.3.89 St John's Smith Square. Metanoia.

146 **Pimmel** (1988-89) 4'
solo piano [Oxford]
'For Chris Newman.'
fp: 4.11.89 Gonville & Caius College, Cambridge. Nicolas Hodges.
Title: (German child's slang) - 'Penis'.

147 **Stanley Stokes, East Street 1836** (1989/94) 3'
solo piano [Oxford]
fp (first version): 15.7.89 BMIC, London. Composer.
fp (final version): 4.10.96 Conway Hall, London. Ian Pace.
Title: after persecuted Brighton homosexual.
Based on Dies Irae from Berlioz's 'Grande Messe des Morts'.

148 **Ének** (1990) 9'
solo violin [Oxford]
Commissioned by The Carl Flesch Violin Competition.
fp: 6.90, London. Maxim Vengerov.
Title: (Hungarian) - 'Voice'
Test piece for first round of 1990 competition.

149 **More Gershwin** (1989-90) 32'
8 arrangements: may be performed separately [Oxford]
solo piano
'For Joanna MacGregor.'
fp: 10 May 1990, BMIC, London. Composer.
Based on songs by George Gershwin.

149.1 **Limehouse Nights** (1989) 3'
More Gershwin 1 [Oxford]
'For Joanna MacGregor.'
From *Morris Gest Midnight Whirl* (1919).

149.2 **Wait a bit, Susie** (1989) 3'
More Gershwin 2 [Oxford]
'For Joanna MacGregor.'
From *Primrose* (1924).

149.3 **I'd Rather Charleston** (1989) 4'
More Gershwin 3 [Oxford]
'For Joanna MacGregor.'
From *Lady be Good* (1926).

149.4 **Isn't It Wonderful!** (1989) 5'
More Gershwin 4 [Oxford]
'For Joanna MacGregor.'
From *Primrose* (1924).

149.5 **Nobody but You** (1989) 3'
More Gershwin 5 [Oxford]
'For Emma Slade and Jonathan Cross, on their engagement.'
From *Sweet Little Devil* (1924).

149.6 **Swanee** (1989) 3'
More Gershwin 6 [Oxford]
'Friedrich Hommel-zum 60ste Geburtstag.'
From *Capitol Theatre Review/Demi-Tasse* (1919).

149.7 **Someone Believes in You** (1989) 3'
More Gershwin 7 [Oxford]
'For Neil Brown - on his 21st Birthday.'
From *La, la Lucille* (1919).

149.8 **Nashville Nightingale** (1990) 5'
More Gershwin 8 [Oxford]
'For Andrew Worton-Steward.'
From *Nifties of 1923*.

150 **Unknown Ground** (1989-90) 25'
baritone, piano, violin, cello [Oxford]
fp: 15.5.90 Marlborough Pub Theatre, Brighton. Richard Jackson (bar), Roger Redgate (vn), Julia Ryder (vc), composer (pf).
Text: anon: Nick W.; Steve R.; Philip X.; Brent T.; Nicolai Kluyev; Mikhail Kuzmin; Sergei Esenin (in English).

151 **Sometimes I...** (1990) 3'
solo piano [Oxford]
'For Geoffrey Hannan.'
fp: 10.5.90 Winchester. Geoffrey Hannan.
Title: from Negro Spiritual 'Sometimes I feel like a motherless child'.
Written for Children in Need charity concert.

152 **Can't Help Lovin' Dat Man** (1990) 10'
solo piano [Oxford]
'To Joanna MacGregor.'
fp: 1990 BBC early evening concert. Joanna MacGregor.
Arrangement of song from 'Showboat' by Jerome Kern.

153 **Two of Us** (1990) 2'
solo piano [Composer]
'For Aki Takahashi.'
fp: 1990 Buffalo, USA. Aki Takahashi.
Arrangement of song by Lennon & McCartney.

154 **Same as we**
2 versions

154.1 **Same as we** (1990) 10'
Version 1 soprano, pre-recorded tape. [Oxford]
'For Juliet Oppenheimer.'
fp: 10.8.90 Dartington, Devon. Juliet Oppenheimer.
Text: James Joyce: Finnegans Wake.

154.2 **Same as we** (1990) 10'
Version 2 [Oxford]
mezzo-soprano, alto flute, cimbalom
'For Elise, Anne and Mikael.'
fp: 1990 Flanders Festival, Ghent, Belgium.
Zivitar.

155 **Maldon** (1990) 20'
baritone, SATB chorus, 2 trombones, 2 percussion, organ [Oxford]
fp: 15.6.91 Maldon Millennium festivities.
Text: composer, from 'The Battle of Maldon' (anon/Anglo-Saxon).

156 **Kulamen Dilan** (1990) 10'
soprano saxophone, percussion [Oxford]
'For Steve [Cottrell] and Liz [Davis].'
fp: 21.7.90 Darmstadt, Germany. Steve Cottrell (ssax), Steven Schick (perc).
Title: (Kurdish) - 'Love Songs'.

157 **In Stiller Nacht** (1990/96-97) 11'
piano trio: piano, violin, cello [Oxford]
'To Amelia and Barry Mills.'
fp: 17.9.90 QEH, London. The Bekova Sisters.
fp (final version): 18.11.97 Royal Academy of Music, London. Manson Ensemble.
Based on Brahms' folk-song arrangement of the same name.
Revised version has independent parts; no score.

158 **My Love Is Like a Red Red Rose** (1990) 3'
solo piano [Oxford]
'To Philip [Adams].'
Title: afer Burns poem of same name.

159 **De toutes flours** (1990) 4'
solo piano [Oxford]
'For Philip [Adams].'
Based on Machaut work of same name.

160 **How dear to me** (1991) 3'
solo piano [Oxford]
'For P[hilip Adams].'
From 'The Irish Song Book' Air No. 37 (1895).

161 **William Billings** (1990) 4'
solo piano [Oxford]
'For James Clapperton's 22nd Birthday.'
fp: 27.1.91 Maastricht, Netherlands. James Clapperton.

162 **Vanèn** (1991) 3'
solo piano [Oxford]
'For Frits and Nanny Vanèn.'
fp: 3.2.91 Hilversum, Netherlands. Composer.

163 **Rossini** (1991) 3'
solo piano [Oxford]
'To Father Gordon O' Loughlin.'
fp: 18.2.93 BMIC, London. Ian Pace.
Based on Idreno's Aria 'E se ancor libero' - Semiramide Act I.

164 **WAM** (1990-91) 15'
piano and two obbligato instruments: treble & bass. [Oxford]
3 separate parts, no score.
Commissioned by Het Trio.
fp: 29.2.92 Brighton. Ixion (pf, vn, vc).
Title: W[olfgang] A[madeus] M[ozart].

165 **The Cambridge Codex** (1991) 18'
soprano, fl(picc), perc(2 bells), violin, cello [Oxford]
Commissioned by the Cambridge New Music Players.
fp: 13.11.91 University Concert Hall, Cambridge.
Cambridge New Music Players.
Text: Medieval anonymous sacred poems (in Latin and English).

166 **Seven Sacred Motets** (1991) 38'
SATB chorus (or 4 solo voices) [Oxford]
'For Philip Adams.'
fp: 24.9.91 Warsaw Autumn Festival, Poland. BBC Singers (No. 2 only).
Cycle telling the life of the Virgin. Complete cycle unperformed (1996).

166.1 **Hymnos sacrae quos virgini** (1991) 5'
Seven Sacred Motets 1 [Oxford]
Text: St Bede (in Latin).

166.2 **In mense autem sexto** (1991) 7'
Seven Sacred Motets 2 [Oxford]
Text: St Luke 1 (in Latin).

166.3 **Salve Regina** (1991) 4'
Seven Sacred Motets 3 [Oxford]
Text: attributed to Aimar, Bishop of Le Puy (in Latin).

166.4 **Et cum factus esset** (1991) 4'
Seven Sacred Motets 4 [Oxford]
Text: St Luke 2 (in Latin).

166.5 **Ave regina coelorum** (1991) 5'
Seven Sacred Motets 5 [Oxford]

166.6 **Stabant autem iuxta crucem** (1991) 4'
Seven Sacred Motets 6 [Oxford]
Text: St John 19 (in Latin).

166.7 **O Virga, floriditatem tuam** (1991) 6'
Seven Sacred Motets 7 [Oxford]
Text: Hildegard von Bingen (in Latin).

167 **Three Motets, Two Interludes** (1991) 16'
soprano, violin, viola, cello [Oxford]
Interludes for string trio alone, (*c.* 4') unfinished.

167.1 **O quam glorifica luce** (1991) 4'
Motet No. 1 of Three Motets, Two Interludes [Oxford]
soprano, viola
fp: 20.7.91 Cheltenham Festival. Mary Wiegold (sop), Kate Wilkinson (va).
Title: first line of text.
Text: anonymous 12th century hymn (in Latin).

167.2 **Videtis enim interiorem** (1991) 4'
Motet No. 2 of Three Motets, Two Interludes [Oxford]
soprano, violin
fp: 12.6.91 BMIC, London. Nicola Walker Smith (sop), Charles Mutter (vn).
Title: first line of text 'Thus you see the inner [power]'.
Text: Hildegard von Bingen (in Latin).
See also first of Two Motets, 1991.

167.3 **Iam mea certa manent** (1991) 4'
Motet No. 3 of Three Motets, Two Interludes [Oxford]
soprano, cello
fp: 9.91 Amsterdam, Netherlands.
Title: first line of text.
Text: anon. (in Latin).

168 **Anima Christi** (1991) 20'
counter-tenor or contralto, tenor, SATB chorus, organ [Oxford]
'For Philip [Adams].'
fp: 17.4.92 Brighton. Sussex Philharmonic Chorus, dir. Jonathan Cross.
Text: Medieval sacred poem (in Latin).

169 **Two Motets** (1991) 8'
may be performed separately [Oxford]
counter-tenor, guitar
fp: 8.1.92 Purcell Room, London. Jonathan Peter Kenny (ctn), Steve Gibb (gui).

169.1 **Videtis enim interiorem** (1991) 4'
Two Motets 1 [Oxford]
counter-tenor, guitar
Text: Hildegard von Bingen (in Latin).
Arrangement of Motet No. 2 of Three Motets, Two Interludes.

169.2 **Ave Maria** (1991) 4'
Two Motets 2 [Oxford]
counter-tenor, guitar
Text: (in Sardinian).
Arrangement of 3rd of Seven Sacred Motets with new text.

170 **There never were such hard times before** (1991) 2'
solo piano [Oxford]
'In memory of Cornelius Cardew.'
fp: 13.12.91 Purcell Room, London. Composer.
Based on English folk-song of same name.

171 **French Piano** (1991) 6'
solo piano [Oxford]
'For Lesley Young.'
fp: 1995, BMIC, London. Michael Blake.
Title: After Chris Newman drawing of same name.

172 **Willow Willow** (1991) 2'
solo piano [Oxford]
'For Philip [Adams].'
Based on English folk-song of same name.

173 **Nine Romantics** (1992) 25'
solo piano [Oxford]
'For Rolf Hind.'
fp: 1.5.92 Aarhus, Denmark. Rolf Hind.
Bears no relation to withdrawn work with same title.

174 **New Perspectives on Old Complexity** (1990/92) 5'
solo piano [Oxford]
'For Perspectives of New Music.'
fp: 21.4.94 BMIC, London. Ian Pace.
Based on Sanctus super 'Da gaudiorum premia' - John Dunstable; Contrapunctus I (Die Kunst der Fuge) - J. S. Bach; Je tremble en voyant ton visage (Le Promenoir des Deux Amants) - Claude Debussy.
The original central section appeared (1990) in an anthology published for the 'Complexity?' conference in Rotterdam. Whole piece published in *Perspectives of New Music*, Vol. 31, No. 1, 1993.

175 **Cibavit eos** (1991) 3'
solo piano [Oxford]
'For *The Musical Times* Mozart Issue.'
fp: 3.12.91 Sussex University, Brighton. Composer.
Based on Mozart's antiphon of same name, K. 44 (73u).
Published in *The Musical Times*, 1992.

176 **Poor Stuff** (1991-92/96) 2'
solo piano [Oxford]
in preparation

177 **Wenn wir in höchsten Nöthen sind** (1992) 4'
solo piano [Oxford]
fp: 1.10.92 BMIC, London. Nicolas Hodges.
Based on the Chorale-Prelude by J S Bach BWV. 668.

178 **The Cry of the Prophet Zephaniah** (1992) 7'
solo baritone, TB men's choir, 2 tpt, 2 trb, 2 vc. [Oxford]
Commissioned by BBC TV for series 'The Cry'.
fp: 6.12.92 BBC TV. Producer: Chris Mann.
Text: Book of Zephaniah.

179 **Various Nations** (1992) 12'
narrator, fl(pic), cl, hn, perc, gtr, vn, vc [Oxford]
Commissioned by Almeida Opera.
fp: 9.7.92 Almeida Theatre, London. Eleanor Bron (spkr), Music Projects/London, dir. R. Bernas.
Text: from 19th century children's book 'A Peep at Various Nations of the World'.

180 **A solis ortus cardine** (1992) 2'
solo piano [Oxford]
'In memory of Olivier Messiaen.'
fp: 1992 Bratislava. Composer.

181 **Thérèse Raquin** (1992-93/97) 90'
soprano, mezzo-soprano, counter tenor, baritone, piano [Oxford]
Commissioned by The Garden Venture & Eastern Arts.
fp: 1.10.93 Bury St Edmunds. Royal Opera House Garden Venture. Heather Lorimer, Linda Hirst, Andrew Watts, Richard Jackson, Christopher Willis.
Text: composer, after the novel and play by Emile Zola.
Work was revised several times during first production.
1997 revision contains several minor modifications, mainly to Scene 1.

182 **Blessed be**
3 Versions [Oxford]

182.1 **Blessed be** (1992) 3'
Version 1 [Oxford]
soprano, piano, double bass
Commissioned by Kathleen Supové for The Political Songbook.
fp: 1993 Bang On A Can Festival, New York, USA.
D. Ohrenstein (sop), K. Supové (pf), R. Black (db).
Text: St Matthew.

182.2 **Blessed be** (1995) 5'
Version 2 [Oxford]
tenor, flute, horn, guitar, harp, cello
'To Gerald English.'
fp: unperformed (1996).

182.3 **Blessed be** (1996)
Version 3 [Oxford]
soprano, recorder, piano.
fp: 26.10.96 Wilmslow Parish Hall. Alison Wells, John Turner, Keith Swallow.

183 **John Cage** (1992) 2'
solo piano [Oxford]
'In Memory of John Cage.'
fp: 1992 Dartington Summer School. Composer.
Based on fragment of music by Grieg and Satie.

184 **Cozy Fanny's Tootsies** (1992) 2'
solo piano [Oxford]
'Christmas Greeting to Friends.'
fp: 10.5.96 Conway Hall, London. Ian Pace.
Based on Mozart's opera 'Cosi Fan Tutti'.

185 **Mars + Venus** (1993) 14'
fl,ob,cl,bn/hn,tpt,tbn/perc(vib)/pf/2vn,va,vc,db [Oxford]
Commissioned by Antwerpen 93.
fp: 25.5.93 Antwerp. Champ d'Action, dir. Composer.
Title: from Rubens painting of same name.

186 **'What the meadow-flowers tell me'** (1993) 3'
solo piano [Oxford]
'A Valentine for Philip [Adams].'
fp: 23.8.93 Seoul, Korea. Composer.
Based on material from Mahler, Symphony No. 3.

187 **Plain Harmony** (1993)
2 versions [Oxford]

187.1 **Plain Harmony** (1993) 10'
Version 1 [Oxford]
free instrumentation
fp: 3.9.93 Wortley Hall, Sheffield. Members of first COMA residential course.
(COMA: Contemporary Music Making for Amateurs.)

187.2 **Plain Harmony** (1993) 8'
Version 2 [Oxford]
string quartet: 2 violins, viola, cello
fp: 6.2.94 New England Conservatory, Boston, Mass. USA. Amaryllis Quartet.
Shortened version of 187.1 with different final section.

188 **Folklore** (1993-94) 72'
in four sections, may be performed separately [Oxford]
solo piano
fp: 1.12.94 BMIC, London. Composer.

188.1 **Folklore 1** (1993-94) 12'
solo piano [Oxford]
'Lovingly and reverently dedicated to Edvard Grieg.'
Commissioned by Salford University.
fp: 20.4.93 University College, Salford. James Clapperton.
Based on Norwegian folk music, Grieg Slätter Op. 72, and piobaireachd.
Includes material from *Sorabji* (withdrawn).

188.2 **Folklore 2** (1993-94) 28'
solo piano [Oxford]
'For Sir Michael Tippett.'
fp: 27.6.94 Sofia, Bulgaria. Composer.
Includes *Haen* and *Let him answer yes or no* (both withdrawn).
Based on piobaireachd, Rumanian, Chinese and English folk music
and Negro spiritual 'Deep River'.

188.3 **Folklore 3** (1993-94/95) 20'
solo piano [Oxford]
'For Brian Ferneyhough on his 50th Birthday.'
fp: 22.10.93 Taipei, Taiwan. Composer.
Includes *Hier J'ai Recontré* (withdrawn). Based on piobaireachd.
French, Serbian and Swedish folk music.

188.4 **Folklore 4** (1993-94) 12'
solo piano [Oxford]
'For Rodney Lister.'
fp: 11.2.94 University of Sussex, Brighton. Composer.
Based on Indian, Korean, Chinese folk music, Rodney Lister 'The Stones', Sousa marches and Negro spiritual 'Deep River'.

189 **Vertue** (1993/AR) 6'
SA female choir, piano [Oxford]
Commissioned by Finchley Children's Music Group.
fp: 28.3.93 Lockers Park School, Hemel Hempstead.
Finchley Children's Music Group, dir. Murray Stewart.
Text: George Herbert.

190 **The larger heart, the kindlier hand** (1993) 1'
solo piano [Oxford]
'In celebration of Justin Connolly's 60th Birthday.'
fp: 14.4.93 BMIC, London. Composer.
Title: from Tennyson poem.

191 **Silver Morning** (1993) 15'
tenor or baritone, piano, violin, cello [Oxford]
Commissioned by South West Arts.
fp: 15.7.95 Cheltenham Festival.
Text: A E Housman.

192 **...desde que naçe** (1993) 1'
solo piano [Oxford]
'For the ISCM World Music Days in Mexico City.'
fp: 22.11.93, Mexico City, Mexico. Composer.
Based on the Villancico 'Los que fueren de buen gusto' by Francisco de Vidales (c. 1630-1702). Published in OUP volume CSPP2.

193 **Yvaroperas** (1993-95) 9'
5 pieces [Oxford]
solo piano
'In memory of Yvar Mikhashoff.'
fp: 10.6.94 (1-4 only) Almeida Theatre, London. Composer.
fp (complete): 4.10.96 Conway Hall, London. Ian Pace.

193.1 **Yvaropera 1** 3'
solo piano [Oxford]

193.2 **Yvaropera 2** 2'
solo piano [Oxford]
Based on 'The Sun, whose rays...' from Arthur Sullivan, *The Mikado*.

193.3 **Yvaropera 3** 2'
solo piano [Oxford]

193.4 **Yvaropera 4** 2'
solo piano [Oxford]
Based on 'Je crois entendre encore' from Bizet, *Les Pêcheurs de Perles*.

193.5 **Yvaropera 5** 2'
solo piano [Oxford]
fp: 22.6.96 Royal College of Music, London.
Based on material from Arthur Sullivan, *Iolanthe.* Included in 'Spectrum' published by ABRSM (1996).

194 **Quelle** (1994) 3'
4 saxophones: 2 soprano, 2 contrabass [Oxford]
'For Thomas K. J. Mejer.'
fp: Recorded but no concert performance (1996).

194 **Elephant** (1994) 2'
solo piano [Oxford]
'For Luk.'
fp: 4.10.96 Conway Hall, London. Ian Pace.

196 **Traum des Sängers** (1994) 15'
cl, gtr, perc (vib), vn, va, vc, db [Oxford]
'For Andrew Toovey.'
Commissioned by The South Bank Arts.
fp: 24.10.94 Purcell Room, London. Ixion.
Title: From Caspar David Friedrich glass-painting of same name.

197 **Shameful Vice** (1994-95) 45'
2 soprano, mezzo-soprano, tenor, baritone, bass, [Oxford]
2 cl, 2 tpt, gtr, hp, 2 vn, db
Commissioned by Vocem Electric Voice Theatre and Endymion.
fp: 28.3.95 Blackheath Concert Halls, London. Vocem; Endymion Ensemble.
Text: Composer, after letters and diaries of Tchaikovsky.

198 **Two Scenes From Shameful Vice** (1995) 6'
solo harp [Oxford]
fp: 10.1.94 Purcell Room, London. Marshall McGuire.
Based on 'Shameful Vice' material from scenes 5, 12 and 13.

199 **Glad Day** (1994) 13'
2 recorders, 2 trumpets, chamber-organ, theorbo or harp, strings. [Oxford]
Commissioned by the BBC.
fp: 15.1.95 Town Hall, Birmingham. King's Consort, dir. Robert King.
Title: from William Blake painting of same name
(sometimes called 'The Rise of Albion').

200 **Sefauchi's Return** (1994) 1'
flute, oboe, clarinet, piano [Oxford]
'For Sounds Positive and The Purcell Tercentenary.'
fp: 8.2.95 St John's Smith Square, London. Sounds Positive.

201 **Ethel Smyth** (1995) 4'
solo piano [Oxford]
fp: 26.10.95 Durham University. Composer.

202 **Liturgy of Saint Paul** (1991-95) 30'
counter tenor, 2 tenors, baritone, chamber organ [Oxford]
fp: 1.8.96 (incomplete) Cambridge. Hilliard Ensemble.
Text: Latin mass. Eusebius, The Acts of the Apostles (in Greek).
Includes *Missa in Commemoratione Sancti Pauli* and *Missa in Festo Conversionis Sancti Pauli* (withdrawn).

203 **Violet, Slingsby, Guy and Lionel** (1994-96) 18'
22 short pieces for beginners and their teachers: [Oxford]
1. A long while ago.
2. They all thought they should like to see the world.
3. For the first ten days they sailed.
4. Violet chiefly occupied herself in putting salt-water into a churn while her brothers churned it violently.
5. A single tree, 503 feet high.
6. Red parrots with blue tails, all fast asleep.
7. Extreme noise made by the Arctic bears.
8. Oranges falling down on their heads.
9. Lionel continued to stand on one leg and whistle to them.
10. They gradually recovered their spirits.
11. Sitting in a great circle slowly eating custard pudding.
12. Copious and rural harmony.
13. A fizzy extraneous utterance.
14. A subdued simultaneous snuffle.
15. Nothing particular occurred.
16. The co-operative cauliflower.
17. On the brink of the western sky.
18. Some wide and deep pits full of mulberry jam.
19. Pursuing their wanderings by land.
20. Four small beans and three pounds of mashed potatoes.
21. A sort of profuse and triumphant procession.
22. As for the rhinoceros....
solo piano
fp: 4.10.96 Conway Hall, London. Ian Pace.
Title: from story by Edward Lear.

204 **Violet, Slingsby, Guy and Lionel** (1995-96) 7'
tuba quartet [Oxford]
fp: 11.1.96 Purcell Room, London. Tubulaté.
Arrangement of sections 14, 15 and 17 from piano piece of same name.

205 **Tracey and Snowy in Köln** (1996) 2'
solo piano [Oxford]
'In memory of Tracey Chadwell'
fp: 14.3.96 Chapel Royal, Brighton. Composer.

206 **Prelude Op. 23 No. 4 by Sergei Rachmaninoff** (1996)
Instrumentation by Michael Finnissy [Oxford]

207 **Honky Blues** (1996) 1'
solo piano [Oxford]
'For Marcel Worms.'
fp: 11.1.97 Bimhuis, Amsterdam. Marcel Worms.

208 **Georghi Tutev** (1996) 4'
solo piano [Oxford]
'To Mara Chapanova, in memory of Georghi Tutev.'
fp: 17.6.96 Musica Nova, Sofia, Bulgaria. Composer.

209 **Golden Sleep** (1996) 12'
solo tenor, baritone, SATB choir [Oxford]
'For Zöe, Gary and the Vasari Singers.'
Commissioned by Steyning Music Society
Text: Homer's Iliad XXIII, 93-101 in translation by Alexander Pope.
Unperformed but broadcast by the BBC Singers (1997).

210 **Different Things** (1996) 6'
clarinet quartet [Oxford]
Independent parts, no score.
'For No Strings Attached.'
fp: 28.7.96 Leasowes Bank, Shropshire. No Strings Attached.
Title: after David Hockney's 'Three Different Things'.
Based on songs of Schumann and Gounod.

211 **Speak its Name!** (1996) 22'
2222/2210/2vib,timp/hp/quartertone keyboard/strings (min. 8.8.6.6.3) [Oxford]
Commissioned by the Brunel Ensemble
fp: 26.10.96 Victoria Rooms, Bristol. Brunel Ensemble, dir. Christopher Austin.
Title: 'The love which dare not speak its name' (Lord Alfred Douglas).

212 **his voice/was then/here waiting** (1996) 8'
two pianos [Oxford]
Independent parts, no score.
fp: 14.11.96 Durham University. Ian Pace, composer (pfs).

213 **Ten Tangos** (1962-96) 14'
10 Tangos, can be performed separately [Oxford]
solo piano

213.01 **Tango 1** (1994) 1'
'For Belkiss Carneiro de Mendonça.' [Oxford]
fp: 29.2.96 Conway Hall, London. Ian Pace

213.02 **Tango 2** (1968-69) 1'
fp: 29.2.96 Conway Hall, London. Ian Pace. [Oxford]

213.03 **Tango 3** (1962) 1'
fp: 29.2.96 Conway Hall, London. Ian Pace. [Oxford]

213.04 **Tango 4** (1983-84) 3'
fp: date and venue unknown. Yvar Mikhashoff. [Quadrivium/Oxford]
Originally called 'Tango'.

213.05 **Tango 5** (1994) 1'
'For Richard Steele.' [Oxford]
fp: 29.2.96 Conway Hall, London. Ian Pace.

213.06 **Tango 6** (1976) 1'
fp: 29.2.96 Conway Hall, London. Ian Pace. [Oxford]

213.07 **Tango 7** (1996) 1'
'For Colin Matthews.' [Oxford]
fp: 10.5.96 Conway Hall, London. Ian Pace.

213.08 **Tango 8** (1996) 1'
'For Paul Driver.' [Oxford]
fp: 10.5.96 Conway Hall, London. Ian Pace.
Based on songs of Sibelius.

213.09 **Tango 9** (1996-) 1'
'For Elliott Schwartz on his 60th birthday.' [Oxford]
fp: 11.12.96 BMIC, London. Composer.

213.10 **Tango 10** (1996-) 3'
'For Howard Skempton (to honour his 50th birthday).' [Oxford]
fp: 5.12.96 Conway Hall, London. Ian Pace.

214 **Selected Movements of Great Masters** (1996) 10'
Spohr tugs at his forelock; Schubert brushes his teeth; [Oxford]
C.P.E. Bach scratches his bottom; Beethoven blows his nose;
J. Ludwig Bach sticks a finger in his ear; Mendelssohn heaves up his leg;
Haydn bites his nails; J.S. Bach folds his arms;
Handel touches his shoulders and toes; Dvorák closes his eyes.
saxophone quartet: 2 altos, 2 tenors.
fp: 30.11.96 Huddersfield Festival. Delta Saxophone Quartet.

215 **Tu me dirais** (1996) 3'
solo piano [Oxford]
'In memory of Elizabeth Abercrombie.'
fp: 5.12.96 Conway Hall, London. Ian Pace.
Based on Cécile Chaminade song of same name.

216 **Meeting is pleasure, parting a grief** (1996) 45'
solo piano [Oxford]
'An 'encore' for the concluding concert in Ian Pace's
series of 'The Complete Piano Music.''
fp: 5.12.96 Conway Hall, London. Ian Pace.
Title: from Sussex folk-song set by George Butterworth

Works in progress (1997)

217 **History of Photography in Sound** (1996-) 270'
in five sections may be performed separately [Oxford]
solo piano

217.1 **Le démon de l'analogie**
History of Photography in Sound Book 1

217.2 **Landscapes**
History of Photography in Sound Book 2

217.21 **The wakening of intractable reality** (1997)
'To Marc Coroux.'

217.22 **North American Spirituals** (1997)
'To Marilyn Nonken.'

217.3 **Portraiture**
History of Photography in Sound Book 3

217.31 **Alkan-Paganini** (1997) 15'
'To Nicolas Hodges.'

217.32 **Seventeen Immortal Homosexual Poets** (1997) 40'
'To Ian Pace.'
fp (Part 1): 21.3.97 Conway Hall, London. Ian Pace.
fp (Complete): 1.5.97 BMIC, London. Ian Pace.

217.321 **Portrait of Frank O'Hara as Orpheus in Hell** (1997) 3'
Part of *Seventeen Immortal Homosexual Poets*, performable separately.
fp: 7.3.97 Monnaie Opera House, Belgium. Ian Pace.

217.33 **Eadweard Muybridge - Edvard Munch** (1997) 25'
'To James Clapperton.'
fp: 21.9.97 'An Tasten' Festival, Germany. James Clapperton.

217.4 **Documentation**
History of Photography in Sound Book 4 (in two parts)

217.41 **Unsere Afrikareise** (1997-)

217.42 **Click!**

217.5 **Etched bright with sunlight**
History of Photography in Sound Book 5

218 **Sehnsucht**
'To Christopher Fox.'
2 violins, viola, cello
fp: 18.11.97 Royal Academy of Music. Manson Ensemble.
Title: after Brahms' song Op. 14, No. 8.

219 **L'Union Libre** (1997) 11'
alto horn or other E flat instrument, 2 pianos (quartertone apart), 3 ocarinas, kazoos or jews' harps, viola, accordion, 2 de-tuned zithers, 4 large drums.
fp: 11.97 Moscow.
Title: from Michel Foucault *History of Sexuality*.

220 **Recent Britain** 25'
clarinet, bassoon, piano, cello, conductor, tape [OUP]
all are theatrical parts and involve recitation of texts
'For Apartment House.'
fp: 25.1.98, ICA, London (for BBC *Hear and Now*). Apartment House.
Andrew Sparling, Philip Gibbon, Ian Pace, Anton Lukoszevieze, Mikel Toms.

221 **Multiple forms of constraint** (1997) 14'
violin, string trio (violin, viola, cello)
'For Peter Sheppard and the Kreutzer Quartet.'
Title: from Michel Foucault *History of Sexuality*.

CLASSIFIED INDEX

Orchestra

Large Ensemble (8 or more instruments)

Small Ensemble (5-7 instruments)

Instrumental Soloist and Ensemble

Song 4 (1968) 4.04
Piano Concerto No. 1 (1975/1983-84) 32
Piano Concerto No. 2 (1975-76) 35
Piano Concerto No. 3 (1978) 54
Piano Concerto No. 5 (1980) 73
Piano Concerto No. 7 (1981) 80
Jisei (1981) 83
'above earth's shadow...' (1985) 126
Obrecht Motetten III (1989) 142.3

Quartet

n (1969/1972) 11
Nobody's Jig (1980-81) 78
Australian Sea Shanties Set 3 (1983) 114.3
String Quartet (1984) 124
East London Heys (1985-86) 127.2
Plain Harmony (1993) 187.2
Quelle (1994) 194
Sefauchi's Return (1994) 200
Violet, Slingsby, Guy and Lionel (1995-96) 204
Different Things (1996) 210
Selected Movements of Great Masters (1996) 214
Multiple forms of constraint (1997) 221

Trio

Quem Pastores Laudavere (1962/65/66) J10
Untitled Piece to Honour Igor Stravinsky (1971) 7.2
Keroiylu (1981) 89
Aijal (1982) 94
Independence Quadrilles (1982/83/86/88/95) 103
String Trio (1986) 132
Obrecht Motetten II (1988) 142.2
In Stiller Nacht (1990/96-97) 157
WAM (1990-91) 164

Duo

Cantet nunc aula caelitum (1962) J9
Alice (*c.* 1975) 15.3
Kagami-Jishi (1979) 61
Mississippi Hornpipes (1982/97) 99

Dilok (1982) 100
Delal (1984/88) 120
Quabara (1988) 138
Kulamen Dilan (1990) 156

Solo Instrument

Song 12 (1972-73) 4.12
Song 13 (1971) 4.13
Song 17 (1976) 4.17
Song 18 (1976) 4.18
Untitled piece to honour Igor Stravinsky (1967) 7.1
Alice (1974-75) 15.1
Alice (*c.* 1975) 15.2
Ru Tchou (1975) 34
First Sign A Sharp White Moon, as if the cause of Snow (1968/75) 36
All the trees they are so high (1977) 40
Doves Figary (1976-77) 41
Runnin' Wild (1978) 51
Pavasiya (1979) 63
Sikangnuqa (1979) 65
Hinomi (1979) 67
Stomp (1981) 87
Andimironnai (1981) 88
Yalli (1981) 90
Terekkeme (1981/1990) 91
Marrngu (1982) 97
Nasiye (1982/AR) 98
Gerhana (1981-82) 101
Cirit (1982) 104
Uzundara (1983) 106
Sepevi (1982-83) 108
Ulpirra (1982-83) 111
The Eureka Flag (1983) 115
Obrecht Motetten III (1989) 142.3
Ének (1990) 148
Two Scenes From Shameful Vice (1995) 198

Solo Piano

The Chinese Bridge (1950) J1
Juvenilia (1953-58) J2
Polskie Tance Op. 32 (1955/62) J3
Two Mazurkas Op. 142 (1957) J4
Two Pasodobles (1959) J5
Vieux Nöel Op. 59 No. 2 (*c.* 1958-59) J7

My Love Is Like a Red Red Rose (1990) 158
De toutes flours (1990) 159
How dear to me (1991) 160
William Billings (1990) 161
Vanèn (1991) 162
Rossini (1991) 163
There never were such hard times before (1991) 170
French Piano (1991) 171
Willow Willow (1991) 172
Nine Romantics (1992) 173
New Perspectives on Old Complexity (1990/92) 174
Cibavit eos (1991) 175
Poor Stuff (1991-92/96) 176
Wenn wir in höchsten Nöthen sind (1992) 177
A solis ortus cardine (1992) 180
John Cage (1992) 183
Cozy Fanny's Tootsies (1992) 184
'What the meadow-flowers tell me' (1993) 186
Folklore (1993-94) 188
The larger heart, the kindlier hand (1993) 190
...desde que naçe (1993) 192
Yvaroperas (1993-95) 193
Elephant (1994) 194
Ethel Smyth (1995) 201
Violet, Slingsby, Guy and Lionel (1994-96) 203
Tracey and Snowy in Köln (1996) 205
Honky Blues (1996) 207
Georghi Tutev (1996) 208
Ten Tangos (1962-96) 213
Tu me dirais (1996) 215
Meeting is pleasure, parting a grief (1996) 216
History of Photography in Sound (1996-) 217

Two Pianos

Wild Flowers (1974) 26
his voice/was then/here waiting (1996) 212

Voice(s) and Ensemble

Forget-me-not (1959) J6
Le Dormeur du Val (1963-64/66/68) 1
From The Revelations of Saint John the Divine (1965/1970) 2
Horrorzone (1965-66/1971/1987) 3
Song 3 (1969) 4.03
Folk Song Set (1969-70) 12.1

Folk Song Set (1969-70/75-76) 12.2
Folk Song Set (1969-70/75-76) 12.3
Jeanne d'Arc (1967-71/AR) 13
World (1968-74) 16
Babylon (1971/AR) 17
Gorõ (1978) 55
Sir Tristran (1978) 57
Talawva (1979/AR) 64
Warara (1982/91) 93
Celi (1984) 123
The Cambridge Codex (1991) 165
The Cry of the Prophet Zephaniah (1992) 178
Various Nations (1992) 179
Blessed be (1995) 182.2
Sehnsucht (1997) 218

Voice and 1-3 instruments

Song 11 (1969-71) 4.11
Moon's goin' down (1980) 74
Lord Melbourne (1980) 75
Duru-Duru (1981) 86
Le Lay de la Fonteinne (1983/90) 110
Botany Bay (1983/89) 113
Cabaret Vert (1985) 125
Beuk o'Newcassel Sangs (1988) 139
Unknown Ground (1989-90) 150
Same as we (1990) 154.1
Same as we (1990) 154.2
Three Motets, Two Interludes (1991) 167
Two Motets (1991) 169
Blessed be (1992) 182.1
Silver Morning (1993) 191
Songs from the Exotic (on the rocks) 4 songs (with Judith Weir) (1989) 144
Blessed be (1996) 182.3

Voice and Piano

Mine Eye Awake (1977) 46
... fairest noonday ... (1979) 66
Green Bushes (1980) 76
Anninnia (1981-82) 102
Lyrics and Limericks (1982-84) 121

Solo Voice

Song 1 (1966/69-70) 4.01
Song 14 (1974) 4.14
Song 15 (1974) 4.15
Song 16 (1976) 4.16
Ohi! ohi! ohi! (1978) 50
Mountainfall (1978) 53

Vocal Ensemble and Instruments

Ngano (1983-84) 117
Haiyim (1984) 119
Maldon (1990) 155
Anima Christi (1991) 168
Vertue (1993/AR) 189
Liturgy of Saint Paul (1991-95) 202

Vocal Ensemble

Cipriano (1974) 28
Kelir (1981) 81
Australian Sea Shanties Set 1 (1983) 114.1
Seven Sacred Motets (1991) 166
Golden Sleep (1996) 209

Theatre, Stage Work and Dance

Irma Cortez (1970-72/96) 19
Tsuru-Kame (1971-73) 20
Circle, Chorus and Formal Act (1973) 21
Mysteries 1-8 (1972-79) 22
Commedia dell'incomprensibilie potere che alcune donne hanno sugli uomini (1973-75) 24
Medea (1973-76/AR) 25
Orfeo (1974-75/AR) 30
Bouffe (1975) 31
Mr Punch (1976-77/79) 39.1
Tom Fool's Wooing (1975-78) 48
Vaudeville (1983/87) 109.1
Soda Fountain (1983) 116
The Undivine Comedy (1985-88/95) 135
Thérèse Raquin (1992-93) 181
Shameful Vice (1994-95) 197
Recent Britain (1997) 220

CYCLES

Cycles for Piano

Ives-Grainger-Nancarrow

English Country-Tunes

Boogie-Woogie-Jazz-Fast Dances, Slow Dances

B.S. - G.F.H.

Verdi Transcriptions

Gershwin Arrangements-More Gershwin

Folklore 1-4

Yvaroperas 1-5

Ten Tangos

History of Photography in Sound

Other Cycles

Songs 1-18

Mysteries 1-8	*1. The Parting of Darkness From Light* *2. The Earthly Paradise* *3. Noah and the Great Flood* *4. The Prophecy of Daniel* *5. The Parliament of Heaven* *6. The Annunciation* *7. The Betrayal and Crucifixion of Jesus of Nazareth* *8. The Deliverance of Souls*
***Australian Aboriginal*:**	*Teangi, Warara, Aijal, Banumbirr, Marrngu, Ulpirra, Hikkai, Ouraa, Quabara*
***Australian Colonial*:**	*Botany Bay, Australian Sea Shanties Sets 1,2,3, The Eureka Flag*
***Azerbaijani*:**	*Keroiylu, Terekkeme, Uzundara, Sepevi*
***Hopi Indian*:**	*Sikangnuqa, Talawva* (currently awaiting revision), *Pavasiya*
***Japanese*:**	*Tsuru-Kame, Gorõ, Kagami-Jishi, Hinomi, Jisei*
***Kurdish*:**	*Yalli, Nasiye, Dilok, Cirit, Delal, Kulamen Dilan*
***Sardinian*:**	*Duru-Duru, Andimironnia, Anninnia, Taja*

Obrecht Motetten 1-5

INDEX OF TITLES

WITHDRAWN WORKS

1. *23 Poems/Fantasies* (various instrumentations).
2. *Make-Up* (free instrumentation) used as a dance score by Henrietta Lyons.
3. *Xunthaeresis* (solo organ).
4. *9 Romantics* music-drama (voices and ensemble). No relation to later *Nine Romantics*.
5. *Duet* (piano, percussion).
6. *Some other day of my life* (piano); material to be re-used in *History of Photography in Sound*.
7. *Light Matter* music/dance theatre (tenor, oboe, guitar, 2 perc, 4 dancers).
8. *Forest* (8 instruments).
9. *Theseus* dance score (oboe, ?guitar, ?2 perc).
10. *Long Distance* (solo piano, 3tpt, 3trb, 2vn, 2va, 2vc, db, offstage flute); material re-used in *Verdi Transcription no. 11*, *Piano Concerto No. 4* and *...above earth's* shadow....
11. *Piano Concerto no. 8* (piano and ensemble).
12. *Spirituals* (solo electric organ).
13. *Guwark* (solo piano); material re-used in *Verdi Transcription no. 14*.
14. *Jive* (violin, piano).
15. Further fragmentary *Verdi Transcriptions* (piano).
16. Two more *Gershwin Arrangements* (piano).
17. *Sorabji* (piano, unfinished); material used in *Folklore 1*.
18. *Haen* (piano); now last section of *Folklore 2*.
19. *De contrapuncto* (piano, unfinished); was to include *Haen*. The D minor fugue from *New Perspectives on Old Complexity* was to have been part of this work.
20. *Hier J'ai Recontré* (violin, piano); material used in *Folklore 3*.
21. *Missa in Commemoratione Sancti Pauli Apostoli* (voices, chorus, organ); incorporated into *Liturgy of Saint Paul*.
22. *Missa in Festo Conversionis Sancti Pauli* (choir, organ); incorporated into *Liturgy of Saint Paul*.

APPENDIX A

The following is a list of piano pieces written as fiftieth birthday tributes to Michael Finnissy. They were commissioned and first performed by Ian Pace on 11 July 1996, British Music Information Centre, Stratford Place, London.

DAVID ALDRIDGE	Only Love
GHEORGI ARRAIDUDOV	Sonnett 50
RICHARD BARRETT	the light gleams an instant
LUC BREWAEYS	Nobody's Perfect - Finnissy's Fifty
JAMES CLAPPERTON	They're writing songs of love
JAMES CLARKE	Étude
JUSTIN CONNOLLY	MPF - In Rebus
LAWRENCE CRANE	Birthday Piece for Michael Finnissy
RICHARD EMSLEY	Finnissy's Fifty
JAMES ERBER	You Done Torn Your Playhouse Down
CHRISTOPHER FOX	Complimentary Forms
EDWARD DUDLEY HUGHES	Orchid 4
RODNEY LISTER	Monday Music
DAVID MAW	For Michael Finnissy at 50
CHRIS NEWMAN	Untitled Combine
IAN PACE	Aldeburgh Lullaby
MICHAEL PARSONS	Jive
JONATHAN POWELL	Skazka
ALWYNNE PRITCHARD	Spring
RODNEY SHARMAN	Canonic Toccata
HOWARD SKEMPTON	Starlight
GERHARD STÄBLER	Internet 1.1
LUKE STONEHAM	Counting Crows
MARK TAYLOR	Gallagher Transcriptions; Study
ANDREW TOOVEY	To Sappho
JOHN WHITE	Piano Sonata No. 131
IAN WILLCOCK	The Persistence of Melody

APPENDIX B

The following programmes formed the series of concerts in 1996 in which Ian Pace played the complete piano music of Michael Finnissy at Conway Hall, Red Lion Square, London.

1. FINNISSY THE ROMANTIC 26 January 1996

Autumnall; Snowdrift; Sometimes I; My Love is like a red red rose; How dear to me; What the meadow-flowers tell me; Nine Romantics; Verdi Transcriptions

2. FINNISSY THE JAZZMAN 29 February 1996

Freightrain Bruise; Two of Us; Gershwin Arrangements; Can't Help Lovin' Dat Man; Six Tangos; We'll get there someday; To & Fro; Boogie-Woogie; Jazz; Fast Dances, Slow Dances

3. FINNISSY THE TRANSCRIBER AND TRIBUTER 10 May 1996

Romeo and Juliet are Drowning; De Toutes Flours; Wenn wir in höchsten Nöthen sind; Cibavit eos; Cozy Fanny's Tootsies; Rossini; More Gershwin; There never were such hard times before; The larger heart, the kindlier hand; A solis ortus cardine; Strauss-Waltzer; Ives; Grainger; Nancarrow; B.S; G.F.H; Liz; Ethel Smyth; Tangos 7 & 8; Tracey and Snowy in Köln; William Billings; John Cage

4. FINNISSY THE FOLKLORIST 28 June 1996

Three Dukes went a-Riding; Willow Willow; Kemp's Morris; Polskie Tance Op. 32; Svatovac; Taja; Lylyly li; Terekkeme; Australian Sea Shanties Set 2; Hikkai; Folklore 1-4.

5. FINNISSY THE VERSATILE 4 October 1996

Piano Concerto No. 6; Valse Burlesque; Tambourin; Air and Variation; Preambule; Vêpres; Two Mazurkas Op. 142; Two Pasodobles; Vieux Nöel; Romance (with Intermezzo); Vanèn; ...desde que naçe; Georghi Tutev; Pimmel; French Piano; White Rain; Short but...; Free Setting; Stanley Stokes, East Street 1836; New Perspectives on Old Complexity; Wee Saw Footprints; Four Teaching Pieces; Violet, Slingsby, Guy and Lionel; Elephant; Five Yvaroperas; Piano Concerto No. 4.

6. FINNISSY THE VIRTUOSO 5 December 1996

Song 5; Song 6; Song 7; Song 8; Song 9; Tango 10; Tu me dirais; all.fall.down; English Country-Tunes; Meeting is pleasure, parting a grief.

Bibliography

Writings about Michael Finnissy

This list generally does not include the multitude of reviews that have appeared in newspapers and magazines.

Arntzen, K. (1991), 'De lijn van gecompliceerde muziek', *Entr'acte* 8, October.

Barrett, R. (1995), 'Michael Finnissy - An Overview', *Contemporary Music Review*, Vol. 13 (1), Harwood Academic Publishers, Amsterdam.

Bialosky, M. (1989), *'Ngano' Notes*, December.

Bowling, I. (1989), 'British Piano Music since 1945', Dissertation, Chapter 4 (pp. 77-98).

Clements, A. (1988), 'Finnissy's *Undivine Comedy*', *Musical Times*, Vol. 129, Musical Times Publications, London.

Cross, J. (1991) 'The Repertoire Guide: Michael Finnissy', *Classical Music*, 26 January, Rhinegold Publishing, London.

Cross, J. (1996), 'Vive la différence', *Musical Times*, Vol. 137, Musical Times Pubications, London.

Driver, P. (1980), 'Finnissy's *Alongside*', *TEMPO* 132, March, Boosey & Hawkes, London.

Ferneyhough, B. (1978: 1995), 'The Piano Music of Michael Finnissy', originally written to accompany Australian recording of *English Country Tunes*, reprinted in Boros, J., Toop, R., (eds) *Brian Ferneyhough - Collected Writings*, Contemporary Music Studies, Vol. 10, Harwood Academic Publishers, Amsterdam.

Halbreich, H. 'Michael Finnissy and his Undivine Comedy', included in programme for Almeida Festival premiere of *The Undivine Comedy*

Jameson, M. (1993), 'Till death do us part', (on *Thérèse Raquin*), *Classical Music*, Rhinegold Publishing, London.

Johansson, O. (1985), 'Between Bel Canto and Jazz. On Michael Finnissy's *Songs 14 and 15*'. Article and interview.

Knussen, O. (1977), 'Finnissy's *Pathways of Sun & Stars*', *TEMPO* 120, Boosey & Hawkes, London.

Molineaux, S. (1994), 'The Finnissing Touch', *Keyboard Review*, March.

Pace, I. (1996), *Michael Finnissy - An Introduction* - Promotional article for United Music Publishers, London.

Pace. 1 (1996) ,'The Panorama of Michael Finnissy (I)', *TEMPO*, No. 196, Boosey & Hawkes, London.

Pace, I. (1997), 'The Panorama of Michael Finnissy (II)', *TEMPO* No. 201, Boosey & Hawkes, London.

Pace, I. (1996), 'Finnissy the Romantic', 'Finnissy the Jazzman', 'Finnissy the Transcriber and Tributer', 'Finnissy the Folklorist', 'Finnissy the Versatile', 'Finnissy the Virtuoso', articles to accompany each concert in 'The Complete Piano Music of Michael Finnissy' series in London. Some material from these articles used in 'The Piano Music' in this volume.

Pedersen, M.E. (1990), 'Michael Finnissy i samtale med', *Ballade* No. 3, Oslo.

Potter, K. (1979) 'Michael Finnissy', *Classical Music*, 1 December, Rhinegold Publishing, London.

Reeve, S. (1980) 'Of Finnissy and Ferneyhough', *Classical Music*, 7 June, Rhinegold Publishing, London.

Titcomb, S. 'Following the paths to 'York' (by Malcolm Singer) and *Unknown Ground* (by M.F.)'. Dissertation with extensive analysis and interview.

Toop, R. (1988), 'Four Facets of The New Complexity', substantial article on Finnissy, Dillon, Dench, Barrett, *Contact 32*, Contact, London.

Warnaby, J. (1988), 'Michael Finnissy', *Music and Musicians*, February.

Watson, B. 'Michael Finnissy', biography for UMP leaflet.

Williams, L. (1988), 'Finnissy's *Undivine Comedy*', *Opera*, Vol. 39, London.

Williams, L. (1995), 'Reinstating 'The Spritual Quest'', *Contemporary Music Review*, Vol. 13 (1), (on Finnissy's theatrical works), Harwood Academic Publishers, Amsterdam.

'A Happy Melancholia (a portrait of Michael Finnissy)' - Presenter: Lynne Williams, Producer: Andrew Kurowski. Winner of Category 2 of the 22 Prix Musical de Radio Brno. Programme-book containing interviews with Finnissy, Roger Wright, Judith Weir and Chris Redgate. BBC Publications 1988, London.

Writings by Michael Finnissy

(1977), 'Ferneyhough's Sonatas', *TEMPO* 121 (June) pp. 34-6.

(1980), 'Nancarrow: Complete Studies for Player Piano Volume 2', *TEMPO* 133/134 (September) pp. 85-6.

(1987/88/89), Editorials (with Roger Wright), *New Music 87/88/89*, Oxford University Press.

(1987), 'Composers in Education', *New Music 87*, Oxford University Press.

(1987), 'View from Japan - Interview with Jo Kondo' *New Music 87*, Oxford University Press.

(1988), 'Conversation with Josephine Nendick', *New Music 88*, Oxford University Press.

(1989), 'Piano Concerto and works for piano-duet and two pianos' and 'A Reminiscence of my teacher' in *Bernard Stevens and his Music - A Symposium*, complied and edited by Bertha Stevens.

(1991), 'Those Twentieth Century Blues - Michael Tippett', review in *Gay Times*, November.

(1992), 'Andrew Toovey', *TEMPO* 181, Boosey & Hawkes, London.

(1995), 'Music Breaks Free...from issues of Gender and Sexuality', Introduction to lecture and concert series at the University of Sussex, March, (Programme-book), University of Sussex, Brighton.

Discography

Australian Sea Shanties Set 2	Metier (1998), Michael Finnissy - piano
Autumnall	NMC D002, Michael Finnissy - piano
Beuk o'Newcassel Sangs	BML 012, Tapestry
B.S.	CD Nova 7, James Clapperton - piano
Can't help lovin' dat man	Collins 11372, 'MacGregor on Broadway', Joanna MacGregor - piano
Câtana	ETC K1098, Uroboros Ensemble, dir. Gwyn Pritchard
Contretänze	ETC K1098, Ensemble Exposé, dir. Michael Finnissy
Delal	ATTACCA BABEL 9476 DDD, 'Ladder of Escape 7', Jonathan Impett - trumpet, Martin Allen - percussion
Delal	Forthcoming, Christopher Redgate - oboe
Dilok	Forthcoming, Christopher Redgate - oboe
Dove's Figary (first version)	NMC D019, 'Wavesongs', Alexander Baillie - cello
Ének	NMC D043, Charles Mutter - violin
English Country-Tunes	ETC K1091, Michael Finnissy - piano
English Country-Tunes (Movts 2, 3, 8 only)	FACD 326, Rolf Hind - piano
Fast Dances, Slow Dances	CD Nova 7, James Clapperton - piano
Folklore 2	Metier (1998), Michael Finnissy - piano
Freightrain Bruise	NMC D002, Michael Finnissy - piano
Gershwin Arrangements Nos 3, 7, 8	Collins 12992, prev. LDR CD 1004, Joanna MacGregor - piano. Also included on 'The Music of George Gershwin', Collins 13622
G.F.H.	CD Nova 7, James Clapperton - piano
How dear to me	Metier (1998), Michael Finnissy - piano
Kemp's Morris	NMC D002, Michael Finnissy - piano
Lylyly Li	Metier (1998), Michael Finnissy - piano
Mars + Venus	NMC D043, IXION, dir. Michael Finnissy

Multiple Forms of Constraint	Metier (1998), Kreutzer Quartet
My love is like a red red rose	Metier (1998), Michael Finnissy - piano
Nobody's Jig	Metier (1998), Kreutzer Quartet
Pavasiya	Forthcoming, Christopher Redgate - oboe
Plain Harmony	Metier (1998), Kreutzer Quartet
Polskie Tance Op. 32	Metier (1998), Michael Finnissy - piano
Quelle	ear*up* CD1003, Thomas K. J. Mejer - saxophones
Red Earth	NMC D040S, BBC Symphony Orchestra, dir. Martin Brabbins
Reels	NMC D002, Michael Finnissy - piano
Runnin' Wild	Forthcoming, Christopher Redgate - oboe
Sehnsucht	Metier (1998), Kreutzer Quartet
Short but...	NMC D002, Michael Finnissy - piano
Sikangnuqa	Polygram - ABC Classics, ABC 446 738-2, 'The Flute in Orbit', Laura Chislett - flute
Songs of the Exotic (with Judith Weir)	BML 012, Tapestry
Stabant autem iuxta crucem	ECM New Series 453259-2, Hilliard Ensemble
Stanley Stokes, East Street 1836 (original (now withdrawn) version)	NMC D002, Michael Finnissy - piano
String Quartet	Metier (1998), Kreutzer Quartet
Svatovac	Metier (1998), Michael Finnissy - piano
Traum des Sängers	NMC D043, IXION, dir. Michael Finnissy
Two of Us	EMI Japan TOCE-7345, Aki Takahashi - piano
Videtis enim interiorem	KWCD 017, Nicola Walker Smith - soprano, Charles Mutter - violin
Vieux Nöel	Metier (1998), Michael Finnissy - piano
WAM	NMC D043, Rowland Sutherland - flute, Andrew Sparling - clarinet, Ian Pace - piano
Warara	KWCD 017, Nicola Walker Smith - soprano, IXION

Filmography

The Cry of the Prophet Zephaniah (1992), First Broadcast BBC2, 6 December 1992, producer Chris Mann

Dust in the Road (1986-88), First Broadcast, BBC2 'Sound on Film', 11 December 1988, producer Barrie Gavin

Index